FINANCIAL REPORTING IN JAPAN

This work was commissioned by the Research Board of the Institute of Chartered Accountants of England and Wales.

Financial Reporting in Japan

Regulation, Practice and Environment

T. E. COOKE and M. KIKUYA

Copyright © ICAEW, 1992

The right of T. E. Cooke and M. Kikuya to be identified as authors
of this work has been asserted in accordance with the
Copyright, Designs and Patents Act 1988.

First published 1992

Blackwell Publishers Ltd
108 Cowley Road
Oxford OX4 1JF
UK

Three Cambridge Center
Cambridge, Massachusetts 02142
USA

British Library Cataloguing in Publication Data
A CIP catalogue record for this book is available from
the British Library.

Library of Congress Cataloging in Publication Data
Financial reporting in Japan: regulation, practice, and environment/
T. E. Cooke and M. Kikuya.
   p.   cm.
Includes index
ISBN 0–631–18299–3
  1. Corporations—Accounting—Law and Legislation—Japan.
  2. Corporation reports—Law and legislation—Japan. I. Kikuya. M.
KNX1072.F56 1992
346.52'066—dc20
[345.20666]
91–29561
CIP

Typeset in 10 on 12pt Plantin
by Wearside Tradespools, Boldon, Tyne and Wear
Printed in Great Britain by
Billing & Sons Ltd, Worcester

Contents

Foreword

Since the Second World War the Japanese economy has developed rapidly and the country has now established itself as one of the most advanced nations. With the growth of Japanese companies into multinational enterprises and the globilization of capital markets it is important that the world of accounting has a greater understanding of financial reporting in Japan.

An important aspect of the growth in internationalization of capital markets, in which the Tokyo stock exchange has become the second largest in the world and Japan has become the world's leading creditor nation, is that securities should be priced in accordance with international rather than domestic factors. As part of the pricing mechanism, information is of particular importance and international investment often involves understanding accounting in a variety of different countries. To ease the burden of such comparisons the process of harmonization seeks to make financial statements more compatible. This has been one of the objectives of the International Accounting Standards Committee.

This book serves the needs of those wishing to gain an insight into corporate reporting issues but it offers much more than that. The text provides an extensive description and analysis of the factors influencing accounting and reporting in Japan. Indeed, the striking feature of the book is the placing of accounting issues in their environmental context. Whilst the world has witnessed growing internationalism in which some cultural differences have diminished, comparative studies like this one serve to provide a greater insight into what has been referred to as 'enclaves of uniqueness'. This book also provides an important insight into disclosure practices by Japanese companies by the provision of data, examples and discussion. The analyses are enhanced further by comparisons of Japanese practices with those in the UK and the US and also comparisons with international accounting standards.

This book is the product of collaboration between a British accountant and a Japanese accountant and was funded by the Research Board of the Institute of Chartered Accountants in England and Wales. I commend the support offered by the Research Board and recommend this book as an important contribution to the literature on financial reporting in Japan.

Eiichi Shiratori
Chairman Designate,
The International Accounting Standards Committee

Preface

It is generally agreed among international accountants that Japan and the UK are among the eight most vital countries so far as international harmonization of accounting standards is concerned. The achievement of harmonization depends in part on accountants in these countries understanding the accounting regulations and practices in the others. This is made difficult not only by differences of language but also by important differences in the respective economic, social and cultural environments. It is encouraging, therefore, to observe the increasing literature on Japanese accounting in English and on British accounting in Japanese.

Our objective is to add to the literature by the provision of a book with both technical and research content, which is placed in context by a discussion of the economic, social, political and cultural environment. The research aspect of this publication involves a survey of 48 corporate annual reports. Annual reports prepared in accordance with the Commercial Code and the Securities and Exchange Law were scrutinized and, when available, English versions of the companies' accounts were analysed. The English version accounts are not translations of the reports prepared in accordance with the Commercial Code or the Securities and Exchange Law but, rather, a report based on corporate perceptions of the needs of international readers. The orientation of English version accounts is very much towards the US reader, including the use of American terminology. In the main, this publication uses British terminology; so, for example, 'stock' is used instead of 'inventories'. Since the book is, in part, a reference work each chapter contains a summary to highlight the important points. In addition, the final chapter provides a summary of the whole book.

We are indebted to a number of individuals and organizations for their support. Most importantly, the Institute of Chartered Accountants in England and Wales which funded the project and their two anonymous referees who received the manuscript enthusiastically and made a number of useful suggestions. Other organizations that assisted include Hitachi, the Japanese Institute of Certified Public Accountants, Matsushita Electric Industrial, Minolta Camera, Mitsubishi Kasei, Nippon Steel, Nissan, Shōwa Denko, the Tokyo Stock Exchange and Toshiba. We are grateful to JICPA for permission to reproduce the material found in appendices F, G and H. In addition, we would like to thank Mr F. Kogomori, Miss K. Matsuda, Miss K. Suzuki and the professional and academic accountants we met in the summer of 1988. The final manuscript remains, of course, the responsibility of the authors. It is our hope that this publication will prove to be a useful research report and reference book.

T. E. Cooke
University of Exeter
M. Kikuya
Asia University, Tokyo

1

Introduction

This book is intended to assist our understanding of financial reporting in Japan. It tries to achieve its objective by considering the major environmental factors that have influenced the evolution of accounting and reporting practices as well as investigating the specific accounting principles and practices prevalent in Japan. 'Like other business practices, accounting is to a large extent environmentally bound. That is, it is shaped by and reflects particular characteristics unique to each country's environment. The list of these characteristics is virtually infinite, ranging from personal traits and values to institutional arrangements, and can even extend to climatic and geographic factors' (Arpan and Radebaugh, 1985, p. 13). The framework used to consider factors influencing the evolution of accounting and reporting practices is a modification of the conceptual framework developed by Radebaugh (1975, p. 41) to consider the development of accounting objectives, standards and practices. Part I of this book considers the evolutionary factors and Part II consists of an analysis of accounting principles and practices, based in part on a survey of accounts.

The conceptual framework used in Part I is shown in figure 1.1. Such a framework adds a level of sophistication to the study of accounting in other countries because it permits dynamic as well as static comparisons of accounting (Radebaugh, 1975). Whilst Arpan and Radebaugh (1985) have argued that countries have 'unique' attributes we believe that many characteristics are far from being nation-specific.[1] Indeed whilst the Japanese seek to emphasize their homogeneity and uniqueness such cultural arguments are often used as surrogates to justify power and economic motives. Consequently, there is an element of revisionist thought underlying Part I which has been advanced by van Wolferen (1989) and Dale (1986) – the latter has written a book entitled *The Myth of Japanese Uniqueness*. Van Wolferen argues that

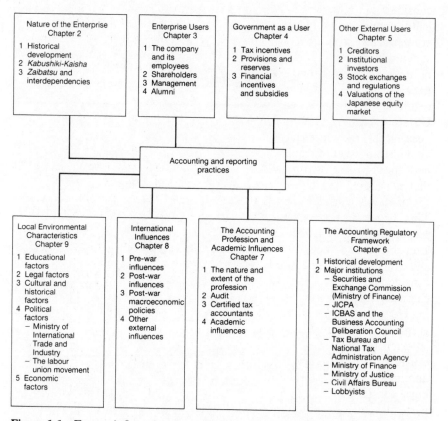

Figure 1.1   Factors influencing the evolution of accounting and reporting practices

it is almost an article of faith among Japanese that their culture is unique, not in the way that all cultures are unique, but somehow uniquely unique, ultimately different from all others, the source of unique Japanese sensibilities and therefore safe from (if not off-limits to) intellectual probes by outsiders. Japanese are constantly persuaded of the specialness of their nation in their schools and corporations and through the media and speeches by functionaries, whenever an opportunity arises for comparisons from the outside world.

(van Wolferen, 1989, p. 14)

Part I begins with a chapter on the nature of enterprises within Japan, since most capitalist countries have a range of business organizations. In terms of economic significance the limited liability company is most important in Japan as it is in the UK and US. This chapter is then followed by a consideration (chapters 3–5) of the users of financial statements of limited liability enterprises. Institutional investors, business organizations and government have a number of sources of information, including the financial statements. Because of interdependency between companies and domination of the financial institutions the small investor has in effect been disenfranchised. These three chapters are followed by a consideration of the accounting regulatory environment and how it has changed since its imposition by the US after the Second World War. Chapter 6 will emphasize the dominant position of the bureaucracy, a theme reinforced by chapter 7, which demonstrates that bureaucratic domination of the accountancy profession has kept the Japanese Institute of Certified Public Accountants a pale shadow of that considered desirable by the post-war occupation forces.

Chapter 8 considers international influences over Japanese accounting. This began in the nineteenth century by the importation of German accounting ideas, followed by a US influence which was imposed upon Japan after the Second World War. Local environmental characteristics – specifically educational, sociocultural, legal and political and economic factors – are considered in chapter 9. Great emphasis is placed upon education in Japan, a characteristic of Confucian values common to Sino-culture countries including Hong Kong, Korea, Singapore and Taiwan. Whilst the education system is egalitarian and co-educational with a national curriculum, the existence of an extensive network of private tutoring schools means that a wealthy elite is separated off at a very early age. Traditionally, Japan has been a male-dominated society in which the great divide begins at the age of 18. Whilst boys consider a college education studying engineering and business in particular, girls begin to prepare themselves for their subsequent responsibilities of marriage, looking after the home and bringing up the children and fostering their education. Since the large corporations concentrate on a graduate intake it becomes inevitable that such enterprises are also male-dominated. Industry likes to recruit graduates to train them for their future responsibilities within the corporation. Since the concept of lifetime employment is important in the large-firm sector individuals must be able and willing to adapt to changes demanded by their employer. Whilst aspects of the management style of major corporations have been described as part of the Japanese cultural environment it is remarkable how quickly they can be adapted to changing circumstances. For example, table 1.1 summarizes present and future management styles. Characteristics such as lifetime employment, company labour unions, in-house training and education and the welfare of employees are expected to be retained but the seniority system of promotion is expected to change to a meritocratic basis. Note that these characteristics apply to large corporations, and concepts such as lifetime employment are not usually relevant to medium and small-sized companies. Table 1.1 also demonstrates that corporations are likely to invest further in

Table 1.1 Japan's management style for the 1990s

	Present management style	*New management style*
Strategic action	Development research	Basic research
	Emphasis on efficiency	Emphasis on innovation
	Emphasis on principal line of business	Diversification in related fields of business
	Emphasis on operation	Emphasis on strategy
Organization	Power base in production division	Power base in research and development division
	Large head office	Small head office
	Bureaucratic structure	Innovative structure
	Centralization of authority	Decentralization of authority
	Bottom-up-type decision-making	Top-management-led decision-making
	Class pyramid	Horizontal division of labour network
Practices	Lifetime employment	(Retain)
	Seniority system	Meritocracy
	Company labour union	(Retain, but redefine)
	In-house training/education	(Retain)
	Welfare of employees	(Retain)
Human resources	Homogeneous personnel	Heterogeneous personnel
	Collectivism	Tolerance of individualism
	Loyalty to company	(Retain)
	Equality	Individuality

Source: Keizai Doyukai (The Committee for Economic Development)

research and development (R & D) to produce more high-technology goods since the R & D function is expected to increase in importance. This is inevitable in that Japan's high wages cannot compete with other Far Eastern countries. It also seems likely that bottom-up decision-making which emphasizes collective responsibility will be replaced by top-management-led decision-making based on tolerance of the individual.

Chapter 9 also considers legal influences over financial reporting, followed by a discussion of the link between culture and accounting. It will be argued that the Japanese accounting system is based on statutory control, uniform disclosure, flexible measurement practices, conservatism and secrecy. Despite conservatism in Japanese accounting pre-tax profitability is higher than some of Japan's major competitors (see table 1.2). Furthermore, the profit

Table 1.2 International comparisons of pre-tax profitability: net rate of return on fixed capital, 1972–1985

| | *Non-financial corporations (% rate of return)* | | | | | |
	US	*Japan*	*France*	*UK*	*Canada[a]*	*Germany*
1972	14	25	15	8	10	15
1973	14	22	15	8	12	15
1974	12	17	13	5	12	13
1975	12	15	10	3	9	11
1976	13	15	10	4	9	13
1977	14	16	10	7	9	13
1978	13	17	10	7	9	13
1979	12	17	10	6	11	14
1980	10	17	9	5	11	12
1981	11	16	8	5	9	10
1982	9	16	8	6	7	11
1983	11	15	8	8	8	12
1984	13	16	9	9	9	13
1985	13	16	n/a	10	n/a	n/a

[a] Industry plus transport.
Sources: OECD, US Department of Commerce, UK Central Statistical Office (*United Kingdom National Accounts 1987*), Survey of Current Business and Shearson Lehman Hutton

rate is less cyclical than competitors' even though there has been a substantial appreciation of the yen over the period covered by the table. Perhaps the extensive range of provisions and reserves available to Japanese companies permits the smoothing of income more readily than in other countries.

The political environment in Japan is essentially that of a one-party state in which the labour unions have been rendered impotent. What makes Japan so interesting to many is its outstanding post-war growth. Based on an effective educational system, political stability and government support – not least in controlling imports and capital flows – Japan enjoyed phenomenal growth in the 1960s, and even its subsequent lower growth rate has consistently exceeded that of its major competitors. The revisionist school of thought argues that the interdependency between Japanese corporations and the bureaucracy serves to ensure that it is difficult for imports to enter the country but that every encouragement is given for its exports. There is an element of truth in this; yet Japan's ability to obtain foreign market shares has been based on high-quality mass-produced goods which are competitively priced. Japanese companies demand subcomponents of a similar standard, delivered at the time and place demanded, and which are assembled in highly automated factories. Emphasis on quality has enabled Japanese companies to produce high-quality finished products in foreign countries as well as its own. However, its aggressively priced exports, based on a limited number of products, are a source of trade friction, particularly to the US.

As Japanese companies invest heavily to produce high-technology goods in highly automated factories, pay low dividends and seek to increase their foreign market shares, however, Anglo-Saxon companies seek to increase dividends to placate their institutional investors, whose managers' performance is assessed on the basis of short-term profitability. The latest (1989) Organization for Economic Co-operation and Development (OECD) report on research and development found that in the 1981–5 period the UK was the only OECD country where growth in R & D expenditure was lower than growth in gross domestic product. Japan, Spain, Norway and Finland led the R & D growth table with compound increases of about 9 per cent a year. Another aspect of US and UK listed companies is that they are constantly seeking to ensure that they can defend themselves against unwelcome predators, whereas major Japanese corporations accept the status quo of mutual existence and co-operate with the bureaucracy to achieve national objectives. Nevertheless, Japan is sensitive to international criticism and is careful not to exacerbate friction. If it really wanted to, Japanese industry could turn many industries – including the UK car market – upside down.

Who gains and who loses from this economic success is a different question. Since lifetime employment probably applies to only 25 per cent of the workforce, primarily located in the large corporations, it is left to the medium and small firms to provide flexibility in response to changing economic circumstances. It is these workers who suffer lower wages, poorer benefits and much less security of employment than their large-firm counterparts. Furthermore, the level of annual hours worked in Japan is much higher than in other OECD countries. The OECD estimates that in 1987 average hours worked in Japan exceeded those worked in the UK and US by more than 10 per cent, and those of Germany and France by nearly 25 per cent (OECD, 1988–89). The OECD summarizes other differences as follows (p. 53):

- the share of workers having two days off each week was still only 30 per cent in 1988;
- paid annual leave taken was, on average, only 7.5 days per year out of an entitlement of 15 days compared with 20 to 30 days typically taken in the United States and Europe respectively;
- average regular hours worked per week were 44 hours in 1988, compared with 36 to 39 hours in Europe, although Japan was only slightly longer than the UK.

The distribution of national income is, however, a problem faced by all governments. What *is* certain is that economic development by Japan in the twentieth century has been quite remarkable, elevating the country to one of the leading industrial nations in the world.

Note

1 Note that Cooke and Wallace (1990) conclude that the level of corporate financial disclosure regulation in many developed countries is determined more by internal factors, while those of many developing countries is determined more by external factors. In Japan the Commercial Code and the Securities and Exchange Law have been the strongest influences on financial accounting and reporting (Kikuya, 1989, pp. 98–9).

PART I

Factors Influencing the Evolution of Accounting and Reporting Practices

2
Nature of the Enterprise

Historical development of the forms of business organization

The foundation of regulation of corporate reporting in Japan was the introduction of the Commercial Code[1] in 1899. Until the middle of the nineteenth century bookkeeping systems were based, in general, on single-entry. However, the restoration of the imperial regime in 1868 heralded the move away from Tokugawa feudalism towards a capitalist economic system (McKinnon, 1986, p. 118). Prior to 1868 a succession of shogunates held political power over fairly autonomous provinces. 'These commanded the allegiance of bodies of hierarchically organised supporters to whom, in turn, they granted rights to parcels of land. The farmers who worked the land were obliged to provide their superiors with rice and other foodstuffs, and in exchange they were supposed to receive protection. In practice farmers often suffered incidentally in battles waged between lords for supremacy over a particular area' (Hendry, 1987, p. 14).

During the latter half of the nineteenth century the West had an increased influence over accounting. This was due both to the import of a number of books on double-entry bookkeeping and to the number of Western teachers in Japan. These included Vincente E. Braga from Portugal, Alexander Allan Shand from Great Britain and William Goswell Whitney from the United States, all of whom played important roles in the early development of 'modern' bookkeeping in Japan (Fujita, 1966, p. 51).

Another factor in this development was the national banks' adoption, in December 1873, of Shand's treatise on bookkeeping, *The Detailed Method of Bank Bookkeeping*. Acceptance of Shand's[2] system was formalized in the National Bank Act 1872. The Act required banks to maintain proper books of account and prepare and submit financial statements to both shareholders and government.

The Commercial Code of 1899, issued under the authority of the Ministry of Justice, marked the beginning of the system of corporate report regulation in Japan. The main forms of business organization authorized under the Code include the sole proprietorship, an unlimited liability company (*Gomei-Kaisha*), a company with limited and unlimited liability (*Goshi-Kaisha*) and the corporation (*Kabushiki-Kaisha*). In addition, there are other forms of business organization such as the private limited company, *Yugen-Kaisha*, whose regulation is provided by the Yugen-Kaisha Law 1938; a law based on the German *Gesellschaft mit beschränkter Haftung Gesetz* (1892). Business can also be conducted in Japan through a branch of a foreign enterprise.

Gomei-Kaisha is a general form of unlimited partnership, a form of business organization characterized by the *zaibatsu*, a financial combine initially governed by several families such as Iwasaki (Mitsubishi), Mitsui, Sumitomo and Yasuda. One of the goals of the MacArthur regime after the Second World War was to dissolve the *zaibatsu* as they were considered too powerful both politically and economically. *Goshi-Kaisha* is a limited partnership resembling *Gomei-Kaisha* except that it has both unlimited and limited partners.

The major types of business organization in Japan are the *Kabushiki-Kaisha* (*KK*) and *Yugen-Kaisha* (*YK*). A *KK* is a company limited by shares, the liability of each shareholder being restricted to his or her capital contribution. Foreign business enterprises normally adopt this form of business organization when establishing a subsidiary in Japan. In contrast to the *KK*, the *YK* is a limited company which requires no public financing. The *YK* is a common type of business organization for small and/or closed companies because the formation procedures and other formalities are fairly simple in comparison to those of the *KK*. The minimum called-up capital is ¥3 million by the par value.[3] In addition, a statutory auditor (described below) is not required and only one director is necessary when forming a *YK*.

In June 1991 the number of each type of *Kaisha* (or company) was: *KK* 1,265,347; *YK* 1,574,297; *Goshi-Kaisha* 77,897; and *Gomei-Kaisha* 19,246. Table 2.1 shows the number of *KK*s by the amount of paid-up share capital as at February 1990. It should be noted that the great majority of *KK*s are small-sized enterprises, defined by the Commercial Code as below ¥10 million (in mid-1991 the exchange rate was £1 = ¥235). To the surprise of the government a large number of small-sized enterprises have been formed as *KK*s, not *YK*s. On the other hand, large-sized enterprises whose share capital is ¥500 million or more, or whose liabilities as at the latest balance sheet date are at least ¥20,000 million, total around 6,500 companies only. It is important to note that in Japan *KK*s range in size from multinational enterprises to very small companies.

What is crucial in influencing the disclosure of information and accounting in general is the predominant type of business organization and its ownership

Table 2.1   Analysis of *Kabushiki-Kaisha* by share capital, 1990

Share capital (¥m)	Existing	Liquidated
below 1	42,441	242,885
1–10	719,436	359,939
10–50	355,900	44,138
50–100	35,446	1,866
100–300	16,503	485
300–500	5,022	112
500–1,000	2,049	36
1,000–5,000	2,916	34
5,000+	1,509	6
	1,181,222	649,501

Source: Ministry of Justice

structure. In general, limited liability companies have a broader investor base than sole traders and partnerships. As a result, disclosure by limited liability companies tends to be more extensive than, say, sole traders. In terms of economic significance, like the US and UK, the limited liability company is the most important type of business enterprise. Consequently the focus of this research is accounting and reporting by *KK*s.

Kabushiki-Kaisha

Formation requirements

According to the provisions of the Commercial Code, a *KK* can be formed by at least one founder, who may be resident or non-resident Japanese nationals or companies. In order to form a company, the founders must prepare and sign the articles of association, which must contain the following information:

1 the objectives of the company;
2 the trade name;
3 the total number of shares which the company intends to issue;
4 the par value per share;
5 the total number of shares to be issued on the occasion of the formation and the classification by par value and no-par value shares;
6 the address of the head office;
7 the method of public notice;
8 the name(s) and address(es) of the founder(s).

Since the 1981 amendment to the Commercial Code the amount of par value shares to be issued on formation may not be less than ¥50,000. In addition, if no-par value shares are issued, the amount to be paid in must be at least ¥50,000 per share. In order to complete the formation of a company, at least 25 per cent of the total number of authorized shares must be issued and paid. A public notice of the formation of a company must be made either in the official gazette or a daily newspaper. Unless the founders underwrite a portion of the shares to be issued at the time of the formation, subscriptions are normally necessary. Where the founders acquire shares through investment in property which can be made only by them, details must be provided of the founders, the real value of the property and the type and number of shares to be issued.

The formation meeting at which the company is legally constituted must elect at least three directors and one statutory auditor. The formation of a *KK* must be registered with the local office of the Ministry of Justice within two weeks of the formation meeting. The particulars for registration contain the following information in addition to (1) to (4) and (7) of the articles of association described above:

1 the location of the head office and branches;
2 the total number of shares issued by type and number;
3 the amount of paid-in capital;
4 names of directors and statutory auditors;
5 name and address of the representative director.

Once a company is registered it becomes a legal entity which takes over responsibility for any pre-incorporation contracts including formation costs. A tax-deductible registration duty of ¥150,000 or, if greater, 0.7 per cent of capital is imposed on the formation of a company.

Before a foreign investor may acquire shares in a newly formed *KK* it is necessary to file a report with the Ministry of Finance and other relevant ministries before the investment is made. The report must provide details of the investment, including its objectives, amount and timing.

Capital structure

The minimum called-up capital that must be fully paid on issue is, ¥10 million.[4] Shares are normally issued for cash although they may also be issued in exchange for property. If shares are issued for property and the number of shares to be issued to the investor is more than 5 per cent of the total number of shares issued, an independent valuation of the consideration must normally be undertaken by an examiner, whom the court elects at the request of the directors.

The Commercial Code specifies that shares issued and outstanding must be a minimum of 25 per cent of the total authorized capital. In order to increase the number of authorized shares it is necessary to amend the articles of association at a general meeting. For approval to be valid, the majority of shares issued must be represented and a special resolution – requiring a two-thirds majority – passed.

A *KK* may issue par value shares, no-par value shares, registered shares or bearer shares. Provided a bearer shareholder deposits his or her share certificate with the company, all shareholder rights may be exercised. Provided the articles of association allow, it is permissible to issue classes of shares with different rights to dividend income and/or residual assets in the event of a liquidation. It is also permissible to issue non-voting shares with dividend income privileges, provided that the total number of non-voting shares does not exceed 25 per cent of the total number of shares issued. However, it is normal for a *KK* to issue only ordinary shares.

Before the 1981 amendment to the Commercial Code the par value of shares could be ¥20, ¥50 or ¥500. Since 30 September 1982, however, shares issued at the formation of a *KK* must be for ¥50,000 or more, in the form of either par value or no-par value shares. Existing *KK*s were obliged to group shares together to match this new par value. All *KK*s listed on a stock exchange are required to adopt the unit-share system, whereby one unit of shares constitutes the number of shares calculated by dividing the existing par value by at least ¥50,000. Shares of less than one unit have no voting rights but other beneficial rights exist. These include the right to dividends, redemption payments and pre-emption rights where applicable.

Companies formed after 30 September 1982 apply a fractional-share system in which shares are issued equal to one-hundredth of one share or multiples thereof. Consequently a minor share may not be less than one-hundredth of one share. Fractional shares, which must have a minimum value of ¥500, should normally be registered with the company, and share certificates issued may be bearer shares. Consequently, fractional shares may be transferred on delivery although such shares do not have voting rights.

Share capital may be increased through a combination of new issues and stock dividends or transfers from capital reserve and/or legal earned reserve (described later). The issue of new shares is subject to approval by the board of directors, subject to the restriction that shares may not be issued in excess of authorized capital. In contrast, a stock dividend requires retained earnings to be capitalized, for which shareholder approval is required. Any new shares must be issued in accordance with the articles of association. The articles may grant pre-emption rights to new shareholders.

Share capital may be decreased by offsetting an accumulated deficit, by the redemption of shares or by a reduction in the par value of shares. To protect creditors, the Commercial Code specifies the conditions and circumstances of a capital reduction.

In general, it is not possible for a company to acquire Treasury stock and consequently the frustration of a hostile takeover bid by this method is prohibited.

Legal earned reserves and distribution policy

The concept of legal earned reserves is familiar in continental Europe. Since the original Japanese Commercial Code was based on the German model it is not surprising that there is a regulation in Japan to provide for a legal earned reserve. In Germany all stock corporations (*Aktiengesellschaften – AG*) are required to maintain a legal earned reserve by appropriating 5 per cent of annual net profits until the reserve equals 10 per cent of share capital. Such reserves are common in Europe. For example, in Sweden every company must appropriate 10 per cent of annual net profits to a legal reserve until the reserve equals 20 per cent of share capital. Prudence in Swedish financial reporting means that the rate of appropriation and level of the legal earned reserve are twice those applicable to German companies. The requirement in Japan is somewhat different. Rather than a percentage of annual net profits, the Commercial Code stipulates that an amount equal to at least 10 per cent of appropriated annual profits (i.e. cash dividends plus bonuses paid to directors and auditors) must be set up as a legal earned reserve until the reserve equals 25 per cent of capital stock.

The legal earned reserve may be used to reduce accumulated losses provided shareholder approval has been obtained. It may be capitalized provided approval from the board of directors is obtained. However, the reserve may not be used for a dividend distribution.

A *KK* may pay an interim dividend in the form of cash provided the directors approve and provided there are available brought-forward surpluses less legal earned reserve provisions and any anticipated current losses. In contrast, a final dividend may be in the form of cash, or in shares (shareholder approval is required for a dividend distribution which is not in the form of cash). The Commercial Code specifies that the maximum dividend distribution is the net asset value of the company – as shown on the balance sheet – less issued paid-in capital and less the larger of two amounts: the total capital and earned surplus appropriated for the legal earned reserve including the current year's appropriation; and the total deferred costs, comprising pre-operation and research and development expenditure.

Auditors

The Commercial Code specifies that all *KK*s, but not other types of business (a *YK* may have statutory auditors if its articles of association provide), should have a statutory auditor (*Kansayaku*) of one or more individuals. There is no upper limit as to how many statutory auditors a company may have. A statutory auditor cannot be a director, officer or employee of the company or of any of its subsidiaries.[5] A statutory auditor is not required to be a professional accountant (CPA) and his role is similar to an internal auditor in companies in many Western countries. The appointment of a statutory auditor requires approval from shareholders, and the term of office is normally two years before further approval is required.

The Commercial Code also contains special provisions for the audit of large *KK*s – often referred to as Commercial Code audits. All *KK*s with capital stock of at least ¥500 million or with total liabilities of at least ¥20,000 million should provide an independent auditor's report on the financial statements which are prepared in accordance with the Code under the requirements of the Law Concerning the Special Case of the Commercial Code for the Audit of Kabushiki Kaisha, promulgated in 1974. Another change brought about by that revision was the procedure for appointing independent auditors. Until 30 September 1981 the independent auditor was appointed by the board of directors with agreement with the statutory auditors. From 1 October 1981 the appointment of independent auditors requires approval from shareholders. The independent auditors must be qualified accountants under the Certified Public Accountants Law (CPA Law) and be members of the Japanese Institute of Certified Public Accountants (JICPA).

If a *KK* offers shares or bonds amounting to ¥500 million or more, or has its own shares listed on the Stock Exchange or registered over the counter, the Securities and Exchange Law (SEL) requires that the financial statements be prepared in accordance with Japanese generally accepted accounting principles. Usually the independent auditor appointed to conduct a Commercial Code audit will also undertake the SEL audit. Where applicable the consolidated accounts must also be audited.

The relationship between managers and the statutory auditors is explored in chapter 3.

The zaibatsu, *interlocking shareholdings and directorships*

In order to understand fully the organization of industry in Japan it is necessary to appreciate the historical role of the *zaibatsu* (family combines). The rise and fall of the *zaibatsu* took place over a very short period, from 1920 to 1950, although the foundations of the *zaibatsu* were laid during the period of Meiji government. Businessmen such as Iwasaki of Mitsubishi, Minomura of Mitsui and Yasuda had been offered financial subsidies and materials to start new enterprises, with the added advantage that profits were tax free (Clark, 1979, p. 42). In addition, non-strategic state-owned industries had been sold off cheaply during the recession of the 1870s. Entrepreneurs, particularly from the same family, founded companies in several different industries. With common origins and common ownership together with money from the same bank the core of the *zaibatsu* was formed. Four main groups developed – Mitsubishi, Mitsui, Sumitomo and Yasuda. Trading within such combines was on favourable terms and the groups continued to

> benefit from government influence in, for example, the allocation of import licences for technology. They also gained immeasurably from their privileged access to capital since each zaibatsu had a bank, which acted as a money pump. Deposits from the public were channelled towards the other member companies of the group, by loans or by the underwriting of share and debenture issues. The ability to raise capital easily allowed the zaibatsu to take the lead in the development of heavy, capital industries like engineering and chemicals between the two World Wars. (Clark, 1979, p. 42)

The structure of each *zaibatsu* was hierarchical, with a central holding company controlled by a founding family (see figure 2.1). The holding company would own the majority of shares in a number of core companies including the bank, the trust company, trading company and insurance company. These core companies would own shares in many other corporations so that the *zaibatsu* as a group would control somewhere between 40 and

Figure 2.1   Hierarchical structure of a *zaibatsu*

100 per cent of the share capital of the major members (Clark, 1979).

Since each one of up to 12 core companies held investments as affiliations, associates or subsidiaries in perhaps two or three other companies, the conglomerate structure was considerable. The *zaibatsu* were held together not only by share ownership, including cross-ownership, but also by interlocking presidencies and directorships. In addition, considerable central management co-ordination was exercised over the group, which included a substantial amount of intergroup trading and use of other members of the group as agents. 'So great was their collective power and so wide their interests that the zaibatsu had some pretension to economic self-sufficiency' (Clark, 1979, p. 43). Sufficient information was reported to the holding company to enable the *zaibatsu* family to control and effectively manage these almost self-sufficient groupings. Since there was never any need to raise external capital – which might require the disclosure of information – the *zaibatsu* were based on secrecy; disclosure was restricted to the minimum level required by the law.

In the final quarter of the nineteenth century and the early part of the twentieth militarism began to rise. In 1904 Japan was at war with Russia and two world wars followed, interspersed with frequent skirmishes with the Chinese about Manchuria, on the mainland. In fact, between 1868 and 1945 Japan was involved in five major wars. Whilst the political influence of the *zaibatsu* families declined somewhat over this period their economic power grew. Hadley (1970, p. 45) estimates that by 1941 the *zaibatsu* controlled 32 per cent of investment in heavy industry and 50 per cent of Japan's banking sector. Indeed, the military encouraged the formation of cartels among the *zaibatsu*. For example, Roberts (1973, p. 187) reports that in 1908 'well before hostilities began in China, war minister Terauchi Masatake summoned representatives of Mitsui Bussan, Okura-gumi, and a Mitsubishi affiliate, and instructed them to establish a joint organization for overseas arms transactions. Thus the Taihei Kumiai (Pacific Union), better known as the Taiping Company, was established. The three parent organizations were guaranteed a profit of five per cent on their sales.'

Despite co-operation between the traditional *zaibatsu* and the military the cartel was cautious about the former because of their ties with the conservative government. Consequently the military created new *zaibatsu* – industrial capitalists – who would be loyal to them. 'In this way such companies as Nissan, Nihon Chisso (Japan Nitrogen), Nihon Sōda (Japan Soda), Shōwa Denko (Shōwa Electrical), boomed under the protection of the military. The capital for their enterprises was raised from the public or the open capital market. Through their close connections with the military they gained various concessions, and were therefore loyal to the military' (Morishima, 1982, pp. 95–6).

Japan was occupied by the allied forces from 1945 to 1952 and one of the objectives of the occupation authorities was to dismantle the *zaibatsu*. The Law Concerning Prohibition of Private Monopoly and Presentation of Fair Trade, usually referred to as the Anti-Monopoly Act, was promulgated in 1947 with the purpose of protecting consumer interests by facilitating effective enforcement of free and fair competition. The Law prohibited private monopolies, unfair trade and anti-competitive arrangements and there were also restrictions on mergers, acquisitions and business transfers. The Anti-Monopoly Law was based on the US model, which tried to maintain a competitive environment. In the US the Sherman Act 1890 tried to outlaw monopoly and the Clayton Act 1914 prohibited companies from acquiring other companies 'where in any line of commerce in any section of the country, the effect of such acquisitions may be substantially to lessen competition, or to tend to create a monopoly'. In 1914 the US government set up the Federal Trade Commission, by an Act of that name, with the purpose of overseeing the competitive environment and prohibiting anti-competitive behaviour (Cooke, 1988a, p. 421). The Americans introduced an organization called the Fair Trade Commission on Japan. This Commission can order necessary measures to be taken to prevent abuse of a dominant position and may bring a lawsuit against the merger (Anti-Monopoly Law, s. 17–2). In order to prevent illegal mergers, any company intending to undertake a merger must report the proposal to the Commission. There is then a 30-day suspension period during which the merger cannot be completed. It is up to the Commission to decide whether a merger has been accomplished by unfair means or has resulted in a restriction of free competition. The Commission decides whether a further review is required.

Despite the apparent rigours of the Anti-Monopoly Act,

> Japan has an impressive number of laws exempting cartel activities from the application of the Anti-Monopoly Act. Most (thirty-four) of these laws were enacted in the early post-war period, from 1947 to 1960. During the last twenty-three years, only eight cartel exemption laws have been added. Although one-third of the cartel systems have never been used, cartels were heavily employed up through the late 1960s. Following 1970, Japan attempted to eliminate unnecessary cartels, and it became difficult to form new cartels. For international comparative purposes, the number of cartels enforced as of March 1982 was only 121. (Uesugi, 1986, p. 392)

The cartel system in Japan is often used as part of the adjustment process, particularly with respect to dealing with excess capacity. Economists in the West often argue that such arrangements are not likely to lead to an efficient solution to the problem of excess capacity (see, for example, OECD, 1982). However, the Japanese view is that cartelization allows companies in difficulty to reach a consensus in solving mutual problems. Again, the concepts of harmony and consensus are important in the resolution of a particular problem (Amaya, 1980). Indeed, 'Japan's policy of using cartel systems to promote adjustment is by far the most extensive of all the developed countries' (Uesugi, 1986, p. 390).

In addition to the Anti-Monopoly Act, the occupation authorities issued directives prohibiting 'the zaibatsu families from involvement in management activities, and as a result of the new property tax they also lost a large proportion of their assets. At the same time those who had acted as their loyal "foremen" before and during the war, i.e. the top managers of zaibatsu enterprises, were also purged. Thus, in these enterprises management and ownership were separated in one stroke' (Morishima, 1982, p. 169).

After the occupation forces left Japan, many of the large firms which had been divided began to reconstitute themselves and core companies of the *zaibatsu* began to make arrangements with one another (Clark, 1979, p. 43), this time without holding companies.

> Even today, therefore, there are constellations of companies with a common name – Sumitomo Metal, Sumitomo Chemical, Sumitomo Real Estate, and so on – each constellation including a bank and a trading company. Within each, also, companies trade together and co-operate, and there are cross-holdings of shares and common directorships. Yet even though these constellations are commonly called zaibatsu, and even though their constituent companies are usually descended from the pre-war zaibatsu, they are very much more loosely co-ordinated than were their defunct progenitors. (Clark, 1979, pp. 43–4)

Such groupings are often referred to as *keiretsu*, although at their origin there was a distinction between the *keiretsu* and the *gurupu*. The former was a term originally used for a type of conglomerate in which heirarchical systems incorporated not only a number of subsidiaries but also suppliers, subcontractors and distributors associated with a particular manufacturer. In contrast, the *gurupu* consist of highly diversified conglomerates with banks, insurance, property and trading arms to their corporate groups. Cross-shareholdings are a characteristic of this type of organization, which is controlled by a presidents' council (*shachokai*) based on share ownership of other group companies. In practice, the term *keiretsu* is often used to cover both types of conglomerate organization.

The prohibition on the holding companies has effectively prevented the re-formation of family groups with central management direction. Whilst the new *zaibatsu* – such as Mitsubishi, Mitsui and Sumitomo, which were companies within giant groups – now exist, they are characterized by minority shareholdings rather than the majority shareholdings which existed before the war. Furthermore, whilst there is still a preference to deal with one another the links are much less formal and perhaps even less common.

A second major type of industrial organization in post-war Japan is that centred around a bank. For example, Sanwa is similar in many respects to the German Deutsche Bank or Dresdner Bank (Clark, 1979, p. 77). The group consists of about 15 major companies in which Sanwa owns shares and to which it provides finance. Associations are not as close as the early *zaibatsu* and cross-ownership of shareholdings is less common.

A third major form of industrial organization in Japan centres around major manufacturing groups such as Nissan, Hitachi and Toyota. Such groups are characterized by specialized operations in industry and largely independent subsidiaries. One advantage of such a relationship is that a group subsidiary can be listed on the Stock Exchange.

Groups and mergers

Mergers can take place between companies formed under the Commercial Code provided that the surviving company is a *KK* when either or both parties to the merger are themselves *KK*s (s. 562). A *YK* may also merge or be merged with another company provided certain conditions are fulfilled. When either company survives after a merger it must issue new shares to the shareholders of the acquired company (s. 409).

In Japan there are two main schools of thought with regard to mergers.[6] One viewpoint considers an amalgamation to be a unity of juristic persons supported basically by the Corporation Tax Law, and the other is that it represents an investment in property (assets), a view generally suggested by accounting theorists and the Commercial Code. According to the former viewpoint, the essence of a merger is regarded as a union of one juristic person with another to form a new legal entity. The following characteristics therefore are prevalent:

1 assets and liabilities in the merged companies should be carried forward at their book values;
2 capital surpluses and earned surpluses, etc. in the merged companies should remain intact and be transferred to the new juristic entity.

On the other hand, the essence of a merger might be recognized as a contribution of capital in the form of an investment in property. Therefore its characteristics are as follows.

1 Fixed assets should be stated at fair market value.
2 When the amount of net assets valued at fair market value exceeds the amount of shares issued to shareholders of the merged company (including cash delivered) at the time of the merger, the difference should be treated

as a capital surplus. This capital surplus is merely an additional paid-in surplus.

3 Capital surpluses, earned surpluses, etc., will not remain intact. These capital items disappear at the time of the merger and should be transferred to a capital surplus.

One of the myths about Japan is that mergers and acquisitions are rare. Indeed, there are now some 1,300 transactions each year (see figure 2.2) that may be categorized as mergers and acquisitions, compared with 902 acquiring companies in the UK in 1988. In addition, there are now over a thousand business transfers (figure 2.3) each year in Japan. The value of such

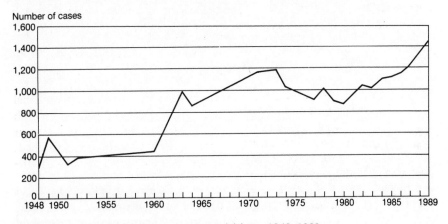

Figure 2.2 Number of mergers and acquisitions, 1948–1989

Source: FTC Annual Report, 1989

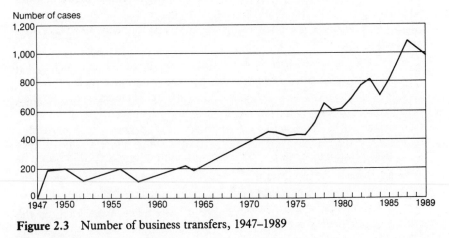

Figure 2.3 Number of business transfers, 1947–1989

Source: FTC Annual Report, 1989

Table 2.2   Number of mergers, acquisitions and business transfers, 1983–1988

Financial year	Amount of total assets after transaction (¥ billion)						
	below 1	1–5	5–10	10–50	50–100	100+	Total
Mergers and acquisitions							
1983	584	261	78	64	13	20	1,020
1984	626	271	88	78	17	16	1,096
1985	575	336	89	87	12	14	1,113
1986	608	302	83	114	19	21	1,147
1987	571	347	125	119	19	34	1,215
1988	592	382	154	157	22	29	1,336
Business transfers							
1983	511	76	25	60	8	22	702
1984	559	118	27	38	12	36	790
1985	586	92	29	47	18	35	807
1986	671	108	36	49	26	46	936
1987	773	142	47	54	7	61	1,084
1988	729	130	42	61	12	54	1,028

Source: FTC Annual Reports 1986–9

transactions is shown in table 2.2. It is apparent that the majority of mergers and business transfers involve assets of less than ¥5,000 million. It is also apparent that there has been a substantial increase in completed transactions since 1970. The Economic Research Institute of Daiwa Securities Limited has attributed this change to six major factors:

1 *The needs of conglomerates*   As the rate of growth in the Japanese economy has slowed and the rate of return has declined, many companies have turned to acquisition as a preferred route to new investment in order to protect margins.
2 *The shortening in the life-cycle of commodities*   As the pace of innovation has grown faster the product life-cycle has become progressively shorter. One way of gaining market share quickly is through a merger rather than through new investment.
3 *Countermeasure to the friction of foreign trade*   As Japanese foreign trade has expanded so the trade imbalance has become a political subject. To redress some of this imbalance and to avoid the possibility of retaliation, Japanese companies have begun to shift emphasis from conventional exports to production abroad. One way of achieving this quickly is through acquisition. The substantial rise in the yen against the dollar has necessitated a change in companies' strategy.
4 *Funding*   To undertake mergers, acquisitions and business transfers it is

essential that sufficient funding is available. Liquidity ratios of Japanese companies have been increasing since 1975.

5 *Changes in management's view of cross-shareholdings*   In order to maintain a close relationship between one company and another it has been traditional for Japanese companies to own shares in one another. Such close relationships are being modified somewhat and divestments are quite common. For example, heavy industrial companies that have fallen into a state of decline are having to sell off their shares in order to cover operating losses.

6 *Mitigation of legal controls*   The Act Concerning Control of Foreign Exchange and Foreign Trade was revised in December 1980, giving effect to a policy of liberalization of its foreign investment policy rather than prohibition.

Whilst the above factors help explain the increase in mergers and business transfers, there are some aspects which characterize Japanese transactions. For example, mergers involving Japanese companies are invariably friendly and brought about as a result of the initiative of a third party. Indeed, a characteristic of doing business with the Japanese is the important role of the intermediary. Intermediaries are used not just for the initial introduction but also in negotiation between companies. However, whilst transactions involving Japanese companies are normally reported as 'friendly' or 'agreed' mergers, several have in fact begun as hostile acquisition attempts. Obvious hostile takeovers are more difficult to find although Koshin's successful takeover of Kokusai Kogyo, an aerial survey group, clearly comes within that category.

Another feature of mergers and acquisitions is that takeovers of Japanese companies by foreigners are rare and may encounter cultural difficulties. For example, in April 1989 the Texan corporate raider, T. B. Pickens, became the single largest shareholder in an automobile lighting company, Koito Manufacturing. Pickens denied allegations that he had acquired his 20.2 per cent stake in the company for purposes of 'greenmail' and emphasized his long-term investment in the company. Nevertheless, he did acknowledge that he had purchased his stake from a Japanese investor with a reputation for 'greenmail'.[7] Despite such events, there are few prospects of such procedures being readily accepted in Japan. It is also likely that Japanese companies will continue to make friendly acquisitions rather than hostile takeovers. On 28 September 1989 the *Japan Economic Journal* (usually referred to as *Nikkei* in Japanese) published the results of a questionnaire which asked: What is your opinion on the acquisition of shares by Mr Pickens? The question was put to top management. Seventy per cent stated that they were against hostile acquisitions.

The Anti-Monopoly Act and the Act Concerning Control of Foreign

Exchange and Foreign Trade both impose restrictions on share acquisitions. Share acquisition may be undertaken by:

1 a transfer by a private sale agreement by a small number of major shareholders;
2 a purchase of newly issued shares by share quotas to third parties; and
3 by purchasing shares in the market.

In Japan either or both of the first two procedures are normally adopted in practice; purchasing shares through the market is not usual as it leads to a sharp rise in the share price.

The Anti-Monopoly Act aims to prevent shareholdings that may harm competition in a specific market. As part of this overall aim the Act stipulates that if one company (or individual) owns in excess of 10 per cent of the issued and outstanding shares of two or more competing companies, the investor must notify the Fair Trade Commission within 30 days of the share acquisition.

Under the Securities and Exchange Law promulgated by the Ministry of Finance in 1948 (and subsequent amendments) with the purpose of protecting investors and enhancing the administration of the Japanese economy, consolidated accounts for listed companies should be prepared (from 1977), audited and filed with the Ministry of Finance as supplementary information. It should be noted that the Commercial Code and the Corporation Tax Law do not require consolidated accounts to be prepared. A company in which more than 50 per cent of the votes are substantially owned by a parent company may be treated as a subsidiary. The criterion of control over the composition of the board of directors cannot be adopted. The equity method of accounting is appropriate in consolidated accounts where investments of 20 per cent or more of the votes is made in an investee. Although tax-effect accounting cannot be generally used at the individual company level, the allocation of income taxes may be permitted when timing differences arise on consolidation. The accounting aspects are dealt with in more detail in Part II.

Liquidation of a company

Companies may be liquidated by mergers, bankruptcy, special decision at a shareholders' general meeting, expiration of the operating period provided in the articles of association, or by court decision. Normally, a director must become the liquidator to the company except in the cases of a merger or a bankruptcy. The liquidator is required to report to the court, within two weeks of the liquidation, the reason for and date of the liquidation, and the name and address of the liquidator. Section 419–1 of the Commercial Code provides that the liquidator must prepare an inventory and a balance sheet without delay, and submit it to a shareholders' general meeting for approval.

After approval, the inventory and balance sheet should be submitted to the court as soon as possible. Usually, the liquidator must distribute residual assets to shareholders in proportion to the number of shares held.

Branch of a foreign corporation

According to the provisions of the Commercial Code, a foreign company, duly registered abroad, is required to appoint a representative to establish a branch in Japan. It is necessary to register a branch of a foreign corporation with a local office of the Ministry of Justice within two weeks of its formation. Items to be registered are as follows:

1 the company's name;
2 the addresses of the head office and the branch in Japan;
3 the objectives of the business;
4 the authorized, issued and outstanding share capital of the company;
5 the date of formation of the company;
6 the names of the directors of the company;
7 the name and address of the representative in the Japanese branch.

Under the Law Concerning Control of Foreign Exchange and Foreign Trade, governed by the Ministry of Finance, establishment of a branch of a foreign company is regarded as a direct inward investment. The foreign company must prepare a report on the proposed direct inward investment showing the objectives of the business and the amount and timing of the investment. At least three months before the scheduled day of the investment, the report should be filed with the Ministry of Finance and the competent authorities by way of the Bank of Japan.

A branch of a foreign company does not have an obligation to publish accounts. However, tax regulations require submission of the accounts of the branch in addition to those of the foreign company. If a foreign corporation takes the form of a branch, the foreign corporation will be taxed on its entire income from all sources within Japan, including dividends, interest, royalties, rents and capital gains, unless an applicable tax treaty stipulates otherwise. Dividends, interest, royalties, technology fees and rents received by a foreign corporation from a Japanese subsidiary or other company are subject to withholding income tax at a flat rate of 20 per cent. This may be reduced to a lower rate as the result of an applicable tax treaty. Under the tax treaty between Japan and the UK, for example, the withholding tax rate is reduced to 10 per cent, except for certain types of dividends that are taxed at 15 per cent. Under the Japan/Zambia treaty, the withholding tax rate is reduced to nil for dividends, while for other types of income it is 10 per cent. The treaty tax rates apply to foreign branches as well as to foreign subsidiaries only if the income is not attributable to a permanent establishment in Japan by a foreign company. Otherwise, an ordinary withholding rate of 20 per cent applies as a general rule.

Books and accounting

Section 32 of the Commercial Code requires any person carrying on business activities to keep proper books of account, including the balance sheet, in accordance with fair accounting conventions. This provision applies to sole traders as well as to *KK*s.

The books of account usually consist of cash books, journals and general ledgers. Accounting books and important material for business activity must be kept in an orderly manner and must be maintained for a period of at least ten years from the end of the financial year. According to section 34 of the Commercial Code assets must be stated in the books of account on a systematic basis, as follows:

1 current assets must be valued at either historical cost, production price or current value provided that, in cases where the current value is considerably lower than historical cost or production cost, the current value should be adopted except where the value is expected to recover historical cost or production price;
2 fixed assets must be valued at historical cost or production price less reasonable accumulated depreciation and reasonable deductions for any diminution in value;
3 the value of receivables cannot exceed the amount obtained by subtracting a reasonable estimate of loss from uncollectable amounts.

Summary

The majority of limited liability companies are small in size, i.e. below ¥100 million share capital, and are often family-run. However, the small-firm sector provides great flexibility for the medium and large firms since small companies act as subcontractors to their big brothers. Such flexibility has its costs since Japan has a high level of corporate bankruptcy.

Influences over the regulation of companies arose from both Europe and the US, particularly the former where experience in such matters extended well beyond that of the Japanese. Whilst prudence became a fundamental underlying concept, particularly with respect to legal earned reserves, Japan did not adopt the concepts of 'restricted' and 'free shares', a characteristic of some European countries such as Sweden. Legal earned reserves in Japan are based on appropriations of cash disbursements rather than on annual net profits as in Germany and Sweden.

The audit function in Japan has been described as largely perfunctory and ceremonial (Arpan and Radebaugh, 1985, p. 27), based on unqualified statutory auditors who may not be described as independent. However, the Commercial Code stipulates that large firms must also be audited by qualified certified public accountants who are members of the Japanese Institute of Certified Public Accountants. Furthermore, those companies that have sold securities to the public are subject to more extensive disclosure under the Securities and Exchange Law.

Whilst the *zaibatsu* were purged by the allied forces after the Second World War, they have been replaced by the *gurupu* and *keiretsu*. Features of these 'headless' groups include interlocking directorships and reciprocal shareholdings. Such groups are characteristic of Japan in many ways – no ultimate authority, no board of directors, no mastermind, no 'Japan Inc.'. Furthermore, it may be surprising to some that mergers and acquisitions do occur in Japan, although hostile takeovers are rare since they smack of disloyalty to the workforce.

Notes

1 The first Commercial Code was promulgated in 1890 and amended in 1899. The Code established in 1899 (which was amended in 1911, 1923, 1938, eight times in 1947–51, 1962, 1974, 1981 and 1990) dominated financial reporting in Japan until the end of the Second World War.

2 Yukichi Fukuwaza was also influential in the process of moving away from single-entry bookkeeping to Western double-entry. In June 1873 he published the first book in Japanese on Western bookkeeping, a translation of Bryant and Stratton's *Common School Bookkeeping*, which had been published two years earlier.

3 The Yugen-Kaisha Law was amended in 1990 to provide that the minimum called-up capital should be ¥3 million for all *YKs*. However, existing companies have a transitional period of five years in which to change from the earlier minimum of ¥100,000.

4 An amendment to the Commercial Code in 1990 permits only one founder on formation and provides that the minimum called-up capital for all *KKs* is to be ¥10 million. Existing companies have a five-year transitional period in which to change from the earlier minimum of ¥350,000, since a *KK* had to be formed by at least seven founders, each with shares of not less than ¥50,000.

5 Before the Second World War the statutory auditors could be employees of the company. For instance, Alletzhauser (1990, pp. 78–9) notes the appointment of one of the first auditors to the Nomura Partnership in the 1920s. Kamata was given an auditor's salary of ¥70 a month at first, compared with experienced bank branch managers of the big *zaibatsu*, who earned ¥100 a month. Such high salaries were paid to protect auditors against the temptations of fraud.

6 In essence, the debate in Japan is similar to that prevailing in the UK and US, which compares pooling-of-interests (merger) accounting with purchase (acquisition) accounting.

7 A term used to describe the purchase of a sufficient number of shares to be able to threaten a full takeover bid if the company does not buy back the shares – at a substantial profit to the 'greenmailer'.

3
Enterprise Users

'Within the enterprise there are many users of information. The quantity and quality of information provided depend on the level of sophistication of the users as well as the technical competence of the accountants. Managers require specialized information to assist in decision making, and a whole branch of accounting has resulted from this need' (Radebaugh, 1975, p. 43). This chapter identifies and discusses the key users of corporate information and considers the interrelationship between these groups. According to the provisions of the Commercial Code the main elements of a corporation consist of shareholders, particularly at a general meeting, the board of directors and the statutory auditors. However, for a better understanding of a Japanese company it is necessary to consider both employees and alumni (the 'old boys').

The term *Kabushiki-Kaisha* is normally considered to correspond to the limited liability company in the UK and the joint-stock company in the US. However, in Japanese *kaisha* denotes something beyond the concept of the company:

> Kaisha does not mean that individuals are bound by contractual relationships into a corporate enterprise, while still thinking of themselves as separate entities; rather kaisha is 'my' or 'our' company, the community to which one belongs primarily, and which is all important in one's life . . . That company A belongs not to its shareholders, but rather to 'us', is the sort of reasoning that is involved in Japan and which is carried to such a point that even the modern legal process must compromise in face of this strong value orientation.
>
> (Nakane, 1970, pp. 3–4)

The determination of the relationship between the individual and the company has its roots in the concept of the *ie*. The *ie* is sometimes translated as the 'family' although this does not adequately convey the full meaning of the term. The Japanese concept of the family extends beyond the nuclear family to cover the entire line, including descendants, embracing the unborn, as well as the recently dead and also ancestors, those who cannot be remembered (Hendry, 1987, p. 23). The *ie* was hierarchically structured, based 'on age, sex, and expectation of permanency in the house' (1987, p. 24). Relations between members of the same group were based on Confucian principles of benevolence and loyalty with the aim of achieving order and continuity. One permanent heir would be chosen as the head of the *ie* and a non-inheriting son may take the option of setting up his own house to develop a new *ie*. In certain parts of Japan the original *ie* would co-operate in economic matters with a new *ie*. These *dozoku* (related houses) were not restricted to family life but extended to the large companies.

After the Second World War the allied forces abolished the *ie* in favour of the nuclear family in an attempt to transform Japan from its feudal heritage towards a modern democracy. Nevertheless, certain characteristics of the *ie* persist in many parts of Japan (Horie, 1966, p. 15; Nakane, 1970, pp. 7–8; Hendry, 1987, p. 27). A characteristic of Japanese companies is that employees' lives are taken over to a much greater extent than in Western companies. Consequently, 'the modern corporation remains an important focus of group consciousness in Japan' (McKinnon, 1986, p. 83). In Japan great value has been placed on the concept of *wa* (harmony) within a group, whereas in the West there is more emphasis on individuality and independence.

The company and employees

It is difficult to generalize about companies that, in Japan, range in size from the very small to some of the largest in the world. Morishima (1982, p. 174) argues that there is a substantial difference in rewards between the large corporations and the smaller companies. 'Even today in Japan the well-being of a person's whole life is virtually decided by whether or not he is able to obtain employment within a large enterprise ... In a Western type capitalist economy the most difficult problem is that of class, and in Confucian–capitalist Japan the problem of dual structure, a sort of segmentation of labour market, is no more than the class problem in another guise.' The rewards offered are not merely in terms of remuneration. Large companies are able to offer better pensions, higher bonuses, better health care and in many cases accommodation too. In addition, large companies extend their role to the provision of sports facilities, hobby clubs, and holiday homes.

As a result of the duality of employment there is fierce competition to join large firms. This competition takes place only once in a lifetime, after leaving school or college. 'Since in a Confucian society people are ranked in the hierarchy according to the education they have, or have not, received, the large enterprises wish to recruit graduates from what one might term the more prestigious institutions, as this is clearly the most appropriate way to preserve the standing of the enterprise' (Morishima, 1982, p. 174). In return for greater rewards, based on a seniority system, the large companies expect loyalty through a lifetime's work. Leaving a large company without one's employer's agreement would render a person a 'traitor' and unfit to work for another large firm.

The contractual relationship between the firm and employee is formalized by signing a document which pledges the individual to obey company rules. The rules are not stated, however, so that contractual obligations are implicit rather than explicit. Consequently, disagreements are resolved by reaching a consensus through negotiation rather than by resorting to litigation. Alston (1986, p. 243) argues that since the contractual obligations are so vague a resolution through litigation is not appropriate: 'This is one reason why America has more lawyers and litigation than Japan.'

A feature of the contractual relationship between employers and employees is flexibility. Rohlen (1974, p. 19) states that there is an obligation on an employee to be flexible both in the type of job undertaken and with respect to pay, attributes which allow large companies to respond quickly to changing circumstances. In return the company offers lifetime employment. Another important difference between a Japanese company and a Western corporation is in response to an economic depression. 'During times of economic depression all workers will receive reduced pay if necessary, and since higher-level employees receive higher pay, they will also be expected to receive larger percentage pay decreases than the lower-level workers' (Alston, 1986, p. 244). In times of economic prosperity employees would receive not only increased bonuses but also improved fringe benefits. Thus, members of the 'family' gain or lose according to the performance of the company, thereby enhancing the concept of *wa* within the group.

Flexibility in the type of job an employee undertakes means that the employer is acquiring the services of an individual rather than a particular skill. A dissatisfied employee in a Western company, or one whose skill is no longer needed, will leave or perhaps be dismissed. The Japanese employee has a lifetime obligation to serve and be served by the company. Note that the concept of lifetime employment is not as prevalent as some would believe. First, as has already been pointed out, there is a substantial difference between large Japanese corporations, where lifetime employment exists, and medium and small firms, where such practices are not commonplace. In reality the majority of employees work in medium and small companies, a situation more prevalent in Japan than many other major countries (see table 3.1). Information from a 1986 government white paper (*Chusho Kigyo*

Table 3.1   Distribution of employment by establishment size: 1981 percentages

| | Establishment size (number employed) | | | |
	Very small (1–19)	Small (20–99)	Medium (100–499)	Large (500+)
Austria[a]	33.6	27.9	23.1	15.4
Belgium[b]	22.2	22.6	26.0	29.2
France[b]	32.1	28.0	23.4	16.5
Italy[c]	43.4	30.4	14.2	12.0
Japan	49.4	27.7	14.6	8.3
Great Britain[d]	26.1	22.6	26.1	25.2
United States	20.1	28.4	24.0	21.5

[a] Wage and salary earners.
[b] 1983.
[c] The first two bands are 1–9, 10–99.
[d] The first two bands are 1–24, 25–99.
Source: OECD, *Employment Outlook*, September 1985

Hakusho) and Statistics Bureau publication (*Nihon no Tokei*) reveals that the majority of employees work in companies with a maximum of 300 employees. 'Of manufacturing industries alone, 99.5 per cent fall into this category, and they account for 74.3 per cent of people employed in manufacturing. Of these enterprises 87 per cent employ fewer than 20 people, and more than 50 per cent employ four or less. In wholesale and retail trade, nearly 97 per cent of the total number of organizations employ less than 20 people, which accounts for nearly 70 per cent of the employees' (Hendry, 1987, p. 139).

Second, women are expected to marry and in many cases leave their jobs to concentrate on the home. 'Japanese women take very seriously the roles of wife and mother and probably a majority feel that they should be at home during the early child-rearing years. The business of rearing children is regarded almost as a profession in itself by some mothers' (Hendry, 1987, p. 148). Consequently, the concept of lifetime employment does not apply to most women, a fact which can prove advantageous to a large Japanese corporation. For example, about 60 per cent of Matsushita's Japanese employees are women, the majority of whom work in relatively unskilled jobs in the factories. Thus, girls leave school, join the company and then in their early to mid-20s leave to concentrate on the home. Such women are often employed in assembly work where they are still more dexterous than robots. Consequently, the corporation has a pool of loyal women workers for a relatively short period of time, to be replaced by other young, agile and nimble women. Third, those employees who have lifetime employment are usually expected to retire between the ages of 55 and 60. And fourth, it is common practice for companies to have a pool of 'temporary' workers who may work for the company for several years but are excluded from the lifetime employment system. As a result of these features Sumiya (1981, p. 2) has estimated that only about 20 per cent of Japanese workers are part of the lifetime employment system.

Employees may constitute a user group which can have a significant effect on the disclosure of information. 'Employees have a vested interest in the enterprise and may have an impact on the disclosure of financial data. This can be made manifest through unions that require certain types of information prior to the negotiation of labour contracts' (Radebaugh, 1975, p. 43). We have already emphasized the nature of the enterprise as a family in which there is a strong desire for consensus. However, labour participation in management through unions and councils is not common, particularly since most unions are company unions rather than skill (trade) unions. Consensus within a Japanese company is reached by disseminating information widely. Information is disseminated to individuals within the firm even if they are not directly concerned. The *ringi* is a procedure used in Japanese organizations, by which suggestions and proposals for changes or improvements are formulated by departments and agreed by junior managers before being shown to senior management. Senior management hold regular discussion groups with junior staff which provide details of performance. Such information flows enhance corporate understanding, team spirit and participation in the decision-making process (Clark, 1979).

It is a characteristic of Japanese companies, particularly large corporations, that employees are kept fully informed not only of developments in the corporation but also of its financial position. Consequently, there is no need for information to be disseminated through corporate annual reports or special employee publications. Furthermore, employees can exert considerable influence over decision-making despite the lack of works councils, such as in Sweden, or board representation, as in West Germany. The labour unions in Japan are different from those prevalent in the UK or US because they represent employees of only one company. Japanese unions have a feeling of belonging towards the company where their members are employees. Ishizumi (1988) provides an example which highlights the importance and influence a labour union can exert. In January 1988 there was confrontation between management and the labour union. For many years Okuma Machinery Works, a quoted company and one of Japan's leading machine tool manufacturers, had had a company chairman from the Okuma family. The *Japan Company Handbook* for 1974 reveals that the company president at that time was Koichi Okuma. Subsequently the president passed his position on to Takeo Okuma, who in 1988 in turn tried to pass on the presidency to his first son, who was already an executive vice-president of the company. The labour union objected on the grounds that whilst the financial institutions where the biggest shareholders the Okuma family was treating the company as if it were their own. Legally only the shareholders are entitled to vote to appoint or dismiss members of the board. However, the labour unions attempted to have both Takeo Okuma and his son dismissed from the company. The matter was resolved through the mediation of the company's major lender, the Tokai Bank. The Bank appointed one of its own employees to the position of company president.

Ishizumi (1988) states that the success of a merger or acquisition is largely determined by the extent to which the workforce's co-operation is obtained.

It should be apparent from the above discussion that employees of Japanese companies, particularly large companies, can be a significant force within a company. This is achieved not by strong trade unions but by the acceptance that a company, including its management, is a family of employees. The company is a community in which there is usually no major distinction between managers and workers and where shareholders are associated with the company for a long period. Consequently, short-term profits and dividends are not reasons for share purchase, unlike Western corporations where shareholders are primarily interested in the company as a financial investment – particularly a short-term investment. Profits in a Japanese company are pursued to ensure the financial viability and expansion of the corporation rather than for the benefit of shareholders. In summary, 'companies in Japan are said to be essentially "communal organizations". Large companies in particular seem to exist for their workers; workers have lifetime ties to their firms, for which they seem to work incessantly. This factor is said to be a reason for Japanese companies' entertainment expenses (spent largely by management on employees and viewed as an important fringe benefit) often exceeding shareholder dividends' (Ames, 1981, p. 551). The effect of the importance of employees in Japanese companies is that information is disseminated through channels other than corporate annual reports or special reports. The impact of employees on financial disclosure in corporate annual reports is minimal.

Shareholders

In theory shareholders can have an impact on the disclosure of information by raising questions to the board of directors during the year or by raising issues at a shareholders' general meeting. In reality Japanese companies are largely unconcerned about the small shareholder. In contrast, the institutional shareholder can exert considerable influence but as a business associate rather than as a shareholder.

The interests of shareholders are represented by the board of directors and at a general meeting. A shareholders' general meeting must be held at least once a year within three months of the end of the financial year (or at the closing date in the case of a six-month fiscal period). The notice convening a general meeting must be issued to the shareholders at least two weeks before the date of the meeting. At a general meeting shareholders approve the accounts and the proposed appropriation of retained earnings (or disposition of accumulated deficit). An extraordinary meeting may be called at any time necessary by a representative director, or by a shareholder owning at least 3 per cent of shares provided that such shares have been continuously held for a period of six months. Normally a quorum to constitute a valid meeting is at least 50 per cent of the issued shares and decisions are adopted by a single majority of the voting rights although shareholders may vote by proxy separately for each meeting. However, decisions on the following matters must be accepted by a two-thirds majority vote of the shareholders present:

1 alteration of the articles of association;
2 sale or purchase of a significant part or the whole of a business;
3 merger contract;
4 capital reduction;
5 issue of new shares or convertible bonds with advantageous conditions to third parties;
6 dismissal of a director or statutory auditor;
7 dissolution of the company.

The 3 per cent threshold and the requirement for a two-thirds majority in certain instances may suggest that shareholders have more power than enterprises in the West. However, the directors of most Japanese companies emerge from the ranks of employees after having spent some 20 to 30 years working through various levels of management. The fact that they have served the company for many years may mean that they favour employees' rather than shareholders' interests. Such behaviour is reinforced by the fact that most Japanese directors also own part of the business. Non-executive directors form only a small minority of the board of directors and often consist of company allies. Sometimes individuals are appointed because of their connections and contracts. 'Notable among these are retired civil servants who have "come down from heaven" from Ministries concerned with the company's business' (Clark, 1979, p. 100). Such appointments are not uncommon in the West; witness the number of civil servants and politicians from a variety of ministries, including the Ministry of Defence, who have been appointed to the board of directors of UK defence contractors. In Japan such non-executive directors are often sympathetic to the management directors, unless the company is unprofitable, in which case dissatisfaction may be expressed – which is consistent with shareholders' interests. In reality, therefore, ordinary shareholders may have little real impact on the board of directors.

The second avenue for expression of shareholders' concerns is at the annual general meeting. Again, the fact that institutional shareholders and other business corporations own the majority of shares is significant. Table 3.2 shows a steady trend of increased share ownership by the institutions since 1951. Notice also a decline in foreign ownership since the crash in October 1987. Institutional investment will be dealt with in more depth in chapter 5. As table 3.3 reveals, the growth of institutional shareholdings in the UK is very similar to developments in Japan (table 3.2). What is different between the two countries is the objective of the major institutions. In the UK an investing institution looks for a return in the form of a dividend plus capital gain. Consequently its objective is the same as that of individual shareholders. In Japan institutional shareholders, consisting of banks, their associates and trading partners, often hold investments in the form of cross-holdings. 'In general, therefore, Japanese institutional shareholders invest as a means of doing business with companies' (Clark, 1979, p. 102). Indeed, Franklin at UBS Phillips and Drew has estimated that up to 75 per

Table 3.2   Share ownership by type of investors (%), all listed Japanese companies

Type of investor	1951	1961	1971	1981	1986	1988	1990
Government and local government	3.1	0.2	0.3	0.2	0.8	0.8	0.7
Financial institutions	12.6	23.1	30.9	37.3	40.9	42.2	42.3
Investment trusts	—	7.5	1.4	1.5	1.3	2.4	3.7
Securities companies	11.9	3.7	1.2	1.7	2.0	2.5	2.0
Business corporations	11.0	17.8	23.1	26.0	24.1	24.9	24.8
Individuals and others	61.3	46.3	39.9	29.2	25.2	23.6	22.6
Foreigners	—	1.4	3.2	4.0	5.7	3.6	3.9

Source: Ministry of Finance, The National Conference of Stock Exchange, *TSE Fact Book 1991*

Table 3.3   International comparison of shareholding structure (%), 1985

	Japan	*Germany*	*France*	*Italy*	*US*	*Canada*	*UK*
Non-financial corporations	30	43	41	66	—	1	10
Banks	17	8	4	3	0	4	0
Non-bank financial institutions	22	9	8	3	28	21	52
Households	23	18	24	13	67	69	24
Government	0	9	10	9	—	2	5
Others[a]	7	13	13	5	4	4	10
Total	100	100	100	100	100	100	100

[a] Mainly non-residents.
Source: Bank for International Settlements, *BIS Review*, 1989

cent of the shares quoted on the Tokyo Stock Exchange are held for such long-term relationships. Since such institutions aim to foster business relations they are unlikely to support any conflict with management that could endanger that relationship.

At a general meeting directors are not very forthcoming when questioned by shareholders. Indeed there is almost a tacit understanding that no questions will be asked. Voting is invariably on a 'follow-the-leader' basis, the leader being the institution with the largest shareholding. Where there is the potential for embarrassing questions directors can make use of *sokaiya* (a general-meeting 'fixer' – a type of gangster) who, for a fee, will discourage the inquisitive.

In effect, therefore small shareholders have been effectively disenfranchised. Large shareholders wish to maintain their existing business relations and so are in reality very passive. The extent of shareholder influence over corporate disclosures is thus minimal.

Management

Management of Japanese companies is the responsibility of the board of directors, subject, in theory, to the rights of shareholders, creditors and other interested parties. An essential difference between the management structure of a Western corporation and a Japanese company is the decision-making process. In the West the process may be described as 'top to bottom' whereas in Japan emphasis is on 'bottom to top'. In a Japanese corporation those on the bottom rung of the management structure are required to prepare a *ringisho* (*ringi* report) and submit it to the next rung of management. The *ringisho* is a corporate document recommending a particular course of action and which requires approval from the immediate superior. The document is modified where necessary and submitted to the next rung of the management ladder. Such a procedure suggests that decision-making is a collective responsibility rather than attributable to a particular individual. However, whilst Clark (1979, p. 127) provides some evidence for this assertion, he states that a comparison between companies in Japan and those in the West is not at all simple. One of the inherent difficulties of a hierarchical management structure based on a 'bottom-up' process is that managers at the bottom may put forward ideas and policies that they believe will be acceptable to their immediate superiors even if alternative courses of action may be more beneficial to the company. 'In this way, when things go wrong, they can still be safe and avoid responsibility for any detrimental consequences by saying that under the objective circumstances in which they were forced to make the decisions they made, they had no alternative but to do what they did' (Ishizumi, 1988, p. 127).

In essence, then, a Japanese company belongs to its workforce, from which most of the members of the board of directors will emerge. The 'insider' group includes not only employees but extends to the banks, insurance companies and other companies with cross-shareholdings, and all are likely to have access to information in excess of that reported in the corporate annual report. Indeed, some argue that the very essence of Japanese stock markets is the availability of market-sensitive information to brokers, bankers and large shareholders. 'This means that altering the system [to establish effective insider dealing legislation] would prejudice the interests of a very large section of the Japanese business community, and not only a few individuals who make spectacular profits by flouting the law. And in a market moved more by fundamentals, the Japanese brokers' inside track on the news is clearly a major selling point with clients' (Waldmeir, 1989).

Since Japanese companies have generally been more highly geared than Western corporations the banks have been more influential and are likely to support management provided interest and principal repayments on debt are fully met. Thus, management, employees and major shareholders have sufficient inside information for their purposes, and consequently there will be little lobbying for an increase in disclosure in corporate annual reports beyond meeting their obligations. Continuity of the enterprise is all-important and in some ways 'the company itself has taken over the traditional role of the *ie*' (Hendry, 1987, p. 35). There is little internal pressure to extend disclosures in corporate annual reports since information is for family members, not outsiders. In contrast, in the 'United States as well as other countries, the board of directors is a powerful policy-making group that can have a strong impact on the nature and quality of reported information' (Radebaugh, 1975, p. 44).

The objectives of management also differ between Japanese and Western companies. Japanese companies pursue policies of long-term market share and growth based on development research and efficiency whereas Anglo-Saxon corporations often pursue goals, including asset-stripping, to achieve short-term profits and dividends for short-term investors.[1] Reischauer (1988) argues that

> whereas the American executive must keep his eye on stock prices and the quarterly bottom line, his Japanese counterpart can take a more Olympian view, seeking to maintain a sound company and to lay the basis for growth that may not pay off for a decade, long after he himself has retired. This longer time horizon for Japanese business permits a wiser strategy for growth and is probably the single greatest advantage it has over business in the West. (p. 332)

Managers and the statutory auditors

The statutory auditor is empowered to supervise the directors' conduct of business. In addition, the statutory auditor can request the directors or employees to report their operations and, when necessary, investigate the affairs of the company and the status of its property. The statutory auditor of a parent company may request a subsidiary to provide a report on its operations and, where necessary, the statutory auditor may examine the report to verify that the company has fulfilled its statutory obligations. It is necessary for the statutory auditor to examine the financial documents which the directors intend to present to the ordinary shareholders' general meeting for approval. If the directors violate the regulations or the articles of association, the statutory auditor must state his opinion at the shareholders' general meeting.

The statutory auditor is elected, normally for a period of two years, at the company's shareholders' general meeting. There is no requirement that the statutory auditor be a qualified accountant (CPA) although the Commercial Code does stipulate that a statutory auditor may not be a director, officer or employee of the company or of its subsidiaries. The role of the statutory auditor is similar to that of an internal auditor in the West and, before the Second World War, was to serve the needs of the *zaibatsu* rather than external users. The role of the statutory auditor today is to ensure that fraud or illegal acts do not take place. 'The statutory auditor is obliged to monitor the fiduciary responsibilities of the directors and to ascertain whether they follow the law and the articles of incorporation for the benefit of shareholders' (Toba, in Choi and Hiramatsu, 1987, p. 81). In addition, the statutory auditor is responsible for auditing the financial statements as well as the operations of the company. Where the share capital does not exceed ¥100 million the duties and responsibilities of the statutory auditor include an examination of the financial statements and report prepared by the directors that will be submitted to shareholders at a general meeting. Where the share capital is at least ¥100 million the responsibilities include not only the audit of financial statements but also the supervision of the performance of directors. Thus, statutory auditors have considerable powers, which may include a request for any information from directors, managers and employees. The statutory auditors' job is onerous since negligent performance of their duties may render them jointly liable with the company for damages incurred by third parties.

Alumni

It is also a feature of Japanese companies that certain shareholders can exercise a degree of control well above that commensurate with their shareholding. Directors can exercise considerable influence even though they are not shareholders and 'many companies are controlled by other companies that own minimal stock or none at all, through "old boys" (alumni) placed in key positions on the board of directors or as president' (Ames, 1981, p. 552). Such a feature led Nishiyama (1981) to argue that Japan is not really a capitalist country. In the West ownership of a company is determined by ownership of voting shares, whereas in Japan many other factors must be taken into consideration. This difference in perception can be gleaned from corporate annual reports. Western corporate reports emphasize that the company belongs to its shareholders with regular statements about 'your company'. In contrast, Japanese corporate reports refer to 'our company'. For example, the 1987 annual report of Shōwa Denko KK contains a 'message from the management' which refers to

> the orientation of *our* research and development . . . We're intensifying *our* R & D in items that should underpin *our* tomorrow, namely, specialty products. *Our* broad range of materials and vast repository of technology, and *our* in-depth experience too, should ensure success of that effort. *Our* emphasis on specialties . . . *We*, at Shōwa Denko, are confident that the directions *we've* chosen and the strategies *we're* pursuing will serve *us* well in attaining sustained growth over the years ahead [emphasis added].

No greater difference from that extract can be seen than by scrutinizing a UK defence document to a hostile takeover bid. For example, Peachey Property Corporation plc issued a defence document opposed to a takeover bid by Wereldhave UK. Typical of the document are the following:

> The offer document gives no commercial reasons for the offer and no information about Wereldhave's intentions for the future of *your Company*.
>
> *Your* Directors believe that property values . . .
>
> None of *your* Directors will accept Wereldhave's offer in respect of their own holdings [emphasis added].

It is this essential difference between Western companies and Japanese corporations that makes it almost impossible for a hostile bid for a Japanese company to succeed. Indeed, the Japanese word for takeover is *'nottori'*, which also means hijacking. However, mergers and acquisitions do take place where there is agreement (consensus) between both parties, a fact highlighted in chapter 2.

Summary

The nature and extent of information discussed in corporate annual reports depend on a number of factors, including enterprise users. In Japan employees' lives seem to be taken over to a much greater extent than in the West. Perhaps this has an effect on the degree of participation and access to information. It is important to note, however, that there is a dichotomy between large and small firms. Substantial differences exist in salaries, perquisites and lifetime employment. The concept of 'lifetime employment' is not as prevalent as many would believe since a high proportion of married women leave the workplace to fulfil their role in the home, male workers retire at a relatively early age, and there are many temporary workers.

The *ringi* system ensures participation in decision-making, and information flows are considerable – with the consequential effect that there is less need to communicate information via corporate annual reports or special employee publications. Perhaps this system assists in ensuring that there is harmony between management and labour. However, in the 1950s quite a few unions were neutralized, with the support of the US, to ensure that there was no threat from the left (van Wolferen, 1989). Nevertheless, consultation with the workforce is important, particularly in determining the outcome of a merger or acquisition (Ishizumi, 1988).

A similarity between Japanese, UK and US corporations is the effective disenfranchisement of small investors. Stock exchanges in all three countries have shown a steady decline in the proportion of shares held by individuals and a growth in institutional investment. However, in Japan the institutional investor exerts considerable influence as a business associate whereas in Anglo-Saxon countries emphasis is placed on returns to the shareholder investor. Consequently, the information flow is fundamentally different.

Another interesting characteristic of Japanese companies is that certain shareholders, including 'alumni', can exercise a degree of control well above that consistent with their shareholding. Nishiyama (1981) has argued that the influence of companies through minimal shareholdings renders Japan so fundamentally different that it is not really a capitalist society.

Note

1 In a comparative study of the UK and Japan, Kono (1984) found that the long-term goals of UK companies emphasized financial aspects, including return on total assets, earnings per share and cost reduction. In contrast, Japanese companies emphasized sales, amount of profit (both as indicators of growth), employee compensation, value added and labour productivity, i.e. emphasis on growth and employee welfare.

4

Government as a User

'The government is one of the most persuasive forces in the development of accounting objectives, standards and practices' (Radebaugh, 1975, p. 49). The government can influence accounting and reporting practices in two main ways: as a user group and as a regulator. This chapter considers government as a user and chapter 6 deals with government as a regulator, although they are interrelated in many ways: 'government regulators often act in response to the needs of government users' (1975, p. 50). One way in which this relationship could occur is for regulators to influence disclosure to meet government's need for political stability and economic development.

Post-war economic policies adopted by government – or more realistically the bureaucrats – have been to develop its industry within a protectionist framework. Since the *zaibatsu* had been disbanded by the occupation forces, industry had no central driving force. This allowed four large business federations to form, namely, Keidanren (the Federation of Economic Organizations), Nikkeiren (the Japan Federation of Employers' Associations), Keizai Dōyūkai (the Committee for Economic Development) and Nihon Shōkō Kaigisho (the Japan Chamber of Commerce and Industry); these organizations are considered in chapter 6. The role of the main federation, Keidanren, has been particularly important since funds raised by this organization helped to bring together a number of political factions to form the Liberal Democratic Party (LDP), the ruling party for virtually the whole of the post-war era. Not only was business ensuring its political influence but employers' organizations were consolidating their positions with the bureaucracy. The objective of large firms was to secure domestic market share based on high prices with minimum effective competition – although aggressive price competition did break out periodically – in order to secure the ultimate, foreign market share. This was assisted by interdependence between firms and banks so that shareholders need receive only low dividend payments. Indeed, whilst gearing in Japanese firms has been

Table 4.1   Ratios of gross debt to total assets (market values[a])

Countries	1970	1975	1980	1985	1986	1987
Low leverage						
United States	0.45	0.52	0.50	0.50	0.49	0.51
United Kingdom	0.51	0.64	0.63	0.52	0.48	0.48
Canada	0.50	0.58	0.54	0.47	0.45	0.45
High leverage						
Japan	0.86	0.83	0.84	0.73[b]	0.63	0.59
Germany	0.72	0.76	0.81	0.71	0.70	0.77

[a] Private non-financial corporations (all producing enterprises for Germany), with total assets calculated as gross debt plus equity at market value.
[b] Break in the series.
Sources: National flow-of-funds statistics, BIS estimates and Bank for International Settlements 59th Annual Report

traditionally much higher than many Western nations (table 4.1 demonstrates this point but note that gearing in Japan, in terms of market values, has declined substantially as the Japanese stock markets became buoyant in the second half of the 1980s), the stock market has not been the major contributor to raising new capital. The dividend payout ratio over time is shown in figure 5.4 (see chapter 5), demonstrating that Japanese firms pay a low fixed rate of dividends on shares irrespective of an increase or decrease in profits.

The government offers a number of incentives to business including tax incentives, financial incentives and subsidies. The key elements of the government's taxation policy will be considered in this chapter. A detailed analysis of personal and corporate taxation in Japan may be found in Gomi (1989).

Tax incentives

Tax incentives affect financial reporting by the extent to which tax adjustments must be put through the financial statements to qualify for relief. The general principle of the Corporation Tax Law is that all companies are subject to corporation tax based on the financial statements prepared in accordance with generally accepted accounting principles. In general, income should be determined on an accruals basis although the percentage of completion method may be used for construction contracts where there are no anticipated losses, and profits may also be taken where sales are on an instalment basis. Whilst there is considerable interdependence between companies, the general rule for taxation purposes is that transactions must be conducted on an arm's length basis.

In general, corporations are classified into domestic or foreign entities. A domestic corporation is taxed on its worldwide income whereas a foreign company generally pays tax only on its Japanese-source income. Another distinction is made between corporations completing 'blue form' tax returns and those filing 'white form' returns. Any corporation, including a foreign company, may obtain 'blue form' tax return status by applying to the appropriate tax authority and demonstrating that proper accounting records are maintained. Thus, the tax return concessions influence accounting to the extent that proper accounting records are maintained.

All corporations in Japan must prepare accounts in accordance with the Commercial Code. However, in some respects the Code is vague and consequently choices made by corporations may affect the tax assessed. Thus, the Corporation Tax Law affects financial reporting to the extent that it specifies accounting procedures. The following sections list the major items where the Corporation Tax Law is more specific than the Commercial Code and consequently affects financial reporting.

Standard depreciation

Depreciation should be provided on the acquisition or manufacturing cost of an asset together with any costs of making the asset available for use. Depreciation is tax-deductible on both tangible or intangible assets, except for certain assets such as land and certain precious items, provided the charge is brought into the books of account.

A corporation may elect to use either the straight-line or declining-balance method (or other approved method) for calculating depreciation on tangible fixed assets, but intangibles should be amortized by the straight-line method (although again it is possible for other methods to be used subject to approval). The election of the method to be used for each tangible fixed asset classification should be notified in advance to the tax office. Where notification is not made a corporation must use the declining-balance method for tangible fixed assets. The method should be applied in a consistent manner and changes in method must receive advance approval from the tax authorities.

The amount of depreciation or amortization allowable for tax purposes is determined by ministerial ordinance. In practice companies will try to obtain the maximum immediate benefit. Table 4.2 lists some of the major tax depreciation rates. Allowances are provided for a whole range of tangible assets, from manufacturing machinery and equipment, vehicles, buildings to intangible fixed assets. Note the considerable variety in rates applicable to machinery and equipment.

Table 4.2   Tax depreciation rates

	Rate per annum (%) Straight line	Declining balance
Goodwill	at discretion of corporation	n/a
Patents	12.5	n/a
Offices	1.6	3.5
Factories	2.3	5.0
Cars	16.6	31.9
Lorries	20.0	36.9
Machinery and equipment		
Petrochemical plant	11.1	22.6
Oil refinery plant	12.5	25.0
Semiconductor manufacturing equipment	14.2	28.0
Automobile manufacturing plant	10.0	20.6
Automobile parts manufacturing equipment	8.3	17.5
Electric appliance manufacturing plant	9.0	18.9
Steel pipe, cold strip manufacturing equipment	7.1	15.2
Clothing and textile product manufacturing equipment	10.0	20.6
Cement manufacturing equipment	7.6	16.2
Radio and TV broadcasting equipment	16.6	31.9

Source: Price Waterhouse, *Doing Business in Japan*

Special accelerated depreciation

In addition to standard or ordinary depreciation, corporations in certain industries who file 'blue form' tax returns may claim special accelerated depreciation as provided for under the Special Taxation Measures Law 1957. The introduction of this Law was aimed at stimulating certain sectors of Japanese industry so the conditions that need to be fulfilled are quite stringent. One particular problem is that there is an inconsistency in treatment of special depreciation between the Corporation Tax Law and the Commercial Code. The former treats it as an expense, the latter an appropriation.

Special depreciation comes in two forms: increased initial allowances and accelerated depreciation (over a period of five years). Increased initial allowances in the year of purchase are in addition to ordinary depreciation spread over a number of accounting periods. Accelerated rates of depreciation apply to designated assets, which may vary according to ministerial ordinance. The following are included in the initial allowance scheme (as at July 1990):

1 machinery designed to improve energy conservation;
2 plant and equipment purchased by small or medium-sized companies in certain industries provided the business is a member of an industrial association and is undertaking a modernization programme;
3 anti-pollution machinery;
4 water service machinery;
5 machinery used to reclaim scrapped materials;
6 some new ships;
7 some aircraft;
8 expenditure incurred on assets to make them resistant to earthquake.

Accelerated rates of depreciation do not affect the total tax paid over a period of years; rather, they represent a deferment since the total amount of depreciation that may be taken over the useful life of any tangible asset is normally 90 per cent (sometimes as high as 95 per cent) of its total cost, with the residual 10 (or 5) per cent being tax-deductible at the time of disposal. Initial and accelerated depreciation result in the write-off of assets over a shorter period of time.

Amortization of deferred assets

A number of expenses are deferred and amortized over a period in excess of one year. The major expenses are those identified by the Commercial Code although the Corporation Tax Law also specifies five categories. The Commercial Code categories are:

1 organization expenses;
2 pre-operating costs;
3 research and experimentation expenses in new product design or new technology inventions;
4 development expenses;
5 new share issue expenses;
6 bond-issuing expenses;
7 bond discounts;
8 interest during construction.

The additional five Corporation Tax Law categories are:

9 the cost of building or improving public facilities, including the cost of installation of appropriate equipment;

10 key money for the leasing of property;
11 cost of fixed assets provided to customers for advertising purposes;
12 payments made for future benefit, such as the purchase of know-how;
13 other expenditure for the benefit of the business.

Under the Commercial Code, expenditure classified under headings (1) to (4) should be amortized over a period not exceeding five years, and those in categories (5) and (6) over a period not exceeding three years. In contrast, whilst the Corporation Tax Law specifies the period of amortization of deferred assets, including immediate write-off, the periods differ from those stipulated in the Commercial Code.

Provisions and reserves

Provisions may be provided for by all companies in accordance with the Corporation Tax Law. In contrast, reserves may be established only by companies filing blue form returns as specified in the Special Taxation Measures Law. Again, the important point is that provisions and reserves must be included in the books of account and therefore the financial statements if tax relief is to be allowed.

Provision for bad debts
The amount allowed against tax depends upon the type of business and varies between 0.3 per cent in banking and 1.3 per cent of receivables outstanding in the instalment sales business. This limit is increased by 16 per cent for companies whose share capital does not exceed ¥100 million.

Provision for returned sales
This provision applies to particular businesses such as publishers, manufacturers or wholesalers of pharmaceuticals, agricultural chemicals and a number of other businesses where goods are sold subject to repurchase.

Provision for bonus
It is common practice in Japan for bonus payments to be made both at the year-end and half-way through the year. The Corporation Tax Law specifies the extent to which these bonuses are allowable. Note that such provisions (like directors' emoluments) are shown in the profit and loss account on a cost basis and are not accrued.

Provision for retirement allowance
The working regulations of all organizations with at least ten employees must be approved by the Labour Standard Office. These regulations specify the retirement entitlement and such payments are allowable against tax with the

exception of payments to directors, who are not covered by this indemnity provision. Provided the approved regulations have been filed with the tax authorities the deductible provision is limited to the net increase in the pension liability during the period; otherwise, a limit of 6 per cent of the total salaries and wages paid during the accounting period is imposed.

Provision for warranty

Industrial and construction industries offering warranty on their goods are allowed to provide for the actual repair expense ratio during the previous two-year period or at a set percentage depending on the type of goods (for example, 0.1 per cent for construction of buildings and vessels, 0.5 per cent for many electric goods and cars and 0.2 per cent for microwave ovens).

Other than the provision for retirement allowance, all provisions allowed in one accounting period must be reversed in the following period. The following important tax-deductible reserves are allowable against tax in accordance with the Special Taxation Measures Law provided they are recorded in the books of account:

1 reserve for development of overseas market by small and medium-sized enterprises (whose share capital amounts to ¥500 million or less);
2 reserve for loss on overseas investment;
3 reserve for investment loss in the free trade zone in Okinawa;
4 structural improvement project reserve for small and medium-sized enterprises;
5 depreciation reserve for construction for atomic power generation;
6 depreciation reserve for specified gas constructions;
7 forestation reserve;
8 reserve for losses from repurchase of electronic computers;
9 reserve for computer programs;
10 reserve for liability on transactions in securities or commodities;
11 drought reserve;
12 unusual risks reserve for insurance companies arising from earthquake damage or damage related to atomic power;
13 reserve for prevention of mineral pollution from mining;
14 depreciation reserve for specific railway construction;
15 reserve for reprocessing spent nuclear fuel.

Computation of taxable income

To arrive at taxable income, profit before income taxes should be adjusted by adding items that are not tax-deductible and deducting tax-allowable reserves appropriated from retained earnings. In particular, the tax-deductibility of entertainment expenses is limited by reference to the amount of paid-in capital. For companies whose paid-in capital does not exceed ¥10 million, the maximum deduction is ¥4 million; between ¥10 and 50 million, it reduces to ¥3 million; if paid-in capital exceeds ¥50 million, no deduction may be made.

Tax rates

Up to 1 April 1990 the rate of corporation tax depended upon whether net income was retained or distributed. This split rate system provided a reduced rate of tax on distributed income with the retained portion being taxed at the regular rate. An important point is that the reduced rate is not available to foreign companies. The rates applicable, for example, to a corporation with paid-in capital of ¥150 million based on the location of headquarters in Tokyo (apart from corporation tax, rates vary with location) were as shown in table 4.3.

The effective rate of tax is lower than the aggregate nominal rate by the extent to which enterprise tax is tax-deductible. This bringing together of national corporation tax with two local taxes, enterprise tax and inhabitants tax, makes the rules somewhat complex. With effect from April 1990 the dual system of taxation was scrapped, to be replaced by a system in which there is no discrimination between retentions and dividend payments. The new single rate of tax is 37.5 per cent, giving an effective combined rate of tax of 51.64 per cent.

In addition to the above taxes, family or closely held corporations are liable to a special additional 10–20 per cent tax on industrial profits. This tax does not apply to foreign corporations.

The tax reform programme of 1988–9 aimed at widening the tax base and

Table 4.3 Tax rates from 1 April 1989 to 31 March 1990

	Regular rate (%)	*Reduced rate %*
Statutory rates		
Corporation tax	40.00	35.00
Enterprise or business tax	13.20	13.20
Inhabitants tax:		
$40 \times 20.7\%$	8.28	
$35 \times 20.7\%$		7.25
	61.48	55.45
Effective rates		
$61.48 \div (1 + 0.132)$	54.31	
$55.45 \div (1 + 0.132)$		48.98

reducing the relatively high marginal rates of income tax; measures which moved towards other OECD countries. The statutory and average effective tax rates, together with international comparisons, are shown in table 4.4

Table 4.4 Statutory and average effective tax rates

Japan: national tax statutory rates (%)	FY 1988	FY 1989	FY 1990
Personal income tax			
Highest bracket of taxable income	70.0	50.0	50.0
Lowest bracket	10.5	10.0	10.0
Number of bracket	15.0	5.0	5.0
Corporate income tax[a]			
(profits)			
Basic rate	43.3	40.0	37.5
Reduced rate[b]	31.0	29.0	28.0
(dividends)			
Basic rate	33.3	35.0	37.5
Reduced rate[b]	25.0	26.0	28.0
General consumption tax[c]	—	3.0	3.0

	International comparison: national and local tax rates 1988 (%)					
	Personal income tax			*Corp. income tax*		*VAT*
	Statutory[d]	*Brackets (no.)*	*Effective[e]*	*Statutory*	*Effective[e]*	*Standard*	*Effective[e]*
Japan	10–50[f]	5	7.4	52[g]	47.2	—	—
US	15–28/33	3	10.5	34	19.3	—	—
Germany	19–53	—[h]	10.8	56	9.3	14	10.7
UK	25–40	2	11.5	35	30.4	15	9.4
New Zealand	24–33	2	25.4	28	8.1	10	6.8
Spain	25–56	16	6.5	35	4.5	12	6.4

[a] Corporate income which is paid out as a dividend is first taxed at corporation level, then also taxed as personal income (no imputation).

[b] The reduced rate applies to corporations with capital less than ¥100 million.

[c] Exemptions are sales and leasing of land, sales of financial securities, sales of postage stamps, provision of medical services under insurance laws, social welfare services, nursery schools, maternity clinics, and tuition and entrance examination fees for school, etc.

[d] National tax statutory rates.

[e] Average effective tax rates are calculated as the tax revenue as a percentage of the tax base (personal income, operating surplus, personal consumption expenditure in the National Accounts, respectively) on average of five years 1982–6.

[f] From FY 1989.

[g] Combined national and local rax rates for income more than ¥8 million. The rates will be 50 per cent from FY 1990.

[h] Continuous progression up to a maximum of 53 per cent.

Source: Ministry of Finance, *Financial Statistics Monthly*, OECD, *Economies in Transition*, 1989

Other tax principles

1 Losses may be carried back for one year and carried forward for five years.
2 There is no concept of consolidated tax returns.
3 Any dividends, interest or royalty payments paid to a non-resident corporation are subject to a 20 per cent withholding tax.
4 Legal provisions exist to avoid tax evasion through inter-company transactions.
5 Traditionally, direct taxation has been a more substantial provider of funds to the authorities than indirect taxation (see table 4.5). However, a consumption tax was introduced with effect from 1 April 1989. The general rate is 3 per cent except for motor vehicle sales, for which the rate is 6 per cent. All business enterprises, including importers, are subject to the tax although there is exemption for small businesses whose annual sales do not exceed ¥30 million. There is marginal relief for enterprises with sales of between ¥30 million and ¥60 million. The reform programme being introduced is trying to shift part of the tax burden from direct to indirect taxes. Such reforms are aimed at rectifying some existing anomalies in the indirect taxation of goods, and additional money raised is aimed

Table 4.5 Structure of central government revenue

| | General account, per cent | | | | |
	FY 1975	FY 1980	FY1985	FY1988	FY1989[a]
Direct tax	71.4	72.9	74.7	75.2	75.4
of which:					
Personal income tax	38.9	39.0	40.4	35.3	35.6
Corporate income tax	30.3	32.2	31.5	36.3	36.0
Inheritance tax	2.2	1.6	2.8	3.6	3.7
Indirect tax	28.6	27.1	25.3	24.8	24.6
of which:					
General consumption tax	—	—	—	4.3	7.1
Liquor tax	6.5	5.1	5.1	2.7	3.5
Gasoline tax	5.8	5.6	4.1	4.0	2.7
Exercise Tax	4.8	3.8	4.0	4.2	0.0
Securities transaction tax	0.5	0.8	1.8	9.6	2.2
Others[b]	11.0	11.8	10.3		9.1
Total	100.0	100.0	100.0	100.0	100.0
Memorandum (Index 1980 = 100):					
Total tax revenue	50.9	100.0	138.0	183.6	184.3
Nominal GNP	62.1	100.0	131.1	151.5	159.0

[a] Initial budget, other figures are from settlements.
[b] Includes stamp revenue and monopoly profits.
Source: Ministry of Finance, *Financial Statistics Monthly*, EPA, *Quarterly Estimate of National Income*, OECD

to increase welfare benefits in particular as Japan has one of the world's most ageing populations. The consumption tax allows companies to base their assessment of tax paid on the preceding stage of production or distribution instead of the way tax is collected through VAT systems prevalent in Europe.

Financial incentives and subsidies

The second way in which the government offers incentives to business is through financial incentives and subsidies. The government offers a number of subsidy schemes which are invariably not available to foreigners. Furthermore, organizations like the Japan Regional Development Corporation, the Hokkaido-Tōhoku Development Corporation and the Japan Development Bank (JDB) generally do not provide funds to foreign businesses, although the JDB may do so.

Other schemes serve to subsidize ailing industries. For example, the Structurally Depressed Industries Law (SDIL) was enacted in 1983 with the aiming of reducing domestic capacity to regain international competitiveness. 'When it is remembered that designated industries are by legal definition suffering from structural weaknesses that render them unable to compete internationally, the failure of imports to capture a major share of the domestic market in most designated products raises justifiable doubts as to whether the SDIL is an instance of successful Positive Adjustment Policy or a form of sophisticated protectionism' (Upham, 1986, p. 142).

Whilst financial incentives and subsidies have economic implications, effects on accounting are minimal. Rather, such incentives demonstrate the extent of administrative guidance given to the business sector.

Discussion and summary

The objective of large firms has been to secure domestic market share, based on high domestic prices with minimum effective competition, in order to assist their efforts to obtain foreign market share based on high-quality, low-priced mass-produced goods. Keidanren was one of the large business federations instrumental in raising funds which helped to produce the LDP party; the LDP political hegemony has been virtually uninterrupted since the Second World War. There is substantial interdependence between companies, particularly large companies, the banks and the bureaucracy. 'The role of the large companies as the team chosen to represent Japan in the achievement of the national aim of building a strong country able to compete with the West meant that more than any others it was they who had to be conscious of this national purpose, keep in mind the views of government and at all times support the government' (Morishima, 1982, p. 122).

Indeed, it can be argued (see, for example, van Wolferen, 1989) that a characteristic of Japan is that there is an interdependent relationship between the LDP, the bureaucrats and big business, with no central power, little accountability and full of contradiction. The LDP subcontracts the running of the country (including its budgets) to the bureaucrats, leaving the politicians to concentrate on securing political support for re-election. The bureaucrats – recruited in the main from the Universities of Tokyo and Kyoto, and in particular the Law Faculty of the former – run the country and assist business in its objective of securing foreign market share. In turn big business, supported by the newspapers in particular and the media in general, funds Keidanren, which lobbies for its own cause and funds the LDP party. This scenario reflects the equilibrium status quo of a system based on reciprocal relationships that seems to run itself. Indeed, there is no 'Japan Incorporated' but, rather, a political system on autopilot in which recalcitrant members are forced to act in a way that ensures that the system remains intact.

Such a political arrangement has taxation implications. For example, in 1959 Okumura became Nomura Securities' first chairman and in many ways it was he who advanced the career of Hayato Ikeda, who eventually became party president and consequently prime minister (Alletzhauser, 1990). The reciprocal relationship 'brought Japanese stockbrokers to power. Ikeda showered the securities industry with benefits throughout the rest of his career. Any hint, for example, of a capital gains tax in Japan during the reign of Ikeda was immediately dispelled and investment trust laws were strengthened to increase Nomura's sway over the securities markets' (1990, pp. 147–8). Before the 1988–9 tax reform capital gains attributable to individuals were in principle tax-exempt but the reforms introduced changes which, in effect, tax the sale of securities rather than the capital gain. Consequently, capital gains are still favourably treated in Japan when compared with the West.

In order to achieve its macroeconomic objectives the government uses the tax system to influence investment decisions. Investment by companies is influenced by tax concessions that are allowed only if allocations to reserves are made in the books of account and consequently the financial statements. In the accounts the reserves are treated as appropriations of retained earnings and presented as a component of shareholders' funds. Fiscal incentives include depreciation, accelerated depreciation, amortization of deferred assets and the use of provisions and reserves. In particular, there are reserves to develop overseas markets and to cover losses on overseas investment. Such an array of reserves is not unique to Japan; they are common in many European countries. Sweden, for example, has a considerable number of reserves, some of which require government permission to use. Such control is not quite so pervading in Japan in a formal sense but through administrative guidance the government can 'encourage' important companies to conform to its viewpoint.

5
Other External Users

Users or user groups, other than those internal to the firm or government, can affect the development of accounting and disclosure of information in corporate annual reports. For example, where companies rely on well-developed stock markets for capital it is essential that quality information is available on which to base investment decisions. Examples of this would include the US, UK and Sweden. In contrast, where banks and institutional investors are important – especially so where companies are highly geared such as in Japan[1] – creditors are important users and represent an important influence over accounting information production.

Creditors

McKinnon (1986) traces the important role of creditors as far back as the Meiji period. In 1867 the first Japanese companies were incorporated and this form of business organization was promoted vigorously by the Meiji government, who saw it as essential to the development of a modern Japan. These early trading companies lasted only a few years, but in the 1870s a number of new corporations were formed and these lasted somewhat longer. They included a number of banks and the Kansai Railway Company. The motivation for company legislation was mainly to gain international respect and promote modern institutions.

Although the Tokyo Stock Exchange Company Limited was established on 15 May 1878 the major companies, the *zaibatsu*, rarely used these markets. Little pressure was exerted by the banks for improved financial disclosure in corporate reports because the Commercial Code 1899 was itself 'creditor-orientated, and, therefore, consistent with the nature of the relationship between the banks and the corporations' (McKinnon, 1986, p. 135). This was not surprising because the Japanese Commercial Code was based on the German Commercial Code, which was itself based on the French *Ordonnance de Commerce* of 1673. The *Ordonnance* required a stock check every two years to attempt to protect creditors, by the provision of detailed information on assets and liabilities, from fraudulent disposal of property. Such information was provided periodically or at the time of a petition for bankruptcy. This concept was introduced in the *Code de Commerce* 1807 in France, *Das allgemeine Handelsgesetzbuch* 1861 in Germany and commercial codes in other countries.

The second reason the banks failed to demand increased corporate disclosure in annual reports was because their business association provided access to both the board of directors and internal financial information (Murase, 1950, p. 335). This point was emphasized in chapter 3. Consequently, the annual reports prepared in accordance with the Commercial Code merely served as confirmation of the internal information already available to major creditors.

Little seemed to change until the allied occupation. Pressure was 'exerted by the allied forces for the establishment of a "democratic" framework of corporate reporting regulation in Japan' (McKinnon, 1986, p. 174). In an attempt to democratize Japanese companies, and recognizing the inadequacies of the Commercial Code, a new regulatory system was introduced which included, *inter alia*, the formation of the Securities Exchange Commission. (The regulatory framework will be considered in more depth in chapter 6.) The allied forces attempted to improve the disclosure of information to shareholders. There were three amendments to the Code in 1947, one in 1948, one in 1949 and two in 1950. The 1950 amendments revised certain provisions of the Commercial Code including those relating to the auditors, the rights and duties of shareholders, the general meeting and in relation to the individual shareholder (McKinnon, 1986, p. 180). These important new provisions marked the first move away from accounts prepared primarily for creditors towards recognizing the importance of shareholders. Whilst there have been several subsequent amendments, 'the underlying objective of financial statements prepared in accordance with Commercial Code requirements is to protect creditors and current investors. Accordingly, disclosures relating to availability of funds for dividends, creditworthiness and earning power are emphasized' (Robins, 1987, p. 241). The other significant event in providing more information for investors was the introduction of the Securities and Exchange Law in 1948 together with the establishment of the Securities Exchange Commission.

Institutional investors

There is no doubt that the financial institutions are important investors in Japanese listed companies. Table 5.1 shows the percentage breakdown of share ownership in terms of market value for 1986 to 1990 (table 3.2 showed share ownership by number of shares). It is noticeable that the financial institutions and business corporations together hold in excess of 70 per cent of shares. For a historical breakdown in terms of units of share ownership and for an international comparison see chapter 3. According to Hodder and Tschoeg (1985, p. 178) the shareholdings of private domestic institutions increased fairly consistently from 28.1 per cent of total shares in 1950 to the 66.7 per cent in 1983. The comparable figure for 1980 is 73 per cent.

Table 5.1   Share ownership by market value (percentages)

	1986	1987	1988	1989	1990
Government and local government	0.3	0.9	0.5	0.4	0.3
Financial institutions	39.8	41.5	42.5	44.1	43.5
Business corporations	28.8	30.1	30.2	29.0	29.5
Securities companies	1.9	2.1	2.3	2.3	2.0
Individuals and others	22.3	20.1	20.4	19.9	20.5
Foreigners	7.0	5.3	4.1	4.3	4.2

Source: *Tokyo Stock Exchange Fact Book 1991*

An issue of some importance is the extent to which financial institutions and business corporations are active in trading securities. Hodder and Tschoeg, when referring to trading in 1983, state that

> the major institutional holders (banks, insurance companies, and nonfinancial business corporations) collectively held 61.2 per cent of listed shares, but engaged in only 10.7 per cent of trades. By contrast, member security firms, individuals, and foreigners accounted for 81.5 per cent of trading, despite holding less than 35 per cent of the listed shares. If we exclude trades by member security firms acting as dealers (23.9 per cent of the total), individuals and foreigners accounted for 75.7 per cent of remaining trades. Thus, we get a rather clear picture of an economy where over 60 per cent of listed shares are held by institutions that do very little trading. (Hodder and Tschoeg, 1985, p. 178)

In contrast, Franklin (1988) estimates that the non-trading sector may be as high as 75 per cent. Sakakibara et al. (1988, p. 138) suggest that 'on the average, less than 30 per cent of outstanding shares of Japanese common stocks are available to the ordinary investor'. Futatsugi (1986) has argued further that reciprocal shareholdings are unjust and represent a 'dividend swindle'. This is because all shareholders have the right to vote and receive dividends. Whereas the individual expends real economic resources to acquire shares, reciprocal shareholdings result in inter-company transfers of capital.

It is possible that the attitude towards cross-shareholding may be changing somewhat. For example, the Economic Research Institution of Daiwa Securities put forward a number of reasons to explain why strategic mergers were becoming more acceptable. Perhaps due to trade friction and the rising yen Japanese industry has been undergoing considerable restructuring. Part of this restructuring process has involved the disposal of cross-shareholdings (Cooke, 1988a, p. 278). Evidence for this assertion comes from block transactions and transactions executed by integrated securities companies. One source of evidence available on turnover relates to block transactions, a method for executing large orders in which 'one and the same member acts as a seller and a buyer of one transaction within the framework of the auction market principles. The ratio of block trade volume by crossing, each involving 300,000 shares or more, to the total trading volume in the 1st section was 6.5% in 1988' (*Tokyo Stock Exchange Fact Book 1989*, p. 16). ('1st section' companies are those that satisfy the criteria set out in table 5.7 – i.e. larger ones.) Table 5.2 shows the substantial increase in the proportion of block trade transactions undertaken by the financial institutions and business corporations between 1983 and 1988. The volume of block trades trebled in the same period (see table 5.3), which underlines the rapidly increasing influence of the institutions.

Table 5.2 Block trades by crossing (1st section) (percentages)

	1983	*1984*	*1985*	*1986*	*1987*	*1988*
Members' accounts	35.3	38.5	37.7	33.0	30.9	23.3
Financial institutions	13.5	11.1	19.2	22.0	22.6	25.8
Investment trusts	2.5	2.9	4.2	2.7	2.5	2.5
Business corporations	19.1	25.5	23.4	28.5	30.7	36.0
Individuals	5.7	5.5	5.7	5.9	6.3	8.6
Foreigners	23.9	16.5	9.8	7.9	7.0	3.8

This table has been calculated from the raw data in the *Tokyo Stock Exchange Fact Books 1988/1989*

Table 5.3 also shows that between 1983 and 1985 the financial institutions were net buyers of shares whereas between 1986 and 1988 they were net sellers. Business corporations were net sellers over the entire period. Thus,

Table 5.3 Block trades by crossing (1st section) (millions of shares)

	Members' accounts		Financial institutions		Investment trusts		Business corporations		Individuals		Foreigners	
	Buy	Sell	Buy	Sell	Buy	Sell	Buy	Sell	Buy	Sell	Buy	Sell
1983	2,000	2,424	768	704	140	180	1,086	1,159	321	173	1,357	1,030
1984	2,112	2,119	610	574	157	178	1,400	1,443	304	175	897	990
1985	1,756	1,690	888	740	192	184	1,089	1,276	267	134	458	627
1986	4,977	4,951	3,332	3,496	406	384	4,298	4,549	883	456	1,186	1,245
1987	6,127	5,425	4,475	5,400	499	417	6,079	6,459	1,256	652	1,378	1,460
1988	4,229	4,067	4,701	5,053	458	367	6,555	7,071	1,562	841	682	787

Source: Tokyo Stock Exchange Fact Books 1988/1989

there is some evidence that the financial institutions and business corporations have indeed become more active.

The second source of information on share turnover relates to stock transactions executed by 'integrated' securities companies (table 5.4) – companies with a licence to undetake all four of the major categories of investment business (discussed later in this chapter). The proportion of transactions undertaken by the financial institutions (insurance companies, banks and investment trusts) and business corporations has increased steadily between 1983 and 1988; in 1983 the percentage share was 14.4, compared with a figure of 38.3 for 1988.

As reported in chapter 2, the fact that institutional shareholders and business corporations have been long-term investors, have traditionally voted with management and have had access to inside information has meant that there has been little pressure from major shareholders to improve the disclosure of information in corporate reports. A fundamental change in investment behaviour might radically alter the pressures for improved accounting information.

Table 5.4 Stock transactions by investment sectors (percentages)

	1983	1984	1985	1986	1987	1988
Members	23.9	21.2	24.2	26.3	25.2	26.5
Individuals	43.7	42.8	36.9	29.2	26.0	23.7
Foreigners	13.9	14.1	12.5	10.9	10.0	7.4
Insurance companies	0.9	0.8	0.9	1.0	1.0	1.1
Banks	2.8	4.5	8.1	12.7	16.8	18.9
Investment trusts	3.7	4.2	4.3	4.7	5.1	5.9
Business corporations	7.0	8.7	8.7	10.9	11.5	12.4
Others	4.1	3.7	4.4	4.3	4.3	4.1
Total (¥billion)	95,288	123,310	145,318	320,007	490,673	562,542

Source: *Tokyo Stock Exchange Fact Books 1988/1989*. All figures are based on the 1st and 2nd sections of the Tokyo, Osaka and Nagoya Stock Exchanges

Stock exchanges and regulations

In terms of both turnover and market capitalization the Tokyo Stock Exchange (TSE) was the world's largest exchange as at 31 December 1989. Table 5.5 shows that the TSE overtook the New York Stock Exchange in 1987; in 1990, however, prices began to fall and it is now, again, second to New York. It is also interesting to note that the overseas proportion of sales turnover is very low in Japan, particularly when compared with Singapore, the UK and Belgium.

Table 5.5 Market capitalization of listed domestic equities 1986–1988 and sales turnover 1988

Country	Exchange	Market capitalization (£m) as at end			Value of sales turnover 1988	Overseas equities % of
		1986	1987	1988	(£m)	total
Europe						
Belgium	Brussels	25,146	23,013	32,487	5,905	22.2
Denmark	Copenhagen[a]	11,744	10,840	58,706	2,567	n/a
France	Paris	116,667	92,117	123,729	37,809	5.4
Germany	Fed. of Exchanges[b]	178,791	116,710	139,307	101,996	5.9
Greece	Athens	763	2,393	2,380	167	0.0
Ireland	Dublin (ISE)	3,389	3,267	5,298	1,363	0.0
Italy	Milan	95,859	64,425	75,245	17,561	0.0
Luxembourg	Luxembourg	n/a	3,828	4,662	164	14.0
Netherlands	Amsterdam[b]	56,721	46,106	63,036	19,106	0.9
Portugal	Lisbon	n/a	3,320	4,662	355	0.0
Spain	Madrid	31,544	38,399	50,300	11,835	0.0
Sweden	Stockholm	46,365	41,156	55,617	10,463	0.5
Switzerland	Zurich[c]	87,664	68,301	77,768	214,682	n/a
UK	ISE[b,d]	304,865	349,239	377,162	202,620	22.9
North America						
Canada	Toronto	124,495	284,866	134,287	31,879	0.5
USA	AMEX	49,430	20,875	41,522	17,220	8.1
	NASDAQ	235,114	208,803	196,345	194,796	4.2
	NYSE[a]	1,436,242	1,130,998	1,307,602	794,199	n/a
Asia Pacific						
Australia	Association of Exchanges	63,652	54,532	77,098	23,276	2.0
Hong Kong	Hong Kong	36,270	33,014	41,074	13,047	0.9
Japan	Tokyo	1,189,861	1,451,322	2,121,322	1,273,933	0.3
Singapore	Singapore	27,066	23,082	27,600	3,481	29.0

[a] NYSE and Copenhagen Stock Exchange statistics include both domestic and foreign equity transactions.
[b] These exchanges normally count both sales and purchases in their turnover statistics. Only sales are included in the table.
[c] Zurich Stock Exchange statistics include both domestic and foreign equity and bond transactions: a breakdown is not available.
[d] Investment trusts have been excluded from ISE capitalization.
Source: European Stock Exchange Statistics

There are eight stock exchanges in Japan: Tokyo, Osaka, Kyoto, Nagoya, Fukuoka, Sapporo, Hiroshima and Niigata. All the exchanges have their own listing and delisting regulations although they are, in reality, very similar. The aim of the listing regulations is 'to ensure fair and orderly transactions in listed securities and protection of investors' (*Tokyo Stock Exchange Fact Book 1989*). The criteria for a stock listing on the Tokyo Stock Exchange are shown in table 5.6. In addition, the criteria for 1st section assignment and delisting of domestic stock are shown in table 5.7 and the schedule of listing fees is provided in table 5.8. An important point is that whilst Japanese investors prefer capital gains to dividends there is a delisting provision if no cash dividends are paid for the last five years and the company has excess liabilities for the last three years. Delisting may occur only if approval is obtained from the Minister of Finance.

Supervision of listed companies on the TSE is through standards of behaviour of participants. These standards require companies to inform the Exchange

of a material fact having an impact on investment judgement, such as suspension of banking accounts or business activities. They also require them to file various documents with the TSE on matters concerning rights of shareholders, such as the issuance of new shares and the closure of the stockholder's register ... Where the TSE finds it necessary to make public the fact in the notice or document submitted, the TSE requires the listed company to disclose it to the public investors at an appropriate time in an appropriate way. (*TSE Fact Book 1989*, p. 37)

Despite the TSE being the largest in the world, it is relatively unsophisticated. Historically, the equity markets have been very restrictive with, for example, fixed price commissions, no market makers, no effective insider dealing rules and being unable to sell stock short. Furthermore, the big four securities houses – Daiwa, Nikko, Nomura[2] and Yamaichi – dominate probably half of the total turnover on the TSE. The securities houses are able materially to affect prices by 'their ability to place stock and promote rumours' (Robins, 1987, p. 123).

Growth in Japanese equity markets

One of the most important factors in the growth of Japanese equity markets is liquidity availability. Equity market growth was fuelled by 'one of the largest household savings rates in the industrial world (17% compared with an average 9.2% for all OECD countries). Moreover, during the first half of 1987, Japan generated 54.8 trillion yen, yielding excess domestic savings of

Table 5.6 Criteria for a listing on the Tokyo Stock Exchange, April 1991

	Domestic stock	*Foreign stock*
Application	All of the following criteria must be met	All of the following criteria must be met
No. of shares to be listed	If the issuer is based: 1 In or around Tokyo: 6 million shares or more 2 Elsewhere: 20 million shares or more	If the stock is to be traded in a unit of: 1 1,000 shares: 20 million shares or more 2 100 shares: 2 million shares or more 3 50 shares: 1 million shares or more 4 10 shares: 200,000 shares or more 5 1 share: 20,000 shares or more
No. of shares held by 'Special Few' (i.e. 10 largest shareholders and persons having special interest in the issuer)	Provisional criteria: 80% or less of the number to be listed by the time of listing, and also 70% or less by the end of the first business year after the listing	Not applicable. The stock is instead required to have a good liquidity in the home market
No. of shareholders holding 1 'unit' or more (excluding 'Special Few')	If the number of shares to be listed is: 1 Less than 10 million shares: 1,000 or more 2 10 million shares or more but less than 20 million shares: 1,500 or more 3 20 million shares or more: 2,000 plus 100 per each 10 million shares in excess of 20 million shares up to 3,000	Not applicable. The stock is instead required to have 1,000 or more shareholders in Japan
Time elapsed after incorporation	5 years or more with continued business operation	As for domestic stock
Shareholders' equity	¥1 billion or more in total and ¥100 or more per share	¥10 billion or more in total

| Net profit before taxes | 1 Annual total for each of last 3 business years:
  (a) 1st business year: ¥200 million or more
  (b) 2nd business year: ¥300 million or more
  (c) The last business year: ¥400 million or more
2 Per share amount: ¥15 or more for each of last 3 business years and ¥20 or more for last business year | Annual total for each of last 3 business years: ¥2 billion or more |
| Dividends | 1 Dividend record: paid in cash for the business year ended within the latest year
2 Dividend prospect: able to maintain ¥5 or more in cash per share after listing | 1 Dividend record: paid for each of last 3 business years
2 Dividend prospect: able to pay continuously after listing |

The TSE also has listing regulations for straight bonds, convertible bonds, bonds with warrants, etc.

All criteria above are for a company which provides 1,000 shares as the number of one 'unit' of shares.

Source: TSE Fact Book 1991

7.2 trillion yen. This surplus has been invested abroad to make Japan the largest creditor nation in the world' (Nagourney, 1988b, p. 10).

One of the reasons for Japanese thrift may be attributed to culture. The savings ethic begins at an early age. 'A traditionally exciting event of the lives of young people is going away for a few days with their age mates on the proceeds of regular savings begun at an early age by their mothers' (Hendry, 1987, p. 60). Thrift has been encouraged by political and economic means. The economic reality is that land prices in Japan are, by any standards, astronomical. To a certain extent this is a function of the population, some 123 million, in a land mass of 377,800 square kilometres, 67 per cent of which consists of mountains and forest. On average, each resident of Tokyo has 100 square metres of living space – one third of that in London. For some the prospects of owning a house may not be realized until later in life and for many young people owning a home has become an abandoned dream. In fact a recent development in the housing market is the introduction of three-generation mortgages. Few fiscal incentives are available to encourage home

Table 5.7. Criteria for 1st section assignment and delisting of domestic stock, April 1991

	Assignment of listed stock to 1st section	*Delisting*
Application	All of the following criteria must be met	If falling under any of the following criteria
No. of shares listed	20 million shares or more	Less than 6 million shares
No. of shares held by 'Special Few' as of each end of last 2 business years	70% or less of the number of shares listed	More than 70% of the number of shares listed (provisionally 80%)
No. of shareholders holding 1 'unit' or more (excluding 'Special Few') as of each end of last 2 business years	If the number of shares listed is: 1 Less than 30 million shares: 3,000 or more 2 30 million shares or more but less than 200 million shares: 3,000 plus 100 for each 10 million shares in excess of first 20 million shares, or more 3 200 million shares or more but less than 220 million shares: 4,800 or more 4 220 million shares or more: 4,800 plus 100 for each 20 million shares in excess of first 200 million shares, or more	If the number of shares listed is: 1 Less than 10 million shares: less than 500 2 10 million shares or more but less than 200 million shares: less than 750 3 20 million shares or more: less than 1,000 plus 100 for each 10 million shares in excess of first 20 million shares, up to 2,000
Average monthly trading volume	For each period of last 6 months and preceding 6 months – if the stock is listed on: 1 TSE only: 200,000 shares or more 2 TSE and either of Osaka or Nagoya SEs: 200,000 shares or more on any of 2 SEs, or 250,000 shares or more in total of 2 SEs	1 For last 1 year: less than 10,000 shares; or 2 No trades during last 3 months

	3 TSE, Osaka and Nagoya SEs: 200,000 shares or more on any of 3 SEs, or 300,000 shares or more in total of 3 SEs	
Dividends	1 Dividend record: ¥5 or more in cash per share for each of last 3 business years 2 Dividend prospect: able to maintain ¥5 or more in cash per share after listing	No cash dividends paid for each of last 5 business years and excess liabilities continued for last 3 business years

Source: TSE Fact Book 1991

ownership and down payments on houses tend to be very large. Whilst there are regional differences the value of land in Japan is extremely high in historical terms as well as by international comparison:

> The aggregate value of Japanese real estate is 'worth' more than that of the United States, Canada and France put together. About 40 per cent of all real estate values in 1987 has materialized in two years, between the end of 1985 and 1987. In 1987 the capital gains accruing to real estate owners exceeded the value of GNP, implying significant accruals of unearned incomes. As a result, the wealth disparity between those who already own urban real estate and those who do not has risen dramatically. This is considered to threaten some basic tenets of Japanese society, in which a relatively equal distribution of incomes has historically been important in providing social cohesion. (OECD, 1988/89, p. 51)

Savings, then, are essential for house purchase. This, together with a traditional six-day working week, limits the ability of the Japanese to consume. Pressure from the US and concern by the Prime Minister, Toshiki Kaifu, that there has been a loss of confidence in the LDP political party since the Recruit bribery scandal may mean that increased attention will be given to individuals as consumers rather than as producers. Indeed, in his opening speech to the Diet (2 October 1989), Kaifu expressed concern about high land prices and the inability of many to purchase their own homes and the growing disparity between the 'haves' and 'have nots'.

Another factor of importance has been the tax treatment of certain interest income. Whilst interest income from deposits, debentures and public bonds is taxable, interest from postal savings and special deposits of reserve funds has been tax free. In addition, where interest income is deemed to be taxable,

Table 5.8   Listing fees, April 1991

Classification	Fees for domestic issuer	Fees for foreign issuer
Stocks		
Original listing	*Fixed fee* ¥5 million per issuer *Proportional fee* For the number of shares listed: ¥0.045 per share	*Fixed fee* ¥2.5 million per issuer *Proportional fee* If the total number of shares held in Japan is: 1 More than 20% but 50% or less of total listed shares: ¥0.0225 per share 2 More than 10% but 20% or less of total listed shares: ¥0.009 per share 3 10% or less of total listed shares: ¥0.0045 per share
Additional share listing	9/10,000 of the amount of the issuing price multiplied by the number of shares additionally listed	The same formula and rates as for the 'Original listing' are applied
Non-convertible bonds		
Life of less than 10 years	¥300,000 per issue (if the issuer's stock is not listed on TSE: ¥800,000 for the first liting of an issue. From the second listing and on, ¥300,000 per issue)	
Life of 10 or more years	¥400,000 per issue (if the issuer's stock is not listed on TSE, ¥900,000 for the first listing of an issue. From the second listing and on, ¥400,000 per issue)	
Convertible bonds and bonds with warrants	4.5/10,000 of listed amount in par value	
Warrants	4.5/10,000 of listed amount	
Preferred stocks	4.5/10,000 of the amount of the issuing price multiplied by the total number of shares listed	
Subscription rights	If the amount of issuing price multiplied by the number of additional shares which will be issued by exercise of the rights is: 1 ¥5 billion or less: one half of the amount derived by applying the formula for 'Additional share listing' above or ¥170,000, whichever smaller 2 More than ¥5 billion: ¥340,000	

Source: TSE Fact Book 1991

the 20 per cent withholding tax need not be paid if the total deposit does not exceed ¥3 million. However, from 1 April 1988 tax-free interest on small deposits (*maruyu*) in Japan's Postal Savings Bureau (PSB) was terminated, a privilege enjoyed since 1875. The PSB is the world's largest retail deposit-taking institution and accounts for about a third of all Japanese household savings, estimated to be ¥750 trillion at the end of 1988. Nomura Research Institute estimates that the immediate effect of the change in taxation was that deposits with the commercial banks were reduced by ¥1.8 trillion between March and June 1988 while postal savings accounts were reduced by ¥131 billion. An effective publicity campaign by the Post Office reversed the immediate reaction, however, to leave deposits at the end of 1988 at ¥124 trillion. In contrast to interest income, dividend income is taxable although certain exemptions have applied here also. For example, dividend income not exceeding ¥50,000 from any one company is tax free.

The purpose of investing in the PSB has been to obtain a risk-free return to provide for future house purchase and children's education. As noted in chapter 3, obtaining a good education can mean a substantial difference in the security and remuneration an employee can obtain.

The effect of the high propensity to save has been to provide what appears to be an endless supply of capital. Some of these savings have been channelled into the stock market. At the end of 1987, 45.5 per cent of the total financial assets of individuals (¥703,136 billion) was held in the form of time deposits compared with 20.1 per cent in securities. The comparable figures for 1983 (¥479,705 billion) are respectively 49.9 per cent and 18.3 per cent (*TSE Fact Book 1989*).

For much of the post-war period up to the end of 1983 interest rates were kept at low levels. Since 1984 there has been considerable financial deregulation in Japan – a summary of the key events is shown in table 5.9. Liberalization of interest has enabled investors to seek more favourable yields, particularly by international portfolio investment. Early interest in the purchase of foreign bonds has moved to participation in international equity markets, particularly by insurance companies and trust banks. Japanese holdings of financial securities at the end of August 1987 were estimated by the Bank of Japan to be US$223.8 billion, making the country the world's largest overseas portfolio investor. Much of the pressure for deregulation has come from the US:

> First there was Donald Regan in the early 1980s, urging the Japanese when he was at the US Treasury to liberate capital flows on the assumption that it would somehow help reduce the US trade deficit with Japan. When Japanese savers were offered an overseas alternative to low domestic returns the resulting capital outflow exacerbated an existing currency misalignment and caused the US trade deficit to soar

Table 5.9   Financial deregulation in Japan

Interest rates	
1/1984–4/1988	Progressive reduction of the minimum denomination of CDs, from ¥500 million to ¥50 million
4/1984–10/1987	Progressive enlargement of the ceiling on CD issues from 75 to 300 per cent of each bank's net worth, with the ceiling finally being lifted
3/1985–6/1989	Introduction of Money Market Certificates (MMCs) with a minimum of ¥50 million and progressive reduction to a minimum of ¥3 million
10/1985–10/1987	Progressive enlargement and final lifting of the ceiling on MMC issues
10/1985–11/1988	Progressive decontrol of interest rates on deposits of ¥1 billion or more, to those of ¥30 million or more
10/1985–10/1989	Minimum denomination of large time deposits progressively reduced from ¥1 billion to ¥10 million

Over the same period the minimum and maximum maturities for CDs, MMCs and time deposits were progressively reduced and extended, respectively

Financial and capital markets	
3/1985	Removal of restriction forbidding banks to be both borrower and lender at the same time in bill discount market
4/1985	Establishment of bond rating companies
6/1985	Start of yen-denominated BA market
8/1985	Start of 2- and 3-week loans in call market
10/1985	Start of bond futures market
2/1986	Start of public auction of short-term government bond
12/1986	Start of Japan Offshore Market (JOM) (initial size of market: US $51.5 billion, with 181 participants)
3/1987	Reduction of the minimum denomination of yen-denominated bankers acceptances (from ¥100 million to ¥50 million)
6/1987	Start of package-type stock index futures at Osaka Stock Exchange market
11/1987	Start of CP market
9/1988	Stock index futures transactions approved
11/1988	Start of 1-, 2- and 3-week deals in bill discount market; start of 1–6-month loans in unsecured call money market
6/1989	Option trading in the stock price index starts in the Osaka Stock Exchange
6/1989	The Tokyo International Financial Futures Exchange (TIFFE) starts trading

Business segmentation	
4/1984	Start of domestic sales of foreign CPs and CDs; approval of

	participation in syndication of Japanese government bonds by eligible foreign banks and securities firms in Japan
6/1984–4/1986	Progressive extension of approval to dealing in Japanese government bonds to banks (including, in October 1984, foreign banks in Japan)
12/1984	Permission for Foreign securities firms to lead-manage in Euroyen bond issues
3/1985	Approval of issues of foreign currency convertible bond by Japanese banks
6/1985	Approval for securities firms to deal in CDs and advance stand-by loans under collateral of government bonds; approval of direct entry into trust business by 9 foreign banks
11/1985	Allocation of 6 seats to foreign securities firms in Tokyo Stock Exchange
12/1985–5/1987	Approval of participation in securities business by European and US banks in Japan
6/1986	Approval for securities firms to participate in yen-denominated BA market, and for trust funds to invest in short-term government bonds
8/1986	Approval of participation in public auction of medium-term government bonds by foreign securities firms
4/1987	Increase of shares for foreign securities firms in underwriting syndicate of long-term government bonds
5/1987	Approval of access to overseas financial futures markets by Japanese financial institutions
12/1987	Expansion of membership on Tokyo Stock Exchange
3/1988	Approval of access to overseas option transactions by Japanese financial institutions
1/1989	Adoption of standard rate of short-term loans interest-linked with market interest rates
2–8/1989	Conversion of 65 *Sōgo* (mutual savings) banks into ordinary banks

Cross-border transactions

4/1984	Liberalization of yen-denominated loans with maturities over one year to non-residents; approval of Euroyen bond issue by Japanese residents
4/1984–4/1985	Progressive relaxation of guidelines and qualification standards of Samurai bonds
6/1984	Liberalization of Euroyen loans with a maturity of one year or less to Japanese residents
7/1984	Elimination of the designated company system limiting the total percentage of stock which foreign investors are permitted to purchase in any of 11 companies in defence-related and other fields
4/1985	Removal of withholding tax on non-residents' interest

	earnings on investment in Euroyen bonds issued by Japanese residents; relaxation of restriction on seasoning period of Euroyen bonds (shortened from 180 to 90 days)
1/1988	Approval of domestic CP issue by non-residents
12/1988	Relaxation of guidelines for domestic CP issues by non-residents

Euroyen market

12/1984	Approval of short-term Euroyen CDs with maturities of 6 months or less, not to be purchased by Japanese residents
12/1984–4/1985	Relaxation of guidelines and qualification standards for Euroyen bonds issued by non-residents
4/1985	Liberalization of Euroyen loans with maturities over one year to non-residents
4/1986	Relaxation of restriction on maturities of Euroyen CDs (from up to 6 months to up to 12 months)
6/1986	Approval of Euroyen bond issued by foreign banks
10/1986	Approval for Japanese bank-affiliated foreign securities firms to deal in Euro-CP (except Euroyen CP)
2/1987	Approval for foreign branches of Japanese banks to deal in Euro-CP (except Euroyen (CP)
11/1987	Approval of Euroyen CP issues by non-residents
4/1988	Approval of Euroyen CDs with maturities of 2 years or less, not to be purchased by Japanese residents
12/1988	Relaxation of guidelines for Euroyen CP issues by non-residents

Source: OECD (1988/89), Bank of Tokyo, *Tokyo Financial Review*

. . . And what are we to make of the American attempt to loosen up Japanese financial markets through the so-called Structural Impediments Initiative? The proverbial alien from Mars would surely feel that the move is inspired by a remarkable insular vision. After all, the larger Anglo-Saxon economies are scarcely attractive models. They all have trade deficits, which is partly a consequence of liberalization; their financial markets are thoroughly unstable; their corporate sectors are constantly subjected to external shocks and disruptive takeovers; and their individualistic commitment to free markets often stands in the way of social cohesion. (John Plender, *Financial Times*, 18 December 1989)

Organizational structure

Figure 5.1 shows the organizational structure of the TSE. The membership of the Exchange consists of regular members, numbering 93 corporations or less, and *saitori* (or *nakadachi*) members (brokerage or intermediary

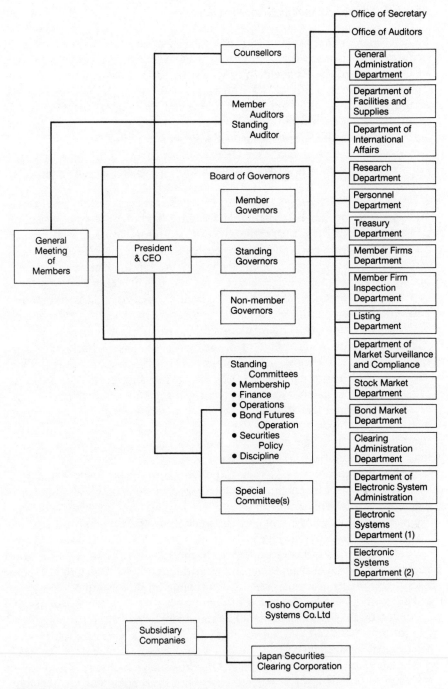

Figure 5.1 Organization structure of the Tokyo Stock Exchange

Source: Tokyo Stock Exchange Fact Book 1991

members), numbering four or less. A regular member is a securities company or foreign securities company whose primary business involves transactions in the market of the Exchange. A *saitori* member is a securities firm whose business involves acting as an intermediary for the purchase or sale of securities listed on the Exchange. The general meeting of members has a regular meeting in November each year and special meetings are convened according to needs. The chairman of a general meeting is elected by the governors each time it convenes. For a quorum there must be a majority attendance by members or voting rights must be exercised and lodged by letter.

Officers of the Exchange consist of the president, 23 governors, and three auditors. The president is appointed for three years by the governors and non-member governors with the consent of two-thirds or more of all regular members. Thirteen governors are appointed by regular members from their own ranks, and four from individuals not involved in the securities business but with sufficient knowledge to give a fair judgement; the president selects and appoints the other six with the consent of member and non-member governors. Two auditors are appointed by representatives of regular members and one is appointed by regular members from non-members.

The president's main role is to preside over the general business of the Exchange and to ensure independence. The Constitution of the TSE stipulates that the president may not be engaged in the securities business or act as an officer of another commercial entity during his tenure of office. The executive vice-president and senior managing governor assist the president in managing the business of the Exchange. Article 73 of the Constitution stipulates that it is the duty of auditors to 'inspect the business of the Exchange and audit the accounts of the Exchange'.

Whilst the government is very important in business matters and the interrelationship between the bureaucracy and business is very significant, the TSE works with some independence within the framework of the Securities and Exchange Law, which is administered by the Ministry of Finance. If we compare Japan to Sweden, where there is also a close relationship between business and government, it is apparent that the organization of the exchanges is somewhat different. The Stockholm Stock Exchange consists of a chief executive, appointed by the board of directors, and 23 member firms. The board of directors has 11 representatives, seven appointed by the government including the chairman and vice-chairman, two by industry, and two by member firms. The Exchange is supervised by the government's Bank Inspection Board. Thus, the involvement of the two governments in the main exchanges of their respective countries is different. In Japan the Ministry of Finance oversees activities although the TSE has some independence, whereas in Sweden direct representation to the board of directors ensures overall control.

Historical development

Both the TSE and the Osaka Stock Exchange (OSE) were established in 1878. These markets undertook some bond trading but their development was limited by the existence of the *zaibatsu*, which had their own banks to provide necessary capital. In 1943 the Japan Securities Exchange was formed, which effectively merged all stock exchanges in Japan into a quasi-governmental organization. The united exchange was officially dissolved on 16 April 1947 although all trading had been suspended on the stock exchanges by the occupation forces from August 1945 to 1949.

One of the policies of the occupation forces was to try to increase the democratic ownership of corporations, by the abolition of the *zaibatsu* and the wide distribution of their shares. To protect shareholders it was considered necessary to improve the quality of corporate reporting. To achieve this objective the occupation forces considered it essential to change the system of regulation, particularly because the Commercial Code was considered to be inadequate. However, all Japanese companies were still subject to the requirements of the Commercial Code, which specifies that the three organs of the company are the directors, the general meeting of shareholders and the statutory auditors. The revised Commercial Code specifies the rights and duties of the organs of the company and the information that should be disclosed to shareholders.

After the Second World War the regulatory system was drastically altered, with the introduction of:

1 the Securities Exchange Commission in 1948;
2 the Japanese Institute of Certified Public Accountants in 1948;
3 the Investigation Committee on Business Accounting Systems in 1949;
4 the Tax Bureau and National Administration Agency in 1950.

The role of these regulatory bodies will be discussed in chapter 6.

Another feature of the reforms introduced by the occupation forces was the reorganization of the stock exchanges, which had been united before the Second World War. This involved splitting the united exchange into independent exchanges to be run on a non-profit-making basis. Legislation was introduced which banned futures trading and controlled the establishment of investment trusts. The effect was that there was a large flow of personal savings into the investment trusts during the 1950s.

Despite the attempts at democratization of share ownership of Japanese corporations the equity markets never really flourished as either a primary or secondary market until probably the 1980s. Indeed, state intervention has been apparent on a number of occasions. For example, within three months of the evacuation of the occupation forces, the Diet had dissolved the

Securities Exchange Commission and transferred its role to the Ministry of Finance. Second, during a deflationary period and balance of payments crisis in 1961 there was a loss of confidence in the securities markets. In an attempt to stabilize markets, in 1964 a number of large institutions, encouraged by the Bank of Japan, set up the Japan Joint Securities Company, which purchased shares to assist demand. However, the company became the major buyer in the market and its funds were quickly exhausted. In 1965 the Japan Securities Holding Company was formed to try to bolster demand. Two securities companies, Yamaichi Securities and Ohi Securities, needed special financial assistance from the Bank of Japan.

Trading practices

There is considerable anecdotal evidence that share prices on the TSE bear no relationship to fundamentals because trading is based on rumour and gossip, in which insider dealing is rife (see, for example, the *Financial Times*, 13 March 1984, p. 21). Qualities of a stock market trader seem to range from being a tic-tac man to natural physique – long arms and height help clinch the deals. The Exchange itself describes the trading mechanism as a 'two-way, continuous pure auction market where buy and sell orders directly interact with one another' (*TSE Fact Book 1989*, p. 12).

The TSE does not have the equivalent of the UK's market makers. However, to avoid substantial short-term price fluctuations two measures are adopted. First, there is the concept of special bid or asked quotes. Where there is an imbalance in orders for a listed stock the TSE posts special prices which are a little higher or lower than the last sale price, in order to generate counter-orders. These quotes may be revised every few minutes until an equilibrium in demand and supply is reached. The second approach is the daily price limit: an absolute yen limit that prevents any listed stock being traded in excess of the limit fluctuation from the previous day's closing price.

Out of 1,700 listed stocks, 1,550 are electronically traded through the Computer-assisted Order Routing and Executive System (CORES). Manually traded domestic stocks total about 150. By the mid-1990s all stocks will be traded electronically and there is the possibility that the two trading sessions (0900–1100 and 1300–1500) will be replaced by one.

As well as trading stocks and shares the TSE also trades in bonds (since 1956), government bonds (since 1966), convertible bonds (since 1970), yen-based foreign bonds (since 1973), foreign stock (since 1973), 10-year government bond futures (since 1985), 20-year government bond futures (since 1988) and stock index futures (since 1988).

Admission of securities

The TSE has regulations on the listing of securities which fall under seven main headings (*TSE Fact Book 1991*):

1 procedures for original listing application and documents to be submitted;
2 procedures for listing of additional shares;
3 alterations to listed status;
4 obligations of listed companies to file various information with the TSE;
5 assignment of listed stocks in 'sections';
6 delisting;
7 listing fees.

The requirements for a listing are onerous. The criteria for a stock listing, and for 1st section assignment and delisting, are shown in tables 5.6 and 5.7 respectively. In essence, companies applying for an original listing are required to meet criteria based on the scale of business, the liquidity of the securities and their business results. In addition, the TSE will wish to ensure that the price and the likely liquidity of the shares are warranted. Once approval is obtained from the TSE the application is submitted to the Ministry of Finance for final approval.

In making an application to the TSE for listing the following major items of information will need to be disclosed on the application form:

1 description of the stock for which the application is being made;
2 a list of other securities issued by the company;
3 detailed information on the number of shares outstanding and the amount of capital;
4 purposes of the company;
5 outline of the business;
6 the terms and conditions of any public offering or secondary distribution conducted during the three-year period preceding the listing application date;
7 the number of shares held by directors;
8 the number of shares held by principal stockholders;
9 the distribution of share ownership by type of holder, size of holding and geographical distribution.

In addition to the application form for listing of stock there is an extensive list of other documentation required, from the articles of association to a securities report providing detailed business information including the annual report for the last five years and a semi-annual and quarterly report for the last two years.

Valuation of the Japanese equity market

To try to understand the level of Japanese equity markets, the high price–earnings (P/E) ratios and low yields is like explaining the inexplicable. Indeed, on Monday 30 January 1989 Nomura Securities had a one-page advertisement in the *Financial Times* claiming that the school of thought which considered Japanese P/E ratios to be sky-high, the TSE much too expensive and the market unstable is as credible as the Ptolemaic theory that the sun revolved around the earth. We do not propose a definitive answer to the Japanese P/E riddle but offer a summary of the factors that may be market determinants.

The problem

The problem is that for investment to be global comparisons between national equity markets must be rational. On the basis of conventional methods of valuation comparisons appear somewhat odd. For example, on the basis of P/E ratios (see table 5.10) French equities are valued 7.6 per cent higher than UK equities, German 53 per cent higher and Japanese 248 per cent higher. Compared with the US, German equities are valued 16.8 per cent higher and Japanese equities 165 per cent higher. Using the price–cash earnings (defined as earnings plus depreciation) ratio the pecking order is changed with the exception of Japan. However, the Japanese price–cash earnings ratio is 114 per cent higher than the UK market compared with 248 per cent based on P/E ratios.

The share price movements in early 1990 did bring Japanese equities more into line with other leading markets since differences in P/E and price–cash earnings ratios were more significant in 1988. Considerable trading in Japanese equities in the final quarter of 1989 led to an 11 per cent increase in the Nikkei index, or more than 3,900 points, from 34,996 on 17 October to 38,916 on 28 December, the last day of trading in 1989. However, the Nikkei

Table 5.10   International equity markets – June 1990

Market	P/E ratio	Price–cash earnings ratio
UK	11.8	7.3
US	15.5	7.9
France	12.7	6.0
Germany	18.1	5.5
Japan	41.1	15.6

Source: Morgan Stanley Capital International

index fell substantially in early 1990, and by October had slumped to 20,211 – a five-year low.

Economic factors

Nomura Securities has offered an explanation of the Japanese phenomenon:

> Since Black Monday, the Tokyo market has clearly outperformed the New York and European stock markets. As the largest of the world's stock markets, Tokyo constituted 44.2% of their entire capitalization as of December 1988. Analysis shows that Tokyo's quick rebound was a factor of market determinants which have always existed: strong corporate earnings performance, low and stable interest rates and ample liquidity. The Nikkei 224, like the New York Dow, has always been a mirror of the economic and financial market conditions of the nation. Further analysis of the Nikkei stock average shows that the three principal market determinants are industrial production, which is tied to corporate earnings, and the two monetary factors of long-term interest rates and real money supply.

This argument was supported by two graphs showing an analysis of market determinants and their contributions on the Nikkei 225 and the Dow Jones Industrial Average (figure 5.2). The conclusion offered is that P/E ratios measure the relative value of stock reflecting changes in financial factors such as real money supply, long-term interest rates, economic strength and corporate earnings performance.

There is no doubt that economic factors are important. Throughout the 1980s Japan has enjoyed a low rate of unemployment (averaging approximately 2.5 per cent), low rates of inflation (approximately 2 per cent), and a current account surplus. Characteristics such as growth expectations and consequently capital gains, which have been higher in Japan than the UK and US, and interest rates much lower, which has not deterred savings, are all aspects of a strong economy. Indeed, the gross savings ratio (gross national disposable income minus private and government consumption) for Japan in 1987 was 32.3 per cent of GDP, the highest of the OECD countries with the exception of Luxembourg, compared with 17.2 per cent in the UK and 14.7 per cent in the US. Strong growth and high levels of liquidity are important factors in explaining the level of share prices in Tokyo, not least because for a given level of debt Japanese companies have lower interest charges than their Western counterparts.

An alternative explanation is offered by Smithers (1989b), who argues that the 'liquidity' explanation is unsatisfactory since monetary growth has been modest in the 1980s. Furthermore, financial liberalization and the massive

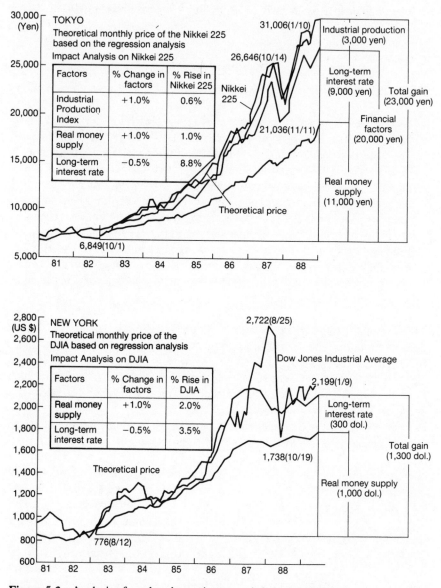

Figure 5.2   Analysis of market determinants and their contributions

Source: Hideo Nakazawa Equity Department, The Nomura Securities Co. Ltd

growth in overseas assets have occurred fairly recently and are 'too small to be a satisfactory explanation of the high returns achieved in the Tokyo market since 1982 . . . The main causes of the multiple expansion have been Japan's change from a capital importing to a capital exporting nation, superimposed on a general decline in real interest rates, which has served to boost returns worldwide' (Smithers, 1989a, p. 1). Smithers contends that the implication is that a capital-importing country requires expected real returns to exceed world rates in order to compensate capital exporters for the apparent risk of overseas investment with a different currency, whereas a capital-exporting country requires expected real returns below world rates to compensate for the reversed risk. Smithers's argument is somewhat suspect in as much as Japan has been a capital exporter in every year since 1965 with the exception of 1980 (see table 5.11 for trends over the 1970–88 period).

An analysis of the figures, however, reveals that from 1984 onwards Japan became a massive capital exporter, a period consistent with the explosion in asset prices of both land and securities. What seems apparent is that a decline in real interest rates over the period has assisted the switching process from government bonds to equities. If exchange controls had prevented the capital-exporting explosion, part of such outflows would presumably have been invested in domestic equities, thereby enhancing the upward movement in values. Figure 5.3 provides a useful summary of those asset price developments.

Table 5.11   Japanese capital movements 1970–1988 ($ billion)

Year	Outflow	Inflow	Net outflow(inflow)
1970	2.0	0.4	1.6
1971	2.2	1.1	1.1
1972	5.0	0.5	4.5
1973	8.5	− 1.3	9.8
1974	4.1	0.2	3.9
1975	3.4	3.1	0.3
1976	4.6	3.6	1.0
1977	5.2	2.1	3.1
1978	14.9	2.5	12.4
1979	16.3	3.3	13.0
1980	10.8	13.1	(2.3)
1981	22.8	13.1	9.7
1982	27.4	12.4	15.0
1983	32.5	14.8	17.7
1984	56.8	7.1	49.7
1985	81.8	17.3	64.5
1986	132.1	0.6	131.5
1987	132.8	− 3.7	136.5
1988	149.9	19.0	130.9

Source: OECD *Economic Surveys*

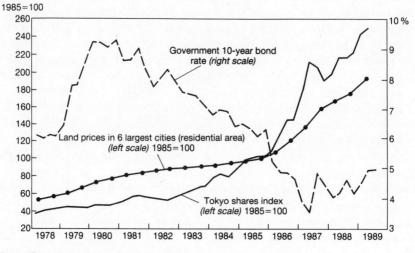

Figure 5.3   Asset price developments

Source: Japanese Real Estate Institution, OECD, *Main Economic Indicators*

Asset values

Fundamentalists argue that Japanese companies should be viewed as a mix of a commercial business, an investment trust and a property company. Just as P/E ratios in London and New York are poor indicators of the fundamental values of investment trusts and property companies, so they have limited application to Japanese companies. It is important to note that land values in the financial accounts are expressed in historical terms in both Japan and the US but in the UK periodic revaluations are common. It is also noticeable that there was steady growth in the Tokyo shares index and land prices in the period from 1978 to 1985 but rapid growth in both between 1986 and 1989. 'The value of real assets owned by Japanese corporations is grossly undervalued; land and shares owned by corporations are usually valued at purchasing prices, not replacement prices, so that the unrealized capital gains in the corporate sector accumulated over time amounted to some ¥500 trillion at the end of 1988, i.e. over 130 per cent of GNP. The ratio of the total market value of shares to the estimated asset value at market prices was calculated to be near unity at the end of 1987' (OECD, 1988/89, pp. 22–3). As the survey also points out, highly valued assets may not be reflected in the earning power of those assets.

Because of the investment trust and property aspects of Japanese companies fundamentalists maintain that the P/E ratio is inappropriate and that the price–book value ratio (PBR) is more relevant particularly since managers attach at least as much importance, if not more, to increasing assets rather than earnings. Such information is published in the *Tokyo Stock Exchange Fact Book*, reflecting the importance attached to the ratio (see table 5.12). Differences in Japanese and Western corporate objectives is one explanation for very low dividend yields in Japan.

Japanese companies regard stock like bonds in which the obligation to pay a dividend is maintained but there is a general unwillingness to increase it. Consequently, average payout ratios of listed companies (see figure 5.4) fall when after-tax profits rise and rise when after-tax profits go down, thereby maintaining a fixed rate of dividends on the face value of a share regardless of the level of profits.

Table 5.12 Price–earnings and price–book value ratios on the Tokyo Stock Exchange (1st section)

Year	Price–earnings ratio[a]	Price–book ratio[b]
1980	20.4	2.2
1981	21.1	2.1
1982	25.8	2.0
1983	34.7	2.5
1984	37.9	2.8
1985	35.2	2.9
1986	47.3	3.4
1987	58.3	3.7
1988	58.4	4.2
1989	70.6	5.4
1990	39.8	2.9

[a] average PER = $\dfrac{\text{Arithmetic stock price average}}{\text{Simple average of after-tax EPS}}$

[b] average PBR = $\dfrac{\text{Arithmetic stock price average}}{\text{Simple average of shareholders' equity per share}}$

Source: *Tokyo Stock Exchange Fact Book 1991*

Cross-holdings

Long-term cross-holdings in shares could mean that Japan's claim to having the largest stock market in terms of capitalization is overstated since the 'locked away' shares reflect a premium based on 'thin' trading. Estimates of

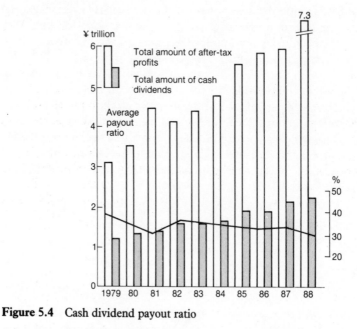

Figure 5.4   Cash dividend payout ratio

Source: Tokyo Stock Exchange Fact Book 1991

the extent of cross-holdings vary from 45 per cent (Japan Securities Research Institute) to 75 per cent (UBS Phillips and Drew). In a paper published in 1988, Gideon Franklin of UBS Phillips and Drew calculated a free-market P/E ratio by eliminating shares held for long-term relationships. As a result, Tokyo's 1987 year-end ratio fell from 58.3 to 13.9 compared with 10.8 for the FT All-Share Index and 15.9 for the S & P 500.

In another paper by Smithers (1987) an adjustment was made for cross-shareholdings which reduced the P/E ratio from 60 to 40. Whilst the explanation is consistent with increased cross-shareholdings from 1960 to 1980 it does not help to explain the post-1988 surge in share prices since there is no evidence that cross-shareholdings increased over that period.

Accounting adjustments

Consolidated accounts
Consolidated financial statements became a requirement for all listed companies for the financial year beginning on or after 1 April 1977. However, non-material subsidiaries are excluded from consolidation and, since 1 April 1983 (when equity accounting for associates became compulsory), there has been a tendency to lower shareholdings so that associates become trade

investments. (For further details see chapters 11 and 12.) The effect of such policies is to lower earnings, since the whole of the group is not consolidated, whereas the market capitalization reflects the value of the entire group.

Depreciation

The use of accelerated rates of depreciation is far more common in Japan (here it is a majority practice) than in the US, where it is a minority practice. The effect of this is to reduce earnings of Japanese companies artificially, thereby reducing one component of the P/E ratio. To compensate for this some analysts add back depreciation but this creates a further distortion since Japanese depreciation charges are high, not least because the purchase and scrapping of plant and equipment are more rapid than in the West. This is important when comparing Japanese P/E ratios with those in the UK since depreciation in Japan is based on historical cost, unlike the UK where it is often based on revalued amounts.

Other allowances/reserves/provisions

An extensive range of reserves, provisions and allowances is available to Japanese companies and are allowable against tax provided they are recorded in the books of account (see chapters 4, 11 and 12). These allowances include a provision for doubtful debts which is usually taken up to the extent of the limit prescribed by the tax laws and regulations. Table 5.13 shows the maximum percentages that may be applied to outstanding receivables. As with many other allowances and provisions there has been a tendency to replace them during the 1980s, due in part to international criticism but also due to the fact that Japanese companies no longer need this form of protection.

Inventory valuation

The valuation of inventories may also have an effect on earnings and,

Table 5.13 Maximum tax-allowable doubtful debt provisions

	Percentage applied to outstanding receivables offset with related payable to each customer, if any	
Type of business	*1983*	*1990*
Whole and retail	1.3	1.0
Instalment sales	1.6	1.3
Manufacturing	1.0	0.8
Banking and insurance	0.3	0.3
Other	0.8	0.6

consequently, P/E ratio comparisons. In practice, FIFO (first in, first out) is more extensively used in the UK and US, unlike Japan where only about 15 per cent of companies adopt such an approach. In inflationary times FIFO has the effect of boosting earnings, thereby lowering the P/E ratio, other things being equal. Higher rates of inflation in the UK and US compared with Japan also have the effect of boosting profits under the historical cost method.

Valuation of the Japanese equity market – summary

The relatively brief analysis given above merely serves to highlight the factors that may be important in explaining differences in P/E ratios between Japan and Western nations. No definitive answer is put forward in this chapter because a number of factors are important in explaining differences in P/E multiples. It is extremely difficult to explain why, even after the capitalization of Nippon Telegraph and Telephone fell by 30 per cent as a result of the Recruit scandal, the market value of the company still exceeded that of the entire German stock market.

Summary

The limited liability form of business organization did not develop until the Meiji period, and then mainly to gain international respect. Like the German and French Commercial Codes the Japanese Commercial Code of 1899 was creditor-orientated. There was little change in corporate reporting regulation until the allied occupation, when the Commercial Code was amended and the Securities and Exchange Law introduced. The US insisted on more disclosure for shareholders.

There have been few pressures from major shareholders to improve disclosure in corporate annual reports. Like the UK, investment on the domestic stock exchanges is dominated by institutional investors. Both institutional investors and business corporations (often with reciprocal shareholdings) tend to vote with management and often have access to inside information.

At the end of 1989 the Tokyo Stock Exchange was the largest in the world in terms of both turnover and market capitalization, although, as mentioned earlier, this position changed somewhat in early 1990. The growth of the Tokyo Stock Exchange has been enhanced by ample liquidity which has flowed to the financial institutions as a result of the high savings ratio.

Explaining why Japanese equities have such high market prices is extremely difficult. This chapter has raised some issues that are contributory factors, including economic factors such as the high savings ratio, low long-term interest rates, expansionary industrial production and real money supply. Accounting factors are also important. The extent of cross-shareholders is also significant but it is difficult to judge, with any precision, the extent of such holdings and their effect on market prices. Confidence, particularly about economic growth, is also a factor which contributes to explaining high P/E ratios in countries such as Japan, South Korea and Taiwan.

Notes

1 Note that Alletzhauser (1990, p. 21) makes the point that in the 1980s 'while Americans were turning equity into debt, the Japanese turned debt into equity. While Americans tapped their bankers on the shoulder for capital, thus saddling their company with debt, the Japanese tapped their brokers for equity, which was virtually free since Japanese companies paid nominal dividends and cared little about dilution of earnings per share.' See pages 45–6 for a discussion on gearing.
2 According to Alletzhauser (1990, pp. x–xi) Nomura accounts for 15 per cent of all traded volume on the TSE and when its brokerage subsidiaries are included the group transacts in excess of 20 per cent of the shares traded in Japan. Nomura has more assets 'than the Daiichi Kangyo Bank, the world's largest bank; makes more money than any financial firm in the world; controls 20 per cent of the Japanese bond market; and dominates the Eurobond underwriting tables . . . [Nomura] has the nation's fifth largest real estate firm and its second largest software firm, while its research operation, the largest in Japan, was known by Japanese as "the brain of Nakasone", the prime minister until 1987.'

6
The Accounting Regulatory Framework

This chapter covers the institutional framework governing financial reporting in Japan. Key historical developments are briefly mentioned (for a summary of key events see Appendix I) followed by a consideration of the role of the major institutions in influencing financial reporting in Japan.

Historical developments

The first Japanese company was formed in 1867 yet the real impetus for this type of trading came from the modernization of trading organizations instituted during the Meiji regime (1868–1912). At first, attempts to advance the corporate entity encountered difficulties, not least because such organizational structures were at odds with Japanese merchant houses. Nevertheless, 'the Meiji government continued to propagate the idea of a company as a form of business organization with almost missionary zeal' (Clark, 1979, p. 31). Such 'missionary zeal' was a reaction to the 200-year period of isolation from the rest of the world during the Edo Period. The Meiji government considered the Western company to be modern and therefore in a sense a desirable attribute. Furthermore, the government considered that such a business structure had both financial and administrative advantages.

The rise of the joint-stock company in Japan was met with legal progress. Early regulation was on an *ad hoc* basis, pending the preparation of a comprehensive commercial code (Clark, 1979, p. 33). The Code was eventually promulgated in 1899 and provided companies with their legal status. The Commercial Code consisted of five books: General Provisions; Companies and Partnerships; Commercial Acts; Bills; and Maritime Commerce (Takayanagi, 1963, p. 32). The Code permitted the formation of joint-stock companies without special arrangements, provided there was a mechanism for dissolution when considered necessary, and established the duties of directors. 'Perhaps the greatest difference between the history of commercial law in Japan and in the West was that in Japan the law was created to serve rather than master the company. The moving spirit of company legislation was not so much, as in England and America, to curb private influence or prevent fraud, but to establish laws that would earn international respect and at the same time promote modern institutions' (Clark, 1979, p. 33).

The four major disclosure articles (190–3) introduced in 1899 covered the following areas:

1 preparation of accounting documents (article 190);
2 publicity of accounting documents and annexed specification (article 191);
3 approval of accounting documents and public notice of balance sheet (article 192);
4 release from liability of directors or auditors (article 193).

Specifically the articles required the following:

Article 190
The directors submit to the auditors one week before the day set for an ordinary general meeting the following documents:

(1) an inventory;
(2) a balance sheet;
(3) a business report;
(4) a profit and loss account;
(5) proposals relating to the reserve fund and the distribution of profits or interest.

Article 191
The directors shall, before the day set for each ordinary general meeting, deposit at the principal office of the company the documents mentioned in the preceding Article and also the report of the auditors.

Any shareholder or creditor of the company may, at any time during business hours, demand inspection of the documents mentioned in the preceding paragraph.

Article 192
The directors shall submit the documents mentioned in Article 190 to each ordinary general meeting for approval.

After obtaining the approval mentioned in the preceding paragraph, the directors shall give public notice of the balance sheet.

Article 193
When the ordinary general meeting has given the approval mentioned in the first paragraph of the preceding Article, the company shall be

deemed to have released the directors and auditors from their responsibility, except where there has been some dishonest act on the part of
any of the directors or auditors.

The preparation of a commercial code was marred by disagreements
between English-trained and French-trained jurists. This lack of harmony
and consensus was resolved by commissioning Hermann Roesler to draft a
commercial code based on the German model, which was in fact modelled on
the French *Ordonnance de Commerce* of 1673. Roesler's proposals were
modified by Japanese jurists – demonstrating the country's ability to absorb
Western ideas and modify them to their own needs.

As mentioned in chapter 5 the Commercial Code 1899 was creditor-
orientated, reflecting the European continental influence in its drafting. The
Code itself was administered by the Ministry of Justice, a situation that
prevails today.

The next major change in the regulation of accounting in Japan occurred in
1934 when, due to the lack of guidance in the Commercial Code, the
Temporary Industrial Rationalization Bureau of the Ministry of Commerce
and Industry issued the Working Rules for Financial Statements. The 1920s
and 1930s might be characterized as a period of growing nationalism instilled
and imposed on government by the military.

The great earthquake of Tokyo, in 1923, which killed over 140,000 people,
also proved important. To assist the process of reconstruction the government issued bonds, but these were misused and in 1927 a financial crisis
developed. As a consequence, the Banking Law of 1927 was introduced,
which resulted in more than 50 per cent of the 1,400 banks being disqualified
from banking activities. This compared with the peak number of banks of
1,867 in 1901.

Towards the end of the 1920s the government planned extensive industrial
expansion steered by the Ministry of Commerce and Industry. However, the
Ministry was concerned about the lack of information disclosed by companies. Furthermore, the military were embarking upon a war with China
which required munitions. To provide the munitions the government
assisted new *zaibatsu* (for example Nissan) to develop, as well as the
traditional ones such as Mitsubishi, Mitsui and Sumitomo. A series of laws,
ordinances and plans were passed to try to ensure that the economy was
strong enough to fulfil the war aspirations of the military. The aim of these
initiatives was to introduce some degree of uniformity in reporting, which
would enhance national planning. This aim was supported further by the
*Manual for Preparing Financial Statements in the Factories of Munitions for the
Navy*, and the *Working Rules for Preparing Financial Statements in Factories of
Munitions for the Army*. Both manuals were issued in 1940. Central planning
was increased further during the inter-war period with the issue in 1941 of

Tentative Standards for Financial Statements of Manufacturing Companies. The Tentative Standards, issued by the Uniform Financial Statements Council of the Central Planning Board, were aimed at enhancing macroeconomic control by the provision of firm specific information on pricing and production policies, rather than integrating standards with the Commercial Code. The standards represented a statement of standardized accounting rather than a set of accounting standards (Fujita, 1966, p. 124).

The other major events in Japan's accounting history are the regulatory measures introduced by the post-war occupation forces, the formation of the Japanese Institute of Certified Public Accountants, the revision of the Commercial Code in 1974 and the ministerial ordinances on consolidation accounts. The driving force behind the occupation forces was the US, which sought to democratize Japan. Since the Japanese were unaccustomed to investing on the stock exchange the US considered it essential to provide some level of investor protection, not least because it wished to distribute the shares of the *zaibatsu*. Thus, the interests of shareholders were considered for once to be as important as those of creditors.

The US disbanded the Temporary Industrial Rationalization Bureau and the Planning Board but retained the Commercial Code and thereby control by the Ministry of Justice. However, the occupation forces recognized deficiencies in the Commercial Code, particularly with respect to the extent of information disclosure for investors. Consequently, the Commercial Code was revised seven times between 1947 and 1950. The two 1950 amendments revised certain provisions which related to the role of auditors, the rights and duties of shareholders, the general meeting and the individual shareholder (McKinnon, 1986, p. 180). In addition, the 1950 revisions included the following new accounting provisions:

1 *Article 286-4* Expenses involved in a new share issue may be treated as an asset and amortized over a three-year period.
2 *Article 288* A company shall set aside an amount equivalent to at least 10 per cent of cash dividends paid with respect to each fiscal period until this legal reserve equals 25 per cent of stated capital.
3 *Article 288-2* A transfer should be made to a capital surplus reserve when shares are either issued in excess of their face value or when shares are issued without a par value, of the amount not credited to share capital.
4 *Article 293-2* A company may make the whole or a part of a distribution of profits in the form of newly issued shares, i.e. a stock dividend.
5 *Article 293-3* A company may capitalize legal reserves provided a resolution has been approved by the board of directors.
6 *Article 293-4* A company has the power to introduce a share split provided a resolution has been approved by the board of directors.
7 *Article 293-6* Any shareholder holding not less than 10 per cent of the

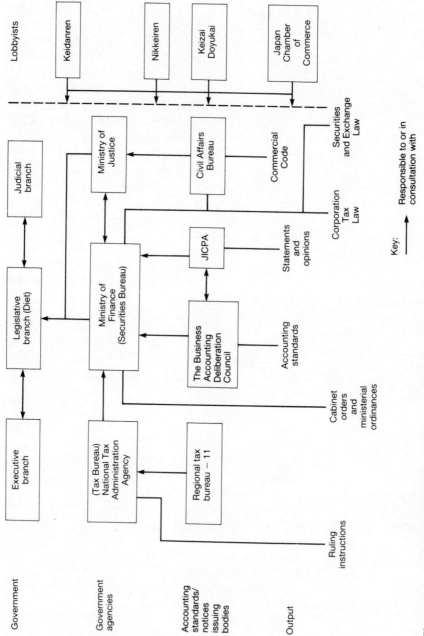

Figure 6.1 Institutional framework governing financial reporting in Japan

total number of the issued shares may demand to inspect the books, records and documents of account.

Whilst the Commercial Code was modified, the occupation forces introduced a completely new system of regulation, based on that prevailing in the US. This involved the formation of the Securities Exchange Commission in 1947; the introduction of the Securities and Exchange Law 1948 (promulgated first in 1947 and subsequently amended in 1948 and 1950); the formation of JICPA in 1949; the formation of the Investigation Committee on Business Accounting Systems in 1948 and the establishment of the Tax Bureau and National Tax Administration Agency. Other than the dissolution of the Securities Exchange Commission in 1952, the regulatory system introduced by the US still exists (see figure 6.1). The role of each of the important organizations will be identified.

Major institutions in Japan's financial reporting system

The Securities Exchange Commission (SEC) and Securities and Exchange Law

The SEC, and the Securities and Exchange Law of Japan established in 1948, were based on the Securities Exchange Commission and the Securities and Exchange Acts effective in the US. The implementation of these elements of regulation was part of the democratization programme advocated by the US. Within a few months of the departure of the occupation forces, however, the SEC had been abolished and its role transferred to the Finance Bureau of the Ministry of Finance (effective from 1 August 1952). Thus, within a very short time a regulatory body, independent of government, had been fundamentally changed. McKinnon (1986) argues that the abolition of the SEC was not a reaction to its external imposition since other requirements introduced during the occupation remained intact; rather, it reflects an aspect of Confucianist philosophy of the existence of the 'ruled' and 'ruler'. 'This cultural philosophy is realized in a greater level of active involvement of government and bureaucracy at all levels of social and economic policy formulation and administration in Japan than in Anglo–American nations' (1986, p. 186). But is the cultural explanation in fact a rationalization of a pervading central government influence more akin to economies in continental (Germany, France) and northern Europe (Sweden) than of Anglo–American values? Whatever the explanation, the abolition of the SEC reflected the first stage of the Japanization of the imposed regulatory framework.

The introduction of the Securities and Exchange Law (SEL) was a major change in the orientation of corporate financial reporting since 'disclosure required by the SEL is oriented to general investors' (JICPA, 1984, p. 32). The requirements of the SEL affect about 2,500 corporations out of a total of some 1 million joint-stock companies. The disclosure requirements of the SEL fall into three major categories: disclosure at the time of issuing securities; continuous disclosure; and further disclosure of reports.

Disclosure at the time of issuing securities

All companies issuing securities in excess of ¥500 million are required to file registration statements with the Ministry of Finance. The registration statement must include: the issuing company's objective for a securities issue; the trade name of the company; details of the capital issue; important matters surrounding the issue such as business and accounting policies; the officers of the company; and any other matters considered appropriate by the Ministry of Finance Ordinance.

The form and content are prescribed by Ministry of Finance Ordinance No. 2 for domestic companies and No. 7 for foreign corporations. The important accounting disclosure items are as follows:

1 Financial statements:
   (a) balance sheet;
   (b) profit and loss account;
   (c) statement of appropriations of retained earnings;
   (d) supporting schedules:
       (i) schedule of investments in affected joint-stock companies;
       (ii) schedule of investment in associated companies other than joint-stock corporations;
       (iii) schedule of bonds payable.
2 Breakdown of major accounts of assets and liabilities and description of short-term borrowings.
3 Performance and plan of cash flow.
4 Subsequent events, lawsuits (if any) and other information.
5 Information regarding parent company (name, address, amount of capital stock, description of business, ownership, etc.).
6 Information regarding subsidiaries (as in (5) above).

Continuous disclosure

Securities reports must be filed on a semi-annual and annual basis with the Securities Department of the Ministry of Finance and also with the appropriate securities exchange or the Securities Dealers Association of Japan (SDAJ). The contents of the reports are similar to those of the registration statement. In addition to these reports a company is obliged to inform the above authorities if:

1 it offers securities for subscription overseas;
2 there is a major change in the shareholders;
3 any other major event takes place.

Further disclosure of reports
The registration statement and other documents listed above must be made available to the public at the issuing company's offices, the Ministry of Finance, the securities exchange or SDAJ, and be made available for purchase at government publication centres.

Detailed aspects of accounting disclosure will be dealt with in chapter 10.

The Japanese Institute of Certified Public Accountants (JICPA)

According to Iino and Inouye (Holzer et al., 1984, p. 377) the first group of professional accountants to organize themselves did so in 1907. Undoubtedly, this was a reaction to the requirements of the Commercial Code 1899. The first formal body of accountants was established in 1927 by the Registered Accountants Law but the occupation forces considered the body to be inadequate for the new regulatory environment (Fujita, 1966, p. 67). Consequently, the Registered Accountants Law was repealed and replaced by the Certified Public Accountants Law 1948. JICPA was formed the following year as a voluntary body, and in 1953 the Institute became incorporated under the Civil Code. However, both the profession and the professional body were of little importance until 1966 when the Certified Public Accountants Law was amended to make it compulsory for all CPAs to be members.

JICPA has no authority to issue accounting standards, that role being given to the Business Accounting Deliberation Council. In essence the JICPA offers a sort of administrative guidance in the form of statements, opinions or working rules. Such guidance is not backed by law but, as in the UK, the JICPA has authority over its members. A detailed consideration of the role of the JICPA will be provided in chapter 7.

The Investigation Committee on Business Accounting Systems

Due to the lack of detail and variety of practices in Japanese accounting the occupation forces established the Investigation Committee on Business Accounting Systems (ICBAS) of the Economic Stabilization Board in 1948. The following year ICBAS issued the Working Rules for Preparing Financial Statements and the Business Accounting Principles.[1] There was considerable US influence over these accounting statements, which continued with the issue of a Tentative Statement of Auditing Standards in 1950. In July 1952 the government changed the role of ICBAS: from being independent, it

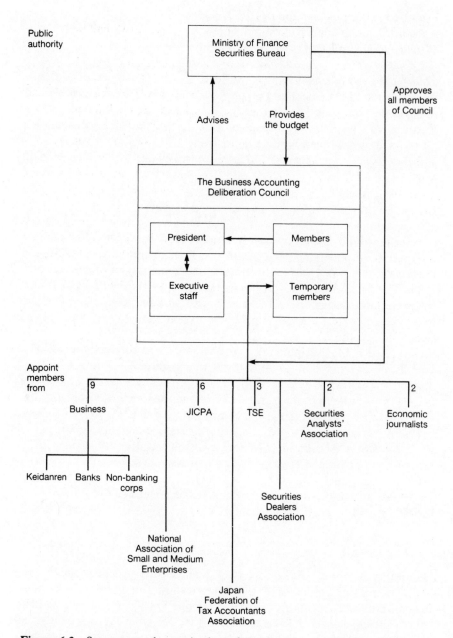

Figure 6.2 Structure and organization of the Business Accounting Deliberation Council

became, in effect, part of the Ministry of Finance. Thus, within a short time both the Securities and Exchange Commission and ICBAS had become part of the government machinery, the bureaucracy.

ICBAS was renamed the Business Accounting Standards Deliberation Council in 1950 and, in 1952, the Ministry of Finance changed its name to the Business Accounting Deliberation Council (BADC), charged with the role of sole originator of accounting standards in Japan. Like all Japanese deliberation councils, BADC acts as an advisory body to the Ministry. BADC consists of some 43 members including technical staff drawn from business, academe and the professional accounting communities, as well as from the Ministry of Finance itself. Indeed, the Ministry has to approve the appointment of all members of the BADC. The structure and organization of the BADC are shown in figure 6.2 and its role is highlighted in figure 6.3. As far as financial reporting is concerned, Section One is responsible for the issue of accounting standards and recommendations – which consist of opinions and interpretations. Both standards and recommendations are mandatory, having the authority of ministerial ordinances.

The role of the Business Accounting Principles issued by ICBAS in 1949 was threefold:

1 Accounting conventions should be followed, even if they are not covered by ministerial ordinance, because they are considered to be 'fair and proper'.

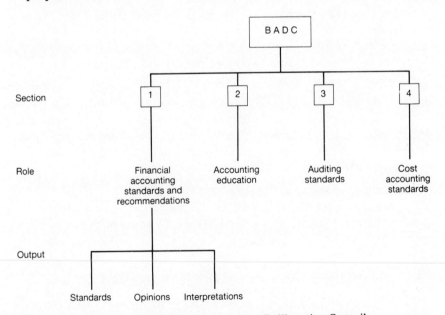

Figure 6.3 The role of the Business Accounting Deliberation Council

2 CPAs should follow such standards in the audit of financial statements under the Securities and Exchange Law and the requirements of the Certified Public Accountants Law.
3 Accounting standards should be given full consideration in any amendments to the law affecting financial statements, e.g. the Commercial Code or tax laws.

The purpose of the Business Accounting Principles is to provide a guide to the establishment of generally accepted accounting principles which must be adhered to by all business enterprises. They consist of three main sections dealing with general principles, profit and loss account principles, and balance sheet principles. The general principles section summarizes the seven fundamentals:

1 financial accounts should provide a true report of the financial position of the company and its operational results;
2 financial accounts should be based on accurate accounting records in accordance with the principle of orderly bookkeeping;
3 capital surplus and earned surplus should be separately disclosed;
4 the financial statements should incorporate accounting which should not mislead users;
5 accounting principles and practices should be consistently applied and changed only if there is good reason;
6 a prudent approach to accounting should be adopted in providing for possible unfavourable effects upon the financial condition of a business enterprise;
7 accounts should be prepared on a consistent basis in accordance with the accounting records and facts and not with regard to the receiver of the statements, e.g. shareholders, creditors, tax authorities.

A list of the accounting standards and recommendations issued by BADC is provided in appendix D, and the Business Accounting Principles in appendix F (although there described as 'standards', they are essentially principles). Important accounting standards will be discussed in chapters 11 and 12, with particular regard to the following statements:

1 Semi-annual Financial Accounting Standards 1977;
2 Accounting Standards on Consolidated Financial Statements 1975;
3 Accounting Standards on Foreign Currency Translation 1979.

Tax Bureau and National Tax Administration Agency

The introduction of the Tax Bureau and National Tax Administration Agency to the regulatory system was the result of the Shoup Committee's recommendations, based on tax theory in the US. One important and lasting innovation was the system of tax returns. In order to encourage good record-keeping and honest self-assessment the tax authorities introduced a dual system of tax returns (see chapter 4 for details). Privileged taxpayers (blue tax returns) receive additional tax deductions – particularly in the areas of losses, research and development and accelerated depreciation – and the authorities can adjust tax assessments only for errors in the books of account and records.

To obtain tax relief for provisions and reserves they must be incorporated into the financial statements. As a result, deferred taxation is rarely practised although permanent and timing differences do occur. Tax law is based on the Corporation Tax Law and the Special Taxation Measures Law. The latter provides the government with special measures considered necessary to achieve its social and economic goals. The influence of taxation on financial statements is dealt with in more depth in chapter 4.

The power to tax and make people responsible for payment is vested in the Diet as provided by the Japanese Constitution. Proposed legislation is drafted by the Tax Bureau which is part of the Ministry of Finance. The actual administration of the tax laws rests with the National Tax Administration Agency (NTAA), which is also part of the Ministry of Finance. The Ministry issues regulations and rules, called cabinet orders or ministerial ordinances, which in effect implement the national tax laws. The director of NTAA issues ruling instructions or directives to the regional tax bureaux, with the aim of ensuring uniformity in the interpretation of tax law. However, as with all legal matters definitive interpretation rests with the courts.

Ministry of Finance

This Ministry is probably the most important influence on accounting in Japan, a position gained since the Second World War. Prior to then the Ministry of Justice had occupied this role, since it administered financial reporting based on the Commercial Code of 1899 as subsequently amended. 'The underlying objective of financial statements prepared in accordance with Commercial Code requirements is to protect creditors and current investors. Accordingly, disclosures as to the availability of earnings for dividend distributions, creditworthiness and earning power are of prime importance. The emphasis is on proper presentation of the company's financial position and results of operations in accordance with the law' (JICPA, 1984, pp. 4–5). The Ministry of Justice's role in influencing financial reporting remains important since its requirements apply to all *KK*s rather than to listed companies only.

The new regulatory environment gave the Ministry of Finance new powers which elevated it to its predominant position. The purpose of reporting under the Securities and Exchange Law (SEL) is 'adequate and appropriate disclosure for the protection of general investors' (JICPA, 1984, p. 38). Whilst reporting under the SEL is mainly limited to listed companies, such corporations represent a significant proportion of economic activity. The Ministry of Finance must be kept informed, not only through disclosures at the time of issuing securities by a registration statement for which Ministry approval must be obtained by the issuing corporation, but also by continuous disclosure. The form and content of the registration statement and securities report are prescribed by the Ministry of Finance Ordinance. Since both the form and content of the financial statements prepared under the SEL are more detailed than under the Commercial Code there has been considerable uneasiness between the two Ministries. Furthermore, there are, at times, contradictions between the SEL and the Commercial Code. In addition, SEL accounts must be filed with the Ministry of Finance. Control over BADC and the Tax Bureau and National Tax Administration Agency together with effective control over JICPA place the Ministry of Finance in a particularly strong position. Discussions have taken place between the two Ministries to reconcile some of the differences between accounting standards and the Commercial Code. Whilst conflict was common in the 1950s and 1960s the two Ministries now enjoy a stable relationship based on sectionalism.

Ministry of Justice

As has been pointed out earlier in this chapter, the Commercial Code was established in 1899[2], under the auspices of the Ministry of Justice, and provided companies with their legal status. Consequently, the Ministry has been influential in setting minimum levels of disclosure in the annual reports of Japanese companies. The Commercial Code tried to ensure a reasonable level of disclosure in the annual reports distributed to shareholders. Emphasis was placed on financial position, although a statement of changes in financial position has never been a requirement of the Commercial Code.

The three most significant regulatory influences are now the Ministry of Justice, the Ministry of Finance and the Tax Bureau. Their relative importance varies, subjectively, with a company's size. The position may be summarized, in order of priority, as:

1 for *small* companies – Tax Bureau, Justice, Finance;
2 for *medium* companies – Justice, Tax Bureau, Finance;
3 for *large* companies – Finance, Justice, Tax Bureau.

As in most other countries, the Tax Bureau is the most significant regulatory authority for small companies. The financial statements are prepared in accordance with the Commercial Code but managers attach considerable importance to the role of the accounts in establishing tax liability. With few shareholders – and those that do often have access to inside information – the Ministry of Justice is of less importance than the Tax Bureau, and the Ministry of Finance is of little consequence to such organizations. In contrast, medium-sized companies often have a reasonable shareholder body and therefore reporting to them via the annual reports prepared in accordance with the Commercial Code is probably most important. A secondary, but nevertheless important role is establishing tax liability, whereas the Ministry of Finance is again not of great significance unless the company has aspirations to become a listed corporation. The significant large company sector is dominated by the requirements of the Securities and Exchange Law and Ordinances issued by the Ministry of Finance.[3] Since a second set of accounts, those prepared in accordance with the Commercial Code, is also produced and distributed to shareholders, the Ministry of Justice remains an important regulatory authority. Preparation of accounts for tax purposes is less important than meeting the legal requirements administered by the two Ministries.

It should always be borne in mind that the three regulatory bodies are not independent but interdependent. The Tax Bureau is responsible to the Ministry of Finance and the Ministry of Justice is responsible for all laws including the Corporation Tax Law.

Civil Affairs Bureau

The Civil Affairs Bureau is part of the Ministry of Justice and is responsible for the Legal Affairs Bureau and the District Legal Affairs Bureau. It is the responsibility of the Civil Affairs Bureau to draft both laws and ministerial ordinances which relate to commercial or civil matters. Consequently, it is also responsible for drafting amendments to both the Commercial Code and such ministerial ordinances.

Lobbyists

The four major business lobbyists, in descending order of importance, are Keidanren, Nikkeiren, the Keizai Dōyūkai and the Japan Chamber of Commerce and Industry. Keidanren is a powerful body of major industrialists, particularly automobile manufacturers, shipbuilders, iron and steel, petrol companies and the chemical industry, as well as trading companies, wholesale businesses, banks, and insurance and securities companies. So powerful and influential is this employers' organization that the chief of Keidanren is often referred to as the 'prime minister of business' (van Wolferen, 1989, p. 354). Keidanren is brought within the political system by regular consultation with the most important ministries. Furthermore, Keidanren is able to appoint members to BADC in order to ensure that the interests of its federation are protected. Whilst this organization has been influential in determining changes in accounting principles it does not always get its own way. For example, Keidanren has never been in favour of extending the nature and scope of the audit function. Despite such opposition the 1974 amendment to the Commercial Code involved an extension of the scope of audit and consequently an increase in responsibility for auditors.

By comparison the other lobbying bodies pale into insignificance. For example, Nikkeiren, the Japan Federation of Employers' Association, was set up by 'business bureaucrats formerly in the forefront of wartime industrial organizations, for the specific purpose of combating the labour movement' (van Wolferen, 1989, p. 68). The organization has been successful in lobbying for changes in the national education curriculum as well as in influencing business policy. The Keizai Doyukai, Committee for Economic Development, 'has provided a forum in which elite zaikai members can formulate a theoretical basis for business policies; it attracted attention in the mid-1950s with proposals for a Japanese style "reformed capitalism"' (van Wolferen, 1989, p. 34). Keizai Doyukai has emphasized the need for economic mobilization and the interplay between corporations, effectively public institutions, and the administration. Furthermore, this organization has consistently taken a national interest point of view in which profit may not be consistent with that objective. As in all these lobbying organizations, former bureaucrats serve in senior positions, not least because of their good connections. The Japan Chamber of Commerce and Industry, the last of the four lobbyists, protects the interests of small businesses. It is important to appreciate that these lobbying organizations are not independent of one another but interdependent. Consequently, each can influence accounting by lobbying the most effective body. For example, the Chamber of Commerce and Industry may try to protect the interests of its members by lobbying Keidanren, which has direct access to the appropriate regulatory authority.

Summary

After the Second World War, the allied forces imposed a new system of corporate reporting regulation based on multiple authorities. Shortly after the allies' departure, the system was changed so that effective control lay with the bureaucracy rather than with the government. The Securities Exchange Commission was abolished and its responsibilities subsumed by the Ministry of Finance, the JICPA was incorporated into the system by giving it a voice, admittedly small, in the development of accounting standards, and the independent ICBAS became an advisory body to the Ministry of Finance rather than an independent organization. Furthermore, qualification to become a CPA was, and still is, effectively controlled by the Ministry of Finance.

Capture theory and the life-cycle theory of regulation advanced by Stigler (1971) and Bernstein (1955) just do not apply to the Japanese system of regulating accountants. The result is that the accounting profession does not earn oligopoly profits.

Qualified CPAs in Japan concentrate on CPA audit work whereas much of the tax work is undertaken by certified tax accountants. In some respects the CPA independent audit, a concept introduced by the US, fits uneasily with certain aspects of Japanese culture – which emphasizes interdependence and reciprocal relationships. However, the independent audit does apply to listed and large unlisted corporations whereas in the US it applies to listed companies only.

If the cultural factor has some validity it may seem odd that the independent audit was extended to large unlisted companies. The explanation stems from a number of major bankruptcies, particularly that of Sanyo Special Steel in 1965, and the emergence of dubious financial dealings by the prime minister, Kakuei Tanaka, who was forced to resign in 1974. Generally, the executive and consequently the legislative branches of government leave the process of regulation to the administrators unless an event occurs which might damage their ability to be re-elected. Consequently, financial dealings by the prime minister and subsequently the Lockheed scandal which emerged in 1976 were of considerable concern. Reaction to the more recent Recruit scandal has yet to emerge. Another factor was that some Japanese unlisted companies had grown extremely large and yet their financial statements remained outside the scope of the CPA audit.

The system of regulation of financial reporting is typical of the bureaucratic control which pervades Japan. As figure 6.1 shows, the number of horizontal lines demonstrates interdependency between institutions. There is no one organization which dominates the regulatory framework but, rather, two major ministries. The Ministry of Finance is the more important organization to large companies, a situation that does not please the Ministry of Justice. Filing SEL accounts with the Ministry of Finance is jealously guarded by that organization. Indeed, the fact that investors concentrate more on the SEL accounts than the Commercial Code accounts has led the Ministry of Justice to consider extending disclosure in the accounts over which it has control. However, in practice only shocks to the system, both internal and external, are likely to extend disclosure in the annual reports of Japanese corporations since confidentiality and secrecy pervade the regulatory system. Japan has never come to terms with the concept of a corporation with limited liability protection providing full and adequate disclosure. This is allowed to persist because there is no pressure to change since major shareholders have access to inside information and thereby possess a valuable asset.

Notes

1 Based on *A Statement of Accounting Principles* by Sanders, Hatfield and Moore (1938) for the American Institute of Certified Public Accountants.
2 Note that the first Commercial Code in Japan was introduced in 1890 but was amended in 1899. It is the 1899 Commercial Code that is considered to be the foundation of financial reporting in Japan before the Second World War.
3 This is based partly on the fact that English versions of Japanese accounts, prepared for the international reader, exhibit levels of disclosure similar to the SEL accounts rather than the Commercial Code accounts.

7
The Accounting Profession and Academic Influence

Another important factor influencing the evolution of accounting and reporting practices is the accounting profession. Indeed, 'the accounting profession can be an important influence on the development of accounting objectives, standards and practices. Three phases (aspects) of the profession are important: the nature and extent of the profession, the existence of professional associations, and the auditing function. The mere existence of a profession is not as important as the level of sophistication of that profession' (Radebaugh, 1975, p. 45).

The nature and extent of the profession

Whilst the accounting profession in Japan can be traced back to 1907 the first formal body emerged in 1927, when the Registered Accountants Law was enacted. Those who graduated from a university with some credits in accounting had the title of registered accountant. In general, the services of a registered accountant were normally limited to bookkeeping, preparation of financial accounts or tax work. However, this body of registered accountants was considered by the allied forces to be inadequate to the new regulatory environment imposed after the Second World War (Fujita, 1966, p. 67). Consequently, the Registered Accountants Law was repealed in July 1948 and replaced by the Certified Public Accountants Law, designed to ensure the quality of professional accountants at a level of competence comparable with the US and the UK, etc. As a result, the Law requires that Japanese accountants be as qualified as those of these countries as well as comparable in status with Japanese lawyers (JICPA, 1983, p. 2).

The services offered by certified public accountants have developed largely from the requirements of the Securities and Exchange Law 1951. The Law required companies with listed securities to have their accounts audited by an independent CPA or independent audit corporation.

Whilst the JICPA was originally formed in 1949 and was incorporated under the Civil Code in 1953, it was not until 1966 that it became compulsory for all CPAs in practice to be members of the Institute. The Certified Public Accountants Law, as amended in 1966, made substantial changes, one of its main aims being 'to promote systematic and standardized examination of financial statements by encouraging and facilitating the organization of individual CPAs into corporate bodies (audit corporations). Partnership as an accounting firm is not permitted in Japan' (JICPA, 1983, p. 4).

In the historical summary of the CPA profession in Japan issued by JICPA (1983, p. 2) it states that as Japanese corporations 'have become multinational so have their methods of financing, such as the sales of equity and debt securities overseas, which have required that the company's financial statements be prepared in accordance with accounting principles generally accepted in Japan or the United States of America and be examined in accordance with generally accepted auditing standards. Certain audit corporations have entered into associations or affiliation agreements with foreign accounting firms.' The comparison with the US is not surprising since the regulatory system of accounting was imposed on Japan by America. However, it will be demonstrated, in chapter 8, that Japanese corporations usually obtain overseas quotations on stock exchanges with disclosure requirements less onerous than New York and London. Thus, whilst Japanese companies have obtained overseas quotations there is also evidence that they are reluctant to comply fully with US generally accepted accounting principles. As far as practice is concerned, some Japanese audit corporations have developed associations or affiliations with the major international accounting firms. Note that these associations are somewhat loose compared with fuller integration in certain European countries. Japanese audit corporations usually trade in their own name, not in the name of the international affiliates.

The role of JICPA

The roles of JICPA under the CPA Law 'are to effectively exercise guidance over, communicate with and supervise over the members in order to uphold professional standards and to improve and advance the profession' (JICPA, 1983, p. 5). The Institute lays down rules in order to uphold professional standards and develop the profession. These rules must be strictly observed by its members.

As part of the standard-setting process in Japan, the Institute has representatives on the Business Accounting Deliberation Council (BADC). In addition, the Institute (JICPA, 1983, p. 5):

1 issues practical guidelines and interpretation on accounting issues;
2 undertakes research and investigations;
3 makes proposals for reforms in the theory and practice of accounting, management advisory services and taxation;
4 sponsors training courses and holds meetings for improving professional services; and
5 issues two monthly publications – *Accounting Journal* and *JICPA News* – and professional publications.

The organizational structure of the JICPA is shown in figure 7.1 and the

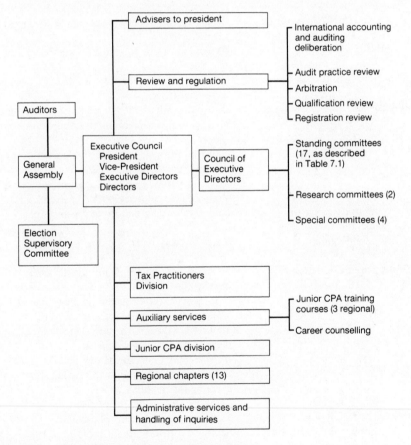

Figure 7.1 Organizational structure of the JICPA

Source: JICPA, 1987d, p. 6

Table 7.1 Main roles of standing committees of the JICPA

Standing committee	Main roles
1 General Affairs	Members' welfare, administration of the Institute's building, revisions of members' rules, and liaison with the local chapters.
2 Professional Ethics	Investigation of members' violations of laws or rules, misconduct, and the interpretation of the rules relating to conduct.
3 Disciplinary	Discipline of a member who has violated laws or rules, has caused disorder within the Institute, has damaged the social creditability of the profession, or has conducted himself in an undignified manner.
4 Certified Public Accounting System	Research work on improvements or advances in the CPA system.
5 Auditing	Research work on general auditing theory and practice.
6 Auditing – Industrial Matters	Research work on auditing problems in various industrial areas.
7 Accounting	Research work on theory and practice relating to accounting problems (accounting standards are set by BADC).
8 Information Systems	Research work on practical problems in computerized accounting and systems audit.
9 School Accounting	Research work on practical accounting standards and auditing problems for schools.
10 Accounting for Non-profit Organizations	Same as above for non-profit organizations.
11 Laws and Regulations	Research work on laws and regulations concerning CPAs.
12 International Relations	Research work on pronouncements being developed by other CPA bodies and professions of foreign countries (including the format in which these bodies are organized and rules applicable to them), the publication and description of the Japanese CPA system of foreign countries' information, and the introduction of American accounting and auditing statements to Japan.
13 Institute's Journal	Planning and editing the Institute's journal.
14 Services Development	Development within the profession.
15 Education and Publications	Seminars for continuing education and technical publications for CPAs.
16 Junior CPA Training	Supervision of junior CPA schools.

17 Assistance to Junior CPAs	Enhancement of the junior CPA education system and guiding the junior CPA association.
18 Research Committees	
1 Taxation and Legislation	Research work on tax laws and impending legislation.
2 Management Advisory Service	Research work on theory and practice of management advisory services performed by CPAs.
19 Special Committees	
1 Accounting for Public Organizations	
2 Award and Citation	
3 Chronicle Editing	
4 Publicity	

Source: JICPA, 1987d, pp. 7–8

main roles of its committees are summarized in table 7.1. Committee members are all CPAs who undertake the work free of charge. Each committee may have a number of sub-committees dealing with a variety of different issues. The president of the JICPA appoints the chairman for each committee and an executive director is assigned to be responsible for the committee. Secretarial support is provided by the Institute.

The organizational structure shown in figure 7.1, which has largely prevailed throughout the 1980s, is formidable bearing in mind that as at 1 March 1990 there were only 8,662 CPAs (US 322,135 in August 1990) and 98 audit corporations[1] in Japan; this despite the fact that there has been increasing demand for the services of CPAs. These figures compare with 6,032 CPAs, 32 foreign CPAs and 63 audit corporations as at 31 December 1980. Note that the number of foreign CPAs is very low and declining. A foreign qualified accountant may become a Japanese CPA by passing both written and oral examinations on Japanese accounting law and practice. An interpreter may be used and the pass rate is high.

Qualification examination system

In order to qualify as a CPA an individual must pass three separate examinations; each set of examinations must be passed at the same sitting.[2] The first is open to anyone – there are no preliminary qualifications and the aim of this examination is to ensure that those who pass have good general literary abilities. The first-level examination consists of assessments in mathematics, the Japanese language and a specified subject in the social sciences. University graduates are exempt from this examination on the grounds that they 'are publicly recognized as having general literary abilities' (JICPA, 1983, p. 11).

Those passing or being exempt from the first-level examination may take the second-level examination consisting of assessments (including a thesis) in bookkeeping, financial accounting, cost accounting, auditing theory, business administration, economics and the Commercial Code. A separate examination paper is taken in each of these subjects although candidates do not have to pass each paper: the overall percentage achieved determines success or failure. The success rate at this examination is usually less than 10 per cent, although it reached 10.6 per cent in 1986 and 10.4 per cent in 1989. A pass at this level means that a person has sufficient expertise to be designated a junior CPA.[3] On 1 February 1990 there were 2,193 junior accountants in addition to full CPAs.

Junior accountants then act as assistants to CPAs for a period of three years, during which one year will be spent training, usually by attending courses run by the JICPA, and two years will be spent gaining practical audit experience. Whilst it is usual for junior accountants to attend the Institute's junior CPA training courses it is possible to undertake the training with an authorized CPA. The training consists of lectures in the evening on the subject areas covered by the final examination as well as on ethics, computers and regulations. Tests are conducted periodically during the training period and reports must be prepared. As well as the academic training, discussions and company visits also take place. All fees are paid for by the candidates themselves.

On the basis of the above level-three training, a report on each candidate is prepared and checked by the Ministry of Finance to assess whether an individual is sufficiently well qualified to sit the final examination. Note that it is the Ministry of Finance that makes the decision, not the JICPA, thereby demonstrating one avenue of control exercised by the bureaucracy over the profession. Those deemed fit to sit the final examination undertake tests of competence in three main areas:

1 auditing practice procedures and reporting;
2 financial analysis;
3 other accounting practices, including:
   (a) bookkeeping;
   (b) accounting systems;
   (c) practices relating to financial statements; and
   (d) taxation.

An important point is that having an open examination system at level one provides the Ministry of Finance with considerable control. Since all examinations are set by the Ministry and those eligible for level-three examinations are approved by the department, the bureaucracy secures monopoly rights over the appointment, and consequently the number, of qualified CPAs.

Continuing professional education

To keep its members abreast of new developments in key areas such as accounting, auditing, taxation, the Commercial Code and management, the JICPA holds seminars and lectures. The *JICPA News* also serves to inform members on both domestic and international developments, particularly new IAS, FASB statements and IFAC guidelines.

Technical training is undertaken extensively by the professional accounting firms and consists of:

1 training of new staff;
2 annual training;
3 lectures with client personnel;
4 on-the-job training.

Types of services rendered

The main service offered by CPAs is the audit and certification of financial statements but they also undertake tax and management consultancy work. Each area of work will be considered separately.

Audit and certification of financial statements

CPAs working on their own account or through audit corporations have monopoly rights over the audit and certification of clients' financial statements. The audit of financial statements under the Commercial Code and the Securities and Exchange Law involves an independent assessment in accordance with generally accepted auditing standards and procedures. It is the function of the audit to express an opinion on the financial statements, as to whether the accounts 'adequately and fairly reflect the financial position and the results of operations of the corporation for the period under examination' (JICPA, 1983, p. 9). The type of companies requiring an audit is specified later in this chapter. Audits undertaken by CPAs consist of those mandated by the Commercial Code or Securities and Exchange Law and voluntary audits. Since the whole basis of audit in Japan is an imposed part of their culture, disliked by the major corporations, voluntary audits are not common other than for joint ventures with foreigners.

The Code of Professional Ethics issued by the JICPA stipulates that a member should not audit an enterprise where a relationship exists which could possibly create doubts concerning his independence and integrity (rule 8). Furthermore, rule 11 stipulates that a member shall maintain a free and independent position and shall always possess a completely fair and impartial attitude when performing an audit and expressing an opinion. Thus, some of the rules emphasize independence, free and independent position and integrity. The introduction of such concepts was part of the new regulatory environment imposed upon Japan by the allied forces after the Second World War. Such notions of independence were Western concepts introduced into a society where trust was assumed and interdependence was more common than independence. To reinforce independence CPAs are paid according to the JICPA fee schedule and members are not allowed to compete for fees against other members (rule 25). Furthermore, a member of the JICPA is not allowed to accept an assignment on the basis of performance-related fee payments (rule 26). Interestingly, since 1951 fee schedules have been fixed periodically (usually every two years) by the JICPA and Keidanren (the role of Keidanren was discussed in chapter 6). Curiously, fees have an element based on the size of the total assets of the corporation being audited plus a time-related charge. Since the two sides are not equally weighted in negotiations – Keidanren being far more influential, both as a body in its own right and in its relationship with the government – fees are fixed at relatively low rates, thereby rendering the audit cartel impotent. Furthermore, the size of many of the audit corporations in relation to their clients makes fee negotiation and indeed independence itself difficult.

Tax work

Whilst the main work of a CPA is the audit and certification of financial statements many members of the JICPA undertake tax work. CPAs are qualified to become certified tax accountants provided they are registered with and affiliated to the Association of Certified Tax Accountants (articles 3 and 18 of the Certified Tax Accountants Law). Once registered, CPAs may act with power of attorney on tax matters, may prepare tax returns, and can give professional tax advice.

Management consultancy work

At the request of clients, CPAs undertake the following types of assignments:

1 perform investigations;
2 prepare financial plans relating to profits, funding programmes, budgeted

investment planning, capital raising, profit analysis, and other financial analysis;

3 advise on reorganization and computerization of accounting systems.

Audit

The extent and type of audit under the Commercial Code depend upon the type and size of the company. The Commercial Code classifies companies into three size groups:

1 large – those whose capital stock is not less than ¥500 million *or* whose total liabilities are not less than ¥20 billion;
2 medium – those whose capital stock exceeds ¥100 million but is less than ¥500 million *and* whose total liabilities are below ¥20 billion;
3 small – those whose capital stock does not exceed ¥100 million *and* whose total liabilities are below ¥20 billion.

The financial statements and supporting schedules of large corporations are subject to audit by both statutory auditors – a 'member' of the corporation – and by an independent external auditor (a CPA or audit corporation). The independent external auditor is appointed at the annual general meeting. There is no requirement for small and medium-sized companies to be audited. In addition to the Commercial Code audit public corporations have their financial accounts, prepared in accordance with the Securities and Exchange Law, audited.

The statutory audit is, in effect, an internal audit by individuals who may not also serve as a director, manager or employee. Statutory auditors are not qualified CPAs so that in technical terms they are unqualified investigators. The nature of the audit is to ensure that fraud has not and does not take place, that directors have fulfilled their responsibilities and complied both with the law and the articles of association.

In contrast, the CPA[4] involves an external audit by a highly qualified individual whose role is to express an opinion on the financial statements. To achieve this, CPAs must at all times be free and independent and must exercise due professional care and proper judgement in rendering their services (rules 10 and 11 of the JICPA Code of Professional Ethics). Rule 12 states that when expressing an opinion on financial statements, as an auditor, a member shall not:

1 state that important auditing procedures have been followed while in fact such procedures were disregarded;
2 intentionally overlook misrepresentation, errors or omissions;
3 overlook material misrepresentation, errors or omissions through negligence;

4 state that the financial statements of an enterprise fairly present its financial position and results of operations while in actuality the opposite is the case; or

5 express an opinion when there is a lack of sufficient information to do so.

In the past an auditor's ability to be truly independent has been compromised by the inequality in size of audit practices and the corporation being audited. It was not until 1966 that the CPA Law was amended to enable joint accounting practices to be developed. The 1966 amendment enabled five or more CPAs to form an audit corporation with unlimited liability. Whilst the size of audit corporations has grown over time (see table 7.2) the imbalance in size between Keidanren and the JICPA means that the fixing of the CPA fee schedule may have an effect on independence.

Table 7.2   The growth of audit corporations, 1978–1990

Year-end	No. of audit corporations
1978	50
1980	63
1982	75
1984	88
1986	89
1987	91
1989	99
1990 (1 February)	98

Source: JICPA

Auditing standards

Financial statements should be prepared in accordance with generally accepted accounting principles (GAAP) in Japan, which emanate from the Law (Commercial Code and Securities and Exchange Law), accounting standards issued by the Business Accounting Deliberation Council (BADC), guidelines issued by the JICPA and tax laws. Whereas the elements of Japanese GAAP have been developed throughout this century, generally accepted auditing standards have been developed more recently. The first statement was 'Auditing Standards and Auditing Working Rules of Field Work', issued in 1950 by BADC (then the Business Accounting Standards Deliberation Council) and based on the AICPA's 'A Tentative Statement of Auditing Standards – Their Generally Accepted Significance and Scope', published in 1947. This first Japanese statement has become the standard, and has been modified periodically.

In addition to auditing standards issued by BADC, the JICPA has issued a series of audit releases covering a range from audits in general to specific aspects such as the procedure for confirming receivables (October 1965) and the observation of inventories (October 1965). Consequently, fundamental aspects of the audit undertaken in Western countries form part of the audit process in Japan. However, certain procedures – including representation letters from management and confirmation of balances – do differ between Japan and the US/UK.

There are standard audit reports, issued by the JICPA, for reports prepared in accordance with the Commercial Code and the Securities and Exchange Law (see figures 7.2 and 7.3). The Commercial Code audit report consists of three parts: the first outlines the auditing method and scope, the second the result of the audit, and the third confirms the independence of the audit corporation. The result of the audit deals with:

1 an opinion on the financial statements – profit and loss account and balance sheet;
2 an audit of the figures in the business report;
3 confirmation that the appropriation of profit complies with the articles of association;
4 there being nothing to raise about any supplementary figures provided.

The standard Commercial Code audit report must be modified where:

1 entries are false or missing or where there are discrepancies between the profit and loss account and balance sheet;
2 the financial statements do not comply with the law, the articles of association or do not show a fair presentation;
3 the proposals with respect to dividends, profits or reserves do not conform to the law or articles of association;
4 certain audit procedures could not be carried out satisfactorily.

If any of these situations arises, the facts and reasons, where necessary, should be disclosed in the audit report. The audit report is either 'clean' or 'qualified'; there is no intermediate position of a 'clean' audit report 'subject to' certain matters arising.

In contrast to the standard Commercial Code audit report, the Securities and Exchange audit report is not split into parts. The report states that the audit is in accordance with generally accepted auditing standards, that the accounts are prepared in accordance with GAAP and that the financial statements present fairly the financial position and results of operations. Again a statement of independence is made. The SEL audit report must be modified in the following circumstances:

1 where the auditors of a parent company have relied on the work of other auditors for material amounts a statement must be made to that effect; this is reinforced by rule 17(2) of the Code of Professional Ethics, which states that in such circumstances reliance on the work of others must be stated and the respective areas of responsibilities indicated;

Figure 7.2   Translation of standard audit opinion format: Commercial Code audit report

---

Date
Mr X. Y. President and Director of AB KK   CPA Office
                                                                                                    .... CPA
                                                                                                    .... CPA

1   Outline of auditing method
In accordance with Article 2 of the Law for Special Measures under the Commercial Code with respect to Auditing, etc., of Joint Stock Corporations, we have examined the balance sheet, the related profit and loss statement, the business report (the accounting figures only included therein) and the proposed appropriation of profit and the related supplementary statements of account (the accounting figures only included therein) of AB KK for the tenth fiscal period from 1 April 1989 to 31 March 1990. Accounting figures contained in the report and the supplementary statements of account, which were subject to our examination, are those based on the accounting books and records.

Our examination was made in accordance with generally accepted auditing standards and included such auditing procedures as normally required.

2   Result of audit
As a result of our examination of above-mentioned financial documents, it is our opinion that:

1 the balance sheet and the related profit and loss statement present fairly, in conformity with the applicable regulations and the articles of incorporation, the financial position and results of operations of the corporation;
2 the business report (the accounting figures only included therein) presents fairly the corporation's affairs in conformity with the applicable regulations and the articles of incorporation;
3 the proposed appropriation of profit is presented in conformity with the applicable regulations and the articles of incorporation;
4 there is nothing to point out as to supplementary statements of account (the accounting figures only included therein) in accordance with the provisions of the Commercial Code.

3   Interest and relationship with the corporation
We have no interest in or relation with the corporation, which is required to be disclosed under the provision of the Certified Public Accounts Law.

Figure 7.3   Translation of standard audit opinion formats: Securities and Exchange audit report

	Date
Mr X. Y. President and Director of AB KK	CPA Office
	. . . . CPA
	. . . . CPA

For the purpose of audit certification required under the provision of Article 193, Paragraph 2 of the Securities and Exchange Law, we have examined the accompanying financial statements, namely balance sheet, statement of income, statement of appropriation of profit and supplementary schedules of AB KK for the year ended 31 March 1990.

Our examination was made in accordance with generally accepted auditing standards, and included such auditing procedures as normally required.

In our opinion, based upon the above-mentioned examination, the accounting principles and procedures followed by the corporation are in conformity with generally accepted accounting principles and have been applied on a basis consistent with that of the preceding year, and the presentation of the financial statements is in conformity with the Regulation Concerning Terminology, Forms and Method of Preparation of Financial Statements (Ministry of Finance Ordinance No. 59 of 1963). Accordingly, in our opinion, the above-mentioned financial statements present fairly the financial position of AB KK at 31 March 1990 and the results of its operations for the year then ended.

We have no interest in or relations with the corporation as described in the Certified Public Accounts Law.

2 where the accounts contain material exceptions to GAAP, either in consistency or application, the amounts involved must be indicated;
3 if an auditor is not prepared to provide a 'clean' audit report the appropriate facts and reasons must be clearly specified;
4 any important subsequent events must also be indicated with appropriate explanations.

Certified tax accountants

As was pointed out in chapter 4, corporations demonstrating that proper books of account are being maintained and certain conditions are fulfilled may elect to adopt the 'blue form' tax return for self-assessment. Such a system conveys administrative and taxation advantages and eases the collection of taxes. It may be that because the government needs to ensure that the collection of taxes is easily achieved it has enabled the certified tax accountant profession to grow at a faster rate than the certified public accountants profession. As at 31 July 1991 there were 57,368 certified tax accountants, representing a profession over six times bigger than the CPA body.

As one of the accounting bodies in Japan, the Japan Federation of Certified Tax Accountants has played an important role in the provision of tax services. According to the Certified Tax Accountants Law, which became effective in 1951, the services of a certified tax accountant are to act as a tax practitioner, which includes the preparation of tax documentation for despatch to the authorities. Besides the above tax services, a certified tax accountant can keep accounting books and assist in other matters concerning financial accounting at the client's request. Almost all companies engage certified tax accountants as tax advisers because Japanese tax laws are complex.

Note that, to ensure independence and avoid a conflict of interest between tax and audit, a CPA who acts as an auditor to a corporation may not also render tax advice to that business. The majority (nearly 90 per cent) of certified tax accountants are not CPAs. The majority pass the examinations – set by the Ministry of Finance – which may be either 'normal' or 'special' examinations. The 'normal' examination covers bookkeeping, financial accounting and three options of tax laws – which include the Income Tax Law, the Corporation Tax Law, the Inheritance Tax Law, the National Tax Collection Law and the Local Tax Law; whereas the 'special' examination is an easier path for those who have served as tax advisers to either national or local governments for 15 years. To assist candidates to pass the examinations, papers may be passed on a subject-by-subject basis – a system very different from the CPA qualification. CPAs and lawyers are exempted from the examination.

Academic influences

Chapter 6 discussed the accounting regulatory environment and the historical development of Japanese companies. It was noted that the preparation of the Commercial Code was marred by disagreements between English-trained and French-trained jurists. Such a disagreement was resolved by adopting a German model, which itself was founded on the French *Ordonnance de Commerce* of 1673. Whilst the German model was modified by Japanese jurists, the theories of German accounting scholars are still influential in both teaching and research in Japan.

The new regulatory framework imposed by the US after the Second World War and the way that the US conducts business in general are extremely important to Japan. Accounting statements issued by the American Accounting Association, the Accounting Principles Board and the Financial Accounting Standards Board are all influential; far more so than any standards issued by the International Accounting Standards Committee.

One of the major problems in Japan stems from the size and weakness of the JICPA. Few CPAs go into academic life; not surprising since the number qualifying is so tightly controlled by the Ministry of Finance that it is extremely difficult to qualify. Furthermore, since accountancy fees are controlled by agreements between Keidanren and the JICPA, the fees are held down, salaries consequently are not exceptional, particularly with respect to the number of years and difficulty of the qualification, and as a result highly qualified individuals are not readily lured into the profession. It would not be surprising were Keidanren to describe this as a very happy state of affairs.

Despite the weakness of the profession it is still possible for accounting academics to be influential. However, this is not readily apparent in Japan. Japan's law-based accounting requirements make the Ministry of Justice, and, in particular, law graduates from Tokyo University within that Ministry, more important than academic accountants. It is noticeable that Japanese accounting academics are very concerned with accounting theory and accounting in overseas countries. With no refereed accounting journals in Japan the accounting academic world, like the JICPA, has retreated into a corner of little influence, no doubt to the satisfaction of Keidanren, and the Ministries of Finance and Justice. Without a radical rethink by these two Ministries there are no great prospects for change.

Summary and evaluation

The bureaucracy effectively controls the profession. The Ministry of Finance's advisory body, the Business Accounting Deliberation Council, issues accounting standards, and the Ministry controls the examination pass rate of the CPA qualification. In addition, competition between CPA firms is restricted somewhat by Codes of Professional Ethics which have established fee schedules and limitations on advertising.

There have been few legal cases involving negligent auditors in Japan, reflecting a society which is not highly litigious, a fact which is in stark contrast to the US and, to a lesser extent, the UK.

The appointment of new 'partners' to an audit corporation requires approval from the Ministry of Finance. This is another example of the extent of control exercised by the government. Furthermore, Keidanren has been very effective at representing the large corporations in ensuring that audit fees are kept as low as possible, particularly because their backers inherently dislike the entire basis of audit. Perhaps shocks to the system such as Lockheed and Recruit may modify attitudes somewhat but this is not very likely. Without a strong independent profession Japan is unlikely to become a major influence in the development of accounting worldwide. However, if multinational audit companies had outside equity, Japan has more than sufficient funds to make a real impact by takeover.

The government controls the number of CPAs to such an extent that it is extremely difficult to qualify. With such a low number of qualified accountants it is not surprising that the large companies recruit graduates to train them in their own accounting systems. Furthermore, the small number in the profession means that it would be extremely difficult to extend the external audit to anything other than the larger corporations. Such a feature provides sustenance to the statutory auditor, whose technical skill is often limited but who is charged with the responsibility of detecting improper conduct and expressing an opinion on the work of the external auditor, when one is required to be appointed. Provided the financial statements are not qualified by the external auditor the accounts prepared in accordance with the Commercial Code do not require approval at the annual general meeting, assuming that the statutory auditor concurs with the opinion of the external auditor. If the statutory auditor does not concur with the view expressed by the external auditor the financial statements must be presented at the annual general meeting for a decision to be made.

If the external auditor detects material misconduct there is a requirement that the statutory auditor be informed, since the statutory auditor must express an opinion on the external auditor's report. This may seem somewhat curious in that the external auditor is a qualified CPA but the statutory auditor need not have any accounting qualifications.

Logic might dictate that there should be sufficient highly trained individuals to cover the whole audit function. However, the power of such an organization relative to the Ministry would upset the bureaucracy. Further, Keidanren, representing the large corporations, would not wish to see the role of auditors extended or indeed the development of a substantial independent accounting body. The status quo serves the needs of the Ministry of Finance and Keidanren admirably. Only major scandals or external pressure are likely to change this position.

Notes

1 The 'big four' are Chuo and Shinko, Tomatsu, Ohta and Showa, and Asahi and Shinwa. Note that prior to 1966, when the present CPA Law was amended, external auditing was undertaken by CPAs acting as individuals, whereas audit corporations developed subsequently. The first audit corporation was Ohta Audit Corporation, formed in 1967.
2 The first CPA examination was held in 1949.

3 University professors, associate professors and holders of relevant doctorate degrees are exempt from this examination, provided they are successful in their examinations in specified subjects.

4 Required under the Law Concerning the Special Case of Commercial Code audits of Kabushiki Kaisha, which was promulgated in 1974.

8
International Influences

Whilst national environmental characteristics are an important influence over the development of accounting and the disclosure of information on corporate annual reports, international influences have been increasingly important. It is important to identify these historical influences and examine the major 'new' influences on disclosure in Japanese corporate annual reports. This chapter aims to meet these objectives by examining historical factors and briefly comparing financial reporting in Japanese corporate annual reports with that prevailing in the UK and the US, and also by comparing Japanese financial reporting with international accounting standards. A more detailed summary of the main differences in financial reporting between Japan, and the UK and the US is provided in appendix B. Also, differences between Japanese accounting practices and international accounting standards are considered in some detail in appendix C.

Pre-war international influences

The Japanese Commercial Code 1899 was largely based on the German Commercial Code of 1897[1]. Consistent features of German accounting include the important influence of tax on the financial statements and conservatism. 'The German requirement that financial accounts should agree with the constantly changing tax requirements leads to changes in financial reporting' (Macharzina, 1985, p. 99). For further details on the influence of tax on the financial statements of Japanese companies see chapter 4. Conservatism in German accounting is demonstrated by the provison of *stille Reserven* or *stille Rücklage* – sometimes referred to as 'secret reserves'. Such reserves represent the difference between the actual market value of the business assets and the written-down book value for the financial statements and tax accounts purposes. Since the tax book values and the tax written-down values invariably differ from the book values in the financial statements there are two sets of corresponding figures, namely the hidden tax reserves and the hidden or silent account reserves. Whilst the account reserves, when taken into account, reflect the actual market value of the assets, the tax reserves represent the capital gains which would be subject to tax if the assets were sold or otherwise disposed of by means of a taxable transaction (Cooke, 1988a, p. 193).

Since the Japanese Commercial Code was based on the German model the influence of taxation and the importance of conservatism became features of financial reporting in Japan. 'The most notable accounting phenomenon in postwar Japan has been the systematic under-reporting of accounting income as a result of both the inherent conservatism in business accounting and the unreasonable intervention of tax accounting in business accounting' (Takatera and Daigo, 1989, p. 187). Since these characteristics have always been inherent in Japanese financial reporting it is possible to delete the words 'in postwar Japan'. It must be said, however, that the post-war administration extended the influence of tax accounting by special tax allowances (see chapter 4 for further details).

Chapter 2 discussed, *inter alia*, the role of the *zaibatsu* in pre-war Japan. Since the origin of each major *zaibatsu* was a single family there was no pressure to demand more disclosure of information. Indeed, there still remains an attitude in Japan that information should be kept as secret as possible. Consequently, it is perhaps not surprising that in our request for accounts from unlisted companies by far the majority of companies did not reply. Some of those that did required assurances that the company would not be identified and that as much information as possible should be kept secret. This may seem somewhat odd since the organizations contacted were major unlisted corporations which prepare financial statements in accordance with the Commercial Code and distribute them to shareholders.

In addition to the inherent dislike of the disclosure of information the pre-war relationship between the statutory auditor and the company being audited was almost one of employee/employer. Indeed, it was not until 1950 that the externally imposed regulatory system stipulated that a statutory auditor should not be an employee, director or manager of that corporation. Consequently, relationships between the statutory auditor and the company were characterized by interdependence rather than independence. Identification as a member of a collective group is a national characteristic of Japanese society inculcated right from early childhood:

> In fact, an individual child usually learns to enjoy the advantage of its new identity as a member of a collective group, and sees that it is in fact in its own interest in certain circumstances to put self-interest second . . . The success of the company, for example, is seen to depend on the

co-operation of its individual members, and the success of the members is seen as directly dependent on the success of the company to which they belong. Individuals may also express satisfaction in being part of a greater entity such as this. (Hendry, 1987, p. 49)

The greatest international influence over pre-war accounting in Japan emanated from Germany. The system of accounting developed to serve the needs of the large family-based *zaibatsu* in which secrecy was an important feature. Indeed, accounting was orientated towards the provision of information for internal rather than external use.

Post-war international influences

Whilst German accounting was the most significant influence over pre-war accounting in Japan, the US was the greatest single influence thereafter. Such a situation is very similar to that of Sweden. 'Accounting development in Sweden has generally been influenced by accounting thought and activities in other countries. Although at present an American influence is felt in Swedish accounting, a German influence was dominant in the period before World War II' (Mueller, 1967, p. 108). However, whilst Sweden began to recognize the economic significance of the US in the early part of the twentieth century, the US influence was imposed on Japan after the Second World War. Chapter 6 discussed the imposition by the US of the new accounting regulatory environment. Although the new regulatory system was quickly modified by Japan once the occupation forces had left, the framework still remains. As was explained in chapter 6, effective control over disclosure of information rests with the Ministries of Finance and Justice and the tax authorities. Consequently, the regulatory framework has become part of the bureaucracy over which the major corporations, through their lobbying organization Keidanren, have substantial influence.

Pressures for change in Japanese accounting might come from within the country or be due to external influences. Internal pressures might come from the accounting profession, shareholders, creditors, consumers, the labour unions or from the reporting entities. In previous chapters it has been argued that the bureaucracy has effectively neutralized the JICPA by restricting its membership, fees and effectiveness. It has also been argued that interdependent relationships, cross-shareholdings, multiple directorships and the importance of long-term institutional shareholders are all features which make the need for external financial reporting less pressing because of access to inside information. The orientation of accounts was traditionally towards creditors, who often had access to inside information and thus no great need to lobby for further disclosure. Furthermore, banks would also have access to inside information. Consumers are another ineffective lobbying organization, neutralized by the pretence of absorbing its views. Despite the large number of consumer groups, estimated to be in excess of 13,000 in the late 1980s, and their predominantly middle-class female membership, the head of the Consumers' Union of Japan is a man, Naokazu Takeuchi, a former senior official in the powerful Ministry of Agriculture, Forestry and Fisheries. It 'is inconceivable that he would work against the interests of his former colleagues in this most protectionist-minded segment of Japan's officialdom . . . The Consumers' Union of Japan . . . now fights against the removal of important restrictions on agricultural products, and against the adjustment of product standards to facilitate the import of foreign consumer goods. In other words, the most significant element in the consumer movement is zealously working to keep food prices high and to limit consumer choice to domestic produce' (van Wolferen, 1989, p. 53). Such has been the extent of neutralization of the consumer movement that the organization has little impact on large corporations and is unlikely ever to demand freer disclosure of information by companies.

As will be outlined in chapter 9, the trade union movement is relatively ineffective and has had no discernible effect on the level of information disclosed by Japanese corporations. As for the reporting corporations themselves, they have consistently lobbied through Keidanren against the extension of any disclosure which might be considered detrimental to their interests. Consequently, corporations disclose what they have to by law and often little else.

Whilst there might not be any great internal pressure to extend disclosure or change accounting practices it is still possible that external pressures might lead to change. For example, in Sweden the needs of the major corporations meant that to expand it became necessary to raise debt and equity abroad. This had the effect of improving disclosure by these multinational organizations as such information became incorporated in the corporate annual reports. To an extent such disclosures became a model of good behaviour so that companies listed only on the Stockholm Stock Exchange emulated the Swedish multinationals. As a result some large Swedish corporations produce accounts that are as good as any other country in the world. That this has not happened to the same extent in Japan is due, in part, to the post-war macroeconomic policies adopted by the government. These issues will be pursued in greater depth.

Post-war macroeconomic policies

The ex-post macroeconomic identity for gross national product (GNP) inclusive of depreciation is:

$$\text{GNP} = C + I + G + (X - M)$$

where C = private sector consumption
      I = private sector investment
      G = government spending
      X = gross exports
      M = gross imports

Alternatively, GNP may be thought of as the sum of consumption, savings or payments to government in the form of taxes. Thus, GNP may be expressed as follows:

$$\text{GNP} = C + S + T$$

where S = savings
      T = taxes

Consequently, the following equation must be true

$$C + I + G + (X - M) = C + S + T$$

Rearranging gives:

$$(S - I) = (G - T) + (X - M)$$

The accounting identity does not imply causality. Given the above equation, if investment exceeds savings the deficit would be offset by either a government surplus and/or a current account deficit. The corollary is that if savings exceed investment in the private sector then the surplus will be offset either by a government deficit and/or a current account surplus.

Table 8.1 shows the summarized sectoral savings–investment balances expressed as an average percentage of GNP at current prices for Japan from 1960 to 1985. During the 1960s private investment consistently exceeded savings for the sector. It is noticeable that whilst the household sectors was consistently a net saver corporations were net investors. This deficit on private savings was offset by a government surplus (tax revenues exceeded government expenditure) with a small current account deficit. Lincoln (1988, p. 73) states that both savings and investment levels in the private sector were double those in the US. Thus, corporate investment was very high, funded by both the household and government sectors, who were net savers. If the government had not been a net saver corporations would have needed to raise capital abroad. This is extremely important because had Japanese corporations raised money overseas it may well have been the necessary external stimulus to increase disclosure. Such was the case for Sweden. As Lincoln said:

the government instituted a variety of policies to prevent serious current-account deficits, including high tariffs and widespread import

Table 8.1 Sectoral savings – investment balances

	Average percentage of GNP at current prices Fiscal years		
	1960–9	1970–9	1980–5
Private			
Savings (S)	29.3	30.7	27.3
Investment (I)	31.2	28.3	23.3
Savings less investment $(S - I)$	−1.9	2.4	4.0
Corporations			
Savings (depreciation and retained earnings)	17.2	12.8	11.2
Investment	23.5	20.5	16.4
Savings less investment	−6.3	−7.7	−5.2
Households			
Savings	12.1	18.0	16.1
Investment	7.8	7.8	6.9
Savings less investment	4.3	10.2	9.2
Government			
Savings (tax revenue) (T)	7.1	4.5	3.5
Investment (expenditure) (G)	5.2	6.2	6.5
Savings less investment $(T - G)$	1.9	−1.7	−3.0
Current account $(X - M)$	0.07	0.76	1.4
Discrepancy	0.07	−0.01	0.4

Source: Data calculated from the *Annual Report on National Accounts*

quotas, strict controls on international capital movements (essentially preventing Japanese corporations from borrowing or lending abroad), and periodic tightening of monetary policy to slow the economy and thereby reduce the growth of imports. In this way the imperatives of exchange rate policy strongly discouraged borrowing overseas to accommodate the private sector's demand for investment funds ... The strict control of imports and capital flow was also strongly influenced by economic xenophobia. Since it began to develop as a modern economy in the late nineteenth century, Japan has striven for an economy owned, operated and supplied by Japanese firms. Policies to that effect proliferated in the 1930s, and postwar policies continued and strengthened the tendency. Xenophobia was given additional impetus in the 1950s by the fear that in the absence of strict controls war-weakened Japanese companies could be quickly overrun by foreign competition. (1988, p. 74)

The 1970s (see table 8.1) show a radically different picture. Corporations continued to invest heavily but this was more than matched by the large savings surplus in the household sector. The net effect was that aggregate private sector savings exceeded investment, which was matched by government deficits and – later in the decade – substantial current account surpluses. After the oil crisis in 1973 corporate sector savings, in terms of depreciation allowances and retained earnings, decreased from the previously very high levels. By 1976, however, savings in the corporate sector were again high. It is also noticeable that investment, as an average percentage of GNP, was lower in the 1970s than in the 1960s. Growth in the economy was inevitably lower, averaging 9.4 per cent annually between 1966 and 1973 and 3.8 per cent from 1974 to 1985.

The trend of reduced investment, as an average percentage of GNP, which characterized the 1970s, continued in the 1980s. Whilst investment in the corporate sector still exceeded savings the deficit was more than matched by the net savings of the household sector, so that overall private sector savings easily exceeded investment. Such a surplus was matched by a combination of a government deficit and a growing trade surplus. The government deficit declined over the period from 1980 to 1985 and, with a substantial private sector savings surplus, this meant a growing trade surplus.

In summary, the heavy corporate investment throughout the period from 1960 to 1985 was matched by flows from the household sector, by the government adjusting to borrowing requirements and by a growing trade surplus. Had the Japanese government allowed corporations to raise more capital abroad there could have been beneficial consequences to the disclosure of information in Japanese annual corporate reports. Instead, with little need for foreign capital, disclosure in corporate annual reports remained at the minimum level necessary to comply with the law. Table 8.2 shows the low level of foreign corporate borrowings over the period from 1975 to 1986.

Table 8.2 Sources of Japanese corporate funds (%)

	1975–9	1980–4	1982	1983	1984	1985	1986
Domestic borrowings	83.8	85.7	84.3	86.6	84.8	81.6	82.6
Private	72.3	76.8	74.2	79.5	79.4	78.1	80.9
Public	11.5	8.9	10.1	7.1	5.4	3.5	1.7
Securities	15.3	15.0	15.7	13.3	16.8	15.9	16.8
Corporate bonds	5.8	3.1	2.8	1.3	3.5	2.3	5.0
Stocks	7.7	8.1	9.0	6.2	7.5	5.5	3.7
Foreign currency bonds	1.8	3.8	3.9	5.8	5.8	8.1	8.1
Foreign borrowings	0.9	(0.7)	0.0	0.1	(1.6)	2.5	0.6
	100.0	100.0	100.0	100.0	100.0	100.0	100.0
¥ billion	14,761.6	21,724.2	22,675.3	22,154.0	24,611.9	29,128.7	31,842.4

Source: Bank of Japan

Whilst there has been little need for Japanese corporations to raise funds overseas some of the larger companies have developed their strategies away from simply export to creating manufacturing units as near as possible to the market-place. For example, NEC's 1988 annual report states that:

> Around the world, NEC companies are working to manufacture and market a wide range of products tailored to their host regions. We believe that the best way to respond to market trends and offer high-quality products is to bring our facilities as close as possible to the end users. In this way, we fulfil another priority: functioning as a responsible corporate citizen by responding to the needs of each community. Thus, to NEC the process of globalization is actually the localization of its operations on a global scale.

As part of their globalization strategies some major Japanese corporations have obtained overseas listings. Previously it has been argued that Japan views the US as its main, and sometimes only, serious competitor. Rivalry between the two countries is intense. However, it has also been argued that

Table 8.3 Listing of Japanese corporations (1st section only), 1987

Stock exchange	No. of Japanese companies listed
Tokyo	1,089
Osaka	794
Nagoya	406
Frankfurt	52
Luxembourg	51
Amsterdam	20
Paris	16
Düsseldorf	10
London	9
Basle	7
Geneva	7
Hong Kong	7
New York	7
Zurich	7
Antwerp	4
Brussels	4
Singapore	4
Pacific	2
Total	2,496

Note that some companies have multiple listings.

Japanese corporations have an inherent dislike of disclosure of information so that it is natural for disclosure listing requirements to be an important factor in obtaining an overseas quotation. Table 8.3 shows the number of listings of domestic corporations, both in Japan and overseas, and was assembled from the *Japan Company Handbook*, First Section, 1987. Japanese corporations are reluctant to meet the more stringent disclosure requirements of the New York Stock Exchange and the International Stock Exchange in London, preferring instead to obtain quotations on much smaller markets with less onerous disclosure requirements. Consequently, Frankfurt, Luxembourg and Amsterdam are popular destinations for Japanese companies seeking overseas quotations. The corollary to this observation is that US and UK companies are not likely to find the disclosure requirements of the Tokyo Stock Exchange more onerous than their domestic exchanges. This seems to be borne out by the fact that US and UK companies formed in excess of 75 per cent of the total number of foreign corporations listed on the Tokyo Stock Exchange in 1987 and 1988 (see table 8.4).

Table 8.4 Country of origin of foreign corporations listed on the TSE at the end of 1987 and 1988

| | 1987 | | 1988 | |
Country of origin	No.	%	No.	%
US	60	68	67	60
UK	10	11	18	16
Canada	6	7	6	5
Australia	3	4	5	4
West Germany	2	2	4	3
Netherlands	1	1	3	3
Sweden	3	4	3	3
Switzerland	2	2	3	3
France	–	–	2	2
Spain	1	1	1	1
Total	88	100	112	100

Source: TSE Fact Books 1988/1989

Other external influences

Whilst the JICPA is a relatively small accountancy body it has nevertheless co-operated as a member of the International Accounting Standards Committee (IASC), the International Federation of Accountants and the Confederation of Asian and Pacific Accountants. In particular, the JICPA was a founder member of the IASC in 1973 and has played a role in preparing international accounting standards (IASs) as well as trying to acquire and harmonize its own rules and regulations with IASs. However, Japanese common practices are often different from IASs, most of which are modelled on FASs and SSAPs – reflecting the leading role that the US and the UK have in drafting international standards. Perhaps because of different customs, conventions and economic and social climate, some significant differences between IASs and Japanese generally accepted accounting principles prevail. It would seem that Japan plays only a minor role in the formulation of IASs (Kikuya, 1989, p. 106). A more detailed summary of these differences is provided in appendix C, but the important ones are:

1 IAS 1 requires the presentation of a two-year financial statement whereas there is no equivalent requirement in the Japanese Commercial Code. However, the SEL requires two-year financial statements.
2 IAS 2 requires valuation of stock on the basis of the lower cost or net realizable value whereas in Japan stocks are valued at either cost or the lower of cost and market value.
3 IAS 3 stipulates that parent companies should issue consolidated financial statements. Such statements are produced as supplementary information by listed companies and filed with the Ministry of Finance.
4 IAS 4 states that major depreciable assets or classes of depreciable assets should be reviewed periodically and depreciation rates adjusted accordingly. There is no such requirement in Japan, practice being dictated by the Corporation Tax Law which is followed by most companies.
5 Information to be disclosed in financial statements in accordance with IAS 5 exceeds the disclosures of many Japanese corporations, particularly unlisted companies.
6 In Japan only listed companies (including companies which issued ¥500 million or more of securities) prepare a statement of changes in financial position whereas IAS 7 (Cash flow statement) applies to all corporations.
7 IAS 9 requires research costs to be charged in the year in which incurred whereas, in Japan, in exceptional circumstances they may be deferred and amortized over a period not exceeding five years.
8 Deferred tax accounting is not normally practised in Japan because it is not legal under the Commercial Code. Consequently, tax effect accounting is optional only when timing differences arise on consolidation.
9 IAS 21 specifies that long-term monetary items at the balance sheet date should be translated at the closing rate whereas in Japan historical rates should be used. Other differences include the translation of financial statements of foreign branches, foreign operations whose activities are integral to the operations of the parent and use of the restate–translate method.
10 The conditions for capitalization of borrowing costs are more extensive in Japan than IAS 23.

11 IAS 25 permits revalued amounts of long-term investments whereas in Japan long-term investments should be generally carried at cost.

Although the JICPA is a member of the IASC our survey (reported in chapter 12) found that not one company mentioned international accounting standards.[1] This is in stark contrast to Swedish corporate reports where such disclosures are common. If a comparison is made in Japanese accounts they always refer to US accounting requirements. A detailed summary of the differences between Japanese and UK generally accepted accounting principles (GAAP) and between Japanese and US GAAP is provided in appendix B. A summary of the major differences is provided here:

1 In English versions of the Japanese accounts terminology is consistently US rather than British.
2 There is no requirement in the Commercial Code to present two-year financial statements, unlike both the UK and US (companies registered under the US Securities and Exchange Law only). Whilst the SEL does not require comparative figures it is usual, in practice, for such information to be disclosed.
3 In Japan income for tax purposes is based on the published financial statements, a practice which differs from that prevailing in the UK and US.
4 In Japan and the US upward revaluations of assets may not be incorporated into the accounts; in the UK revaluations occur quite often with the surplus being credited to a revaluation reserve.
5 The financial statements in Japan should include a separate appropriation statement. This is probably because the statement is quite detailed and includes reserve movements such as arise with special depreciation and allocations to legal earned reserves, directors and statutory auditors.
6 The layout of accounts in Japan follows a US format.
7 Companies may not purchase their own shares in Japan except in special circumstances such as purchase for cancellation or by acquisition resulting from a merger or business transfer.
8 Japanese companies must allocate 10 per cent of cash disbursements paid to a legal earned reserve until it reaches 25 per cent of share capital. Note that the allocation is a percentage of cash disbursements paid and not annual profits as in Germany and Sweden. Furthermore, the level of the legal earned reserve, 25 per cent of share capital, is very prudent since it compares with 10 per cent in Germany and 20 per cent in Sweden.
9 Deferred tax accounting is compulsory in the UK and US in accordance with accounting requirements whereas inter-period income tax allocations are not permitted by the Commercial Code. However, allocations are permitted in the consolidated accounts filed with the Ministry of Finance.
10 A wide range of valuation methods is permitted in Japan when estab-

lishing the cost of stocks. The range is more extensive than in the UK.

11 Long-term contract work-in-progress is calculated on an accruals basis in the UK; in Japan either the accruals or realization basis is permitted. In practice the completed contract method is used.

12 In the UK research costs should be written off in the year of expenditure whereas in Japan they may be treated as deferred assets. In contrast, development costs may be deferred in the UK provided certain stringent conditions are fulfilled. Such costs should be amortized over a period not exceeding five years. In the US, FAS 2 stipulates that all costs are charged as an expense in the year in which they are incurred. In exceptional circumstances research and development performed for others and certain computer software development costs may be capitalized. In Japan the Commercial Code permits development costs to be capitalized and amortized over a period not exceeding five years, although in practice many large companies adopt a policy of write-off in the year in which the expense is incurred.

13 Finance leases in both the UK and US should be capitalized in the lessee's accounts and the obligation to pay future rentals should be treated as a liability. In Japan, leased assets may be either disclosed or capitalized. In practice Japanese companies have not yet adopted the capitalization option.

14 In the UK, SSAP 6 specifies that exceptional items should be separately disclosed. There is no equivalent requirement in Japan or the US. Prior-year adjustments in the UK are limited to items arising from changes in accounting policies and from the correction of fundamental errors. Corrections or adjustments arising from the estimation process should be excluded. In Japan corrections and adjustments may be included as prior-year adjustments.

15 In the UK and US consolidated accounts are considered to be the main financial statements. In contrast, the Japanese Commercial Code stipulates that the accounts should be based on an individual company basis only. Furthermore, the SEL accounts are based on the parent company although there is a requirement for consolidated financial statements to be filed as supplementary information.

16 In both Japan and the US goodwill on consolidation is treated as an asset and amortized. The amortization period should not exceed five years in Japan but may extend to 40 years in the US. In the UK goodwill should normally be eliminated from the accounts immediately on acquisition, against reserves, but may be amortized to the profit and loss account over its useful economic life.

17 When undertaking a foreign currency translation exercise, the UK standard requires that long-term monetary items should be translated at the closing rate at the balance sheet date. Exchange differences thereon

should be recognized in income in the current period. In Japan long-term monetary assets should be translated at the historical rates; consequently, there is no exchange difference.

When translating foreign currency financial accounts whose activities are self-contained and integrated, the closing rate method should be used normally in accordance with SSAP 20. In addition, the temporal method should be used for a foreign operation whose activities are integral to the operations of the parent. The Japanese regulations require the temporal method to be used for a foreign branch provided long-term items are translated at the historical rate. A modified temporal method should be used for a foreign subsidiary or associate provided that long-term monetary items are translated at the historical rates. Under the modified temporal method, net income and retained earnings should be translated at the closing rate and exchange differences resulting from the translation of balance sheet items should be charged or credited to assets or liabilities. In the UK the restate–translate method should be used for the financial accounts of foreign enterprises which are affected by high rates of inflation, but there is no equivalent in Japan.

The requirements in the US are similar to those prevailing in the UK.

18 Whereas a funds statement must be prepared by companies in the US and UK, there is no equivalent requirement in Japan. However, Japanese companies are required to prepare such a statement as part of the registration report for subscription or sale of securities and the securities report and file it with the Ministry of Finance.

19 In Japan and US dividends are dealt with on a cash basis whereas in the UK they are accrued. Furthermore, in Japan directors' bonuses are not accrued whereas they are in the UK and US.

Summary

The Japanese Commercial Code of 1899 was largely based on the German Commercial Code of 1897. Consequently, the influence of taxation regulations and the importance of conservatism became features of financial reporting in Japan. The characteristics still persist although the influence of tax accounting became increasingly important when special tax allowances were introduced. Another characteristic of Japanese financial reporting is the general unwillingness to disclose more than the minimum required by the law and to try to keep as much information as secret as possible. This attitude probably stemmed from the almost self-contained *zaibatsu*, who saw no good reason to disclose information to third parties.

Whilst German accounting was the most significant influence over pre-war accounting in Japan the US was the greatest single influence thereafter. Such a situation is very similar to that of Sweden although the important difference is that Sweden moved in this direction voluntarily, recognizing the importance of the US economy and its importance in accounting, while in Japan the change was imposed. As the driving force behind the occupation forces the US tried to democratize the country, including the accounting regulatory framework.

Pressures for change are not likely to come from institutional shareholders because interdependent relationships, cross-shareholdings, multiple directorships and access to inside information make the need for extensive disclosure less crucial. Since institutional shareholding dominates Japanese equity markets it is unlikely that pressures for increased corporate information will come from small shareholders. Since the 1899 Commercial Code was orientated towards the needs of creditors it is unlikely that pressure will come from this avenue for further disclosure. In addition, banks would presumably have access to inside information well above that disclosed in the financial statements. Finally, both the consumer movement and trade union movement, which could lobby for more extensive disclosure of information, have been so effectively neutralized that they have little real impact on large corporations.

Whilst there has been little internal pressure in Japan to extend disclosure or change accounting policies it is still possible that changes may have arisen from external pressure. That this has not happened is due mainly to the post-war economic policies. Whereas in Sweden the government recognized that major Swedish enterprises could not survive on its home market and encouraged a process of multinational expansion – with consequential advantageous affects on extending disclosure – the Japanese government sought to protect its industry. This was achieved by high tariff barriers, extensive import quotas and strict controls on capital movements which prevented Japanese corporations from borrowing or lending abroad. During the 1960s private investment consistently exceeded savings (depreciation and retained earnings) and this net investment was matched by net savings by the household sector, a government budget surplus with a small current account deficit. This was important because if Japanese corporations had raised money overseas it may well have been the necessary external stimulus to increased disclosure in corporate annual reports as a requirement of foreign markets.

In the 1970s the continued high level of investment was more than matched by the large savings surplus in the household sector. The net effect was that aggregate private sector savings exceeded investment, which was matched by government deficits and later in the decade substantial current account surpluses.

In the first half of the 1980s private sector savings easily exceeded investment as a result of the high net savings of the household sector. This surplus was matched by a combination of government deficit and a growing trade surplus. However, from 1983 the government deficit has been reduced so that in 1988 a small surplus occurred. Whilst the current account surplus increased up to 1986 the surplus began to fall thereafter. 'The fall in the external surplus in Japan since 1986, reflecting higher business investment and a declining household saving ratio, has more to do with successful domestic demand management policies and fiscal responsibility leading to renewed business confidence, than with changes in trade policies' (OECD, 1988/89, p. 100).

As for the future it appears that capital outflows from Japan will continue, reflecting both direct investment in manufacturing and foreign securities. The Japanese will follow the US approach of diversifying its operations geographically so that they become accepted members of foreign countries. Some of the major Japanese corporations have already invested heavily in Europe, particularly the UK. This is likely to continue as companies jockey for position before 1992 but it seems likely that less investment will flow to the UK compared with other European Community countries as Japan tries to reduce trade friction towards itself by diversifying geographically throughout the Community. Perhaps such activity will lead to more overseas quotations for Japanese companies and perhaps even increased disclosure in their corporate annual reports as a consequence.

This chapter has also highlighted major differences in financial reporting between Japan, and the UK and the US. In addition, major differences between Japanese accounting practices and international accounting standards have been considered. Some significant differences still exist between Japanese reporting requirements and those considered acceptable internationally. The disclosure requirements of the Japanese Commercial Code are not nearly as extensive as those that prevail in the UK and US. Whilst the accounts prepared in accordance with the Securities and Exchange Law require more extensive disclosure the requirements still fall short of international accounting standards. Kikuya (1990) has argued that

> Japanese accounting practice is still nationalistic although Japan has made every effort to achieve international harmonization since the formation of IASC in 1973. Japanese accounting standards are often quite different from IASs published by the IASC. Accounting conventions, the economic, social and cultural environment in Japan hinder the international harmonization of accounting standards or the full compliance with IASs. However, financial statements published by Japanese companies should be prepared on the basis of internationally acceptable and understandable accounting standards as a result of the move to globalization of securities markets with the advance of Japanese economic power worldwide. (p. 139)

Note

1 In Japan only Sasebo Heavy Industry presents an English version of its financial accounts, prepared in accordance with IASs.

9

Local Environmental Characteristics

'Local environmental characteristics belong to the broadest and most important of all the categories. This category contains diverse factors such as the nature and state of the economy as well as cultural attitudes' (Radebaugh, 1975, p. 47). Farmer and Richman (1966) have organized environmental characteristics into four major groups: educational, sociocultural, legal and political, and economic. Each of these groups will be considered in the context of the development of accounting objectives, standards and practices in Japan.

Educational factors

An introduction to the educational system

Many of the functions of the *ie* (see chapter 3) have now been incorporated into the education system. The nature of the hierarchical system in business and the duality of employment make the desire for a good education at times overwhelming. 'Many parents see the success of their children at school as of paramount importance for their future prospects' (Hendry, 1987, p. 86). Placing great value in education is a Confucian value common to Sino-culture countries (for example China, Hong Kong, Korea, Singapore, Taiwan and Japan). By the end of the Edo (Tokugawa) period literacy in Japan exceeded that in China and Korea. Whilst private tutoring in Japan was important most feudal domains had official schools for their *samurai* by the middle of the nineteenth century. In addition, there were many schools for both *samurai* and non-*samurai*, the latter being referred to as temple schools. In the middle of the nineteenth century literacy was about 45 per cent for males and 15 per cent for females, figures not far below those prevailing in advanced Western countries (Reischauer, 1988, p. 187).

A centralized education system was first introduced in the Meiji period and since then opportunities have steadily improved. School attendance is in excess of 98 per cent, making illiteracy almost non-existent. The present system of education was introduced after the Second World War and is egalitarian and co-educational, with a national curriculum set by the Ministry of Education. The Ministry states the subjects to be taught, when they will be taught, and what textbooks will be used. Where books do not convey the message approved by the Ministry of Education the author may be asked to rewrite the section.

Before the Second World War approved school history books told of the country's origins as recorded in the eighth-century *Kojiki* (*Record of Ancient Matters*) and *Nihon-shoki* (*Chronicles of Japan*). These records state that the islands of Japan were born from the marriage between the god Izanagi and his sister Izanami. At a later date they gave birth to the sun, in the form of the goddess Amaterasu, who provided the regalia for the Japanese imperial family. The regalia consisted of a bronze mirror, iron sword and jewel. In addition, the Japanese people were encouraged to believe that they belonged to branches of the imperial line and consequently were descendants of Amaterasu.

The allied forces banned the use of these textbooks as they were seen as encouraging Japanese nationalist fervour. Instead, teaching immediately after the war was based on US values although many courses have become Japanized over time. The system of education today is largely that established in 1947. Formal education in the local public schools begins at the age of six and continues for nine years. Whilst attendance at primary (elementary) schools continues for six years, followed by three years at junior high school, in reality the period of education extends for much longer. Before attending primary school, children attend kindergarten for between one and three years. It is here that the concept of 'group life' is introduced and the new 'inside' group (*uchi*) encountered. It is here that an individual child becomes a member of a new *uchi* – a group opposed to the outside world. The *uchi* moves up together, regardless of academic achievement, thereby reinforcing the group at the expense of the individual. Compare the UK system of primary education where pupils within a class do not all move up together but may go into the next year with children of the same age from other classes. This is presumably to widen horizons and avoid introspection. Thus, at an early stage a Japanese child is made to feel part of a group in which all members are considered equal. Order is maintained by peer-group pressure and ostracism of a recalcitrant child (Hendry, 1987, pp. 45–6). Each group has about 40 members and such a large size is maintained throughout the compulsory stages of education and even beyond.

The primary schools continue with the theme of the group rather than the individual but in order to increase the effectiveness of teaching the class is split into a number of smaller groups. Here emphasis is placed on collective responsibility – togetherness. Collective responsibility extends beyond the teaching function, to serving lunch and cleaning the school premises with the children. 'No work, not even the dirty work of cleaning is too low for a student; that all should share equally in common tasks; the maintenance of the school is everyone's responsibility' (Cummings, 1980, p. 117). There is also a considerable emphasis on art and music both at the primary school and also at junior high school.

Whilst the compulsory period of education emphasizes equality of education there is considerable examination pressure on schoolchildren. Indeed, as was emphasized in chapter 3, ability to go to a 'good' university often determines the standard of living obtained throughout life. It is this very pressure that leads to a breakdown of the concept of equality of opportunity since Japan abounds with private tutoring systems. Consequently, families try to place their children in the 'best' primary schools and even the 'best' kindergartens, and supplement their education by classes after school. This burden of privately borne educational costs contributes towards the high propensity to save. 'There is no question here that a wealthy elite is being separated off at a very early age' (Hendry, 1987, p. 94). However, it should be borne in mind that extensive use of private tutoring does not normally occur until children are between 10 and 18 years old.

The pressure even within the period of compulsory education may seem unrelenting – even after examinations in July, lessons continue and the pressure is maintained. Attendance at primary and junior high schools is based on catchment areas but students are able to apply to the high school or technical college of their choice subject to the ability to commute from home. 'The best qualified students are able to continue in the academically orientated schools, which are ranked in any area for their success in placing graduating students in good universities. There are also a number of vocational high schools which include training in commercial and technical skills, domestic science and fields of local importance such as agriculture or forestry, and there is sometimes also a night high school, so that students can work during the day' (Hendry, 1987, pp. 90–1). Despite the pressures, the Japanese education system is very effective at instilling the work ethic into children and at obtaining a high level of attainment in reading, writing and mathematics, even by the bottom half of the ability range.

Somewhere between 94 and 96 per cent of students go on to senior high school (ages 15 to 18). One of the core subjects studied by all students is mathematics; compared with a mere 7 per cent of the school population of England and Wales who take the comparable GCE A-level. Other core subjects include Japanese, English, social science and physical science. Classes in nearly all subjects are again large, with an average of between 40 and 45 students.

As for the teachers themselves, many teacher training courses include about two weeks' teacher practice. Furthermore, whilst some in-service training courses are organized by individual prefectures they are of a limited scope. Indeed, there is an attitude that 'there is no need to train the teachers. The children have to work so hard for their examinations' (*Times Educational Supplement*, 6 October 1989, p. 2). Whilst classes are larger than in British schools, contact time by teachers is only about 55 per cent, allowing time for preparation and marking. Essay writing is not common, exercises being designed so that they can be answered using one word or a short sentence.

There are approximately 490 universities in Japan and about 38 per cent of high school students (compare the UK 8.4 per cent in 1989, with a further 8.4 per cent in other forms of higher education, and the US 45 per cent) going on to a college education. The highly structured regime prevalent in Japan's primary and high schools changes dramatically on entering university. This is because the career path of an individual is largely determined by attendance at a particular college, regardless of subsequent academic performance. Indeed,

one clear tendency among about 90% of the Japanese college students I've taught is their strong determination not to study ... For these students the four years of college life represent a prolonged respite – a kind of moratorium period during which they spend their time trying to make as many social friends as possible, thus working to develop skills they have ignored while arduously preparing over a period of years during high school for college entrance exams ... Most professors thoroughly understand the motivation of their students and accordingly make their requirements quite minimal, often resulting in a mutually satisfying situation for both parties. (Gold, 1988, pp. 3–4)

At the age of 18 the great divide between male and female begins to take place. Three-quarters of university students are men, often studying business or engineering; home economics and education are considered appropriate for girls to take at university or junior college. Thus, girls are preparing themselves for their role in Japanese society – marriage, looking after the home and bringing up the children and fostering their education. No impediments are placed in the path of a girl, however, although being better qualified than a prospective husband is not considered good practice. However, the idea of females working has become increasingly acceptable in recent years.

Again, the *uchi* is noticeable in university life. Those 'active' in the learning process join a professor's seminar programme – the *zemi*. The *uchi* group then is the professor's group, which involves not only seminars but also *compa* – drinking and eating parties. In addition, the professor is influential in the ultimate employment destination of his students. The group continues beyond graduation. For example, on the marriage of a group member it is common for the professor to be the main guest and to be asked to give a speech extolling the virtues of his former student. When a professor dies, it is common for former seminar students to attend. It is this concept of *uchi* that provides a distinction between the Japanese and the UK and US educational systems.

In conclusion, the compulsory education period up to the age of 15 is very effective at teaching core subjects such as reading, writing and mathematics. In addition, the standard of art and music at both primary schools and junior high schools is high. The pressures placed upon children may seem excessive judged from an Anglo-Saxon point of view. 'Articles in British newspapers have tended to emphasize the strain of keeping up, the lack of time to play, and they are quick to report the high rate of suicide among schoolchildren in Japan. [However,] bullying seems to have replaced examination pressure as a major cause of child suicide in recent reports, and special centres have been set up to provide phone-in help for victims' (Hendry, 1987, p. 96).

Japan probably has a comparative advantage over Britain in compulsory education, but this is not due to higher standards of teaching training. Indeed, it is possible that Britain has a comparative advantage here. What is clear, however, is that Britain has a comparative advantage over Japan in university education. The work ethic inculcated during the nine years of compulsory education in Japan is largely abandoned for a four-year period at university, to be taken up again on gaining employment.

Accounting education

It is possible to undertake some accounting tuition in the high schools under the subject head of commerce. Commerce is often divided into four main areas: business economics, accounting, administration and information technology. Accounting generally consists of bookkeeping, including industrial bookkeeping, accounting and tax accounting. However, the better students normally aim to go to university rather than attend such vocational high schools.

Accounting at universities usually follows the reference standards laid down by the University Establishment Standards Board, which stipulates that accounting is a core subject of a commerce degree and business administration degree but only a related subject in economics. Generally, both the commerce and business administration degrees will consist, *inter alia*, of bookkeeping principles, principles of accounting, cost and management accounting, business analysis, and auditing. Tax accounting is also often a component of a commerce degree.

A feature of Japanese accounting education is the emphasis on theory. 'The traditional accounting lecture is given in a large classroom with the instructor expanding on fundamental theory, with little reference to actual practice in entry-making or financial statement preparation. For this reason, most accounting graduates are unable to prepare an income statement or balance sheet if the slightest complexity is involved. This tendency to divorce theory from practice serves to increase the isolation of universities' (Takemura and Takamatsu, in Choi and Hiramatsu, 1987, p. 206). This is not surprising perhaps because very few accounting lecturers are professionally qualified – a feature rather different from that prevailing in the UK. Most Japanese accounting academics have attended graduate school, whose traditional role has been a place where research is undertaken. Many postgraduates then move on to a university post. Industry, in general, is not particularly keen to recruit those with postgraduate qualifications other than engineering and science, preferring those who have completed their undergraduate studies so that the company itself can train them.

Due to the theoretical nature of undergraduate and postgraduate accounting teaching, the courses are of limited value in trying to qualify as a CPA. Training for the CPA examinations is often done alone, in groups, or by attending courses at specialist training establishments. The pass rate in the intermediate examination is often less than 10 per cent. The difficulty in obtaining CPA status may have implications for future accounting teaching at Japanese universities.

Computers and education

The Japanese have shown themselves very adept at manufacturing computers, yet there is some concern that Japan may enter the twenty-first century as a nation of computer illiterates. The problem stems from the fact that there is virtually no exposure to computers in the nine years of compulsory education. Projections of a shortfall of a million software engineers by the end of this century have prompted the Ministry of Education to offer an optional course in information technology to all those in junior high schools. However, over 60 per cent of schools do not possess any computers. This has everything to do with the education system and little to do with the compatibility of the Japanese language and computing (Cross, 1989, p. 16).

It is not surprising therefore that the application of computing to accounting education is in its infancy. 'In Japan, the computer will undoubtedly have a great impact on future accounting education. It is probably safe to say that present computer accounting education is not what it ought to be' (Takemura and Takamatsu, in Choi and Hiramatsu, 1987, p. 216).

Legal factors

As was highlighted in chapter 6, legal factors are an important influence over the disclosure of information and financial reporting in Japan. In many instances there is little difference between tax accounting and financial accounting. Furthermore, the Japanese Commercial Code is administered by the Ministry of Justice and the Securities and Exchange Law is administered by the Ministry of Finance. The Ministry of Finance through its advisory board, the Business Accounting Deliberation Council, has been very influential in developing financial reporting. In contrast, the Japanese Institute of Certified Public Accountants has been less effective, although recommendations on accounting topics which should be followed by publicly traded companies are issued. One reason for this is that there are only 8,662 qualified CPAs, representing the lowest proportion of qualified accountants in virtually any industrialized country. The difficulty in passing the examinations is a major factor in explaining this feature. Accounting is not unique in this respect. The number of qualified lawyers, about 14,000, is also extremely low compared with other industrialized nations. Again the difficulty in passing the examinations – some 500 out of 20,000 candidates pass the examination each year – is the key factor. The Supreme Court delegates authority for the examination to the Legal Training Institute whose responsibility it is to maintain high standards and in fact to restrict entry.

It is a curious feature that most of those employed as accountants and lawyers in large companies are not professionally qualified. The concept of taking on graduates and training them to meet the needs of the company is far more important than being professionally qualified. It also assists the process of lifetime employment in as much as staff are less mobile and therefore perhaps more loyal. Droves of professionally qualified personnel willing to accept positions with other companies is just not part of Japanese culture.

An important influence over the regulation of legal services in Japan is the government. Indeed, Ramseyer (1986, p. 501) argues that the regulatory system 'can best be understood as an attempt by the state, the bar, and the major consumers of legal services to further their respective private interests. Japanese lawyers have actively sought regulation to promote their own economic advantage . . . Because of the government's own concerns and the power and influence of the major consumers of legal services, the regulatory program in some ways reflects more of the government and those major consumers than of the bar.'

Cultural and historical factors

It is rare for any paper written on Japan to exclude a cultural explanation. The Japanese themselves constantly try to emphasize their 'uniqueness' (see, for example, Takatera and Yamamoto, 1987, p. 10) and cultural identity. In trade negotiations with the US the Japanese frequently try to explain their behaviour by emphasizing their unique culture or customs. Resorting occasionally to the ridiculous, the Japanese government and academics use the cultural explanation of uniqueness to stonewall exasperated trading partners.

The myth of Japanese uniqueness has been considered by a number of authors including Dale (1986) and van Wolferen (1989). Indeed, such authors have been designated as forming part of the revisionist school of thought (*Financial Times*, 8 January 1990). As van Wolferen argues (1989, p. 14) Japanese culture is not unique in the way that all cultures are different but uniquely unique, different from all others. The Japanese are inculcated with 'specialness' at school, at work and through the media and reminded when comparisons are made with the outside world.

This section briefly considers cultural factors that may ultimately have some effect on accounting in Japan. However, it must be recognized that to deal with the subject rigorously would require a book in its own right. Two important approaches which are useful in analysing culture are the cross-sectional approach and historical approach. The historical approach is adopted here to try to identify cultural characteristics. Culture in respect of societies, nations or ethnic groups has been defined by Hofstede (1984, p. 13) as a 'collective programming of the mind which distinguishes the members of one human group from another'.

Historical factors

There is evidence that the Japanese archipelago, which then still bordered on the Asian continent, was first inhabited by people from Siberia some 100,000 years ago. The descendants of these so-called Ainu now live in Hokkaido, having been displaced by Mongoloid immigrants from China, Korea and Manchuria. About 10,000 years ago the Japanese archipelago was isolated from the continent of Asia because of the rise of the sea after the end of the glacial period and then the prototype of the Japanese developed through the mixed blood of existing races. They were mainly hunters and collectors of food and it was not until the third century BC that techniques of irrigation, rice cultivation and wheel-made pottery spread from China to Japan. By

AD 300 iron and bronze was being brought from Korea in sufficient quantities to develop agricultural implements. With 67 per cent of the country being mountainous, cultivation of the flatlands was important.

It is possible that relationships between social groups as posited by Dore (1971) and Nakane (1973) can be traced back as far as AD 400 when the dominant *uji* (semi-autonomous tribal units) of the imperial family had subordinate clans who in turn had subordinates of farmers, fishermen and hunters as well as potters and weavers. Dore (1971) suggests that Japan is characterized by attachment of a young person to a senior. The senior person helps the junior's career and in turn the young person offers loyalty. This type of patronage may be thought of as a *oyabun/kobun* relationship (literally, boss and henchman relationship). Nakane (1973) argues that this *oyabun/kobun* relationship is of fundamental importance to understanding social organization in Japan. Thus, Nakane's basic model is an 'inverted V', as shown in figure 9.1. Here B and C are junior to A, similar to Dore's A/B relationship.

Nakane extends her basic model to show more complex relationships (figure 9.2) in which B and C may act as *oyabun* to D and E and F and G respectively. Note that the structure is hierarchical, so that there is no relationship between B and C. Consequently, if A dies there is no obvious successor.

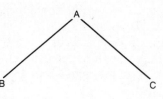

Figure 9.1   Nakane's inverted V

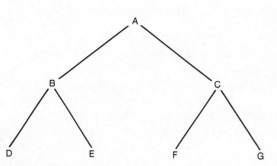

Figure 9.2   Nakane's extended model

By AD 400 the beginnings of these hierarchical relationships had been formed. At that time Japan had a military presence in the south of Korea although it was forced to leave by the sixth century after having given the Yamato court a present of the sacred images and scriptures of Chinese Buddhism. For the following two centuries there was considerable interest by the Japanese in Chinese culture. Interest was shown in the teachings of Confucius (K'ung Fu-tse, 551–479 BC), not because he was reported to be an accountant in a grain store for part of his life, but rather for his moral philosophy (Boughton, 1988, p. 66). His teachings were based on concepts such as respect, loyalty and obedience – ideas still important in modern Japan. Perhaps the most famous saying of Confucious is: 'What you do not wish done to yourself do not do to others.' This concept of reciprocity is very important in Japanese society. Reciprocity 'is a universal characteristic of social interaction, particularly important in long-term relations' (Hendry, 1987, p. 203).

Early religious practices were referred to as Shinto, 'the way of the gods', to distinguish them from Buddhism. Shinto was based on mythology or nature, such as the sun goddess, rather than on ethics. 'The leaders were both high priests and temporal rulers – in fact the same words were used for "religious worship" and "government" and for "shrine" and "palace"' (Reischauer, 1988, p. 42). Respect and cleanliness were and still remain important underlying concepts. Indeed, the Americans after the Second World War described the Japanese as being 'pathologically clean'.

A heavy flow of cultural influences into Japan from China started with a fight at the Yamato court over the acceptance of Buddhism as a religion of equal or greater importance than Shinto, the indigenous Japanese religion based on the divinity of the Tenno (usually referred to as emperor in English), who was supposedly descended from the sun goddess. Supporters of Buddhism won that battle and even a generation later, Prince Shotoku (593–662) advocated Buddhism with obedience to the emperor to ensure national stability. Furthermore, there was pressure to extend the emperor's role into secular matters, as was the case in China. However, in reality Japanese emperors have constantly been 'manipulated by other members of the imperial clan, by the broader court aristocracy, and in time by the feudal nobility of the provinces' (Reischauer, 1988, pp. 44–5).

Centralized government and household taxation were introduced using China as a model, a census of the population was undertaken and the first law codes (including the Taiho Code) were drawn up. The Chinese concept of training the best talents available was modified by Japan to meet the needs of the aristocracy. The concept of importing foreign culture and its modification to meet the 'needs' of Japan is a feature of the country's historical development.

The Nara period (710–94) was characterized by considerable interest in the ritual, art and philosophy of Buddhism. Nara became a permanent residential capital for the imperial court. Many temples were built there to honour Buddha. On the death of Empress Koken (later Shotoku) in 770 attempts were made to move the capital. This was achieved in 794 with a move to Heian-kyo (now Kyoto) by Emperor Kanmu. Like Nara, the city had a right-angled street plan, copying the Chinese style of Chan'an. However, the Chinese influence was less important during this period (794–1192). The foundations of feudalism were laid during this period, with all land belonging to the nation and farmers having to pay a tax to use it. The only exceptions were the granting of tax-free land to the aristocracy and to Buddhist temples. An elaborate system of hierarchical order developed, with the aristocracy or court supporting provincial owners, who employed estate managers, who in turn employed smallholders and then labourers. Perhaps this hierarchical order has never really changed. The Heian period was characterized by an extensive court life with emphasis on the arts. During this period schools tried to integrate the ideograms of monosyllabic Chinese to polysyllabic Japanese and the result was a set of Kana characters.

Despite the considerable cultural influence of the period political activity continued, with two independent landed families, Minamoto and Taira, being prominent. The two families had *samurai*, or *bushi* (retainers and warriors), to protect their interests. A four-year interlude of war between the two families ended with the Taira defeating the Minamoto. The head of the Taira, Kiyomori, became the effective decision-maker although a member of the Fujiwara clan continued as regent. Eventually the head of the Minamoto clan, Yoritomo, took power and set up his headquarters at Kamakura with permission from the emperor, who was only 13 years old at the time. Yoritomo Minamoto became the first national ruler with the title of *sei-i tai-shogun* (barbarian-subduing great general). Military rulers then governed Japan for almost 700 years.

Yoritomo retained central government with the senior posts still being held by court aristocrats. However, he spread loyal supporters from warrior classes throughout the estates of the aristocrats, with central direction from Kamakura based on local rather than Chinese-type law codes (Reischauer, 1988, p. 53).

In 1274 and 1281 the Mongols invaded western Japan only to be defeated by a typhoon. The divine wind (*kamikaze*) created a feeling of divine protection. Japan was not invaded again until 1945. However, the Minamoto regime had been weakened by the two foreign attacks and a new shogun took power. The Ashikaga clan moved the capital to Muromachi, Kyoto (1336–1603) where villas, castles and temples were built. Eventually the central rulers lost their power and the country returned to its feudal system where warlords (*daimyo*) had local political power. Between 1467 and 1568 there was an almost constant civil war. In 1543 Portuguese explorers landed on a Japanese island and Christian ideas began to be absorbed as well as Western military technology.

Many warriors turned to Zen, a type of Buddhism, which emphasized meditation, nature and simplicity, since the underlying philosophy was based on self-discipline. Zen monasteries developed in Kamakura and Kyoto and they became centres of learning based on the Chinese language and literature (Reischauer, 1988, pp. 61–2). Today, the Western businessman, Low (1976, pp. 206–19), advocates Zen Buddhism as a discipline for managers based on acts of creativity.

In 1603 the shogun Ieyasu Tokugawa gained control and set up his military government at Edo (now Tokyo). Whilst peace returned to Japan the government was concerned about the growth of Christianity and its threat to existing religions, language and culture. Language is a characteristic which is often ignored in cultural analysis. Whilst the spirit and structure of the language based on the ideogram may prove difficult for Western nations to come to terms with it is noticeable that far more Japanese try to learn foreign languages than conversely. An inability to decipher codes inherent in a culture may represent a source of misunderstandings between nations.

For 200 years from 1639 the shogun cut off Japan from the rest of the world, except Nagasaki. During this period trade developed based on agriculture, forestry and fisheries, and in the seventeenth century the Mitsui family developed as traders and bankers. In isolation from the rest of the world, however, the country had difficulty in coping with many natural disasters such as earthquakes, famine and drought, and, in particular, crop failures in 1732, 1780 and the 1830s.

European powers had taken over much of the Indian and South East Asian continent by the middle of the nineteenth century. The Russians were pushing southwards and American ships used Japan's coastal waters regularly as part of its trade with China and for whaling (Reischauer, 1988, p. 78). In 1854 the Treaty of Kanagawa was signed which opened up two ports, Shimoda and Hakodate, to the Americans. Such concessions were quickly extended to Russia and Britain. More ports, including Yokohama near Edo, were opened, leading to concern about the Western influence in Japan. There was anguish in Japan about what they saw as a threat from foreigners and as part of its counter-strategy nationalism was emphasized based around the emperor. Some of the *samurai* took action against shogunal officials and some Westerners. 'When Satsuma samurai killed an Englishman near Yokohama, a British fleet in 1863 destroyed Kagoshima, its capital city. Similarly, when Chosu fired on Western ships passing through the Straits of Shimonoseki, an allied fleet in 1864 levelled the Chosu forts' (Reischauer, 1988, p. 80). The Japanese were so impressed by the effectiveness of British ships in destroying much of Kagoshima that an order was placed for them, providing the foundation of the Japanese Imperial Navy.

In 1868 the shogun Tokugawa was defeated by a combination of the Choshu, Satsuma, Tosa and Saga clans and the political authority of the emperor was restored. The emperor occupied the Edo castle and Edo was renamed Tokyo. The emperor was only 14 years old and effective power was placed with the administration, which tried to eliminate feudalism and introduce a more meritocratic society. In effect, power was seized by younger *samurai*, particularly those from Satsuma and Choshu. Recognizing potential problems with Westerners, particularly from a military viewpoint, they accepted the unequal treaties negotiated by the Tokugawa. The new philosophy was to try to make Japan rich and militarily strong (Reischauer, 1988, pp. 80–1). The 260 feudal domains were reorganized into 45 prefectures and the *daimyo* disbanded to form the imperial armed forces. The *samurai* were effectively dissolved. The Meiji period was characterized by a determination to acquire Western skills and technology. Agriculture and industry were modernized and the *zaibatsu* began to form. Comprehensive postal and railway services were introduced based on the British model and schools were developed. In 1889 a constitution was introduced with a bicameral parliament: the House of Representatives was an elected body, the House of Peers was based on aristocratic lines. A new legal system was also introduced based on the French and German models. Part of the liberalization process in trade is still reflected in some corporate annual reports. For example, Minolta's 1988 report states:

> In the 1820s and 1830s, Joseph Nicephore Niepce and Louis-Jacques-Maude Daguerre of France constructed the first camera capable of permanently recording images . . . In 1899, Kazuo Tashima was born in Japan, which was just emerging from over 200 years of isolation from the outside world dating back to 1639, when the Tokugawa Shogunate implemented its isolation policy. However, even before foreign trade was officially restored following the signing of the treaty of amity and commerce in 1858, cameras were introduced in Japan and were used, much as they are today, to record the memories and history of the nation . . . In 1928, at the age of 29, Tashima set up his own business, calling it Nichi-Doku Shashinki Shoten (Japan–Germany Camera Company), and invited Billy Neuman from Germany to help in the construction of the Company's first factory. (p. 4)

Concern was again expressed about the Western influence, however, so that in 1890 an edict on education promoted Chinese and Japanese values at the expense of those from the West. Japanese militarism was still extremely important – between 1868 and 1945 the country was involved in five major wars. In 1945 Japan was occupied for the first time, by the allied forces. (The democratization of Japan was discussed in chapter 6.) Post-war determination has moved away from military ambitions to try to ensure that Japan is not second best as an industrial nation.

The important point of this cursory look at Japanese history is that foreign culture has been an important influence. The people have demonstrated a willingness to import ideas and Japanize them but equally this has often been followed by a reaction phase. Whilst the young are now heavily influenced by the US the traditionalists abhor its cultural incursion. What unites the country is a determination to succeed economically and not to be outdone by the US. To some extent consistency and stability are maintained by the imperial line, not least because the emperor changes less often than Japanese prime ministers. In Japan it has been rare for religious authority (including the Emperor's role as head of Shinto), political and military power, and economic power to be concentrated. Concentrations of such powers is considered to generate instability. Other characteristics that may be drawn out from this historical discussion are those of hierarchy and reciprocity and a willingness by the state to use culture and religion to promote its own political objectives. For example, emphasis on Confucian values of strong family ties, hard work and respect for education – prevalent in Sino-culture countries such as China, Korea, Hong Kong, Singapore, Taiwan and Japan – all assist the process of ensuring economic success for its industry. When these cultural characteristics do not fit an argument they may be modified or found not to be applicable to the particular situation. For example, Buruma (1987 p. 23) quotes the response of Akio Morita of the Sony Corporation when it was suggested that reciprocity in trade should be applied to the Japanese: this 'would mean changing laws to accept foreign systems that may not suit our culture'.

Accounting and culture

Gray (1988, p. 8) has attempted to identify accounting value dimensions based on a review of the accounting literature and practice. Four main value dimensions are identified:

1 *Professionalism versus statutory control* Professionalism emphasizes the exercise of individual professional judgement based on a self-regulated profession whereas statutory control involves compliance with statutory accounting and legal requirements.
2 *Uniformity versus flexibility* Uniformity involves the enforcement of uniform accounting practices on a consistent basis as opposed to flexibility based on the needs of individual entities.
3 *Conservatism versus optimism* Conservatism emphasizes a cautious measurement approach in dealing with uncertain future events whereas optimism is characterized by *laissez-faire* and risk-taking.

4 *Secrecy versus transparency* Secrecy demonstrates a preference for confidentiality and restricting disclosure of information about the business to those closely involved with management and financing operations whereas transparency naturally provides a more open and publicly accountable approach.

Each of these value dimensions will be discussed further to discover the extent to which they are relevant to the development of the Japanese accounting system. For further details on the accounting regulatory environment see chapter 6.

Professionalism versus statutory control

A strong independent accounting profession is a characteristic of both the UK and US whereas in Japan the profession is small and is effectively controlled by the government. Gray (1988, p. 9) argues that 'a preference for independent professional judgement is consistent with a preference for a loosely knit social framework where there is more emphasis on independence, a belief in individual decisions and respect for individual endeavour'. Early on in this chapter we highlighted the importance of the 'inside' group (*uchi*) and in particular that children are probably introduced to the concept when joining a kindergarten. From that early stage collectivism becomes more important than individualism and continues throughout school and university education and characterizes human resource management in Japanese firms. Yet throughout the period of compulsory education the individual is subject to an extremely competitive examination-orientated environment followed later by substantial competition to obtain a position with a large firm.

These seemingly contradictory features are replete throughout society but the Japanese choose not to see them. For example, it is perfectly acceptable and not considered contradictory for an individual to choose a Christian or Shinto wedding and Buddhist burial. The ethics of the Japanese stem, in the main, from Confucianism and popular religious customs are derived mostly from traditional Shinto and Buddhism (Reischauer, 1988, p. 215). Such diversity contrasts with Western monotheism. Such internal contradictions have led many authors, including accounting authors (see for example Takatera and Yamamoto, 1987), to offer a dynamic explanation to the coexistence of both individual responsibility and collective responsibility and co-operation and competition. However, in reality an aspect of culture is chosen to fulfil the requirements of a particular occasion, for in Japan nothing is quite as it seems. The Japanese accounting profession, like the legal profession, is kept small by the state since to have droves of highly qualified mobile professionals is against the principle of company loyalty and a threat to stability. As highlighted in chapter 6 it is the state that controls the development of accounting in Japan – a characteristic which is not likely to change in the near future.

Uniformity versus flexibility

Consistent with state control of accounting in Japan is the requirement to be uniform rather than flexible. For example, the Commercial Code and the Securities and Exchange Law stipulate the format for financial statements, the schedules that should accompany such statements and the content of the business report. Flexibility does exist, however, since measurement requirements often offer alternatives which allow companies to exercise judgement and indeed to indulge in creative accounting from time to time. Gray (1988, p. 9) postulates that a preference for uniformity is consistent with concern for law and order, and rigid codes of behaviour with 'a need for written rules and regulations, a respect for conformity and the search for ultimate, absolute truths and values. This value dimension is also consistent with a preference for collectivism, as opposed to individualism, with its tightly knit social framework, a belief in organization and order, and respect for group norms.'

Conservatism versus optimism

Since the Commercial Code 1899 was largely influenced by Germany, which in turn was influenced by France, it is not surprising that Japanese accounting is strongly conservative. Consequently, assets may not be revalued upwards and legal earned reserves must be provided.

Secrecy versus transparency

'Secrecy would also seem to be closely related to conservatism in that both values imply a cautious approach to corporate financial reporting in general; but with secrecy relating to the disclosure dimension and conservatism relating to the measurement dimension' (Gray, 1988, p. 11). Our empirical work (see in particular chapter 12) suggests that Japanese accounting is conservative with respect to measurement and secretive with respect to disclosure. Despite having the world's largest stock market in terms of turnover and market capitalization (as at 31 December 1989) we found that levels of disclosure were noticeably lower than many European nations and the US. The Commercial Code accounts, which are sent to shareholders, are in most instances a poor excuse for an annual report since they constitute little more than a pamphlet with minimum levels of disclosure. Furthermore, we found no significant difference in the extent of disclosure between unlisted and listed companies. More extensive disclosure is provided in the Securities and Exchange Law (SEL) accounts but these are not distributed to shareholders and are produced by listed companies only and filed with the Ministry of Finance. However, these accounts may be scrutinized at the company's head office and copies may be ordered through many bookshops. Our research found that the extent of disclosure in the SEL accounts differed significantly between those with a domestic listing only and those with at least one overseas quotation.

In summary, disclosure by all companies is characterized by secrecy, uniformity and compliance. Such features, particularly secrecy, may appear somewhat inconsistent with the fact that Tokyo is one of the world's largest stock exchanges. However, other characteristics such as interlocking shareholders and directorships and the fact that dividend payments to shareholders are very low must not be ignored (see chapter 5 for further details). Furthermore, it must be remembered that culture is invariably used as an excuse for bureaucratic control in this one-party state.

Political factors

Political background

Superficially, Japan's political system seems similar in many ways to those that prevail in the West. Indeed, the administration of the Meiji period sought to develop a government machine based more on merit than on ancestry. The foundation of this new parliamentary system was a bicameral structure influenced by Britain, France and Germany. The system was thoroughly revised in 1946 with the promulgation of the Constitution of Japan, effective from 3 May 1947. In order to maintain political stability in Japan the allied forces considered that the retention of the emperor was important. However, the emperor's role was restricted to a diplomatic and ceremonial one – a symbolic head of state like the Queen of England.

The national government is headed by the prime minister, who leads the majority party in the Diet. Administrative power is vested in the cabinet, consisting of 19 ministers appointed by the prime minister. The 12 main ministries are: Justice, Home Affairs, Foreign Affairs, Finance, Education, Health and Welfare, Agriculture Forestry and Fisheries, International Trade and Industry, Transport, Posts and Telecommunications, Labour, and Construction. The cabinet is responsible to the National Diet (elected parliament), which consists of 512 members from 130 districts who are elected for a period of four years. The House of Representatives can vote for no confidence in the cabinet if it chooses and this House has power over the House of Councillors, the second elected body of parliament. The House of Councillors consists of 252 members appointed from the prefectures (152) and from a national constituency (100). Members are elected every six years – half the members every three years.

There are five main political parties in the Diet: the Liberal Democratic Party (LDP) – similar in many respects to Britain's Conservatives and America's Republicans (the LDP has governed Japan continuously since 1955); the Japanese Socialists, the main opposition party; the Komeito; the Japanese Communists; and the Democratic Socialists.

The judicial power of the country is based on a court system headed by the Supreme Court. The cabinet appoints judges with the exception of the chief justice, whose appointment is conferred by the emperor. As well as general responsibility for the laws the courts can rule on constitutional matters.

In essence then, the character of the political system in Japan is familiar to Westerners; however, it has been moulded to fit Japanese culture. For example, like the hierarchical structure of employees in Japanese firms, a young politician will seek a relationship with an established politician in which the former offers loyalty and the latter offers opportunities for advancement. The young politician is introduced to new circles whose members, in the long run, may become supporters. Despite the modernization of the Japanese political system in the Meiji period, ancestry is still an important factor in developing support. A political candidate chosen mainly on the grounds of education and merit may well be at a severe disadvantage. However, this may be compensated by the distribution of wealth, possession of which may well be based on ancestry. An aspiring politician will need to distribute funds to local charities and organizations and be seen to do so. The objective of this is in fact to buy loyalty.[2] Reciprocal relations prevail throughout Japanese life.

Since 1955 Japan has been a one-party state dominated by the LDP. Its support stems from industrialists, professionals and those involved in agriculture. Like Japan, the LDP has been dominated by men. Perhaps a feature of the Japanese political system is that the 'institutions are quite recognizable, but the behaviour within them is not so clear. Indeed, some integral parts of the Japanese version of the system are quite corrupt by the standards of the societies from which the framework was adopted' (Hendry, 1987, p. 183). Such an assertion could not have been more prophetic: as the *Financial Times* reported (13 July 1988), if

> there is a political party in the democratic world eminently capable of riding out a scandal then it is the Liberal Democratic Party in Japan. After all, it has known enough of them in the last three decades, including the conviction on bribery charges of a former Prime Minister, Mr Kakuei Tanaka, and it is still firmly in power. Equally, if there is a political opposition in a major industrialized country so patently unwilling or unable to assume the reins of government, then it, too, is to be found in Japan.

On 24 July 1989 the *Financial Times* had to report a rather different story: 'Japan's ruling Liberal Democratic Party has worked hard during the past two years at repeatedly disgracing itself in the eyes of the public: its efforts were rewarded yesterday with a defeat in national elections. The LDP has lost its majority in the upper house of Diet (parliament) for the first time since it was formed in 1955.'

What is clear from the 1989 election was that the public had grown tired of the level of corruption and deceit as well as being very hostile to the introduction of the 3 per cent consumption tax in 1988. Unusually, Japanese women played an important part in providing victory to Miss Takako Doi, leader of Japan's Socialist party. However, concern has been expressed about the implications for political stability. For example, the *DKB Economic Report* (September 1989) states that 'political instability may undermine competency in economic policy management. The combination of rapid changes in administration, frequent replacement of ministers, the shift in the power balance in the House of Councillors toward the opposition and concerns over the outcome of elections for the House of Representatives (which must be held no later than July 1990) is likely to result in diminished initiative in creating and implementing policy measures.'

Despite the scandals the LDP was returned to power, admittedly with a reduced majority, in the general election held on 18 February 1990. This was not surprising, however, since workers in the major corporations were called upon to demonstrate their loyalty to the firm by voting LDP. Workers with lifetime employment are likely to heed such advice, particularly if there is a perceived threat to their jobs. Indeed, such was the collusion between the major corporations and the LDP party that the former were promising how many votes they could actually deliver.

Despite the current political instability in Japan the strong bureaucratic system offers administrative stability. The three most important ministries as far as accounting, finance and economics are concerned are the Ministry of Finance, the Ministry of Justice and the Ministry of International Trade and Industry (MITI). The role of the first two has been dealt with in chapter 6; that of MITI will be discussed here.

The Ministry of International Trade and Industry

'Some observers think that the Ministry of International Trade and Industry (MITI) controls every aspect of the Japanese economy, as if it were chief executive officer of "Japan, Inc". To others, Japan's industrial policy is a mysterious black box, about which few details are known and only fruitless guesses can be made' (Wakiyama, 1986, p. 467). The mysteries of the Japanese bureaucratic system revolve, in particular, around the nature of administrative guidance. Wakiyama (pp. 469–70) lists the main elements of Japan's industrial policy:

1 to achieve an appropriate industrial structure;
2 to assure a stable and economical supply of natural resources and energy;
3 to promote research and development;
4 to develop small/medium-sized firms;

5 to promote trade and other international transactions;
6 to encourage appropriate industrial location.

Further, Wakiyama (p. 467) states that the major tools to achieve its objectives are:

1 administrative guidance;
2 tax incentives;
3 fiscal investments/loans;
4 subsidy;
5 legal power;
6 direct execution by MITI or its affiliates.

Tools (2), (3) and (4) have been dealt with in chapter 4 and the implications for accounting highlighted. This section highlights the role of administrative guidance in government. To achieve its objectives administrative guidance requires effectiveness of control. Like the City Code on Takeovers in the UK, effectiveness depends on consensus since there are no legal powers to enforce administrative guidance. Also like the City Code, the lack of legal enforcement powers can be an advantage when consensus exists since flexibility and consequently timeliness can be more readily achieved.

Wakiyama (1986, pp. 472–6) classifies administrative guidance into the following seven major types:

1 Administrative guidance accomplished in close connection with other more powerful policy tools: if MITI has some direct or indirect legal control over an industry it is possible to exercise leverage with administrative guidance.
2 Administrative guidance coupled with other powerful tools as a last resort: successful lobbying by the US and European governments led to MITI giving guidance to vehicle manufacturers to restrict exports. MITI made it clear that if its guidance was ignored legal powers would be sought to ensure conformity. Such an approach is sometimes used in Sweden.
3 Administrative guidance supported by tools only partly related to it: for example, if a manufacturer was advised to reduce capacity and refused it might have an import quota placed on the import of essential raw materials.
4 Administrative guidance without leverage: this is the hardest to implement in practice and only MITI's influence may ensure co-operation.
5 Identical interests versus divided interests: MITI can exercise control where the administrative guidance affects all manufacturers within an industry. This is easily implemented where a consensus exists between the major manufacturers but is difficult when interests are divided. If no consensus exists within an industry an individual firm must weigh up the costs and benefits of the guidance, bearing in mind the long-term relationship between the two organizations.

6 Emergency needs versus long-term needs: when there is a particular emergency, administrative guidance may be the only way of dealing with an issue – for example, the oil crisis of 1973. However, if administrative guidance is for long-term needs only, it may be difficult to implement such a policy. Considerable pressure may have to be exercised to be effective.

7 The number of companies affected: administrative guidance normally involves face-to-face persuasion between companies and MITI. Consequently, the effectiveness of its guidance depends upon the degree of concentration within an industry.

In summary, MITI seeks to ensure that Japanese industrial policy is conducted in an orderly manner. Like the Ministry of Finance, administrative guidance assists the process of achieving a mutually agreed long-term strategy, posited by Nagourney (1988a, p. 3) as 'independence of action within the American sphere of global hegemony and where "business is the fountainhead of values"'. Such administrative guidance has been found to be particularly successful in a country where the bureaucracy and the LDP are extraordinarily close. Relationships in Japan are typically reciprocal so that whilst the bureaucracy serves the ruling party well, by exercising a dominant position in the formulation of policy and legislation, the LDP provides the bureaucracy with increased jurisdictional power and generous budgets (Fukui, 1981, pp. 286–8). As McKinnon (1986, p. 98) points out, to understand the regulatory environment in Japan requires an understanding of the relationship between parliament and the bureaucracy.

The labour union movement

Another factor of importance which can have an influence, through the political system, on financial reporting in a country is the labour union movement. Whereas a labour union confederation may be active and effective in lobbying appropriate bodies in the regulatory framework, a combination of the bureaucracy and business has neutralized and accommodated the movement in Japan. The explanation for this lies in the historical development of the trade union movement.

With the development of corporations, in the latter part of the nineteenth century, came an interest in labour unionization, based mainly on European socialist ideas. Recognizing this development as a threat, in 1900 the government introduced the Maintenance of Public Peace Law, which made it illegal for workers to organize themselves. Whilst making it very difficult for organized labour disputes to occur, the Law did not effectively prevent all unrest. Later, during the 1920s and 1930s, companies tried to foster an atmosphere of working for the family corporation. Such a development was encouraged by the Home Ministry, Naimusho, since it enhanced social control by spreading the idea of the company as the family and Japan as a family state. Promotion of this idea was undertaken through 'councils' which consisted of both workers and management. Havens (1978) estimates that by the end of 1940 there were 60,495 'councils' or 'patriotic industrial associations' encompassing in excess of two-thirds of the labour force. The scheme was promoted not only by the Home Ministry and corporations but also by the police. Such a scheme had two main effects. First, an alternative organization had been set up which had the effect of channelling workers away from the idea of labour unions towards the councils. Second, the councils could be used to 'spread enthusiasm for the war effort' (van Wolferen, 1989, p. 66). Van Wolferen (p. 66) argues that the patriotic industrial association 'deserves to be considered one of the milestones of Japanese economic history. The generally accepted culturalist explanation of worker attitudes holds that enterprise unions are a result of a "cultural" Japanese inclination to identify with the interests of one's superior. This interpretation overlooks the fact that Japan's post-war labour unions were formed (and have continued up to the present) as enterprise rather than trade unions largely because [of] their wartime associations.' Such wartime associations 'simply shed their old skins and continued their existence after the war ended' (Nakamura, 1981, p. 18). Among other things, the councils encouraged a sense of loyalty to the corporation and a perception that it is inappropriate to move jobs in mid-career. Consequently, any subsequent developments in the labour movement are likely to be enterprise-based rather than trade-based.

As part of the post-war democratization policy, the allied forces made it legal for workers to organize. Figure 9.3 outlines the history of post-war labour organization. Within a year of the ending of the Second World War three major unions had formed: Sodomei (a pre-war moderate federation) was revived; Sanbetsu-Kaigi was essentially an organization of communists; and Nichiro-Kaigi, an organization that was disbanded in 1950. Industrial action by the unions between 1946 and 1950 was similar to levels in the US and Europe. Concern about the unrest and particularly the activities of the communist trade union, Sanbetsu-Kaigi, led the US to reappraise Japan's strategic position as a capitalist buffer to the USSR. The reappraisal gave permission to the bureaucracy to purge the unions in 1949 and 1950 by removing senior officials. To support the purge, Nikkeiren, the Japanese federation of employers' association, was formed. The role of Nikkeiren is twofold: to control the labour movement and to try to ensure that wage rises do not exceed productivity rises. Nikkeiren 'was formed by business bureaucrats formerly in the forefront of wartime industrial organizations, for the specific purpose of combating the labour movement. A preferred tactic of companies with troublesome unions was to establish a moderate rival union. Within a short time this alternative union would generally attract many more

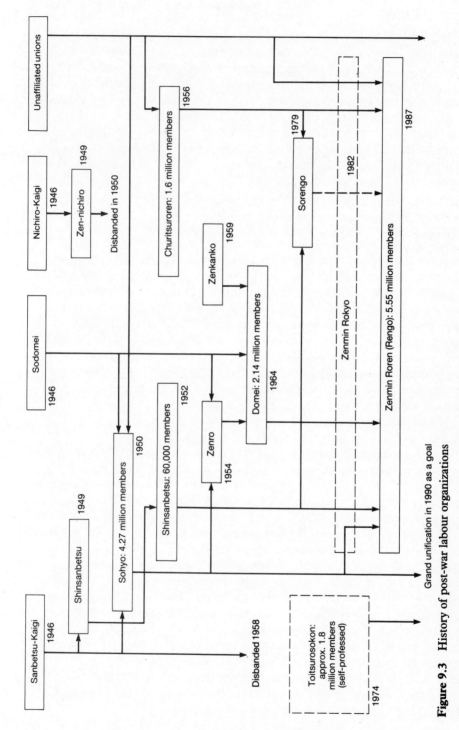

Figure 9.3 History of post-war labour organizations

Note: Number of unionists is based on a January 1986 survey by the Ministry of Labour.

Source: Nikkei Shimbun (Japan Economic Journal), 21 November 1987

members than the activist union, since employees soon realized that not to co-operate would block promotion prospects' (van Wolferen, 1989, p. 68). As part of the attempts to control the unions, the National Public Service Law was amended to prevent public service employees from bargaining collectively and to take away the right to strike.

An interesting feature of figure 9.3 is that on 20 November 1987 Rengo, the Japanese Private Sector Trade Union Confederation, was formed to unify the activities of 62 labour organizations with a total membership of 5.55 million. Such a unified organization, in terms of manpower and financial resources, may produce a more effective lobbying force in the future. To date the unions have been relatively ineffective and have lacked 'the counter power to question management's overly conservative accounting policies, not least in relation to their implications for wage restraint' (Takatera and Daigo, 1989, p. 196).

Economic factors

Of all the environmental factors that influence accounting system development, a strong case can be made that the economic characteristics are the most influential. Economic development affects many sociocultural attitudes and brings about changes in legal, political and educational objectives and sophistication each of which in turn can affect accounting practice. Yet even the pervasive economic influences in isolation do not determine the development and practices of a country's accounting system. One need not only examine the accounting systems and practices of the three dominant market economies of the world – the United States, Germany and Japan – to see that there are considerable differences in accounting among them despite great similarities in their economic sophistication and stature. Thus, there is a need to consider all the environmental factors in analysing a country's accounting system. (Arpan and Radebaugh, 1985, p. 23)

Many of the factors already discussed in this chapter are important in explaining the phenomenal success of the Japanese economy since the Second World War. The Japanese character based on Chinese Confucianism has been described as filial piety, family solidarity and loyalty to the ruler as well as authority in general. Such characteristics coupled with a mutual understanding between industry and central government – based on a strong bureaucracy – have made Japan the second largest economy in the world. However, the phenomenal growth rate in gross national product during the 1960s has slowed down, particularly since the oil crisis of 1973 (see table 9.1). The average growth rate of 7.5 per cent between 1970 and 1973 was

Table 9.1   Average annual real GNP growth rates by country, 1960–1985[a]

Country	1960–9 (%)	1970–3 (%)	1974–85 (%)
Japan	12.1	7.5	3.8
United States	4.1	3.2	2.2
West Germany	5.7	4.2	1.8
France[b]	5.8	5.6	2.1
Great Britain[b]	3.1	3.7	1.3

[a] Based on 1980 prices.
[b] Data are for GDP.
Source: International Monetary Fund, *International Financial Statistics Yearbook*

noticeably smaller than the rate during the 1960s. Despite this, Japan's growth rate in the early 1970s was still noticeably better than its major trading competitors.

Ohkawa and Rosovsky (1973) have argued that post-war Japan lagged far behind Western technology. The country absorbed foreign technology at an extraordinary rate, demonstrating its dynamic ability to assimilate and improve on foreign products. In order to grow rapidly there had to be a pool of available labour, which was forthcoming from the agricultural sector. Success at importing and improving upon technology gave Japanese industry the incentive to invest heavily. Investors preferred to have their money in industry rather than agriculture because it gave a better return. With capital stock growing so quickly economies of scale were readily achieved. Domestic investment was financed by domestic savings rather than by foreign borrowings. The propensity of the Japanese to save has been discussed in chapter 5.

Lincoln (1988, pp. 18–21) lists a number of contributing factors to high economic growth:

1 better post-war education;
2 political stability;
3 supportive government, using tight fiscal and expansionary monetary policies with public works being industrially orientated rather than the provision of social amenities;
4 government imposition of high import barriers;
5 a favourable world environment characterized by changing world trade patterns as a result of the end of colonization;
6 only moderate union activity;
7 reforms implemented by the allied forces, specifically land reforms, the legalization of labour unions and the dissolution of the *zaibatsu*.

In addition to these factors,

> strict control of imports and capital flow was also strongly influenced by economic xenophobia. Since it began to develop as a modern economy in the late nineteenth century, Japan has striven for an economy owned, operated, and supplied by Japanese firms. Policies to that effect proliferated in the 1930s, and post-war policies continued and strengthened the tendency. Xenophobia was given additional impetus in the 1950s by the fear that in the absence of strict controls war-weakened Japanese companies would be quickly overrun by foreign competition. (Lincoln, 1988, pp. 74–5)

The phenomenal growth of the 1960s was ended not only by the oil crisis of 1973 but also by the revaluation of the yen at the end of August 1971. Furthermore, in 1973 the US began its continuing campaign of trade restrictions on Japan with a complete embargo on the export of soybeans. Whilst the embargo was short-lived concern over US–Japanese trade has not been. These factors contributed towards the recession of 1974. Demonstrating its remarkable ability to adapt to new circumstances, Japan has not suffered any further recessions, despite substantial increases in the value of the yen.

Such economic success has generated great confidence in the private sector. 'Despite slower growth, lower profits, and greater uncertainty about the future, corporations in the export sector became increasingly certain of their international competitiveness. Put less politely, many corporate executives became arrogant and contemptuous of foreign competitors. To a certain extent this attitude was reflected by the public, who, for instance, expressed doubt that the United States had anything to export that they would want to buy' (Lincoln, 1988, pp. 40–1). The Japanese would counter such arguments with the view that US executives emphasize short-term goals and effects on share prices rather than long-term investment that tries to secure future growth.

Japan obviously wishes to maintain its economic pre-eminence but the country is sensitive to international criticism. Criticism of Japan's huge trade surplus with the US led to three important developments in the mid-1980s (Tarullo, 1986, p. 343):

1 in 1985 the Group of Five took action to allow the dollar to fall against the yen and other major currencies;
2 the then Prime Minister of Japan, Nakasone, suggested that there might be internal demand stimuli to encourage imports;
3 in May 1986 the Group of Five decided to consult regularly about one another's macroeconomic policies.

Despite such initiatives the Japanese economy maintains a firm expansionary note, with growing domestic demand, and US concern about the trade imbalance has not abated. Indeed, in August 1988 the US Congress approved a new omnibus trade bill intended to strengthen US trade and competitiveness. The US strongly encourages its trading partners to operate under the principle of reciprocity – a concept with which the Japanese are familiar in its domestic interrelationships but consider to be culturally inappropriate for application at the international level. However, the differential between US and Japanese interest rates led to a devaluation of the yen in 1989 thereby making Japan's exports even more competitive and begetting an even greater trade surplus. On 28 April 1989 the US Trade Representative released the Foreign Barrier Report for 1989. The report stated that there were still trade barriers in the high-technology areas such as semiconductors as well as in the service-related sector including information, finance, communication and distribution.

The Japanese distribution system has sometimes been cited, with some justification, as a non-tariff barrier. To defend itself against accusations of bias against foreign goods in its home market Japan used the overworked concept of culture. In a report in 1989 the Japanese Chamber of Commerce and Industry stated that 'the distribution system is a social system with its roots buried deep in history and culture'. There is no doubt that Japan's distribution system is more cumbersome than that prevailing in the UK and US. It is based on small shops – more than 1.6 million – which represent a considerable political lobby since their owners and families account for some 20 million votes, with a heavy bias toward support for the LDP. Protection for small shopkeepers exists in the form of the Large-scale Retail Store Law, which controls the opening of new stores and gives existing shopkeepers the right to delay, sometimes for a period of up to ten years, the opening of new stores. Table 9.2 provides a comparison of retail and wholesale business in Japan, the UK and US.

The main aspect of the retail and wholesale business in Japan which appears to discriminate against foreign goods is that the country's manufac-

Table 9.2   Comparison of retail and wholesale business

	Japan	*US*	*UK*
Number of retail stores	1.62 m	1.5 m	343,000
Number of wholesalers	437,000	376,000	95,000
Retailers per 10,000 people	132	65	61
Wholesalers per 10,000 people	36	16	17
Retailers per wholesaler	3.7	4.0	3.6

Data for Japan 1988, UK and US 1982.
Source: Japan Chamber of Commerce and Industry

turers can exercise considerable control over the retailers. It is perhaps ironic that in the 1988 report from the chairman and president of Matsushita Electric one of the sources of trade friction – the Japanese distribution system – is highlighted some five paragraphs before the comment on friction:

> Matsushita Electric has Japan's largest consumer electronics and appliance sales network. Approximately 25,000 stores carry Matsushita products *exclusively*. Our high domestic sales growth amid increased domestic competition is due to the network's strength. (p. 2, emphasis added)

> the strong yen, trade friction, and our growing corporate commitment to society are making Matsushita's position in overseas markets ever more complex and sensitive. We therefore believe it essential that we think and act as legal corporate citizens in each operating area so that our presence will truly be welcomed. (p. 3)

To make matters worse it appears that Japan's goods in its home market are more expensive than its exports, giving ammunition to accusations of dumping. 'The pricing behaviour has resulted in a large divergence between domestic and export prices (in terms of domestic currency) since 1985 in Japan, unlike the experience of major EMS countries, but similar to that of the United Kingdom' (OECD, 1988/89, p. 93).

Major Japanese corporations have been concerned, particularly during the latter half of the 1980s, about trade friction but also the effects of exports on the rising yen. For example, in its 1987 annual report, Minolta notes the problem of the rising yen and its strategic approach to dealing with it:

> During the year, the yen set new records, appreciating some 18% against the US dollar. With 77% of our sales overseas and a large portion of our sales revenues linked to the dollar, this appreciation put severe downward pressure on profits as calculated in yen. The continued upward trend in the value of the yen has resulted in some benefits accruing from lower prices of components, raw materials, and electric power.

> Minolta has continued to take action in dealing with this new reality of the international market and to compensate for it wherever possible, including increasing overseas production. The company now has production facilities in Malaysia and in the Federal Republic of Germany, and plans to build a production facility in the United States are currently under consideration. (p. 3)

Hitachi also emphasizes the problem of the yen and trade friction and its responsibility to the global community:

> we cannot afford to be complacent: the business environment is fraught with difficult problems including the trade tensions between Japan and the countries of North America and Europe, the strong yen, and the huge national debts of the US and some developing countries. Thus, in working toward future corporate progress, we will be making every effort to fulfil our responsibilities as a global enterprise through farsighted policies that promote our contribution to the communities where we operate and help to achieve deeper international understanding. (1985 annual report, p. 5)

Despite international pressure and resulting trade friction coupled with recent political instability, the Japanese economy remains strong, based on a high level of capital investment and high personal expenditure.

Summary

Local environmental factors are broad but can be important influences over the development of accounting objectives, standards and practices in Japan. This chapter has considered environmental factors, which have been classified into educational, sociocultural, legal and political, and economic.

Placing great value on education is a Confucian value common to Sino-culture countries such as Japan, Hong Kong, Korea, Singapore and Taiwan. The present system of education in Japan was introduced after the Second World War and is egalitarian and co-educational, with a national curriculum set by the Ministry of Education. The Ministry states what will be taught, when it will be taught and which textbooks will be used.

There is considerable pressure on schoolchildren through the examination system to do well since successfully securing a place at a 'good' university often determines the standard of living obtained throughout life. It is this pressure that leads to a breakdown of the concept of equality of opportunity since Japan abounds with private tutoring systems. The financial burden of supplementary education is one factor contributing to Japan's high propensity to save and inevitably the expense means that a wealthy elite may be separated off at a very early age.

Education in accounting can be commenced in school followed by attendance at vocational high schools. However, the better students normally study accounting at universities, where considerable emphasis is given to theory and little concern paid to practice. Perhaps this is not surprising since most accounting academics have been through the same system themselves, including graduate school. In general, those wishing to become professionally qualified accountants – both CPA and certified tax accountants – enter schools which specialize in tutoring for accounting examinations.

Legal influences over financial reporting in Japan are very important since the Commercial Code is administered by the Ministry of Justice and the Securities and Exchange Law is administered by the Ministry of Finance. In practice, the Business Accounting Deliberation Council, an advisory board to the Ministry of Finance, has been far more important than the JICPA. In effect the government has control over the examination system, including the standard of attainment required to qualify, as well as professional fees. Independence is not considered to be culturally acceptable, which is consistent with the widespread emphasis on and use of the cultural explanation although in reality it is an excuse for power and dominance.

In an attempt to link culture with accounting we used the framework proposed by Gray (1988) to analyse the development of the Japanese accounting system. In summary, we argued that in Japan statutory control was more important than professionalism; that disclosure was uniform rather than flexible but that measurement requirements offered flexibility; and that, based on our empirical work, conservatism was very evident.

Superficially, Japan's political system seems similar in many ways to those that prevail in the West. A parliamentary democracy with a bicameral structure seems similar to the UK. However, there are differences between Japan and many other Western nations. The hierarchical structure is important – a young politician will seek a relationship with an established politician in which the former offers loyalty and the latter offers opportunity for advancement. Wealth, often based on ancestry, is usually more important than merit and a good education, a fact which may appear to be a contradiction since respect for education is a Confucian value. Wealth is available to distribute to charities and organizations and an aspiring politician must be seen to do this (in reality it is a way of buying loyalty: a reciprocal relationship develops).

Since 1955 Japan has been a one-party state dominated by the Liberal Democratic Party, whose support emanates from industrialists, professionals and those involved in agriculture. Such is its domination that it is able to shrug off one political scandal after another, even involving prime ministers, who are regularly replaced. The 1989 backlash against the level of corruption and deceit led to defeat for the party in elections for the House of Councillors. Such political instability was short-lived, however, as the LDP won the 1990 general election.

The three most important ministries as far as accounting, finance and economics are concerned are the Ministries of Finance and Justice (covered in chapter 6) and the Ministry of International Trade and Industry. MITI exercises some control over industry by administrative guidance, which requires consensus to be effective since there are no legal powers of enforcement. Such guidance is given to ensure that industrial policy is conducted in an orderly manner in a society in which 'business is the fountainhead of values'.

Labour unions can have important consequences for financial reporting but not in Japan. This is because the labour union movement has been neutralized by a combination of the bureaucracy and business.

Post-war Japan showed great ability to absorb foreign technology and improve on foreign products. Labour was forthcoming from the agricultural sector and investors preferred the higher potential for rewards from the industrial sector. Based on an effective educational system, political stability and government support, not least in controlling imports and capital flows, Japan enjoyed phenomenal growth in the 1960s. The subsequent growth rate has been lower but has consistently exceeded that of its major competitors.

Note

1 The original German Commercial Code was issued in 1861 and substantially revised in 1867 and 1897.
2 The influence of money has been adequately summarized by Alletzhauser (1990, p. 147): 'So powerful was the Tuesday Club and its affiliates that between 1946 and 1972 they controlled the office of the prime minister in eighteen of twenty-six years ... Japan was not like Western democracies where popular vote decided leadership. Control was wielded by the amount of money raised to pay off debtors and not until 1972 did someone outside the Tuesday Club have deeper pockets. This was Kakuei Tanaka who made world headlines in 1976 in the Lockheed bribery scandal.'

PART II

Accounting Principles and Practices

10
Disclosure Principles

The Commercial Code and the Securities and Exchange Law

All *Kabushiki-Kaisha* (similar to the public limited company in the UK and the joint-stock company in the US) must prepare financial statements in accordance with the Commercial Code. The accounts, prepared at the end of each fiscal year, should include a balance sheet, a profit and loss account, a business report, a proposal for appropriation of retained earnings, and supporting schedules. Both the form and content of the accounts are prescribed by the Ministry of Justice, whose responsibility it is to administer financial reporting under the Commercial Code. The requirements are specified in the Regulations Concerning the Balance Sheet, Income Statement, Business Report and Supporting Schedules of Kabushiki-Kaisha, which were first issued in 1963 and are periodically updated by the Ministry of Justice.

The underlying objective of financial statements prepared in accordance with Commercial Code requirements is to protect creditors and current investors. Thus, emphasis is placed on disclosures which provide information on the valuation of assets for solvency purposes, availability of earnings for dividend distributions, and on creditworthiness and earning power. The accounts are prepared for a single year only and on an individual company basis, the traditional form of presentation in Japan. Emphasis is placed on compliance with the law and the articles of association. Whilst the accounts of all companies are audited by statutory auditors, only the largest corporations are required to have an audit by an independent qualified auditor.

As well as preparing accounts in accordance with the Commercial Code, all listed companies and companies that publicly offer shares or bonds amounting to ¥500 million or more must submit, to the Ministry of Finance, financial statements prepared in accordance with the Securities and Exchange

Law (SEL). The form and content of these statements are prescribed by the Ministry of Finance Ordinance, and in accordance with the SEL an annual securities report must be filed. This report includes the articles of association, financial statements prepared in accordance with the Securities and Exchange Law and consolidated financial statements for the most recent fiscal years.

The main objective of reporting under the Securities and Exchange Law is adequate and appropriate disclosure on the results and financial position of the company for the protection of general investors. The accounts are presented in more detail than is required under the financial regulations of the Commercial Code. Whilst the general content of the two sets of accounts is similar, the 'terminology, form and content of these financial statements and supporting schedules are more precisely defined in the SEL financial regulations. This will require, in most instances, additional detail of certain items or, in certain instances, the reclassifying of items as presented in the Commercial Code financial statements in order to comply with the SEL financial regulation requirements. However, the reported net income and shareholders' equity would not change as the result of the reclassifications' (JICPA, 1984, p. 39).

When comparing disclosure under the Commercial Code with disclosure under the SEL the JICPA (1984) distinguishes between 'current investors' and 'general investors'. 'General investors' refers to future potential investors whereas 'current investors' are those who already invest in a listed or unlisted company.

The rest of this chapter is devoted to the key elements of the financial statements and how disclosure differs between the Commercial Code and the Securities and Exchange Law.

The balance sheet

The Commercial Code

According to the Ministerial Ordinance, the Regulation Concerning Accounts, a balance sheet should have three sections – assets, liabilities and shareholders' equity – with each section being totalled. The assets section should be subdivided into current assets, fixed assets and deferred charges. The word 'current' is used to mean a normal operating cycle of the business or, exceptionally, a one-year period. Whilst it is not prescribed in the regulations it is common practice to present current assets in their descending order of liquidity.

The fixed assets heading has three subsections: tangible fixed assets, intangible fixed assets and 'investments, etc.'. Tangible fixed assets consist of land, buildings, machinery, equipment and fixtures and fittings, and intangibles include legal rights and goodwill. The investments, etc. subheading consists of investment in subsidiaries and associates, trade investments and many other receivables not to be collected within the next twelve months. Consequently, monetary assets and accrued expenses over one year are also required to be shown in investments, etc. Outstanding Treasury stock should be disclosed as a current asset at cost. Whilst the assets section is familiar, based largely on US practice, it includes a subheading which covers deferred charges, consisting of pre-operating costs, research and development expenditure and bond issuing costs.

Liabilities are categorized as either current or long-term. Current liabilities, like current assets, are normally presented in descending order of liquidity although there is no requirement to do so. Long-term liabilities are those that are not current. Allowances may be stated individually in the liabilities section in accordance with section 287-2 of the Commercial Code and section 33-1 of the Regulation Concerning Accounts.

Shareholders' equity has three main subheadings: share capital, legal reserves and retained earnings. Capital reserves and legal earned reserves should be shown separately under legal reserves.

Valuation accounts, such as allowances for doubtful accounts and accumulated depreciation, should be separately stated below the related accounts or alternatively be netted against the related accounts. When the accounts are netted, the amounts involved should be disclosed in the notes.

The Commercial Code requires companies to disclose the following items in the notes to the financial statements, although small companies are required to disclose only item (14):

1 significant accounting policies for the preparation of the balance sheet or the profit and loss account, such as the valuation method of assets, depreciation method of fixed assets, method used for allowances, etc.;
2 any changes in the above policies and their effects, if material;
3 accounts receivable and payable relating to subsidiaries and any controlling shareholder (shareholder who owns a majority of the issued shares) unless such amounts are stated independently in the financial statements;
4 estimated uncollectable receivables if such amounts are deducted from the related receivables in the balance sheet;
5 if inventories and marketable securities are valued at acquisition cost but market value is significantly less than acquisition cost, such a fact should be disclosed;
6 the accumulated amounts of depreciation if the related assets are shown net in the balance sheet;
7 change of useful life or salvage value of fixed assets, if material;

Table 10.1 Balance sheet format prepared in accordance with the Commercial Code

[Date and unit of account]

ASSETS			LIABILITIES		
I	*Current assets*	XXX	I	*Current liabilities*	XXX
	Cash in hand and at bank	XX		Notes payable	XX
	Notes receivable	XX		Trade accounts payable	XX
	Trade accounts receivable	XX		Short-term borrowings	XX
	Marketable securities	XX		Accounts payable	XX
	Treasury stock	XX		Deferred income	XX
	Finished goods	XX		Accrued expense	XX
	Work-in-progress	XX		Accrued corporation and	
	Raw materials			inhabitants taxes	XX
	and consumables	XX		Accrued enterprise tax	XX
	Advance payments	XX		Allowance for product	
	Prepaid expense	XX		warranty	XX
	Short-term loans	XX		Other current	
	Other current assets	XX		liabilities	XX
	Allowance for doubtful		II	*Long-term liabilities*	XXX
	accounts	(XX)		Bonds payable	XX
II	*Fixed assets*	XXX		Convertible bonds	XX
	1 *Tangible fixed assets*	XXX		Long-term borrowing	XX
	Buildings & structures	XX		Allowance for	
	Machinery & equipment	XX		severance payment	XX
	Vehicles	XX		Allowance for special	
	Tools, fixtures and			repair	XX
	fittings	XX		Others	XX
	Land	XX	III	*Allowances*	XXX
	Construction in			Allowance for exchange	
	progress	XX		losses	XX
	2 *Intangible fixed assets*	XXX		Others	XX
	Land rights	XX			
	Lease tenant rights	XX		Total liabilities	XXXX
	Patents	XX			
	Telephone rights	XX		CAPITAL	
	Goodwill	XX	I	*Share capital*	XX
	3 *Investment, etc.*	XXX	II	*Legal reserve*	
	Long-term cash at bank	XX		Capital reserve	XX
	Investment in			Legal earned reserve	XX
	subsidiaries	XX	III	*Surplus*	
	Investment securities	XX		Reserve for overseas	
	Long-term loans	XX		investment losses	XX
	Loans to affiliates	XX		Reserve for dividend	
	Long-term prepaid			equalization	XX
	expense	XX		Reserve for expansion	
	Other investments	XX		of business	XX
	Allowance for doubtful			Other voluntary reserve	XX
	accounts	(XX)		General reserve	XX
III	*Deferred charges*	XXX		Unappropriated retained	
	Pre-operating costs	XX		earnings	XX
	Research and development			(Current net income)	(XX)
	costs	XX			
	Bond discounts	XX			
	Bond issuing costs	XX			
				TOTAL LIABILITIES	
	TOTAL ASSETS	XXXX		AND CAPITAL	XXXX

8 total amounts of monetary items relating to directors and statutory auditors;

9 assets and liabilities denominated in foreign currency, if material;

10 assets pledged for mortgages;

11 contingent liabilities for guarantees, notes discounted or endorsed, litigation, etc., unless the contingencies are stated in the balance sheet;

12 if allowances are established in accordance with section 287-2 of the Commercial Code and not shown under the heading 'Allowances', the fact that such allowances were set up under the Commercial Code;

13 amount of net income or loss per share;

14 if the total of deferred pre-operating costs and deferred research and development costs exceeds the legal reserve, the excess should be disclosed;

15 any other items necessary to understand the financial position and results of the company.

Accounts disclosed in the balance sheet, profit and loss account and proposal for appropriations of retained earnings may be stated in thousand yen, omitting any fractional sum. For large companies amounts may be rounded to the nearest million yen.

The format for the balance sheet, as required by the Commercial Code, is shown in table 10.1. The general format is based on the current arrangement method, very similar to the presentation of a US balance sheet. Note also that whilst IAS 1 (paragraphs 16 and 21) requires the disclosure of comparative financial statements and the disclosure of the facts and reasons if the going concern assumption has not been followed, there are no equivalent requirements under the Commercial Code. Furthermore, the notes in the financial statements are limited to the above items while IAS 5 (paragraphs 10–16) requires disclosure of additional items such as pensions and retirement plans.

The Securities and Exchange Law (SEL)

The Ministry of Finance Ordinance specifies the form and content of the financial statements, the notes and relating supporting schedules. In order to fulfil the obligation to make adequate and appropriate disclosure necessary for the protection of general investors, the financial statements should be presented in more detail than those required by the Commercial Code. Whilst the basic financial statements are similar, the terminology, form and content should be more precisely defined in the SEL accounts. This might involve additional disclosure as well as the reclassification of certain items. In particular the following requirements are important.

1 Assets and liabilities should be listed in order of liquidity under the SEL. There is no similar requirement in the Commercial Code although in

practice such a presentation is normal.

2 Balances and transactions with related parties should be separately stated. Four out of the 14 supporting schedules under the SEL require information on investments in and balances with related parties.

3 Under the SEL, any balance sheet item which exceeds 1 per cent of total assets should be disclosed separately.

Additional balance sheet disclosures considered necessary for the protection of investors includes accrued income; short-term loans; loans to officers and employees; other assets; taxes payable; dividends payable; loans from officers and employees; and transactions with related parties.

Section 54 of the Regulation Concerning Financial Statements specifies that liabilities should be split between current and long-term. Whilst the disclosure of current liabilities under the SEL is similar to the Commercial Code, the disclosure of long-term liabilities is more extensive. Under the SEL, liabilities should also include borrowings from affiliates and exceptional allowances or reserves prescribed by the special laws.

In accordance with section 65 of the Regulation Concerning Financial Statements, shareholders' equity should be categorized into share capital; capital reserve; legal earned reserve; and other surpluses. An interesting aspect of Japanese financial reporting is in the treatment of government grants. IAS 20 (paragraph 38) and the UK's SSAP 4 (paragraph 9) require that government grants provided to purchase fixed assets should be recognized in the profit and loss account over the expected useful life of the asset and should not be treated as part of shareholders' equity. Whilst the Commercial Code and the Corporation Tax Law in Japan also adopt such a procedure, the Regulation Concerning Financial Statements and the Business Accounting Principles, both issued by the Ministry of Finance, do not altogether abandon the capital approach to the treatment of such surpluses. Indeed, many municipal undertakings or government-owned public corporations continue to credit government grants or customers' contributions for construction as a capital surplus, thereby adopting a conservative reporting approach (Takatera and Daigo, 1989, pp. 193–4). Due to overseas pressure, and to entities such as the Japanese National Railways which changed their accounting policies to boost income in order to reduce reported losses, the deferred revenue approach has now largely been accepted in Japan (p. 193).

The balance sheet, profit and loss account and statement of appropriation of retained earnings (or statement of disposition of accumulated deficits) are normally presented in the form of a report. With the exception of the rules regarding inventory valuation (5) and monetary items relating to directors and statutory auditors (8), the requirements for the disclosure of information in the notes to the financial statements prepared in accordance with the SEL are similar to those of the Commercial Code. The following additional items should be disclosed:

1 significant events after the balance sheet date;
2 if tangible or intangible fixed assets are revalued, the fact, the reasons, the date of revaluation, the book value of assets before the revaluation, the amount revalued, and the method used for accounting for the revaluation difference should be disclosed. During the ensuing four years, only the fact and the date have to be disclosed, if material;
3 total number of authorized and issued shares;
4 number of new shares to be issued, date of any capital increase, and the amount to be transferred to capital reserve;
5 if there is any deficit that was offset with the capital reserve, legal earned reserve or equivalent reserves within two years prior to the beginning of the current period, the name of the reserve involved, the amount offset and the date of offset should be disclosed;
6 the amount of net assets per share;
7 if the lower of cost and market value method is applied, this fact and the amount written down should be disclosed;
8 the fact and the amount of any stock dividend;
9 if accounting policies, procedures or presentation method of financial transactions in a foreign company are different from those prevailing in Japan, the fact and the details should be disclosed.

The Business Accounting Principles stipulate that the accounting policies for the following items be disclosed in the notes to the financial statements:

1 valuation basis or method of accounting for securities;
2 valuation basis or method of accounting for inventories;
3 depreciation method for fixed assets;
4 the approach adopted to account for monetary items in foreign currency translation;
5 the approach adopted to account for allowances/reserves included in long-term liabilities;
6 the approach adopted to account for expenses and revenues.

In addition to the above items, significant post-balance sheet events should be disclosed. Examples are losses of fixed assets or inventories as a result of fire or flood; issues of significant amounts of shares or bonds; mergers and business transfers; the occurrence or resolution of a lawsuit; the bankruptcy of major customers. Whereas IAS 10 (paragraphs 18, 20–24 and 30–32) and SSAP 17 (paragraphs 19 and 20) in the UK classify post-balance sheet events into 'adjusting' and 'non-adjusting' there is no use of such technical terms in Japan. However, non-adjusting items are permitted and required to be disclosed whereas adjusting items must be incorporated into assets and liabilities in accordance with the regulations of the Interpretative Guideline on the Audit of Post Balance Sheet Events published by the BADC in 1983.

Table 10.2 shows the SEL balance sheet format.

Table 10.2 Balance sheet format prepared in accordance with the Securities and Exchange Law

[Date and unit of account]

ASSETS

I   *Current assets*

Cash in hand and at bank			XX
Notes receivable		XX	
Allowance for bad debts		X	XX
Trade accounts receivable		XX	
Allowance for bad debts		X	XX
Notes and accounts receivable from affiliates		XX	
Allowance for bad debts		X	XX
Marketable securities			XX
Treasury stock			XX
Finished goods			XX
Semi-finished goods			XX
Work-in-progress			XX
Raw materials and consumables			XX
Advance payments			XX
Prepaid expenses			XX
Accounts receivable			XX
Accounts receivable from affiliates			XX
Short-term loans		XX	
Allowance for bad debts		X	XX
Short-term loans to affiliates		XX	
Allowance for bad debts		X	XX
Other current assets			XX
Total current assets			XXX

II *Fixed assets*

1 *Tangible fixed assets*

Buildings		XX	
Accumulated depreciation		X	XX

Structures	XX	
Accumulated depreciation	X	XX
Machinery and equipment	XX	
Accumulated depreciation	X	XX
Vehicles	XX	
Accumulated depreciation	X	XX
Tools, fixtures and fittings	XX	
Accumulated depreciation	X	XX
Land		XX
Construction in progress		XX
Total tangible fixed assets		XXX

2 *Intangible fixed assets*

Mining rights	XX
Land rights	XX
Trade mark rights	XX
Patents	XX
Telephone rights	XX
Goodwill	XX
Total intangible fixed assets	XXX

3 *Investment and other assets*

Long-term cash at bank		XX
Investment in securities		XX
Investment in subsidiaries		XX
Investment in associates		XX
Investment in partnerships		XX
Long-term loans	XX	
Allowance for bad debts	X	XX
Long-term loans to shareholders, officers and employees	XX	
Allowance for bad debts	X	XX
Long-term loans to affiliates	XX	
Allowances for bad debts	X	XX
Doubtful receivables		XX
Long-term prepaid expenses		XX
Other		XX
Total investment and other assets		XXX
Total fixed assets		XXXX

III *Deferred charges*

Organization expenses	XX
Pre-operating costs	XX
Experimental research costs	XX
Development costs	XX
Stock issuing costs	XX
Bond discounts	XX
Interest during construction	XX
Total deferred charges	XXX

Total assets   XXXX

LIABILITIES

I *Current liabilities*

Notes payable		XX
Trade accounts payable		XX
Notes and accounts payable to affiliates		XX
Short-term borrowings		XX
Current portion of long-term borrowings		XX
Current portion of bonds with warrants		XX
Accounts payable		XX
Deposits received		XX
Deferred income		XX
Accrued expenses		XX
Accrued corporation and inhabitants taxes		XX
Accrued enterprise tax		XX
Allowances		
Allowance for bonus payments	X	
Allowance for damages	X	
Allowance for repairs	X	
Allowance for warranty	X	XX
Other current liabilities		XX
Total current liabilities		XXX

II *Long-term liabilities*

Bonds payable	XX
Bonds with warrants	XX
Convertible bonds	XX
Long-term borrowings	XX
Long-term borrowings from shareholders officers and employees	XX
Long-term borrowings from affiliates	XX

Allowances		
Allowance for severance payments	X	
Allowance for special repair	X̲	XX
Other		XX
Total long-term liabilities		X̲X̲X̲
Total liabilities		XXXX

CAPITAL

I	Share capital		XX
II	Capital reserve		XX
III	Legal earned reserve		XX

IV   *Other surpluses*

1 *Other capital surpluses*		
Reserve for government grants	X	
Reserve for gain on insurance claims	X̲	XX
2 *Voluntary reserves*		
Reserve for overseas investment losses	X	
Reserve for dividend equalization	X	
Reserve for business extension	X	
Reserve for additional equipment	X	
Reserve for sinking fund	X	
General reserve	X̲	XX
3 *Unappropriated*		XX
Total capital		X̲X̲X̲
Total liabilities and capital		XXXX

The profit and loss account

The Commercial Code

According to the Regulation Concerning Accounts, a profit and loss account should be divided into ordinary items and extraordinary items before determining profit before income taxes. Ordinary items are further classified as operating and non-operating. Operating items include turnover, cost of sales, distribution and administrative costs and other general operating expenses. The difference between operating revenues and operating expenses must be disclosed as operating profit (or loss). Non-operating income generally includes items such as interest income, discounts earned, interest on securities, dividend income, and gain on sale of marketable securities, and non-operating expenses would cover interest expenses, discounts charged, loss on sale of marketable securities and valuation losses on marketable securities. Ordinary income (or loss) is calculated by adding non-operating income to operating profit (or loss) and deducting non-operating expenses. The ordinary item figure is generally regarded as being the most reasonable and fair indicator of the result of operations for the current period. Note that, unlike the UK, there is no concept of exceptional items.

Profit before income taxes, which indicates the distributable income as at the balance sheet date, is to be calculated by adding extraordinary gains to ordinary income and deducting extraordinary losses from the total. The extraordinary gains or losses include prior-year adjustments, gains or losses on the sale of fixed assets, gains or losses from the disposal or sale of securities or other assets initially acquired for purposes other than for resale, and other losses arising from economic events such as calamities that are considered unusual. The nature and the amount of each unusual gain or loss should be shown as separate items. In Japan extraordinary items consist of prior-year adjustments and unusual items, while SSAP 6 (paragraph 16) in the UK excludes prior period items from extraordinary items because they relate to a prior year. In Japan, there are no definitions of exceptional items, extraordinary items and prior-year adjustments, in contrast to SSAP 6 (paragraphs 36–9).

SSAP 6 (paragraph 31) defines prior-year adjustments as material adjustments applicable to prior years resulting from changes in accounting policies, or from the correction of fundamental errors. In Japan the Business Accounting Principles go no further than listing the following items as prior-year adjustments:

1 adjustments to allowances/reserves;
2 adjustments to depreciation charges;
3 corrections to the valuation of inventories;
4 recovery of bad debts written off in prior years.

It is apparent from these examples that items included in prior-year adjustments in Japan would not qualify as such in the UK. Furthermore, the presentation of prior-year adjustments also differs between the two countries. According to IAS 8 (paragraph 19) prior-year adjustments should be either reported by adjusting the opening balance of retained earnings and restating the prior year's statements, or disclosed in the profit and loss account as part of net income. In the UK, SSAP 6 (paragraph 16) adopts the first method, whereas in Japan the second is stipulated.

Another important difference between Anglo-Saxon and Japanese accounting lies in the definition of extraordinary items. Whereas in the UK and US extraordinary items are identified by their unusual nature and by the infrequency of their occurrence, they are not in Japan. Consequently, even events or transactions which are expected to recur frequently may be considered to be extraordinary in Japan because they are not by their nature ordinary items. Such a wide definition is contrary to the approach adopted in IAS 8 (paragraph 3).

After determining income before income taxes, net income should be stated by deducting corporate income tax and inhabitants tax assessable to the current fiscal year. Enterprise tax, fixed property tax, automobile tax, excise tax and liquor tax are not reported as part of income taxes but are included in administrative expenses. Tax effect accounting cannot be used at the individual company level because the Commercial Code does not permit deferred tax debits. Tax effect accounting is optional only when the timing difference arises on consolidation. In addition, the following items should be stated below net profit in order to calculate unappropriated retained earnings:

1 the opening balance of retained earnings;
2 reversals of appropriated retained earnings in compliance with the special purpose for which it was reserved;
3 interim dividends and legal earned reserves in relation to the interim dividends.

The pro forma profit and loss account under the Commercial Code is shown in Table 10.3. The total amount of sales to and purchase from subsidiaries and controlling shareholders should be disclosed in the notes to the profit and loss account.

The Securities and Exchange Law (SEL)

The profit and loss account prepared in accordance with the SEL is similar in format to that required by the Commercial Code. However, the extent of disclosure is greater under the SEL, and certain items disclosed in the Commercial Code accounts require reclassification. A materiality standard for disclosure is specified at 10 per cent of a major category of the profit and loss account or 20 per cent of total sales. For example, if sales to related parties exceed 20 per cent of total sales that item must be disclosed separately. If losses from the sale of trade investments exceed 10 per cent of total non-operating expenses then that item must be separately disclosed.

In accordance with the requirements of the Business Accounting Principles, the profit and loss account should be segregated into three major divisions: operating profit, ordinary income and net profit. The category of operating profit includes turnover and the related cost of sales to calculate gross profit, which is presented in more detail than that required under the Commercial Code. Distribution costs and administrative expenses are

Table 10.3   Profit and loss account format prepared in accordance with the Commercial Code

[Period and unit of account]

ORDINARY ITEMS

Operating revenue and expenses			
Sales			XXX
Cost of sales	XXX		
Distribution costs and administrative expenses	XX		XXX
Operating profit			XX
Non-operating income and expenses			
Non-operating income			
Interest and dividend income	XX		
Gain on foreign currency exchange	XX		
Other non-operating income	XX	XX	
Non-operating expenses			
Interest and discount charges	XX		
Other non-operating expenses	XX	(XX)	
Ordinary income			XX

EXTRAORDINARY ITEMS

Extraordinary gains			
Gains on sale of fixed assets	XX		
Recovery of bad debts written off	XX		
Gain on sale of shares of subsidiary	XX	XX	
Extraordinary losses			
Adjustment of depreciation provided in prior years	XX		
Fire loss	XX		
Loss on sale of fixed asset	XX	(XX)	XX
Income before income taxes			XX
Income taxes			XX
Net profit			XX
Opening balance of retained earnings brought forward	XX		
Reversal of reserve for self-insurance	XX		

Interim dividends	XX	
Legal earned reserve appropriated in relation to the interim dividends	XX	XX
Unappropriated retained earnings as at the end of the year		XX

subtracted from gross profit in order to determine operating profit. If a company operates two or more lines of business, the revenue and expenses from each of the main businesses should be reported separately.

The cost of sales is stated as opening stock plus purchases, giving a subtotal which is the cost of goods available to be sold during the year, and deducting closing stock, thereby giving the costs of goods sold during the period. Whilst this may seem reasonably precise, considerable flexibility exists in the valuation of stocks. For example, a valuation loss on stock which arises as a result of the application of the lower of cost and market value method may be either reported in cost of sales or stated as a non-operating expense. If a significant decline in market value below cost arises then the valuation loss should be reported as either a non-operating expense or extraordinary loss. The components of distribution costs and administrative expenses should be listed under an appropriate heading.

The format for the profit and loss account prepared in accordance with the SEL is shown in table 10.4. Distribution costs and administrative expenses are deducted from gross profit to produce operating profit. Non-operating profit is added to operating profit and non-operating expenses deducted to establish ordinary income for the period. Extraordinary gains are then added and extraordinary losses deducted to give income before income taxes.

Statement of appropriations of retained earnings

The proposal for appropriation of retained earnings must be prepared by the board of directors and is subject to approval by shareholders at the annual general meeting. The appropriation proposal under the Commercial Code is shown in table 10.5 and the statement of appropriations of retained earnings under the SEL in table 10.6. In order to protect creditors by the maintenance of capital, the Commercial Code imposes legal controls on appropriations of retained earnings: section 288 requires that an amount equal to at least 10 per cent of cash disbursements must be allocated to a legal earned reserve until the reserve has reached 25 per cent of share capital. In principle, this reserve is not available for distribution in order to maintain capital. An additional

Table 10.4   Profit and loss account format prepared in accordance with the Securities and Exchange Law

[Period and unit of account]		
I *Turnover*		
Turnover to affiliates	XXX	
Turnover to other customers	XXX	XXX
II *Cost of sales*		
1 Opening stock	XX	
2 Purchases	XXX	
3 Subtotal	XXX	
3 Closing stock	XX	XXX
Gross profit		XXX
III *Distribution costs and*		
administrative expenses		
Packing and freight	XX	
Commission	XX	
Warehouse	XX	
Advertising	XX	
Directors' remuneration	XX	
Payroll	XX	
Bonuses	XX	
Welfare benefits	XX	
Travelling	XX	
Postage, telephone and telex	XX	
Utilities	XX	
Insurance and maintenance	XX	
Taxes and dues	XX	
Provision for accrued		
enterprise tax	XX	
Depreciation	XX	
Provision for allowance for		
doubtful accounts	XX	
Research and development	XX	
Others	XX	XX
Operating profit		XX
IV *Non-operating income*		
Interest income and dividends	XX	
Interest income from		
affiliates	XX	
Interest income on securities	XX	
Dividend income	XX	

Dividend income from affiliates	XX		
Gain on sale of marketable securities	XX		
Others	XX	XX	

V   *Non-operating expenses*

Interest and discounts	XX		
Interest on bonds payable	XX		
Amortization of deferred charges	XX		
Valuation loss on marketable securities	XX		
Exchange loss	XX		
Others	XX	(XX)	XX

Ordinary income	XX

VI   *Extraordinary gains*

Gain from sale of fixed assets	XX	
Recovery of bad debts written off	XX	
Gain on sale of shares in subsidiary	XX	
Gain from sale of investment securities	XX	XX

VII   *Extraordinary losses*

Adjustment of depreciation provided in prior years	XX		
Fire loss	XX		
Loss on sale of fixed assets	XX	(XX)	XX

Income before income taxes	XX
Corporate income tax and inhabitants tax	XX
Net profit	XX

Unappropriated retained earnings brought forward	XX
Reversal of reserve for self-assurance	XX
Interim dividends	XX
Legal earned reserve appropriated in relation to the interim dividends	XX

Unappropriated retained earnings as at the end of the year	XX

restriction is that a maximum dividend is allowed under section 290 of the Commercial Code, calculated as follows:

Where A = total assets
L = liabilities
C = share capital
R = legal reserves, i.e. capital and legal earned reserves
D = deferred pre-operating costs and research and development costs
P = distributable profit

P is the lower of:

(a) $(A - L - C - R)\dfrac{10}{11}$ and

(b) $A - L - C - D$

Definition of terms in the calculation of maximum permissible dividend payments

Assets
Consists of current assets, fixed assets and deferred charges.

Liabilities
Includes current and long-term liabilities as well as allowances.

Share capital
A capital contribution should, in principle, be accounted for as share capital in its entirety. However, where a capital contribution exceeds par value the excess may be treated as share capital. Where no-par value shares are issued at the time of formation the amount in excess of ¥50,000 can be treated as a capital surplus up to 50 per cent of the total contribution.

Legal reserve
Legal or statutory reserves consist of capital reserves and legal earned reserves. A capital reserve includes share premium and a positive difference which might arise as a result of a capital reduction or merger. The legal earned reserve consists of an allocation of at least 10 per cent of cash disbursements until the legal earned reserve amounts to 25 per cent of share capital.

Deferrals

Consist of deferred assets comprising pre-operating costs and capitalized research and development costs. Such assets are deducted because from a legal point of view they do not constitute assets.

Table 10.5   Proposal for appropriation of retained earnings format under the Commercial Code

Unappropriated retained earnings as at the end of year	XXX
Reversal of reserve for overseas investment losses	XX
TOTAL	XXX
This will be appropriated as indicated below:	
Legal earned reserve	XX
Cash dividends (5 yen per share)	XX
Directors' bonuses	XX
Reserve for overseas investment losses	XX
Reserve for business expansion	XX
Reserve for government grants	XX
Unappropriated retained earnings to be carried forward to the next year	XX

Table 10.6   Statement of appropriations of retained earnings format under the Securities and Exchange Law

I	Unappropriated retained earnings at the end of year		XXX
II	Reversals of voluntary reserves		
	Reversal of reserve for overseas investment losses		XX
	TOTAL		XXX
III	Appropriations		
	Legal earned reserve	X	
	Cash dividends	XX	
	Directors' bonuses	XX	
	Reserves for business expansion	XX	
	Reserve for government grants	XX	
	General reserve	XX	XX
IV	Unappropriated retained earnings to be carried forward		XXX

Supporting schedules to the financial statements

Section 281 of the Commercial Code requires a company to prepare supporting schedules as well as the balance sheet, profit and loss account, business report and proposal for appropriation of retained earnings. Section 47 of the Regulation Concerning Accounts stipulates the disclosure of 17 schedules and specifies that where an accounting policy has been changed the reason for the change must be reported. The Commercial Code does not specify the form of disclosure of the schedules, only the content. Consequently, the JICPA has prepared specimen schedules which may be followed; these are included in appendix G. The schedules which must be prepared are:

1　changes in share capital and legal reserve;
2　changes in debentures, other long-term and short-term borrowings;
3　details of acquisition and disposition of fixed assets, and corresponding depreciation;
4　mortgaged assets;
5　debt guarantees;
6　details, reasons for and method of calculating the amount of allowances provided, other than accumulated depreciation, depletion and amortization (excluding those stated in notes to the balance sheet);
7　amount due from and to a controlling shareholder;
8　equity ownership in subsidiaries and the number of shares of the company's stock held by those subsidiaries;
9　amount due from subsidiaries;
10　transactions with directors, statutory auditors and controlling shareholder (including transactions carried out on behalf of third parties) and those with third parties, which come into conflict with the company's interest;
11　amount of remuneration paid to directors and statutory auditors;
12　treasury stock and the parent company's shares held as collateral;
13　equity ownership of more than a quarter-owned investee companies (excluding subsidiaries) and the number of shares of the company's stock held by these investee companies;
14　transactions with subsidiaries and changes in receivables from and payables to subsidiaries;
15　directors and statutory auditors who also hold posts in other companies;
16　distribution costs and administrative expenses;
17　any additional information which might be considered necessary to supplement the balance sheet, the income statement and the business report of the company.

Whereas the Ministry of Justice does not prescribe the form of the supporting schedules to the accounts prepared in accordance with the Commercial Code, the Ministry of Finance prescribes both the form and content of the supporting schedules prepared in accordance with the SEL. Fourteen schedules must be prepared, which, due to the nature of the SEL, deal mainly with securities or financing. The form and content of each schedule are included in appendix H, and the list of schedules to be prepared is as follows:

1 marketable securities;
2 tangible fixed assets;
3 intangible fixed assets;
4 investments in affiliated companies;
5 investments in equity of affiliated companies other than capital stock;
6 loans to affiliated companies;
7 bonds payable;
8 long-term borrowings;
9 borrowings from affiliated companies;
10 capital stock;
11 capital surplus;
12 legal earned reserve and other appropriations;
13 depreciation, depletion and amortization of fixed assets and deferred charges;
14 reserves and allowances.

The business report

Up until 1982 the Commercial Code had not prescribed the content of the business report. In practice most companies had followed US practice and disclosed business information with their reporting review or financial review. The amended Regulation Concerning Accounts (section 45) prescribes that all companies, with the exception of small companies, should prepare a business report disclosing the following:

1 description of the main business activities, location of offices and factories, description of shares, employees and other information about the company;
2 operations and the results by division (including financing and capital expenditure);
3 relationship with parent company, status of significant subsidiaries and status of other significant business combinations;
4 results of operations and changes in financial position for at least the past three years and related explanations;
5 significant problems facing the company;

6 names of directors and statutory auditors, their position or assignment and main occupation;
7 top seven or more shareholders and their shareholdings, as well as the company's investment in these major shareholders;
8 main lenders, amount of borrowings and number of shares held by these lenders;
9 significant events occurring after the balance sheet date.

Interim financial statements

Those companies who are obliged to file an annual securities report with the Ministry of Finance are also obliged to submit an interim securities report on a semi-annual basis. The aim of such a report is to improve the process of forecasting and to protect investors by disclosing the current position of the company's business activities. The interim report covering the first six months of the accounting year must be submitted to the Ministry of Finance within three months of the end of the interim period.

The interim securities report (Form No. 5 for domestic companies and Form No. 10 for foreign companies) must be prepared in accordance with the Ministerial Ordinance on Regulation Concerning Terminology, Forms and Method of Preparation of Interim Financial Statements. The contents of Form No. 5 are as follows:

Item 1 General information

  1 changes in capital stock;
  2 list of major shareholders;
  3 changes in market price and the transaction value of inventories;
  4 changes in officers;
  5 status of employees.

Item 2 Status of the business and operation

  1 status of the business, e.g. business combinations or business transfers;
  2 status of the business operation, e.g. productive capacity, performance, sales backlog.

Item 3 Conditions of facilities

  1 change in the condition of facilities;
  2 planned capital expenditure.

Item 4 Financial condition

    1 Interim financial statements:
      (a) balance sheet;
      (b) profit and loss account.
    2 Other:
      (a) subsequent events if not already reported;
      (b) litigation;
      (c) interim dividend if approved by the board directors.

The aim of the interim financial statements is to provide a general financial position rather than the final results for a six-month period. Consequently, it is possible that different accounting procedures may be employed from those used at the year-end. This is presumably to ease part of the burden of interim financial reporting since the adoption of different accounting procedures is hardly likely to enhance forecasting. The following may be given special treatment in the interim financial statements.

1 If the business is subject to seasonal fluctuations this fact should be disclosed in a footnote.
2 Deferred or accrued expense items should be estimated based on time, amount of operating income, activity level or some other reasonable basis.
3 Where LIFO is used and inventories have fallen, the expected cost of replacement should be reflected in cost of sales.
4 Although the lower of cost or market value method is adopted for the valuation of inventories such an approach should not be adopted if the fall in value of stock is likely to have recovered by the year-end.
5 The nature of variances should be disclosed where they will be absorbed into inventory cost and eliminated by the end of the fiscal year. Such cost variances may be deferred and reported as an item of current assets or current liabilities.
6 Provision should be made for the period for corporate, inhabitants and other income taxes.

The form and contents of the interim financial statements are prescribed by the Ministry of Finance. The financial statements should consist of a balance sheet and a profit and loss account on a parent-company-only basis and should be prepared on a comparative basis. In addition, the following notes should be disclosed:

1 a summary of significant accounting principles and practices;
2 disclosure of any change in accounting principles or practices and reasons for the change;
3 the amount of trade notes receivable and other notes discounted or endorsed;

4 other contingent liabilities;
5 allowances for doubtful debts and accumulated depreciation where not shown as a deduction from the related assets;
6 depreciation charge for the interim period;
7 subsequent events;
8 other relevant financial information.

Interim dividends

Section 293-5-③ of the Commercial Code provides a ceiling on interim dividend payments. The calculation is similar to the restriction placed on annual dividends with the exception that appropriations of retained earnings during the interim period are deducted from net worth. The ceiling is calculated in relation to assets and liabilities from the last year-end as follows:

Where A = total assets
L = liabilities
C = share capital
R = legal reserves, i.e. capital and legal earned reserves
D = deferred assets including pre-operating costs and research and development costs
P = profit distributed during the interim period (dividends and bonuses to directors)
E = legal earned reserve appropriated from the previous year's profit during this interim period
I = interim dividend

I is the lower of:

(a) $(A - L - C - R - E - P)\dfrac{10}{11}$ and

(b) $(A - L - C - D - P)$

Summary

All *Kabushiki-Kaisha* must prepare financial statements in accordance with the Commercial Code, with the underlying objective of protecting creditors and current investors. Thus, emphasis is placed on disclosures which provide information on the availability of earnings for dividend distributions, on creditworthiness and earning power. The accounts are prepared for a single year only and on an individual company basis, which is the traditional form of presentation in Japan. The extent of disclosure is lower in the Commercial Code accounts than the equivalent in the UK and some European countries such as Sweden. Japanese Commercial Code accounts are effectively compliance statements prepared in accordance with the law and articles of association. In contrast, listed companies must disclose more detailed information and prepare a second set of accounts based on the Securities and Exchange Law (SEL), which are filed with the Ministry of Finance. Nevertheless, this second set of financial statements and supporting schedules is characterized by compliance with the law and articles of association, there being little in the way of voluntary disclosure.

Another important feature of the SEL accounts is that they are individual company based although consolidated accounts must be prepared by listed companies and attached to the basic SEL accounts as supplementary information. The main objective of reporting under the SEL is to provide adequate and appropriate disclosure for the protection of both current and future investors.

The format of the balance sheet is similar to that which applies to US companies, based on the current arrangement method. Assets are shown on the left-hand side and liabilities, capital and surplus on the right-hand side. Whilst IAS 1 requires the disclosure of comparative financial statements and the disclosure of the facts and reasons if the going concern assumption has not been followed, there is no equivalent under the Commercial Code. Furthermore, the disclosure requirements of IAS 5 are more extensive than those stipulated in the Commercial Code.

For listed companies, the Ministry of Finance Ordinance specifies the form and content of the financial statements, the notes and relating supporting schedules. In order to fulfil the obligation for adequate and appropriate disclosure necessary for the protection of investors, the financial statements should be presented in more detail than those required by the Commercial Code. Whilst the basic financial statements are similar, the terminology, form and content should be more precisely defined in the SEL accounts. This might involve additional disclosure as well as the reclassification of certain items.

The format of the profit and loss account under the Commercial Code is stipulated in the Regulation Concerning Accounts. The profit and loss account should be divided into ordinary items and extraordinary items before determining profit before income taxes. In Japan extraordinary items consist of prior-year adjustments and unusual items, while SSAP 6 in the UK excludes prior-period items from extraordinary items because they relate to a prior year. There are no definitions of exceptional items, extraordinary items and prior-year adjustments in Japan similar to those defined by SSAP 6 in the UK.

The profit and loss requirements in the Securities and Exchange Law are more extensive than those of the Commercial Code. The format is similar but disclosure is much greater.

Unlike the UK, Japanese law requires a separate statement of appropriations of retained earnings. To protect creditors the Commercial Code imposes legal controls on appropriations of retained earnings in order to maintain capital. The Code requires an amount equal to at least 10 per cent of cash disbursements to be allocated to a legal earned reserve until the reserve has reached 25 per cent of stated capital. To maintain capital the legal earned reserve is not as a general rule available for distribution.

11

Asset Valuation and Accounting Principles

Asset valuation and income determination

Stock

The acquisition cost of stock comprises its purchase price or production cost, including transport and handling costs, import duties and other material incidental costs, less trade discounts and rebates. When valuing stock (inventories) for purposes of the financial statements considerable flexibility is offered. Consequently, unit cost, FIFO (first in, first out), LIFO (last in, first out), weighted average cost, moving average cost, straight average cost, latest purchase price, and the retail inventory cost method are all acceptable methods of valuing inventories. In the UK, SSAP 9 (appendix 1, paragraphs 12 and 13) stipulates that the base stock method, LIFO and the latest purchase price method are not acceptable whereas in Japan only the base stock method is unacceptable. In contrast, IAS 2 (paragraph 26) permits both LIFO and the base stock method provided that there is disclosure of the difference between the amount of inventories as shown in the balance sheet and either (1) the lower of FIFO or weighted average cost and net realizable value or (2) the lower of current cost at the balance sheet date and net realizable value.

IAS 2 (paragraph 27) permits the standard cost method or the retail method for valuing inventories if the results approximate to the lower of FIFO or weighted average cost and net realizable value. In contrast, if a standard costing system exists in Japan, it is possible to value stock at standard provided that the difference between actual and standard is either included in the profit and loss account or allocated to stocks in the balance sheet.

When valuing stocks at the year-end the rule is either cost or the lower of cost (applying one of the above methods) and market value. In contrast, IAS 2 (paragraph 20) and SSAP 9 (paragraph 26) stipulate that inventories should be valued at the lower of cost and net realizable value. Where there is a substantial and irrecoverable decline in the market value of inventories it is necessary to value them on the basis of the new market value, in accordance with the provisions of the Commercial Code.

Marketable securities

The general rule for valuing marketable securities (classified as both current and non-current assets) is the same as for inventories: cost or the lower of cost and market value. In practice securities are often stated at acquisition cost, which includes commissions and any other incidental charges. The moving average approach is a popular method of cost determination since profit can be recognized on an individual security basis. In contrast, FASB Statement No. 12 requires the carrying amount of marketable securities to be valued at the lower of the portfolio's aggregate cost and market value as at the balance sheet date. Thus, in the US a portfolio approach is adopted whereas in Japan securities are valued on an individual security basis.

In Japan shares in subsidiary companies should be based on historical cost and must be investment securities written down by a charge to income where a permanent decline in value occurs, in accordance with the requirements of the Commercial Code. This rule is consistent with FASB Statement No. 12, which stipulates that any changes in the valuation allowance of equities included in current assets should be charged to income. Where such changes occur and the marketable securities are classed as non-current assets the change should be shown separately in shareholders' funds provided the decline is considered to be permanent, otherwise the charge should be to income.

Thus, whilst there are similarities between Japan and the US in the approach to valuing marketable securities there are also differences. When compared with the UK even more variety exists. Although the general rule for valuing all current assets is the lower of cost and net realizable value, investments classified as fixed may be valued at historical cost or revalued amounts. The classification of investments as fixed usually refers to investments in subsidiaries, associates and other long-term investments.

Accounts receivable

Debtors should be valued at the amount of the claims less normally estimated uncollectables. Under the Commercial Code uncollectable receivables are estimated and a reserve is set up for doubtful debts. The doubtful debt allowance is normally between 0.3 and 1.3 per cent of receivables, in accordance with the Corporation Tax Law.

It is rare in Japan for interest on receivables to be accounted for. Under US GAAP when a receivable, with a repayment period in excess of one year, is not equal to the present value of the consideration, the difference should be amortized as interest income or expense over the life of the receivable to provide a constant rate of interest.

Tangible fixed assets

Japanese accounting, like that of the US, is based on historical cost principles without provision for revaluations. In contrast, both IAS 16 (paragraph 44) and the UK's SSAP 12 (paragraph 21) require that the gross carrying amount of an asset should be either the historical cost or revalued amount. Whilst IAS 16 permits revaluations, the Commercial Code, the Securities and Exchange Law and the Corporation Tax Law in Japan prohibit, as a general rule, the revaluation of plant and equipment.

The acquisition of tangible fixed assets should include incidental costs, such as transport and handling costs. In the case of self-constructed assets it is permissible to include applicable borrowing costs. IAS 23 (paragraph 27) and FAS 34 (paragraph 1) permit a more extensive range of items for capitalization, including amortization of a discount or premium on the issue of bonds, and the amortization of ancillary costs for the arrangement of borrowing. Although borrowing costs of property, plant and equipment, investments in enterprises and inventory, requiring a significant period of time to bring to a saleable condition, real estate and other long-term development projects are all permitted to be capitalized by IAS 23 (paragraph 10), in Japan the capitalization of borrowing costs is limited to tangible depreciable assets only.

Assets acquired in exchange for shares in the enterprise should be valued at the amount issued to the investor. The assets should be recorded at its fair value, or the fair value of the shares issued, in accordance with the provisions of IAS 16 (paragraph 39).

As was discussed in chapter 10, another difference between Japanese financial reporting and international practice lies in the treatment of government grants. Shortly after the post-war occupation forces left Japan the standard treatment to account for government grants was to treat them as part of capital surplus. However, the Corporation Tax Law stipulates that government grants may be accounted for as a deduction from related assets. Whilst it is permissible to deduct government grants from the related assets it is not mandatory according to the Business Accounting Principles.

Depreciation of tangible fixed assets

When depreciating tangible assets, it is permissible in Japan to use the straight-line, the declining-balance, the unit-of-production method or the sum of the year digits method. In practice, it is common to use the declining-balance method applying the rates prescribed by the tax regulations. Land is not normally depreciated in Japan.

According to the provisions of IAS 4 (paragraph 16) and SSAP 12 (paragraph 5) the useful lives of major depreciable assets should be reviewed periodically and depreciable rates should be adjusted for the current and future periods if expectations are significantly different from previous estimates. In contrast, there is no requirement in Japan to review the useful lives of assets periodically. Where adjustments are made to accumulated depreciation resulting from changes in useful lives and depreciation method, Japanese GAAP stipulate that they should be treated as prior-year adjustments. In contrast, IAS 8 (paragraph 19) requires that such adjustments should either be dealt with in arriving at net profit or be reported by adjusting opening retained earnings and restating the prior-year financial statements.

Intangible fixed assets

Intangible fixed assets such as goodwill, patent rights and trade marks should be stated at their unamortized amount. Goodwill should be recognized as an intangible fixed asset in the balance sheet only when purchased or acquired through a business transfer or merger. Purchased goodwill should be valued at acquisition cost. Consistent with international practice, internally generated goodwill is not accounted for in Japan.

Purchased goodwill should be amortized to income on a systematic basis over its estimated useful life. However, the Commercial Code provides that goodwill should be amortized by not less than the average amount within five years of the acquisition and the Corporation Income Tax Law permits voluntary amortization of goodwill. In practice, purchased goodwill is amortized within five years in accordance with the requirement of the Commercial Code. Such an approach is consistent with the prudent accounting policies common in continental Europe. In contrast, APBO 17 in the US stipulates that goodwill, like other intangible assets, should be amortized over its useful life, which should not exceed 40 years. SSAP 22 and IAS 22 specify that goodwill should not be carried as a permanent balance sheet asset, but should be eliminated either by immediate write-off to reserves on acquisition or by amortization over its useful life through the profit and loss account. Although other methods of treating goodwill are permissible, SSAP 22 recommends that the immediate write-off option should be used in normal circumstances. In practice there may be circumstances when an unusually large acquisition would have a significant effect on reserves, however, and in such cases it is reasonable to adopt the amortization option. Where this is done, goodwill should be written off over its useful life, although no maximum period of write-off is stipulated.

Deferred charges

Certain costs may be accounted for as deferred charges in the balance sheet, and in accordance with the Commercial Code should be stated at their unamortized amounts. Such costs include organization costs, pre-operating costs, new share issuing costs, bond issuing costs, bond discounts, research and development costs defrayed for a specific purpose, and construction interests paid to shareholders as dividends during the pre-operation of a company which cannot commence its operations for two years after incorporation. Material losses on assets arising as a result of a natural calamity, which cannot be covered with the net income in the current year or the current retained earnings less appropriated earnings, may also be deferred as an asset in the balance sheet provided that it is permitted by specific laws.

Deferred charges have to be amortized to income on a systematic basis over their estimated useful life or any other basis. Notice the flexibility in approach permitted under Japanese GAAP; often an option is provided which permits alternative methods of accounting. In accordance with the provisions of the Commercial Code, organization costs, pre-operating costs and research and development costs are amortized within five years and share issuing costs and bond issuing costs are normally amortized over a period of three years or, in the case of bonds, the life of the bond if shorter.

In the UK research costs should be written off in the year of expenditure and development costs should be deferred in certain circumstances. Deferred development costs should be stated as an intangible fixed asset and amortized on a systematic basis. Whereas IAS 9 (paragraph 21) and SSAP 13 (paragraph 25) require that deferred development costs should be reviewed at the end of each accounting year, there is no equivalent requirement in Japan.

In Japan the usual practice is to charge research and development costs to income as incurred, e.g. Minolta Camera, Toshiba, Matsushita Electric and NEC. However, some large corporations defer research and development costs and amortize them over a period of five years. For example, Nippon Steel has adopted a policy of capitalizing development costs as deferred assets and writing them off over five years. The accounting policy was applied to the expenditures for 'Medium and Long-term Vision for Multiple-Business Management', i.e. those incurred for the preparation and start-up of new plant test-runs of production facilities and other activities carried out in relation to specific new-type production plants, during the year ended 31 March 1984.

Bond discounts must be amortized over the period to maturity. Construction dividends may also involve deferred charges. Such dividends are peculiar to Japan and involve companies that require considerable sums of money before becoming operational. Such companies are allowed, under the Commercial Code, to pay dividends provided:

1 operation will not commence for two years after formation;
2 the articles of association permit;
3 the court approves.

In effect, payments to shareholders of up to 5 per cent of share capital represent interest on capital and are treated in the accounts as a deferred charge. Whenever profits of the year, in excess of 6 per cent of the share capital, are distributed an amount equal to the excess must be amortized.

Expense and revenue recognition

All expenses and revenue should be stated on an accruals or realization basis in order to present fairly the results of operations for the current period. Unrealized income should not be included in current net profit except for certain transactions. For example, the percentage-of-completion method as well as the completed-contract method may be applied in recognizing revenue from long-term contract work-in-progress. In contrast, revenue arising from hire-purchase (instalment) sales may be recognized at either the due date or the receipt date of the instalment while the revenue should be generally reported in the profit and loss account at the date of delivery of the goods. However, since a number of uncertainties exist concerning the collectability of the debt, collection expenses and after-service costs, it is acceptable to recognize revenue when the payment is received. Since the instalment basis is permitted for tax purposes provided the sales are so recorded in the books of account, it is common for Japanese corporations to adopt such an approach when instalment sales are substantial.

Prior-year adjustments

IAS 8 (paragraph 19) states that prior-year adjustments should either be reported by adjusting the opening balance on retained earnings and restating prior years' statements or should be disclosed in the profit and loss account as part of net income. The UK (SSAP 6, paragraph 16) adopts the first method, Japan the second. Moreover, in Japan extraordinary items are not limited to the events or transactions that do not recur frequently or regularly as defined in IAS (paragraph 3) and SSAP 6 (paragraph 30). Even if the events or transactions are expected to recur frequently, they may be considered to be extraordinary to the extent that they are not by their nature ordinary items.

GAAP

Assets, liabilities, shareholders' equity, revenue and expenses should be stated at gross amounts on the balance sheet or the profit and loss account. Such amounts may not be offset. Accounting principles and procedures should be consistently applied each period and should not be changed without reason.

Capital and liabilities

According to the provisions of the Business Accounting Principles, shareholders' equity should be segregated into capital and reserves/surpluses. Under the heading of 'capital' there should be a further subdivision into share capital and surpluses where the latter include capital reserves, legal earned reserves and other surpluses. For example, share premium, gains from a reduction in share capital and gains from a merger are all to be treated as capital reserves. Items to be included under the heading of 'other surpluses' consist primarily of voluntary reserves and unappropriated retained earnings.

Share premium and share issues

Share premium is defined as capital contributions in excess of the par value of shares or, in the case of non-par value shares, the excess of the capital amount, as designated by the board of directors. An added requirement is that at least 50 per cent of the total contributed, regardless of whether they are par value or non-par value shares, must be treated as share capital.

When forming a company (*KK*), after the 1981 amendment to the Commercial Code, the amount of par value shares to be issued must not be less than ¥50,000. A similar requirement applies to non-par value shares. In order to complete the formation of a company at least 25 per cent of the total number of authorized shares must be issued and paid-in.

Legal reserves

Under the Commercial Code, capital reserves and legal earned reserves are together designated as 'legal reserves'. Whilst legal earned reserves are inherently part of retained earnings, the Commercial Code designates them as legal earned reserves in order to protect creditors and maintain capital. However, legal reserves may be used to cover losses provided a resolution has been passed at a shareholders' general meeting. Alternatively, legal reserves may be capitalized by a resolution of the board of directors in accordance with section 293-3-①. New shares may be issued by capitalization, subject to a resolution of the board of directors in accordance with section 280-2. In practice, the articles of association usually have a pre-emption right clause so that a capitalization issue involves the issue of new shares to shareholders in proportion to their existing holdings.

Expenses or contingent losses

The Business Accounting Principles require that an estimated expense or loss from a contingency may be accrued by a charge to income and should be stated either as a liability or at valuation in the balance sheet, provided the following conditions are met:

1 there is a specific future expense or loss;
2 the occurrence originates from events before the balance sheet date;
3 the outcome has a high probability of occurrence;
4 the amount can be reasonably estimated.

Provided these conditions are met, the following items may be designated as 'allowances':

1 project warranties;
2 sales rebates;
3 sales returns;
4 seasonal employee bonuses;
5 guarantees on construction;
6 severance payments;
7 ordinary repairs;
8 special repairs;
9 guarantee loss;
10 reparations;
11 bad debts.

Provisions for the 'allowances' listed above are regulated by the Corporation Tax Law and, in practice, are also used in Japanese corporate reports. For example, under the Special Tax Measures Law, tax-deductible reserves – such as those for losses on overseas investment, drought, improvement of structures by small and medium-sized corporations, and securities transactions – may be allowed in certain industries. In practice, these tax-free reserves are used by many corporations: both NEC and Toshiba, for example, provide for a 'reserve for losses caused by the repurchase of electronic computers'; Toyota Motor and Minolta Camera both have a 'reserve for overseas investment losses'.

Accounting for mergers

The two main schools of thought for accounting for mergers in Japan – the unity of juristic persons and investment in property (assets) – have been discussed in chapter 2. Both approaches are recognized in law. According to section 288-2-①-5 of the Commercial Code, a positive difference between the merged company's assets on the one hand, and its liabilities and shares on the other, should be set aside as a capital surplus. In such a case the legal surplus and other retained earnings may not be treated as a capital surplus under section 288-2-③. Section 288 of the Commercial Code requires that an amount equal to at least 10 per cent of cash disbursements paid should be set up as a legal earned reserve, which is not available for distribution until the reserve has reached a quarter of the stated capital. Accordingly, the Commercial Code permits the succession of the legal earned reserve in the merged company because the retained reserve is discontinued if it is transferred to capital surplus.

The Corporation Tax Law permits the assets of the merged companies to be valued at their book values, thereby approximating to the viewpoint of unity of juristic persons. However, it is permissible to revalue the assets of the merged companies to reflect their fair value. In contrast, the Business Accounting Principles provide that a merger gain or loss should be stated as a capital surplus whereas the earned reserve may not be treated as a capital surplus. This is consistent with the provisions of the Commercial Code.

Consolidation principles

During the 1960s a number of cases where a large number of investors sustained losses as a result of profit manipulation or window dressing through subsidiary companies, in particular the bankruptcy of Sanyo Special Steel Ltd in 1965, led to considerable criticism of accounting practices in Japan. In addition, the entry of Japanese companies on to the New York Stock Exchange in the early 1960s and the entry of foreign companies on to the Tokyo Stock Exchange in the early 1970s stimulated the Ministry of Finance into the introduction of consolidation accounting. The Business Accounting Deliberation Council was asked by the Ministry to consider the matters closely and in 1975 it published the Accounting Principles for Consolidated Financial Statements. The Ministry of Finance itself issued the Regulations Concerning Consolidated Financial Statements in 1976 and the related interpretive rules in 1977. Consequently, consolidated financial statements became a requirement for listed companies for the financial year beginning on or after 1 April 1977. These statements must be audited by a CPA or an audit corporation and filed with the Ministry of Finance within three months of the end of a financial year. However, consolidated financial statements are prepared as supplementary information in the registration statement or the securities report by large companies required to report under the Securities and Exchange Law in Japan, while IAS 3 and SSAP 14 require that group accounts should be issued by every parent company unless that corporation is itself a wholly owned subsidiary. Furthermore, it is important to note that the Commercial Code and the Corporation Tax Law do not require a company to prepare or report consolidated financial statements.

According to the provisions of the Accounting Principles for Consolidated Financial Statements, a parent company is a company that owns more than 50 per cent of the votes in another company, and a subsidiary company is obviously a company in which more than half of the votes are owned by a parent company. If more than 50 per cent of the votes in a company are owned by a parent company and/or by one or more of its subsidiaries, the company involved is also deemed to be a subsidiary company. The criterion of control over the composition of the board of directors is not permitted in Japan. Further, the following subsidiary companies are excluded from consolidation:

1 a company which is considered to be no longer within a group of common control, for example because of a lack of effective control, such as a reorganized company;
2 a company which is not considered to be a going concern because of bankruptcy or liquidation;
3 a company in which the parent company owns more than 50 per cent of the votes in the company but the investment is only temporary; or
4 a company which, if included in the consolidation, would mislead interested parties.

In addition, a subsidiary whose assets and sales are not material may be excluded from consolidation provided the omission does not hinder a reasonable judgement on the financial position and results of the group. In practice, however, difficulties arise in identifying the subjectivity inherent in the word 'material'. Recently the practice of excluding possible material subsidiaries of Japanese groups from consolidation met with severe criticism from the UK.

Consolidated financial statements prepared in Japan consist of a consolidated balance sheet, a consolidated profit and loss statement and a consolidated statement of retained earnings, or a combined statement of profit, loss and retained earnings. The notes to the consolidated financial statements should disclose the following information:

1 the consolidation policy;
2 any differences in financial year-ends;

3 accounting procedures and practices including:
 (a) the facts, the reasons for and effects of any change in valuation basis
     and method of depreciation for significant assets;
 (b) the policy of eliminating inter-group unrealized profit when applying
     the equity method of accounting;
 (c) any significant differences in accounting principles and procedures
     within the group;
4 the appropriation of retained earnings;
5 the method of foreign currency translation used for foreign entities;
6 other significant matters.

Consideration is taken of the uniformity of accounting periods and of accounting policies. If the difference between the year-end date of a parent and its subsidiary does not exceed three months, the financial statements of the subsidiary for its own accounting period may be consolidated by adjusting for significant transactions within the period. If the difference exceeds three months, the subsidiary must prepare financial statements as at the consolidation date by adjustments for all transactions that have occurred in the period. In contrast, the SEC in the US prohibits the consolidation of a subsidiary whose closing date differs from that of the parent by over 93 days. The cost of investment in subsidiaries and the parent's share in the shareholders' equity of the subsidiary may be eliminated either at the date of acquisition (as a general rule) or at the closing date (exceptionally). The excess of the cost of acquiring a subsidiary over the value of the net assets acquired at that day should be stated as a 'consolidation adjustment' in the consolidated financial statements. Normally, because both the Corporation Tax Law and the Commercial Code permit such an accounting procedure, the difference is based on the book value of the net assets, but some corporations use fair value. In contrast, it is common practice in the UK and the US to take the net assets as their fair value. Where it is possible to trace the cause of such a difference the amount should be transferred to an appropriate account. For example, goodwill should be recognized when it is regarded as arising from the excess earning power of the subsidiary. When a consolidation adjustment account exists with both debits and credits, it may be permissible to offset them in the consolidated financial statements. Where the sums involved in a 'consolidated adjustment' are not material they may be treated as a profit or loss in the current year.

In the UK, SSAP 22 (paragraph 36) states that 'purchased goodwill should normally be eliminated from the accounts immediately on acquisition against reserves'. However, it 'may be eliminated from the accounts by amortization through the profit and loss account' over its useful economic life. In the US the excess of the cost of acquisition over the fair value of net assets must be amortized over its useful life, which must not exceed 40 years. In Japan the Accounting Principles for Consolidated Financial Statements require that the 'consolidation adjustment account' must be amortized by not less than the average amount over its estimated useful life, with no maximum period being specified. However, the Commercial Code provides that goodwill shall be amortized by not less than the average amount within five years after the acquisition. In practice, therefore, goodwill is amortized within five years or written off immediately to the profit and loss account, in accordance with the requirements of the Commercial Code.

Minority interests should be shown as a liability in the consolidated balance sheet, while IAS 3 (paragraph 43) merely requires that they should be stated as separate items and should not be included in shareholders' equity. Minority interests in the consolidated profit and loss account must be shown after corporation tax expense as well as amortization of the 'consolidation adjustment' and investment income or loss computed using the equity method. Needless to say, intra-group sales and intra-group loans should be eliminated in preparing the consolidated financial statements.

As a general rule, investments in unconsolidated subsidiaries or associated companies should be shown in the consolidated balance sheet at an amount calculated using the equity method of accounting, an approach introduced from 1 April 1983. An associated company is not a subsidiary, but an investee in which the consolidated group (the parent company and the consolidated subsidiary companies) holds 20 per cent or more of the votes of the investee, and exercises significant influence over the financial and operating policies through board representation or significant interchange of managerial personnel, financing, dependence on technical information or significant inter-company transactions. Under the equity method of accounting the investment is recorded at cost plus a proportionate share of post-acquisition earnings or losses. Although tax-effect accounting is not generally practised in Japan, inter-period income tax allocations which form part of the determination of the income tax expenses may be provided for in the consolidated accounts.

Foreign currency translation

The Business Accounting Deliberation Council has issued the following specific opinions concerning foreign currency transactions and translation of foreign currency financial statements.

1 Specific Opinion No. 1: 'Opinion on Accounting for Devaluation of Foreign Currency' (2 May 1968).
2 Specific Opinion No. 3: 'Opinion on Accounting for Assets, etc., denominated in Foreign Currency following the Suspension of Fluctuation Limits on Fixed Foreign Exchange Parities' (21 September 1971).

3 Specific Opinion No. 4: 'Opinion on Accounting for Assets, etc., denominated in Foreign Currency following the Change in Fixed Foreign Exchange
   Parities' (24 December 1971).
4 Specific Opinion No. 5: 'Opinion on Accounting for Assets, etc., denominated in Foreign Currency under the Existing International Monetary
   System' (7 July 1972).
5 Specific Opinion No. 6: 'Opinion on Accounting for Assets, etc., denominated in Foreign Currency during the Floating Period in Foreign Exchange
   Rates' (29 March 1973).

These specific opinions were issued to cope with significant changes in
foreign exchange currencies, for example the devaluation of the pound
sterling in November 1967, the suspension of the commitment to exchange
gold for US dollars in August 1971, the establishment of a new system of
fixed exchange rate in conformity with the Smithsonian agreement of 20
December 1971 and the shift to the system of floating exchange rates. On 26
June 1979 the Council eventually published the Accounting Standards for
Foreign Currency Transactions, etc., in order to establish a comprehensive
accounting standard for foreign currency translation and to keep step with
the introduction of consolidated financial statements, which all listed companies were required to prepare for financial years ended on or after 31 March
1978.

The Japanese standard requires that a transaction denominated in a foreign
currency should normally be translated at the actual exchange rate prevailing
on the transaction date or the rates of exchange at which the transaction is
contracted to be settled in the future. Exchange differences arising on
settlement of short-term monetary items must be recognized as part of
income for the current period. Such an approach is consistent with IAS 21
(paragraph 46). According to IAS 21 (paragraph 25), SSAP 20 (paragraph 48)
and FAS 52 (paragraph 15), foreign currency monetary items at the balance
sheet date, irrespective of whether short or long term, should be translated at
the closing rate. In Japan different rates of exchange have to be applied
separately to short- and long-term receivables or payables. Current receivables or payables denominated in foreign currencies are normally translated
at the closing rate. Alternatively, the average rate over a period before or after
the balance sheet date as well as the spot rate at the balance sheet date may be
used as the closing rate. Exchange differences arising on short-term foreign
currency monetary items should be included in income for the current
period. On the other hand, long-term monetary items at the balance sheet
date should be translated at the historical rates. Consequently, no exchange
differences occur. Such an accounting treatment, by which unrealized gains
are not recognized, is consistent with the very prudent approach often
adopted in Japanese financial reporting.

Table 11.1 summarizes the translation methods which must be applied to

Table 11.1   Translation methods of foreign currency financial statements

Method	Foreign branches	Foreign subsidiaries and associates
Principal application	*Temporal Method* Long-term monetary items should be translated at the historical rates. Exchange differences should be included in current income.	*Modified temporal method* Long-term monetary items should be translated at the historical rates. Current net income and retained earnings at the year-end should be translated at the closing rate. Exchange differences should be treated as deferred assets/liabilities.
Exceptional application where long-term monetary and non-monetary items are not material	*Current rate method* Exchange differences should be included in current income.	*Current rate method* Exchange differences should be treated as deferred assets/liabilities.

foreign currency financial statements when preparing consolidated accounts in Japan. An important point is that the translation of financial statements differs between a foreign branch operation and a foreign subsidiary or associated company. The financial statements of a foreign branch are translated using the temporal method. Monetary items and securities are translated using the same method as that adopted by the head office, which would normally be the temporal method. Short-term monetary assets or liabilities are translated at the closing rate of exchange, although for convertible debentures, where the conversion period has not yet expired, the rate of exchange at the time of the issue should be used. Long-term monetary assets or liabilities should be translated at the rate of exchange at the date when the rights were acquired or obligations incurred. Non-monetary assets, advance receipts and deferred credits are all translated at historical rates. All other revenue and expense items are translated at either historical or average rates, with resulting exchange differences being included in current income. Where long-term monetary and non-monetary items are not material the current rate method may be used, with exchange differences being included in current income.

In contrast, SSAP 20, IAS 21 and FAS 52 stipulate that foreign operations conducted through a branch should be accounted for on the basis of the nature of the business operations concerned. Where the foreign branch is an extension of head office's trade and affects its cash flows, the temporal method should be used. Where the branch acts as an independent business with local finance, however, the closing rate/net investment method should be used.

In Japan the translation of foreign currency financial statements of subsidiary or associated companies is based on the modified temporal method. Currencies and short-term monetary assets or liabilities are translated at the closing rate, whereas long-term monetary assets or liabilities are translated at historical rates. Non-monetary assets and liabilities are translated at historical rates. Revenue and expenses are translated at historical rates or an average rate, except that charges to income from non-monetary asset accounts must be translated at historical rates. Net income and retained earnings are translated at the rate applicable at the end of the period. Exchange differences should be treated as deferred assets/liabilities. In exceptional circumstances, where long-term monetary and non-monetary items are not material, the current rate method may be used, with exchange differences being treated as deferred assets/liabilities.

SSAP 20, IAS 21 and FAS 52 require that all assets and liabilities should be translated at current rates if the foreign operation is largely independent of head office. Revenue and expense items should be translated either at historical or average rates, with the resulting difference being treated as a translation adjustment in shareholders' funds. However, when a foreign operation is an extension of the parent company's operations and affects its cash flow directly, or if the foreign operation is in a country with a high rate of inflation, monetary items, marketable securities and inventories should be translated at current rates. Non-monetary items, other than those stated at market value, and associated charges and credits should be translated at historical rates. Other revenue and expense items should be translated at either historical or average rates, with the resulting translation difference being charged or credited to the current period.

Summary

Whilst assets should in general be valued conservatively in accordance with the Japanese law, considerable flexibility in approach is permitted. For example, the general rule for valuing current assets is either cost or the lower of cost and market value. When valuing stock any of the main methods may be used with the exception of the base stock approach. Thus, greater flexibility is permitted than by SSAP 9 and IAS 2, which adopt the general valuation rule of the lower of cost and net realizable value. In other instances, such as when valuing tangible fixed assets, the law requires uniformity by requiring valuation of assets at historical cost and prohibiting revaluations. Furthermore, when considering the appropriate depreciation charge for tangible fixed assets Japanese companies are not required to review their useful lives periodically. This differs from the provisions of both IAS 4 and SSAP 12. However, there is a requirement to adjust depreciation rates for the current and future periods if expectations are significantly different from previous estimates.

Intangible assets such as goodwill, patent rights and trade marks should be stated at their unamortized amount. Purchased goodwill arising from a merger, acquisition or business transfer should be recognized in the accounts and amortized over a period not exceeding five years. Such an approach is consistent with the requirements of some continental European countries but differs from the US, where goodwill may be amortized over a period not exceeding 40 years.

Certain costs such as organizational, pre-operating and research and development costs may be accounted for as deferred charges in the balance sheet and amortized to income on a systematic basis over their estimated useful lives or any other suitable basis; research and development costs should be amortized within five years. When valuing certain assets taxation may be an important factor. For example, the provision for doubtful debts is invariably set at the rate allowable for tax purposes. Further, the Corporation Tax Law permits voluntary amortization of goodwill whereas the Commercial Code stipulates the useful life basis, which should not exceed five years.

Flexibility also exists when recognizing expenses or revenue. For example, either the percentage-of-completion or the completed-contract method may be applied in recognizing revenue from long-term contract work-in-progress. Further, revenue arising from hire-purchase sales may be recognized at either the due date or the receipt date of the instalment while the revenue should be generally reported in the profit and loss account at the date of delivery of the goods.

Flexibility is also a feature when accounting for mergers. Either the purchase method or pooling-of-interests approach may be used in accordance with the Commercial Code or Corporation Tax Law. In practice, the purchase method is used more often but the situation prevailing in Japan is somewhat confusing.

During the 1960s considerable criticism was directed at accounting practices which manipulated profits to such an extent that a large number of investors incurred losses as a result of bankruptcies, e.g. Sanyo Special Steel Ltd in 1965. Furthermore, the entry of Japanese companies on to foreign stock exchanges provided a further impetus to demands for the provision of consolidated accounts. In 1976 the Ministry of Finance issued the Regulations Concerning Consolidated Financial Statements, which subsequently led to the requirement for listed companies to prepare consolidated accounts on or after 1 April 1977. These statements, which must be audited, are supplementary to the main SEL accounts which are still based on the parent company. Criticism has been levied at those supplementary statements because of the exclusion of subsidiaries on the grounds of materiality.

Finally, whilst the UK and US requirements for accounting for the effects of foreign currency transactions and translation of foreign currency financial statements are very similar, the Japanese requirements differ in a number of ways. For example, when accounting for the effects of changes in foreign exchange rates, IAS 21 and SSAP 21 stipulate that long-term monetary items at the balance sheet date should be translated at the closing rate, whereas in Japan historical rates should be used, thereby eliminating the problem of exchange differences. Another difference arises when translating foreign currency financial statements whose activities are relatively self-contained and integrated, since IAS 21 states that the closing rate method or temporal method should normally be used while the Japanese requirements state that the modified temporal or temporal method must be used. Other differences exist between international practice and Japanese practice in this particular area.

12

The Survey of Accounts

Like any other survey of accounts, this chapter seeks to analyse corporate annual reports in a formal way in order to show what companies are doing in practice. A number of general surveys have included Japanese companies as part of their samples: see, for example, Choi (1973), Barrett (1976), Cairns, Lafferty and Mantle (1984), Stilling, Norton and Hopkins (1984), and Tonkin (1989). The latest of these (Tonkin, 1989)[1] ranked the world's major countries by financial reporting practices. Japan ranked 10th out of 16, scoring reasonably on accounting and timeliness but coming last in terms of non-financial disclosures. In contrast, the UK was first and the US sixth. Campbell's (1985) survey was unique in that it was concerned exclusively with Japanese companies. The survey reported here differs in a number of ways. First, the survey covers 48 companies, a sample larger than most previous works. Second, the 48 companies include 13 unlisted firms as well as 35 listed enterprises. Third, the survey is different from Campbell's (1985) research in that it is not based solely on accounts prepared in accordance with the Securities and Exchange Law. Instead this survey covers the annual reports of unlisted and listed companies which prepared their financial statements in accordance with the Commercial Code and were the latest available in June 1988. Such financial statements are distributed to shareholders. In addition, a second set of financial statements was scrutinized for all listed companies we selected, such statements being those prepared in accordance with the Securities and Exchange Law (SEL) and filed with the Ministry of Finance – although they are not usually sent to shareholders. Furthermore, nine companies were willing to supply English versions of their accounts and these were covered in our survey as a special category. These English versions are not straight translations of either the Commercial Code or SEL accounts; rather, they are directed at the international reader, in particular US readers.

Thus, this survey covers nine companies that produced three sets of accounts (Commercial Code, SEL and English version), 26 companies that produced two sets of accounts (Commercial Code and SEL) and 13 unlisted companies which produced only the Commercial Code accounts.

In order to obtain 48 sets of Commercial Code accounts we wrote to 200 Japanese corporations, split between listed and major unlisted enterprises. The companies were selected on a stratified random basis from the *Japan Company Handbook*, which covers all listed and many major unlisted corporations. To obtain accounts from 48 companies proved to be very difficult. It was noticeable that it was more difficult to obtain accounts from Japanese corporations than from Anglo-Saxon companies, used by the authors in other surveys. The level of non-response was considerable and in other cases our requests for all the corporate reports were only partly complied with. For example, 15 listed companies did not provide us with the SEL accounts but supplied instead the Commercial Code and, where applicable, their English version accounts. To ensure that we could obtain a good picture of the overall extent of disclosure and measurement practices we purchased the SEL accounts for those companies from bookshops. In addition, we found it extremely difficult to obtain accounts from major unlisted companies. To obtain the annual reports companies were contacted by letter up to four times in both Japanese and English to obtain our final sample. Curiously, letters in English sent from the UK proved more successful with unlisted companies than letters sent in Japanese from Japan to be returned to a Japanese address. In certain instances assurances had to be given to companies that no information from their accounts would be disclosed and that the name of their company would not be specifically revealed. Consequently, a list of companies included in the survey has not been published. Examples included in this chapter are taken from the English version annual reports of companies not placing any restriction on disclosure. The English version accounts were selected since the format and type of disclosure in the Commercial Code and SEL accounts are dictated by law and, in the case of the SEL accounts, are, in reality, a completion of standard forms for filing with the Ministry of Finance. Examples of the schedules to be completed are included in appendices G and H.

To compare disclosure levels overall a scoring sheet was completed for each set of accounts. The fact that we had obtained multiple sets of accounts for some of the companies included in this survey meant that the number of disclosure scoring sheets completed totalled 92 (48 Commercial Code, 35 SEL, 9 English). Each disclosure scoring sheet had a total of 210 disclosure items.

Financial statements issued by Japanese companies

Under the Commercial Code, the directors of all limited liability companies (*Kabushiki-Kaisha*) are required to prepare a balance sheet, a profit and loss account, a business report, a proposal of appropriation of profit or disposition of loss and related schedules. Copies of these documents, with the exception of the related schedules, must accompany the notice to shareholders of a general shareholders' meeting. Our survey found that two of the 13 unlisted companies did not include the related schedules in the documents distributed to shareholders. Although these schedules – which are an essential component of the accounts – are available for scrutiny by shareholders at the company's head office, to omit them seems inconsistent with the aim of the Commercial Code financial statements: the protection of creditors and current investors.

Listed companies must prepare Commercial Code accounts and file a securities report in accordance with the SEL. As will be demonstrated in this chapter the level of disclosure in the Commercial Code accounts is very low. In general, these accounts are compliance documents which contain mandatory disclosures and little else. Consequently, the criticism is directed first at the Commercial Code because of the low level of disclosure and flexibility in reporting the related schedules and, second, at Japanese companies which treat such accounts as merely compliance documents rather than adopt a wider perspective to financial reporting. With regard to the second criticism, it should also be noted that there was no significant difference between the disclosure in the Commercial Code accounts by listed and unlisted companies, confirming that the general attitude of Japanese corporations is to adhere to minimum levels of disclosure.

The general level of disclosure in the SEL accounts is significantly higher than the Commercial Code accounts. This is not surprising since minimum levels of disclosure required by the SEL are higher than those required by the Commercial Code. It is a pity that the SEL accounts are not distributed to shareholders, however. Such documents are filed with the Ministry of Finance, are available at the company for scrutiny and copies may be purchased from certain bookstalls. In addition, it is possible to photocopy the SEL accounts at the appropriate Stock Exchange.

Asset valuation and income determination

Accounting concepts and policies

The Commercial Code, the SEL and the Business Accounting Principles all require companies to disclose any changes in accounting principles. However, in our survey we found that, whilst it was clear in the SEL accounts whether an accounting policy had been changed it was not so evident in both the Commercial Code and English version accounts. The SEL accounts include a statement in the audit report that 'the accounting principles and procedures followed by the corporation are in conformity with generally accepted accounting principles and have been applied on a consistent basis'. There is no equivalent statement in the Commercial Code accounts. Table 12.1 shows the disclosure of changes in accounting principles. The reader is left to presume that all changes in accounting policies have been reported.

Table 12.1 Disclosure of changes in accounting principles

	CC	SEL	Eng.
Number of companies	48	35	9
Changes in accounting principles or auditors' reference (%)	8	20	22

Stock

Inventories are usually broken down into their respective components and disclosures was very high in all three sets of accounts. However, whereas details of cost and market value were provided in the Commercial Code and SEL accounts less detail was provided in the English version accounts (see table 12.2).

In valuing inventories the cost method is used more than the lower of cost and market value. Table 12.3 shows that there is also an element of non-disclosure, particularly in the Commercial Code accounts. Cost was more popular with listed companies but the difference between method and quotation status was not significant. Interestingly, the English sets of accounts showed that 55 per cent of the sample used the lower of cost and

Table 12.2 Disclosure of inventories

	CC	SEL	Eng.
Number of companies	48	35	9
Breakdown of inventories (%)	90	98	100
Cost/market value of inventories (%)	92	100	22

Table 12.3 Basis of valuation of inventories (%)

	CC	SEL	Eng.
Lower of cost and market value	17	14	55
Cost	67	77	45
Not disclosed	16	9	0
	100	100	100

market value method. In the English sets of accounts, some corporations adjusted their basis of valuation of inventories to comply with the SEC requirement for the lower of cost and market value. In such cases the value of stock is different from that reported in the Commercial Code and SEL accounts. Typical disclosure is provided by Nissan (see example 1).

EXAMPLE 1

Nissan Motor Co. Ltd   Annual Report 1988

Inventory accounting policy
Inventories are stated at the lower of cost or market. The cost of finished products, work in process and purchased parts is determined by the average method and the cost of raw materials and supplies is determined by the last-in first-out method.

In practice, about two-thirds of those companies disclosing their inventory accounting policy used the cost method, often based on monthly moving average, or the weighted average cost method because of the simplified procedures. Whilst the cost method has traditionally been used in Japan the lower of cost and market value is becoming increasingly popular, where market value is interpreted as either net realizable value or replacement cost. For example, Matsushita Electric Company Limited states finished goods and work-in-progress at the lower of cost (average) and market value and raw materials at cost, mainly on a FIFO basis. The Toshiba Corporation values finished products and raw materials at the lower of cost (FIFO and average method used respectively) and market value, whereas work-in-progress is stated at the lower of cost and market method where cost is determined by the specific identification of job order inventories and by the average method for raw materials and other inventories. It should be pointed out that 25 per cent of companies reporting in accordance with the SEL did not disclose the method of cost determination for inventories compared with 37 per cent of companies reporting under the Commercial Code. Perhaps the view was taken that in these particular cases the accounting policy for inventories was not significant in preparing the financial statements. However, no statement to this effect was reported.

Changes in accounting policy in relation to inventories might result from a change in economic circumstances. For example, the Nippon Steel Corporation, a leading steelmaker, changed its method of cost determination during the year to 31 March 1987 from the weighted average cost method to LIFO. The explanation for this was as follows:

The change was made in order to better match the 'cost of sales' with the 'net sales' of the Company, both of which declined materially during the current year. The significant decline of net sales due to lower selling prices and reduced sales volume was caused primarily by the drastic hike of Japanese yen value against US dollars and other foreign currencies. Correspondingly, the cost of imported raw materials and other elements of 'cost of sales' were substantially lowered. Under such circumstances the last-in, first-out basis is believed to more adequately relate 'cost of sales' to 'net sales', for the determination of operating performance during the year. As a result of the change in the inventory valuation method, 'cost of goods sold' for the year ended March 31, 1987 was decreased by ¥50,934 million when compared with the amount which would have been recorded if the previous basis had been applied consistently.

Other inventories are valued at the lower of cost or market, cost being determined by (i) the job order cost method with respect to work in progress, and (ii) the first-in, first-out method or the periodic average method with respect to supplies.

The non-consolidated statement of income of the Nippon Steel Corporation for the years ending 31 March 1987 and 1986 is shown in table 12.4. A cynic might suggest that the change in inventory valuation method had something to do with income smoothing. Certainly the loss in 1987 was reduced from ¥70,937 million before the accounting change to the reported figure of ¥20,004 million – a very material change in accounting policy.

Such changes in accounting policy may be a response to economic events

Table 12.4   Nippon Steel: non-consolidated statement of income

	1987 (¥m)	1986 (¥m)
Operating income and expenses		
Operating income:		
Sales	2,178,537	2,684,721
Operating expenses:		
Cost of goods sold	1,804,902	2,185,377
Depreciation with respect to cost of goods sold	169,412	172,728
Selling, general and administrative expenses	224,227	226,366
Operating profit (loss)	(20,004)	100,250

and a desire to smooth income and, in particular, avoid reporting losses. For example, the Mitsubishi Kasei Corporation changed its stock valuation method away from the moving average cost method to LIFO for finished goods and raw materials in 1982 after the second oil crisis. The company considered such a change to be prudent and tax efficient.

Contracted work-in-progress

Table 12.5 shows the percentage of companies disclosing their accounting policies with respect to work-in-progress. Interestingly, whilst 86 per cent of companies reporting under the SEL disclosed their accounting policy only 22 per cent did likewise in the English accounts. Perhaps such information is material when reporting to the Ministry of Finance but is judged not to be significant to the international reader.

Table 12.5   Accounting policy for contracted work-in-progress

	CC	*SEL*	*Eng.*
Number of companies	48	35	9
Disclosure of policy (%)	63	86	22

Examples 2 and 3 both show disclosure in the English version of the accounts.

EXAMPLE 2

NEC   Annual Report 1988

Work-in-progress: accounting policy
Work in process made to customer specification represents accumulated production costs of job orders. Work in process of mass-produced standard products is stated on an average cost method. The cost of components is determined on a last-in first-out basis.

EXAMPLE 3

Toshiba   Annual Report 1987

Work-in-progress: accounting policy
Work in process is stated at the lower of cost or estimated realizable value, cost being determined by accumulated production costs for contract items and at production costs determined by the first-in, first-out method for regular production items. Advance payments received on contracts are deducted from inventories to the extent of costs incurred.

Fixed assets and depreciation

Whilst fixed assets may be revalued periodically in the UK, such a practice is not allowed in Japan. GAAP in Japan follow the US approach in this respect by using historical cost.

Table 12.6 shows the extent of balance sheet and note disclosure of fixed assets included in each set of accounts. It is apparent that the extent of disclosure is reasonably good with a high level of compliance. However, whilst a detailed schedule of fixed assets, disaggregated into its various components, is disclosed in the Commercial Code and SEL accounts, less detail is shown in the English accounts. For example, in the English accounts the net book value of total fixed assets was shown by all companies. However, no company showed the net book value of each category of fixed assets whereas, in general, this information was disclosed in the Japanese accounts. Moreover, whilst the proportion of fixed assets leased is disclosed in the SEL accounts, such information is not provided in either the Commercial Code or English accounts.

All assets with the exception of land and construction in progress must be depreciated. Based on the SEL accounts, two companies used the straight-line method only, three the reducing-balance basis only and the rest (30) used both the straight-line method and the reducing-balance approach. However, those using two methods applied the reducing-balance approach to most of their fixed assets. Whilst all the companies disclosed the method of depreciation none disclosed the percentage rate applied.

Table 12.6   Fixed assets and depreciation disclosure in the balance sheet and notes

	CC	SEL	Eng.
Number of companies	48	35	9
Balance sheet	(%)	(%)	(%)
1 Gross value of fixed assets	8	71	100
2 Net value of fixed assets	92	29	100
3 Disaggregated into property, plant and equipment	100	100	89
4 More detailed breakdown than in (3) above	100	100	33
Notes			
1 Accumulated depreciation on fixed assets	94	100	100
2 Schedule of movement in fixed assets	98	100	100
3 Proportion of fixed assets leased	0	40	0
4 Proportion of fixed assets pledged	44	63	67
5 Unexpired useful life of fixed assets	0	3	22

On the basis of the Commercial Code accounts it was apparent that whilst listed companies used both the straight-line and reducing-balance methods, unlisted companies had a preference for the straight-line method only. Interestingly, eight out of 48 Commercial Code accounts did not include any information on depreciation, presumably on the grounds that the information was either not material or was included in the schedules.

Research and development

The Commercial Code and the Business Accounting Principles both permit research and development expenses to be deferred and amortized over a period not exceeding five years. The disclosure of such deferred charges is shown in table 12.7. It can be seen from this table that information on the period of disclosure of research and development is poor. This is because there is no requirement to supply this information. Some 80 per cent of companies included in this survey wrote off research and development in the year it was incurred, a finding identical to that of Campbell (1985).

Table 12.7　Disclosure of research and development expenses

	CC	SEL	Eng.
In the profit and loss account (%)	0	60	67
Amortization period disclosed (%)	0	9	22

Taxation

Deferred taxes

Like Sweden, deferred taxation is not normally practised in Japan. Part of the explanation for this is that taxable profits are based on accounting profits so that taxation considerations are often more important than the financial reporting effects. The other part of the explanation is that traditionally the parent company accounts have been considered to be the main accounts rather than consolidated accounts. As in Sweden, 'deferred taxes are rarely recognized. The exception is when purchase accounting is applied to an acquisition. On consolidation the untaxed reserves of the acquired subsidiary are shown as part of acquired equity after deducting deferred taxes. Deferred taxes are also provided on any restatement in the value of assets and liabilities as a result of a revaluation to fair values' (Cooke, 1988b, p. 98). In Japan the main financial statements are the parent company accounts so that deferred taxation may be used only in the supplementary consolidated financial statements. Even then such inter-period income tax allocations are optional rather than compulsory. In practice, deferred tax accounting is quite common in the English accounts. For instance, Minolta Camera summarizes its income tax accounting policy as follows: 'Provision is made in the consolidated accounts to reflect the inter-period allocation of income taxes resulting from certain income and expenses being treated differently for financial reporting purposes than for tax computation purposes in those cases which arise as a result of the consolidation of subsidiaries, such as elimination of inter-company profits.'

Example 4 shows the good note disclosure on deferred taxation provided in the corporate annual report of Matsushita Electric.

EXAMPLE 4

| Matsushita Electric | | | | Annual Report 1988 |

Deferred taxation
Deferred income taxes result from timing differences in the recognition of income and expenses for tax and financial statement purposes. The sources of the deferred income taxes and the related tax effects for the year ended March 31, 1988, the period ended March 31, 1987 and the two years ended November 20, 1986 are as follows:

	Yen (million)				US $000
	1988	1987	1986	1985	1988
Depreciation	(3,300)	(287)	(9,009)	(20,522)	(26,400)
Inventory valuation	(13,495)	2,006	8,963	(12,476)	(107,960)
Expenses and income accrued for financial statement purposes but not currently included in taxable income	(29,426)	3,325	(1,544)	(306)	(235,408)
Other	4,960	(537)	(3,221)	(420)	39,680
	(41,261)	4,507	(4,811)	(33,724)	(330,088

Cumulative net deferred income tax charges at March 31, 1988 and 1987 and November 20, 1986 are reflected in the accompanying consolidated balance sheets under the following captions:

	Yen (million)			US $000
	1988	1987	1986	1988
Other current assets	188,770	152,070	158,133	1,510,160
Other assets	160,666	156,059	153,699	1,285,328
	349,436	308,129	311,832	2,795,488

Income taxes

Japanese corporations are subject to corporation tax, inhabitants tax and enterprise tax, all three taxes being based on reported income (further details are provided in chapter 4). The enterprise tax, which is deductible for inhabitants and corporation tax purposes in the year in which the tax payment becomes due, should be classified as a general and administrative expense in the profit and loss account. Consequently, the tax expense shown in the financial statements consists of corporation and inhabitants taxes payable on taxable income for the period. Any prior-year tax assessments should be separately disclosed in the profit and loss account.

The authors' survey found that approximately 90 per cent of companies disclosed taxes in the profit and loss account and the current tax liability in the balance sheet. However, although all companies producing an English set of accounts disclosed the accounting policy with respect to taxes it was rare for such disclosure to be made in the Commercial Code or SEL accounts. A typical example of disclosure of income taxes is provided by Minolta Camera (see example 5).

EXAMPLE 5

Minolta Camera   1988 Annual Report

Note to the accounts on income taxes
The companies are subject to a number of taxes based on earnings at average normal tax rates of approximately 56% and 58% for the years ended March 31, 1988 and 1987, respectively. The respective effective tax rates of 66% and 52% for the years ended March 31, 1988 and 1987 differ from the average normal tax rates principally because of timing differences, including losses of subsidiaries, in the recognition of income and expenses for tax and financial statement purposes, credits for dividends paid and expenses which are not deductible for tax purposes.

Whilst example 5 appears typical of the type of disclosure in English version accounts, more extensive disclosure is provided by Matsushita Electric, as shown in example 6.

Many of the disclosure requirements for taxation in the accounts of UK companies, such as tax attributable to franked investment income and irrecoverable ACT, stem from the imputation tax system. Since the Japanese taxation system is classical rather than imputation-based, some of the disclosures required by SSAP 8 are not applicable to Japan.

Moreover, US financial statements are far more informative about taxation than are those provided by Japanese corporations. In addition to deferred tax

EXAMPLE 6

Matsushita Electric   1988 Annual Report

Note to the accounts on income taxes
The company and its subsidiaries are subject to a number of taxes based on earnings which, in the aggregate, result in average normal tax rates of approximately 56.0% for the year ended March 31, 1988, and 57.5% for the period ended March 31, 1987 and the two years ended March 20, 1986.

The effective tax rates for the periods differ from the normal tax rates for the following reasons:

	1988	1987	1986	1985
Normal tax rate	56.0%	57.5%	57.5%	57.5%
Tax credits for dividends paid and increased research expenses	(1.3)	(0.7)	(1.7)	(1.2)
Equity in earnings of non-consolidated subsidiaries and associated companies	(4.1)	(2.0)	(2.4)	(2.1)
Expenses not deductible for tax purposes	2.5	2.7	2.3	1.6
Other	(0.5)	(2.8)	(1.6)	(1.1)
Effective tax rate	52.6%	54.7%	54.1%	54.7%

---

accounting, which is commonly applied in the US, other information on operating loss carry-forwards and their expiration dates and a reconciliation between expected and actual tax expenses or benefits are also disclosed. Such disclosures are not normally found in Japanese corporate reports.

Reserves
As reported in chapter 4, a characteristic of Japanese accounting is the substantial influence of taxation. Certain provisions are allowable against tax provided they are incorporated in the financial statements. Table 12.8 shows the proportion of companies disclosing such reserves and the percentage providing an explanation thereon. Notice the improved level of disclosure in the English version of accounts. Such figures mask the underlying nature of disclosure in this area, however, since companies generally disclose only what they are forced to disclose. For example, transfers to legal reserves and bonuses to directors and statutory auditors are shown as appropriations from

Table 12.8　Disclosure of reserves

	CC	*SEL*	*Eng.*
Number of companies	48	35	9
Disclosure of reserves (%)	88	94	100
Companies providing an explanation for its reserves	23	23	100

retained earnings. Provisions for doubtful debts and for retirement and severance benefits are both shown in the balance sheet, with the latter having a note providing a little more detail. However, other reserves prescribed in the Corporation Tax Law are lost in expenses whilst those provided in accordance with the Special Taxation Measures Law do not appear to be extensively disclosed in the English version of accounts. One exception is the NEC Corporation, whose retained earnings are stated as in example 7.

EXAMPLE 7

NEC Corporation   1988 Annual Report

Consolidated statement of income and retained earnings

	1986 (¥m)	*1987 (¥m)*	*1988 (¥m)*
Net income	27,185	15,034	25,363
Retained earnings:			
Balance at beginning of year	193,657	204,088	204,312
Cash dividends applicable to earnings for the year	(12,444)	(12,629)	(13,062)
Transfer to legal reserve	(1,332)	(1,343)	(1,386)
Appropriation for special allowances, net of tax	(2,978)	(838)	(4,306)
Balance at end of year	204,088	204,312	210,921

Pensions

It is common for Japanese companies to provide for employee retirement and severance benefits. In general, employees are entitled to a lump-sum payment based on the current rate of pay and length of service. It is usual to use base pay to apply the service multiple since this excludes various allowances and any bonuses, the latter often given twice a year. Directors are not usually covered by such pension schemes, their remuneration package, including severance and retirement benefits, being charged to income. Similarly, many schemes for employees have not been fully funded although in recent years some companies have decided to fund them partly. Canon provides an interesting example (see example 8).

EXAMPLE 8

Canon   1988 Annual Report

Note on employee retirement and severance benefits
The Company and certain of its subsidiaries have employee retirement and severance benefit plans covering substantially all employees who meet eligibility requirements. The Company funds the costs of its major plans and amortizes prior service costs over twenty years. A comparison of accumulated plan benefits and net assets of a liability accrued for the funded plans, mainly as of May 31, 1988 and 1987, is presented below:

| | ¥ million | | US $000 | |
	1988	1987	1988	1987
Acturial present value of accumulated benefits	57,024	50,921	452,571	404,135
Net assets available for benefits	42,098	35,005	334,111	277,817
Liability accrued	7,806	8,221	61,952	65,246
	49,904	43,226	396,063	343,063

The rate of return used in determining the actuarial present value of accumulated plan benefits was 5.5%. The Company is not required by regulation to report the actuarially computed value of vested benefits, and such information, therefore, is not available.

Provision has been made in the accompanying balance sheets for the estimated accrued liability under the unfunded plans.

Directors and certain employees are not covered by the programs described above. Benefits paid to such persons and meritorious service payments are charged to income as paid since amounts vary with circumstances, and it is therefore not possible to compute the liability for future payments.

Commencing with the year ending December 31, 1989, the companies will adopt a new method of accounting for pension costs to conform with the requirements of Statement of Financial Accounting Standards No. 87. The effect on the consolidated financial statements of that change in accounting has not yet been determined.

Our survey found that no companies disclosed pension costs, as charged to income, in their Commercial Code accounts whilst 43 per cent of listed companies provided such information in the SEL financial statements. In contrast, 90 per cent of companies disclosed their pension liabilities in the Commercial Code accounts compared with 100 per cent of corporations in their SEL accounts. It was also noticeable that disclosures of both pension costs and pension liabilities was very poor in the English version accounts.

Leases

SSAP 21, FAS 13 and IAS 17 all require finance leases to be capitalized in the balance sheet of the lessee, but until recently there has been no similar requirement in Japan. No companies in the survey provided any information on leased fixed assets in their Commercial Code and English version accounts. However, 14 out of 35 companies revealed the extent to which fixed assets were leased in their SEL accounts. Section 18-2 of the Regulations Concerning Accounts, which was amended in June 1988, effective from April 1990, requires finance leases to be either capitalized or disclosed in the notes to the accounts.

Other major accounting issues

Consolidated accounts

The Commercial Code still specifies that financial statements should be prepared on a company-by-company basis. There is, however, nothing to stop a company attaching supplementary consolidated accounts to its main company financial statements. Consistent with Japanese behaviour our survey found that no company adopted such a procedure. Furthermore, despite the Regulation Concerning Consolidated Financial Statements of 1976 and the related interpretative rules of 1977 the basic SEL accounts still remain the parent company financial statements. Consolidated accounts are attached to the parent company financial statements as supplementary information.

Twenty-two of the 35 companies complied with the Ministerial Ordinance to prepare consolidated accounts. It is presumed that the 13 companies that did not comply did so because they did not have any subsidiaries that were considered material. In contrast, none of the 48 companies attached consolidated accounts to its main Commercial Code accounts and only one out of nine failed to include such accounts in its English version financial statements. Whether the fact that the one company which did not produce consolidated financial statements was reporting losses is open to speculation.

The basis of presenting that company's financial statements was stated as follows:

> the accompanying financial statements of [the company] have been prepared in accordance with the provisions of the Japanese Commercial Code and accounting principles and practices generally accepted in Japan. The preparation of statements of changes in financial position is not required in Japan. These statements are, however, presented in the accompanying financial statements together with certain footnote data to provide additional information. The financial statements are not consolidated and the company's investments in affiliates (i.e. subsidiaries and associates) are stated at cost in the accompanying financial statements. Profits of these companies are reflected in the company's books only to the extent of cash dividends received.

It is interesting to note that the statement of changes in financial position is not required in Japan and yet the company decided to produce such a statement for purposes of the English version accounts. In contrast, a consolidated set of accounts is required to be filed with the Ministry of Finance as part of its securities report but such financial statements were not used for the English version of accounts. Such a decision does not assist the international reader and clearly does not present fairly the financial position of the group, which included 51 'principal subsidiaries and affiliates'.

As none of the companies in the survey included a set of supplementary consolidated financial statements in the Commercial Code accounts, there was no information on the group other than the investment in subsidiaries and associates. In contrast, whilst there is a requirement to produce consolidated accounts in the SEL accounts, companies did not disclose the criteria for inclusion of companies in the consolidation. Such a finding was also apparent in the English version of accounts, a feature of US corporate reports as well: 'US companies have become increasingly reticent about full disclosure of their accounting policies, leaving too much as being implied by the US regulatory environment. In consequence, accounting policies in certain "significant areas" are not adequately disclosed' (Cooke and Wallace, 1989, p. 55).

Whilst the regulations require the name of principal subsidiaries to be disclosed there is no obligation to disclose the subsidiaries' activities and location. In practice, however, in excess of 80 per cent of companies disclosed such information; a finding consistent with Campbell (1985, p. 28).

Chapter 11 listed a number of exemptions to the preparation of consolidated accounts. However, such exemptions were not used; instead, the accounting policy with respect to the consolidated accounts normally states that the financial statements include the parent company and either principal subsidiaries or significant subsidiaries. An example of such disclosures is given as example 9.

EXAMPLE 9

Shōwa Denko   1987 Annual Report

Principles of consolidation
Although the Company had 62 subsidiaries as at 31st December, 1987, the
accompanying consolidated financial statements include the accounts of the
Company and 11 significant subsidiaries (the 'Companies') for the fiscal year
ended 31st December, 1987.

The remaining 51 unconsolidated subsidiaries have combined assets, net
income and net sales which in the aggregate are not significant in relation to
those of the Companies.

Example 9 is more precise than most disclosures on the principles of
consolidation. Often explanations lack precision and provide an insufficient
level of disclosure.

The Accounting Standard on Consolidated Financial Statements issued by
the Business Accounting Deliberation Council states that 'uniform accounting policies and practices should preferably by followed by a parent and its
subsidiaries' (section 3-3). Consistent with many of the accounting recommendations in Japan is the use of the word 'preferably'. The words 'uniform'
and 'preferably' may seem somewhat incongruous since 'uniform' conveys
conformity to a rule or practice and 'preferably' may be interpreted as giving
priority to. Consequently, options are available which can be exploited in
consolidation accounting. However, in both the SEL accounts and the
English version accounts the audit report refers to financial statements being
prepared on a consistent basis. Example 10 shows an accounting policy on the
preparation of consolidated financial statements.

EXAMPLE 10

Matsushita Electric   1988 Annual Report

Basis of presenting consolidated financial statements
The Company and its domestic subsidiaries maintain their books of account
in conformity with financial accounting standards of Japan, and its foreign
subsidiaries in conformity with those of the countries of domicile.

The consolidated financial statements presented herein have been prepared in a manner and reflect the adjustments which are necessary to
conform them with United States generally accepted accounting principles.

Our survey found that whilst about 50 per cent of companies disclosed information about uniformity of specific accounting policies in the SEL accounts such a practice was less common in the Commercial Code and English version accounts. In contrast, in excess of 75 per cent of companies disclosed the accounting treatment of unrealized profits or losses on intra-group sales in both the SEL accounts and English version accounts.

Goodwill

There is a very low level of disclosure in this area although it appears that, in practice, goodwill is written off over a period exceeding one year but less than five years. The five-year period is common. For example, the corporate report of Minolta Camera states that 'the difference between the cost and underlying net equity at acquisition date of investments in consolidated subsidiaries is being amortized over a five-year period'. Such a finding is consistent with Campbell (1985, p. 32).

Associated companies

Since 1 April 1983 companies are required to account for investments in unconsolidated subsidiaries and associated companies in the SEL accounts using the equity method. Before this requirement the cost method was more commonly used in Japan (Campbell, 1985, p. 33). Whilst our survey found that the equity method was being used in the majority of cases, a small number of stated accounting policies were somewhat ambiguous or implied the use of the cost method; see example 11, for instance.

EXAMPLE 11

Minolta Camera   1988 Annual Report

Accounting policy for investment in nonconsolidated subsidiaries and affiliates
Investments in nonconsolidated subsidiaries, and affiliates which are owned 20% to 50%, are principally stated at cost, cost being determined by the weighted average method.

It is important to note that despite this change in the SEL accounts, the Commercial Code does not permit equity accounting in the investor corporation's non-consolidated financial statements.

Foreign currency translation

Whilst disclosure with respect to transactions denominated in a foreign currency should be transacted normally at the actual exchange rate at the time of the transaction or when settled in the future in accordance with the BADC standard, our survey found that little information was disclosed in the corporate annual reports. For example, the accounting policy was not stated by the majority of companies and exchange gains or losses on transactions were not normally disclosed. In contrast, the accounting policy with respect to the translation method was reported by the majority of the companies for which such information was relevant.

Based on our survey and the work of Campbell (1985, p. 38) it appears that Japanese companies are gradually moving away from the temporal or modified temporal method towards increased consistency with international practice. Whilst some variations in principle exist between the Japanese standard and FAS 52 (reported in chapter 11) some Japanese corporate reports, in their English versions, actually quote compliance with the US standard in accordance with SEC regulations. One example is Matsushita Electric (see example 12). Example 12 also shows the type of disclosure required in Japan when reporting exchange gains or losses that arise from the translation of foreign subsidiaries' financial statements: the required form is a debit or credit to cumulative translation adjustments shown as part of shareholders' equity.

EXAMPLE 12

Matsushita Electric   1988 Annual Report

Foreign currency translation
Foreign currency financial statements are translated in accordance with Statement No. 52 of the Financial Accounting Standards Board of the United States, under which all assets and liabilities are translated into yen at period-end rates and income and expense accounts are translated at weighted average rates. Adjustments resulting from translation of financial statements are reflected under the caption, 'cumulative translation adjustments', a separate component of stockholders' equity.

Inflation accounting

In response to attempts to account for inflation in the UK and US and by the IASC (IAS 15), in 1980 BADC issued an Opinion on Disclosure of Financial

Information for Changing Price Level Accounting. This opinion stated that it was too early to require Japanese corporations to disclose similar information. In our survey we found that no companies provided any supplementary information on the impact of inflation, a finding consistent with previous work (Campbell, 1985, p. 56).

It is interesting to compare the response of a small country like Sweden with a large country like Japan, both of which have been described (Nobes, 1985, p. 185) as displaying 'macro-uniform' characteristics. Whereas the Japanese response by the BADC in 1980 was firmly against inflation accounting, in October 1980 Föreningen Auktoriserade Revisorer (Swedish Institute of Authorized Public Accountants) issued a draft on current cost accounting with a view to introducing it to large companies. Indeed, a number of large Swedish companies voluntarily provided such information. Thus, the BADC in Japan, controlled by big businesses and the government, was hostile to the development, with the JICPA typically remaining silent, whereas the Swedish professional accounting body was positive, with the government's Accounting Standards Board (Bokforingsnamnden) remaining silent. Campbell (1985, p. 56) provides an explanation as to why inflation accounting may not have been so pressing in Japan: 'The present Japanese attitude to inflation accounting is perhaps a reflection of the recent inflation rate, which has dropped from the double-digit rates of the early 1970s (peaking at 24 per cent in 1974) to a relatively low (by international standards) 3 to 4 per cent a year.' Yet if we compare Japan with Sweden we should note that the latter country achieved single-digit rates of inflation on a consistent basis throughout the 1970s and 1980s. The difference surely lies in the regulatory framework in each country and the ability of accountants and business to respond. Swedish companies and the Swedish Institute have traditionally adopted a positive viewpoint towards international accounting changes whereas Japan acts slowly and negatively to such developments. Swedish listed company reports show a high degree of awareness and willingness to implement international accounting standards whereas Japanese companies and their representative body, Keidanren, adopt a negative attitude to any increased disclosure, for which the costs are apparent but the benefits are not.

However, some accounting theorists, such as Sadaharu Fuwa and Ichiro Katano, argued strongly in favour of inflation accounting. Fuwa, who was influenced by German academicians such as Schmalenbach, Schmidt, Geldmacher and Mahlberg, placed great emphasis on capital maintenance concepts and current value accounting. Fuwa argued that asset valuation was not as important as income measurement. Assets can be stated at historical cost merely as a token value, an argument consistent with Mahlberg's philosophy of 'neutralization in the balance sheet'. However, physical capital must be maintained so that expenses must be stated at current cost. In contrast,

Katano, who was influenced by Sweeny's work, advocated general purchase power accounting.[2]

Accounting for mergers

Since there is no clear distinction in Japan between the purchase method and merger accounting (see chapter 11), a variety of different approaches have been adopted. On balance, it appears that more companies carry forward the assets of the merged companies at their book values. Some companies do, however, revalue assets to fair value – an approach permitted under both the Corporation Tax Law and the Commercial Code. Similarly, the treatment of merger gains or losses varies greatly. Some companies take over retained earnings and keep them intact and others retain only the legal earned reserve of the merged companies. Other companies treat the retained earnings of the merged companies as capital reserves. Retroactive restatements of previous years' financial statements of the combined group to include the operating results of the acquired company for a period prior to the takeover is not acceptable.

Funds flow statements

There is no requirement in Japan to prepare a funds statement in either the Commercial Code or SEL accounts. A statement of changes in financial position is not considered to be one of the basic financial statements and there are no requirements to prepare one as a supplementary schedule. Such a position differs from that prevailing in the UK and US and is not consistent with IAS 7. Although a funds statement is not required, however, a Ministry of Finance Ordinance stipulates that a cash-flow statement should be included in the company's securities report and registration statement, but only as a supplementary statement. Consequently, the statement falls outside the basic financial statements and supplementary schedules and outside the scope of audit.

Consistent with the finding of Campbell (1985, p. 53), our survey found that all 35 listed companies reported the required information in their SEL accounts. However, not one of these companies included the information in its Commercial Code accounts and none of the unlisted companies chose to make such disclosures in its accounts.

The statement required in the SEL accounts is basically a cash statement for the period, commencing with the opening cash balance, listing the major cash receipts and payments and disclosing the closing cash balance.[3] For an example of a cash flow statement see Appendix A. Consequently, the profit for the period is not disclosed and there are no adjustments for items not involving the movement of funds. Only one of the companies disclosed this cash statement in its English version accounts. However, eight of the nine companies preparing English version accounts prepared a statement of changes in financial position consistent with international practice. One is shown in example 13.

Other financial statements

A feature of some of the annual reports of major companies in Europe, North America and Australia is a willingness to reflect changes and developments in international reporting practices. For example, many major European companies produce a value added statement and have in the past produced supplementary statements on price level accounting, and even on transactions with the government as a customer/supplier or money exchanges with the government. Such developments seem to have no impact on Japan. Not one company produced any one of these statements in its Commercial Code, SEL or English version accounts. Furthermore, not one company even mentioned the International Accounting Standards Committee or indeed any of its standards, an approach consistent with US practice. This is not altogether surprising since a feature of Japanese financial accounting is its insularity tempered only by what it sees must be disclosed to comply with US requirements. It appears that the world of financial accounting beyond Japanese and US requirements hardly exists, if at all.

In contrast, Japanese management accounting and management practices are considered to have contributed to the country's economic success. Hiromoto (1988) argues that 'in general Japanese management accounting does not stress optimizing within existing constraints. Rather it encourages employees to make continual improvements by tightening those constraints.' Furthermore, management practices are innovative with respect to physical control and their organization of productive resources (Schonberger, 1982; Hartley, 1987). For example, the Just-In-Time and Kanban materials stock control systems of the Toyota Motor Corporation are often praised, as are other materials management and stock control methods (New and Myers, 1986).

Financial ratios

Whereas earnings per share (EPS) figures have been disclosed by listed companies for many years, not until October 1982 was there a requirement to disclose such information in the Commercial Code and SEL accounts. Earnings per share should be computed based on the weighted-average number of shares outstanding during the year, although the effect of dilution caused by a free share distribution is not to be taken into consideration.

EXAMPLE 13

NEC Corporation   31 March 1988

Consolidated statement of changes in financial position

| | Year ended March 31 | | | |
	1986 (¥m)	1987 (¥m)	1988 (¥m)	1988 (US $000)
Financial resources were provided by:				
Net income	27,185	15,034	25,363	204,540
Add (deduct) income charges (credits) not affecting working capital—				
Depreciation	161,615	156,048	162,407	1,309,733
Provision for severance indemnities, less payments	6,079	4,283	13,727	110,702
Provision (reversal) for other accruals	5,278	(8,164)	10,270	82,823
Minority shareholders' equity in net income	1,936	842	1,869	15,073
Deferred income taxes, non-current	10,774	795	(6,897)	(55,621)
Equity in earnings of affiliated companies, less dividends	(5,867)	(981)	(4,386)	(35,371)
Decrease in long-term receivables, trade	1,621	9,121	524	4,226
Working capital provided by operations	208,621	176,978	202,877	1,636,105
Increase in long-term debt	87,198	214,615	71,002	572,597
Reduction of property, plant and equipment, less accumulated depreciation	24,845	33,079	43,408	350,065
Share conversion of debentures	11,616	15,752	61,767	498,121
Change in interest in subsidiaries and affiliated companies	937	334	5,396	43,516
Increase in minority shareholders' equity	4,040	155	3,475	28,024
Total	337,257	440,913	387,925	3,128,428
Financial resources were used for:				
Increase (decrease) in non-current marketable securities, investments and advances	5,371	(27,567)	14,011	112,992
Additions to property, plant and equipment	293,293	193,623	249,987	2,016,024
Decrease in long-term debt	93,503	109,190	152,543	1,230,186
Cash dividends	12,444	12,629	13,062	105,338
Other, net	9,573	13,689	4,722	38,081
	414,184	301,564	434,325	3,502,621
Changes in exchange rates	(6,742)	(4,130)	(3,570))	(28,790)
Total	407,442	297,434	430,755	3,473,831
Increase (decrease) in working capital	(70,185)	143,479	(42,830)	(345,403)
Changes in components of working capital				
Increase (decrease) in current assets:				
Cash and time deposits	16,671	121,389	(15,948)	(128,613)
Marketable securities	(227,035)	3,803	(31,375)	(253,024)
Notes and accounts receivable, trade	(5,546)	35,567	60,682	489,371
Inventories	23,459	48,979	51,508	415,387
Income tax prepayments, prepaid expenses and other current assets	(32,317)	(4,276)	5,455	43,992
Total	(224,768)	205,462	70,322	567,113

(Increase) decrease in current liabilities:				
Short-term borrowings and current portion of long-term debt	(31,244)	(9,014)	(10,309)	(83,137)
Notes and accounts payable, trade	109,402	(50,243)	(72,813)	(587,201)
Employees' savings deposits	(6,716)	(5,358)	(9,357)	(75,460)
Accrued taxes on income	89,488	(794)	(17,731)	(142,992)
Other current liabilities	(6,347)	3,426	(2,942)	(23,726)
Total	154,583	(61,983)	(113,152)	(912,516)
Increase (decrease) in working capital	70,185	143,479	(42,830)	(345,403)

Common stock equivalents such as convertible bonds and warrant bonds should also be ignored. Table 12.9 shows the disclosure of EPS and other ratios in Japanese corporate reports.

In the SEL and English version accounts it is common to disclose gross profit percentages, operating profit as a percentage of sales, and an occasional balance sheet ratio. Disclosure of accounting ratios is more common in Swedish corporate annual reports than in Japanese accounts.

Table 12.9 Disclosure of accounting ratios

	CC	SEL	Eng.
Number of companies	48	35	9
Disclosures	(%)	(%)	(%)
EPS figure	94	100	78
Method of EPs calculation	94	100	78
Return on capital employed	0	0	0
Return on shareholders' equity	0	0	0
Interest coverage	0	0	0
Other ratios	4	97	89

Summary

The difficulty encountered in obtaining the accounts of Japanese companies reinforced our belief in the cultural characteristic of secrecy rather than transparency. Indeed, the number of corporate reports collected was achieved only through assurances that in certain cases the accounting figures were not disclosed and in others by assurances that company names would not be revealed. One company enclosed a letter with its corporate report specifying that all information published in the financial statements should be considered secret.

The empirical work undertaken resulted in our drawing the following main conclusions.

1   Features of the Commercial Code accounts include a low level of disclosure, flexibility in measurement practices and the provision of information in related schedules that need not be sent to shareholders.

2   Companies treat the Commercial Code accounts as compliance documents since levels of disclosure fulfil the minimum requirements of the law. We found that there is no statistically significant association between quotation status and the extent of disclosure, financial statements being prepared in accordance with the law and the company's articles of association. Voluntary corporate disclosure is not common.

3   There is a significant difference between the extent of disclosure in the Commercial Code accounts and the SEL accounts. This is not surprising since minimum levels of disclosure required by the SEL are higher than those required by the Commercial Code. However, the SEL accounts are not distributed to shareholders although they are available for scrutiny at the company's head office.

4   Changes in accounting policies made by companies are made clear in the SEL accounts but such statements are not so evident in the Commercial Code financial statements.

5   When valuing inventories the cost method is used more often than the lower of cost and market value rule. Cost was usually determined using monthly moving average or weighted average cost. Over time the lower of cost and market value rule is becoming more acceptable.

6   Disclosure of the accounting policy with respect to contracted work-in-progress was high but it was much lower in the Commercial Code accounts.

7   Whilst the general level of disclosure of fixed assets and depreciation was high it was noticeable that less information was included in English version accounts.

8   Disclosure of research and development costs and the amortization period was non-existent in the Commercial Code accounts; in the SEL and English version financial statements disclosure was high.

9   Deferred taxation is not normally practised in Japan, mainly because taxable profits are based on accounting profits. Deferred taxation is sometimes provided for in the supplementary consolidated financial statements attached to the SEL accounts and also in the English version accounts where prepared.

10   Whilst taxes were disclosed in the profit and loss account and the balance sheet it was noticeable that the accounting policy was not normally disclosed in the Commercial Code and the SEL accounts.

11   Employees are usually entitled to a lump-sum payment based on the current rate of pay and length of service. In practice, pension schemes are not

fully funded but recently some corporations have decided to change to a partly funded approach.

12   Although there have not been any requirements in Japan to capitalize finance leases, a characteristic not consistent with SSAP 21, FAS 13 and IAS 17, this situation has changed with effect from April 1990. As a consequence Japanese corporations included in our survey did not capitalize finance leases in their financial statements.

13   The main accounts required by the Commercial Code and the SEL are prepared on a company-by-company basis. However, consolidated accounts are prepared by listed companies and attached to the parent company accounts as supplementary information and filed with the Ministry of Finance. Again, Japanese companies treat the supplementary consolidated financial statements as compliance documents.

14   In the consolidated accounts, forming part of the SEL accounts, we found evidence that the criteria for inclusion of companies in the consolidation were often not disclosed.

15   Companies preparing consolidated accounts disclose information on their subsidiaries in excess of the requirement to disclose merely the names of principal subsidiaries.

16   The Accounting Standard on Consolidated Financial Statements states that uniform accounting policies and practices should preferably be followed by a parent and its subsidiaries. It may appear that terms such as 'uniform', 'preferably' and 'consistently' conflict, but in practice the audit reports refer to consistency being applied.

17   The level of disclosure about goodwill was noticeably low.

18   Whilst the equity method of accounting for associated companies has been mandatory since 1 April 1983, a small number of companies used the cost method.

19   When translating foreign currency financial statements, Japanese companies are gradually moving away from the temporal or modified temporal method towards increased consistency with international practice.

20   Inflation accounting is rarely practised in Japan. None of the companies included in our survey prepared such a statement.

21   There is no clear distinction in Japan between the purchase method and merger method when accounting for acquisitions, mergers or business transfers. Practice is mixed between carrying forward assets at their book value and carrying forward assets at their fair value.

22   There is no requirement to prepare a funds statement in either the Commercial Code or the SEL accounts. This applies also to the supplementary schedules. This position differs from the UK, US and IAS 7. However, whilst a funds statement is not required, a Ministry of Finance Ordinance stipulates that a cash-flow statement should be included in the company's securities report and registration statement but only as a sup-

plementary statement referred to as an auxillary statement, i.e. not subject to audit. All companies comply with this requirement.

23   A feature of some annual reports of major companies in Europe, North America and Australia is a willingness to reflect changes and developments in international reporting practices. Consequently, some European companies produce value added statements, price level accounts and even a summary of transactions with the government as a customer/supplier. Such developments seem to have no impact on Japan. There is little innovation in the corporate annual reports of Japanese companies, whereas management accounting practices are considered to be very innovative.

24   From October 1982 all listed companies must disclose earnings per share figures. Japanese companies comply with this requirement and often disclose gross profit percentages, operating profit as a percentage of sales and an occasional balance sheet ratio. The disclosure of information on segmental reporting is noticeably lower in Japan than in the US. Japan has been seeking to amend this situation, however, and in 1988 a ministerial ordinance entitled Segmental Information Disclosure under the Securities and Exchange Law was passed providing for the introduction of segmental accounting[4]. The JICPA has been preparing general rules which would involve the disclosure of segmental information by types of business based on similarity of category, characteristics, manufacturing processes and sales market. The details have not yet been finalized, but the disclosures will go some way to reducing international criticism of this aspect of Japanese financial reporting.

Notes

1 For a review of this survey, see Cooke and Wallace (1989).
2 Note that Kikuya, who has been heavily influenced by his former teacher Fuwa, also advocates current value accounting.
3 Note that US practice (FAS 95) has moved to cash flows, and UK practice (ED 55) is moving in the same direction.
4 The BADC published the Standard for Disclosure of Segmental Information in May 1988 which became effective in April 1990.

13
Conclusions

Compared with the UK, the development of limited liability companies as a form of Japanese business organization was retarded. It was not until the 1860s and 1870s that Japanese corporations began to develop, and even then most lasted for only a short time. However, the Meiji government saw the Western-type company as modern and worthy of promotion, not least because it was believed that it would gain international respect.

In the late nineteenth and early twentieth centuries the *zaibatsu* emerged as a major commercial force. Some of these family-based firms were assisted by government incentives and others emerged as supporters of and supported by the military. Inevitably, the occupation forces after the Second World War sought to purge the *zaibatsu* and distribute their shareholdings more widely. However, they were replaced by the *gurupu* and *keiretsu*. The *gurupu* are similar in many ways to the *zaibatsu* although they are not family-controlled. In effect they are 'headless' groups with interlocking directorships, and reciprocal shareholdings centred around core companies including banks, trusts, insurance companies and trading companies. Such groups are characteristic of Japan in many ways – no ultimate authority, no main board of directors, no mastermind, no 'Japan Inc.' Instead, each corporate president meets with other *gurupu* members, in their capacity as share owners, at presidential council meetings to discuss investment plans, joint ventures and other areas of mutual interest. Each major member of a *gurupu* forms the apex of a vertical *keiretsu*, consisting of subsidiaries, suppliers, subcontractors and distributors all of whom are associated with a particular major manufacturer.

The nature and extent of information disclosed in corporate annual reports may depend on a number of factors, including enterprise users. Japanese enterprises have a fundamentally different nature from those prevalent in Anglo-Saxon countries, particularly the UK and US. In general, employees in large firms in Japan seem to have much greater access to information concerning the 'corporate family' than in the UK and US. This occurs partly because employees' lives are taken over to a much greater extent than Western companies. The *ringi* system is an effective means of proposals and suggestions which helps to ensure that some degree of participation occurs. Thus, there is less need to communicate information via corporate annual reports or special employee publications. Furthermore, there are no great demands from the unions for information because a considerable degree of apparent harmony exists between management and labour. *Wa* (harmony) within a group has been emphasized and valued in Japanese society. To achieve this harmony it was necessary for employees and the state to neutralize several unions. However, employees are still important to the extent that a company, including its management, is considered to be a family of employees. Thus, an important difference between Japanese and Anglo-Saxon companies is that in Japan the entity is of paramount import- ance whereas in the UK and US directors primarily consider what is in the financial interest of its shareholders. Consequently, Japanese companies pursue strategies of long-term market share and growth – based on develop- ment research, automation and efficiency – whereas Anglo-Saxon corpora- tions often pursue profits and dividends for investors with short-term time horizons.

Historically, Japan had little central government but, rather, factions that fairly regularly disputed power and resorted to war. The Meiji period in the nineteenth century was characterized by a new generation of administrators who set about dismantling the vestiges of feudal rule and tried to Westernize the Japanese economy, stating that 'to maintain equality with foreign nations, words must be made to mean in reality what they claim to signify and the government of the country must enter in a single authority' (Imperial Decree, quoted in Brown, 1955, p. 96). However, the system relied heavily on new administrators such as Toshimichi Okubo and Hirobumi Ito, and once they retired others did not follow to continue the work of strengthening the central administration.

Japan is a one-party parliamentary democracy with a bicameral structure. The Liberal Democratic Party, the ruling party, has been able to shrug off one political scandal after another, even when prime ministers are involved. This is not at all remarkable, however, since the LDP has the support of industrialists, professionals and shopkeepers as well as of those involved in agriculture – and wealth is an important factor in Japanese political life. Once appointed to either the House of Representatives or the House of Councillors politicians concentrate their minds on developing relationships to ensure re-election. Stability is provided by the bureaucracy within those ministries which between them actually run the country. Therefore, an important difference between Japan and Britain is that the politicians in Japan generally concentrate on elections and their extracurricular activities, whereas in Britain they try to run the country as well.

Great ethical worth is placed on Confucian values, not because Confucius was reported to have been an accountant in a grain store for part of his life, but, rather, for his moral teaching which emphasizes concepts such as respect, loyalty and obedience. Furthermore, great value is placed on education – in common with other Sino-culture countries such as China, Hong Kong, Korea, Singapore and Taiwan. The present system of education in Japan was introduced after the Second World War and is egalitarian and co-educational, with a national curriculum set by the Ministry of Education. Characteristically, the Ministry states what will be taught, when it will be taught and what textbooks will be used. The *uchi* group (group opposed to the outside world), first developed at kindergarten, moves through the years of schooling together thereby consolidating the group dimension. Collectivism is reinforced at school by, for example, communal participation by both teachers and pupils in serving lunch and cleaning the school premises.

There is considerable pressure to do well at school and in examinations since securing a place at a 'good' university can often determine one's standard of living for a lifetime. It is this pressure that leads to a breakdown in the concept of equality of opportunity; Japan abounds with private tutoring systems. The financial burden of supplementary education is one factor contributing to Japan's high propensity to save, and inevitably the expense means that a wealthy elite is separated off at a very early age. There is, of course, nothing unique in this. A feature of the Japanese educational system is that it appears to be effective in teaching the whole of the ability range. Whereas less than 10 per cent of the population in England and Wales go on to a sixth-form education, the comparable figure in Japan is about 95 per cent.

Another aspect of Japanese society is that it is male-dominated, with the great divide between males and females beginning at the age of 18. About 75 per cent of university students are men, often studying engineering or business; home economics and education are considered appropriate for girls to take at junior college or university. Thus, girls are preparing themselves for their role in Japanese society – marriage, looking after the home and bringing up and – most important – fostering the education of their children. Such ideas are, however, gradually changing.

The value of the hierarchical system in business and the duality of employment make the desire for a good education at times overwhelming. The hierarchical system is based on a form of patronage in which a senior person helps the junior's career and in turn the young person offers loyalty. Duality of employment exists because of the important dichotomy between large and small firms. Employees in large firms normally form part of the lifetime employment system, in which not only is security of employment virtually guaranteed but also salaries and perquisites well exceed those of the small-firm sector. Employees in the small-firm sector offer considerable flexibility to the Japanese economy since they are often members of family-run businesses that act as subcontractors to large companies. Such family businesses grow during periods of economic prosperity and serve as a flexible source of cheap labour. During economic downtowns they fold (Japan has a high insolvency rate), but often re-emerge in another manufacturing guise, thus providing economic flexibility.

Bureaucratic control over many aspects of Japanese life extends, not surprisingly, to accounting. The post-war accounting regulatory framework imposed by the US was quickly adapted to the needs of society, i.e. control was taken over by the state. Within a few months of the departure of the occupation forces in 1953, the administration began changing the nature of accounting regulation that had been imposed. The Securities Exchange Commission was abolished and its responsibilities subsumed by the Ministry of Finance, the JICPA was incorporated into the system by giving it a voice (admittedly only a small role in assisting the development of accounting standards), and the independent Investigation Committee on Business Accounting Systems became an advisory body to the Ministry of Finance rather than an independent organization. As a result legal influences are extremely important in Japanese financial reporting. The cultural explanation for this might be that collectivism is a more pronounced Japanese characteristic than individualism and so statutory control is preferred to independent professional judgement. On the other hand, a highly competitive, examination-orientated environment, followed by fierce competition to obtain a place with a large firm, places emphasis on the individual and not on the group. These seemingly contradictory features are replete throughout society but the Japanese choose not to see such external contradictions.[1] For example, it is perfectly acceptable and not considered contradictory for an individual to choose a Christian or Shinto wedding and a Buddhist burial. Such diversity contrasts with Western monotheism. Further, reciprocity 'is a universal characteristic of social interaction, particularly important in long-term relations' (Hendry, 1987, p. 203) but such a concept, according to the Japanese should not be applied to international trade as it 'would mean changing laws to accept foreign systems that may not suit our culture' (Buruma, 1987, quoting Akio Morita of the Sony Corporation). Such internal contradictions have spurred some authors, including accounting authors, to offer a dynamic explanation for the co-existence of both individual and collective responsibility and of co-operation and competition. The fact is, however, that an aspect of culture is being carefully selected to fulfil the requirements of a particular occasion – for in Japan reality often differs from the façade.

Statutory control rather than professionalism meets the needs of Japanese industry because a large thriving independent professional sector might be somewhat destabilizing. A large body of highly qualified professionals having job mobility might go against the principle of company loyalty and, furthermore, organized professional bodies could become politically powerful. Consequently, the state exercises control over both the accountancy and legal professions. Examinations are set and regulated by the state, with pass rates so low that Japan has only 8,474 qualified CPAs (at 1 February 1990) and about 14,000 qualified lawyers. This compares with about 140,000 qualified accountants in the UK and about 322,000 in the US. Fee schedules for CPAs are fixed by negotiation between the JICPA and Keidanren, which represents the large corporations, but the two sides are not equally matched so that audit fees are kept at a relatively low level. As a result of the low number of qualified accountants their work is generally restricted to the CPA audit, a form of audit which fits somewhat uneasily with Japanese culture since the audit stresses professional independence whereas Japanese culture emphasizes interdependence and reciprocal relationships. That the independent audit was ever extended to cover large unlisted corporations might seem somewhat surprising, particularly as Keidanren opposed such a move, but major bankruptcies (such as Sanyo Special Steel in 1965) and the emergence of dubious financial dealings involving politicians proved decisive. In addition to the independent audit all companies are subject to scrutiny by statutory auditors, whose functions have been described as perfunctory and ceremonial (Arpan and Radebaugh, 1985, p. 27).

Consistent with state control of accounting in Japan is the requirement to be uniform rather than flexible in the extent of disclosure of information. The Commercial Code and the Securities and Exchange Law stipulate the format for financial statements, the schedules that should accompany such statements and the content of the business report. However, flexibility does exist in the area of measurement, where options exist which permit alternatives and therefore judgement. Gray (1988) argues that uniformity is consistent with concern for law and order and rigid codes of behaviour.

Another aspect of Japanese accounting is that it is conservative rather than optimistic. For example, assets may not be revalued upwards and legal earned reserves must be provided for. Conservatism stems from the Commercial Code 1899, which was largely influenced by Germany, which in turn had been influenced by France. Whilst conservatism applies to the measurement dimension secrecy applies to disclosure. Despite having one of the world's largest stock market our empirical work found that levels of disclosure in corporate annual reports were noticeably lower than in many European nations, such as Sweden and the UK, and the US. The Commercial Code accounts which are sent to shareholders – sometimes without accompanying schedules – constitute little more than a pamphlet with minimum levels of disclosure. Furthermore, we found no significant difference between unlisted and listed companies in the extent of disclosure in the Commercial Code accounts. More extensive disclosure is provided in the Securities and Exchange Law (SEL) accounts but these are not distributed to shareholders and are produced by listed companies only for filing with the Ministry of Finance. These accounts may, however, be scrutinized at the company's head office and copies may be ordered through many bookshops. With two sets of accounts – and sometimes three, as some listed companies produce an English set of accounts – the reader is faced with a rather confusing situation. It would seem eminently sensible for there to be one set of accounts, aimed at current investors, general investors and creditors, available to anyone at the head office. Regrettably, Japanese companies, listed as well as unlisted, are often reluctant to supply financial statements as they like to keep them as secretive as possible.

Our research found that the extent of disclosure in the SEL accounts did not differ significantly between those with a domestic listing only and those with at least one overseas quotation. Furthermore, there was no significant difference in the extent of disclosure between large listed companies on the Tokyo Stock Exchange (1st section) and smaller listed corporations (2nd section). Thus, we conclude that Japanese financial reporting is characterized by secrecy, uniformity and compliance with the regulations.

It may appear odd that secrecy is a characteristic in a country with one of the largest stock markets in the world in terms of both turnover and market capitalization. Historically, secrecy has always been a feature, particularly with the *zaibatsu*, who had no need for external finance and were therefore able to keep information private. The occupation forces after the Second World War attempted to provide a change in direction by disbanding the *zaibatsu*, extending share ownership and imposing more extensive disclosure requirements in the Securities and Exchange Law, aimed at protecting investors. However, secrecy remains a characteristic which is not considered to be incompatible or contradictory with limited liability status.

This book has also considered why Japanese equities have such high market prices relative to those of most other industrial countries. Whilst we did not provide any definitive answers we highlighted what we consider to be important factors – ranging from economic reasons to accounting explanations. Economic factors include a high savings ratio, low long-term interest rates, and expansionary industrial production and real money supply. Whilst accounting adjustments help explain some of the differences between the US and Japan, many of these manipulations would not be necessary when comparing Japanese price–earnings ratios with those that prevail in Germany, particularly with respect to the conservative nature of accounting. Interlocking shareholders and directorships and the fact that dividend payments to shareholders are very low must also be taken into consideration. The effect of interlocking shareholdings is that somewhere between 45 and 75 per cent of the shares on the Tokyo Stock Exchange are held for long-term purposes to enhance business relationships and are not actively traded. Of particular importance is the fact that consistently high economic growth rates compared with other OECD countries provides a confidence and belief in Japanese business. Such confidence also exists in other Far Eastern countries, such as South Korea and Taiwan, where price–earnings ratios are similar to those in Japan.

In terms of detailed aspects of financial reporting in Japan, the traditional form of presentation of financial statements is on an individual company basis. Indeed, the requirements of both the Commercial Code and the SEL stipulate that the individual company basis should be used, although in the SEL accounts supplementary consolidated financial statements should be attached.

Our empirical work was based on a survey of accounts. Our sample consisted of 48 companies which prepared Commercial Code accounts, of which 35 were listed companies and therefore prepared SEL accounts, and nine of the listed companies produced a third set of accounts in English. These English version accounts are not translations of either the Commercial Code or SEL accounts but represent an entirely separate annual report designated for the international reader. As well as the findings already reported our survey found the following. (These are listed and discussed at greater length at the end of the preceding chapter.)

1 A significant difference between the extent of disclosure in the Commercial Code accounts and the SEL accounts.
2 Changes in accounting policies were made clear in the SEL accounts but were not so evident in the Commercial Code accounts.
3 Inventories have traditionally been valued at cost, but it appears that over time the lower cost and market value rule is becoming more acceptable.
4 Deferred taxation is not normally practised in Japan.
5 Employees are usually entitled to a lump-sum payment based on current rates of pay and length of service. In practice, pension schemes are not fully funded.
6 New regulations introduced in 1988 require companies either to capitalize finance leases or disclose the information in the notes to the accounts.
7 In the consolidated accounts we found evidence that the criteria for inclusion of companies in the accounts were often not disclosed.
8 Consolidated accounts disclose more information about subsidiaries than is required.
9 Inflation accounting is rarely practised in Japan.
10 International developments, such as value added statements, seem to have had no impact on financial reporting in Japan. The lack of innovation in financial reporting is in stark contrast to companies' innovatory management accounting procedures.

11 Historically segmental information disclosure has been poorer in Japan than in the US.

Our appraisal of financial reporting in Japan leads us to the conclusion that there have been few internal pressures to extend the disclosure of information in corporate annual reports. Employees and long-term investors have access to inside information so that in reality the small investor, as in the UK, has effectively been disenfranchised. Management of the major corporations emanates from the employee ranks, cross-shareholdings ensure support for management and major companies accept the status quo of mutual existence and co-operate with the government. External pressures can be important, particularly as Japan is sensitive to international criticism.

The role of big businesses in Japan is of fundamental importance since they are central to achieving economic success and they have had to be conscious of the national purpose and support the government at all times (Morishima, 1982, p. 122). Indeed, it may appear that there is an overwhelming interrelationship between the LDP, the bureaucrats and big business, with no central power, little accountability and full of contradiction. Consequently, there is no autocratic leader but, rather, a political system in which recalcitrant members are forced to act in a way that ensures that the system remains intact. Support by business for the LDP party has been rewarded with tax concessions in the form of allocations to reserves and allowable expenses, provided they are entered in the books of account. Fiscal incentives include depreciation, accelerated depreciation, amortization of deferred assets and the use of provisions and reserves. Such incentives together with administrative guidance serve to encourage companies to conform to the government viewpoint.

Japanese economic success in the 1960s was built on protectionism: high tariff barriers, extensive import quotas and strict controls on capital movements. In addition, the household sector has consistently had a high savings ratio – mainly to fund education, housing and retirement – which meant that there were sufficient domestic resources for a high level of corporate investment. The overt forms of protectionism have now gone but as Japan has continued to be successful trade friction, particularly with the US, has developed. To counter such criticisms Japanese corporations have diversified geographically with heavy investment in the US and Europe. In the future more investment is likely to be made in Europe but spread more evenly within the European Community in order to reduce problems of inter-country rivalry which could lead to one country opposing such incursions in general. Cultural excuses no longer seem appropriate since Japan has demonstrated that it can produce high-quality mass-produced goods at affordable prices better than most other industrialized countries.

Note

1 For an interesting discussion of contradictions in Japanese life – and indeed patterns of Japanese culture – see Ruth Benedict's controversial book *The Chrysanthemum and the Sword* (1946).

References and Further Reading

Al Hashim, D. (1980) Regulation of financial accounting: an international perspective, *The International Journal of Accounting Education and Research*, Fall.

Alletzhauser, A. (1990) *The House of Nomura*. London: Bloomsbury.

Alston, J. P. (1986) *The American Samurai*. Berlin: Walter de Gruyter.

Amaya, A. (1980) The ethic of harmony and the logic of the Antimonopoly Law. *Bungei Shunju*, 176, December.

Ames, W. L. (1981) *Police and Community in Japan*. London: Routledge and Kegan Paul.

Arpan, J. S. and Radebaugh, L. H. (1985) *International Accounting and Multinational Enterprises*. New York: John Wiley.

Ballon, R. J. (1979) A lesson from Japan: contract, control, and authority. *Journal of Contemporary Business*.

Ballon, R. J., Tomita, I. and Usami, H. (1976) *Financial Reporting in Japan*. Tokyo: Kodansha International.

Barrett, M. E. (1976) Disclosure and comprehensiveness in an international setting. *Journal of Accounting Research*, 14 (1), Spring.

Barrett, M. E. (1977) The extent of disclosure in annual reports of large companies in seven countries. *The International Journal of Accounting Education and Research*, 12 (2), Spring.

Bavishi, V. B. (1989) *International Accounting and Auditing Trends*. Stoors, Conn: Center for Transnational Accounting and Financial Research, School of Business Administration, University of Connecticut.

Baxter, W. T. (1976) Accounting in Japan. *The Accountant's Magazine*, November.

Benedict, R. (1946) *The Chrysanthemum and the Sword*. London: Routledge and Kegan Paul, 1967 edn.

Bernstein, M. H. (1955) *Regulating Business by Independent Commission*. Princeton University Press.

Biddle, G. and Sandagaram, S. (1989) The effects of financial disclosure levels on firms' choices among alternative foreign stock exchange listings. *Journal of International Financial Management and Accounting*, 1 (1), Spring.

Bloom, R. and Naciri, M. A. (1989) Accounting standard setting and culture: a comparative analysis of the United States, Canada, England, West Germany, Australia, New Zealand, Sweden, Japan, and Switzerland. *The International Journal of Accounting*, 24 (1).

Boughton, S. (1988) *Great Lives*. London: Grisewood and Dempsey.

Brown, D. (1955) *Nationalism in Japan*. University of California Press.

Brown, R. (1963) *Explanation in Social Science*. Chicago: Aldine Publishing.

Buruma, I. (1987) '*We Japanese*', New York Review of Books.

Buzby, S. L. (1975) Company size, listed v unlisted stock and extent of financial disclosure. *Journal of Accounting Research*, 13 (1), Spring.

Campbell, L. G. (1983) Current accounting practices in Japan. *The Accountant's Magazine*, August.

Campbell, L. G. (1985) *Accounting and Financial Reporting in Japan*. London: Lafferty Publications.

Cairns, D. (1984) What is wrong with Japanese reporting? *International Accounting Bulletin*, March, 18–19.

Cairns, D., Lafferty, M. and Mantle, P. (1984) *Survey of Accounts and Accountants 1983–84*. London: Lafferty Publications.

Choi, F. D. S. (1973) Financial disclosure and entry to the European capital market. *Journal of Accounting Research*, 11 (2), Autumn.

Choi, F. D. S. and Hiramatsu, K. (eds) (1987) *Accounting and Financial Reporting in Japan*. Wokingham: Van Nostrand.

Choi, F. D. S. and Mueller, G. G. (1978) *An Introduction to Multinational Accounting*. Englewood Cliffs, NJ: Prentice Hall.

Choi, F. D. S. and Mueller, G. G. (1984) *International Accounting*. New York: Prentice Hall.

Clark, R. G. (1979) *The Japanese Company*. London: Yale University Press.

Cooke, T. E. (1986) *Mergers and Acquisitions*. Oxford: Basil Blackwell.

Cooke, T. E. (1988a) (in conjunction with Arthur Young International) *International Mergers and Acquisitions*. Oxford: Basil Blackwell.

Cooke, T. E. (1988b) *European Financial Reporting: Sweden*. London: ICAEW.

Cooke, T. E. (1989) *An Empirical Study of Financial Disclosure by Swedish Companies*. New York: Garland Publishing.

Cooke, T. E. and Wallace, R. S. O. (1989) Global surveys of corporate disclosure practices and audit firms: a review essay. *Accounting and Business Research*, 20 (77).

Cooke, T. E. and Wallace, R. S. O. (1990) Financial disclosure regulation and its environment: a review and further analysis. *Journal of Accounting and Public Policy*, 9 (2), Summer.

Cross, M. (1989) The fifth generation of computer illiterates. *Computer Weekly*, 15 June, 26.

Cummings, W. K. (1980) *Education and Equality in Japan*. Princeton University Press.

Dai-Ichi Kango Bank (DKB) (1989) *Economic Report*, 19 (9), September.

Dale, P. N. (1986) *The Myth of Japanese Uniqueness*. London: Croom Helm.

Deloitte, Haskins and Sells (1985) *Taxation in Japan*. New York: Deloitte, Haskins and Sells.

Dore, R. P. (1971) *City Life in Japan*. Berkeley: University of California Press.

Dore, R. P. (1973) *British Factory – Japanese Factory. The Origins of National Diversity in Industrial Relations.* London: George Allen and Unwin.

Evans, T. G., Taylor, M. E. and Holzmann, O. (1985) *International Accounting and Reporting.* New York: Macmillan.

Farmer, R. and Richman, B. (1966) *International Business: An Operational Theory.* Homewood, Ill: Irwin.

Firth, M. A. (1979) The impact of size, stock market listing and auditors on voluntary disclosure in corporate annual reports. *Accounting and Business Research*, 9 (36), Autumn.

Firth, M. A. (1981) The relative information content of the release of financial results data by firms. *Journal of Accounting Research*, 19 (2), Autumn.

Franklin, G. (1988) *Japanese Price–Earnings Ratios.* London: UBS Phillips and Drew.

Fujita, Y. (1966) The evolution of financial reporting in Japan. *The International Journal of Accounting Education and Research*, Fall.

Fukui, H. (1981) Bureaucratic power in Japan. In P. Drysdale and H. Kitaoji (eds), *Japan and Australia: Two Societies and their Interaction.* Canberra: Australian National University Press.

Futatsugi, Y. (1986) *Japanese Enterprise Groups.* Monograph No. 4. Kobe: School of Business Administration, Kobe University.

Gold, S. (1988) Inside a Japanese university. *Japan Update*, 6, Winter.

Gomi, Y. (1989) *Guide to Japanese Taxes.* Tokyo: Zaikei Shoho Sha.

Gray, S. J. (1988) Towards a theory of cultural influence on the development of accounting systems. *Abacus*, March.

Gray, S. J., with L. G. Campbell and J. C. Shaw (1984) *International Financial Reporting in 30 Countries.* London: Macmillan.

Haley, J. O. (1982) Unsheathing the sword: law without sanctions. *Journal of Japanese Studies*, 8 (2).

Hadley, E. M. (1970) *Antitrust in Japan.* Princeton University Press.

Harrison, G. L. and McKinnon, J. L. (1986) Culture and accounting change: a new perspective on corporate reporting regulation and accounting policy formulation. *Accounting, Organizations and Society*, 11 (3).

Hartley, J. (1987) *Fighting the Recession in Manufacturing.* Bedford: IFS.

Havens, R. H. (1978) *Valley of Darkness: The Japanese People and World War Two.* London: Norton.

Hendry, J. (1987) *Understanding Japanese Society.* London: Croom Helm.

Hiromoto, T. (1988) Another hidden edge – Japanese management accounting. *Harvard Business Review*, July/Aug.

Hodder, J. E. and Tschoeg, A. E. (1985) Some aspects of Japanese corporate finance. *Journal of Financial and Quantitative Analysis*, June.

Hofstede, G. (1984) *Culture's Consequences.* Beverly Hills: Sage Publications.

Holzer, H. P. and 22 others (1984) *International Accounting.* New York: Harper and Row.

Hopwood, A. G. (ed.) (1989) *International Pressures for Accounting Change.* Hemel Hempstead: Prentice Hall.

Horie, Y. (1966) The role of the IE in the economic modernization of Japan. *Kyoto Economic Review*, April.

Ishida, T. (1964) Pressure groups in Japan. *Journal of Social and Political Ideas in Japan*, December.

Ishizumi, K. (1988) *Acquiring Japanese Companies*. Tokyo: The Japan Times.

JICPA (1984) *Corporate Disclosure in Japan – Reporting*. Tokyo: JICPA.

JICPA (1987a) *Corporate Disclosure in Japan – Overview*. Tokyo: JICPA.

JICPA (1987b) *Corporate Reporting in Japan – Accounting*. Tokyo: JICPA.

JICPA (1987c) *Corporate Reporting in Japan – Auditing*. Tokyo: JICPA.

JICPA (1987d) *CPA Profession in Japan*. Tokyo: JICPA.

Kaplan, D. and Manners, R. A. (1972) *Culture Theory*. Englewood Cliffs, NJ: Prentice Hall.

Katsuyama, S. (1976) Recent problems of the financial accounting system in Japan. *The International Journal of Accounting*, Fall, 121–32.

Kikuya, M. (1989) Comparative analysis of Japanese accounting standards with International Accounting Standards. *The Accounting Research*, 33, (Chuo University).

Kikuya, M. (1990) International environment and Japanese accounting regulations. *Bulletin of Japanese Association for International Accounting Studies*.

Kono, T. (1984) Long range planning of UK and Japanese corporations – a competitive study. *Long Range Planning*, 17 (2), April.

KPMG Peat Marwick Minato (1987) *Banking in Japan*. Tokyo: KPMG.

Lebra, T. S. (1976) *Japanese Patterns of Behaviour*. Honolulu: University Press of Hawaii.

Lincoln, E. J. (1988) *Japan Facing Economic Maturity*. Washington, DC: The Brookings Institution.

Low, A. (1976) *Zen and Creative Management*. New York: Anchor Books.

Macharzina, K. (1985) Financial reporting in West Germany. In C. W. Nobes and R. H. Parker (eds), *Comparative International Accounting*. Deddington, Oxford: Philip Allan Publishers.

McKinnon, J. L. (1984) Application of Anglo-American principles of consolidation to corporate financial disclosure in Japan. *Abacus*, 20 (1).

McKinnon, J. L. (1986) *The Historical Development and Operational Form of Corporate Reporting Regulation in Japan*. New York: Garland Publishing.

Minami, R. (1986) *The Economic Development of Japan*. Houndmills: Macmillan.

Ministry of Justice Ordinance No. 3, March 1963 (1983) *Regulation Concerning Balance Sheet, Profit and Loss Statement, Business Report, and Annexed Specifications of Kabushiki-Kaisha*. Tokyo: EHS Law Bulletin.

Ministry of Finance Ordinance No. 59, November 1963 (1984a) *Regulation Concerning Terminology, Form and Method of Preparation of Financial Statements, etc.* Tokyo: EHS Law Bulletin.

Ministry of Finance Ordinance No. 28, October 1976 (1984b) *Regulation Concerning Terminology, Form and Method of Preparation of Consolidated Financial Statements*. Tokyo: EHS Law Bulletin.

Morishima, M. (1982) *Why Has Japan Succeeded?*. Cambridge University Press.

Mueller, G. G. (1967) *International Accounting*. New York: Macmillan.

Murase, G. (1950) Accounting in Japan and the new Japanese CPA Law. *Journal of Accountancy*, April.

Nagourney, S. H. (1988a) *Japan – Part 1: The World's Largest Capital Exporter*.

Equity Research Publication. New York: Shearson Lehman Hutton.

Nagourney, S. H. (1988b) *Japan – Part 2: The World's Largest Capital Exporter.* Equity Research Publication. New York: Shearson Lehman Hutton.

Nakajima, S. (1973) Economic growth and financial reporting in Japan. *The International Journal of Accounting,* Fall.

Nakamura, T. (1981) *The Postwar Japanese Economy.* University of Tokyo Press.

Nakane, C. (1970) *Japanese Society.* London: Weidenfeld and Nicolson.

Nakane, C. (1973) *Japanese Society.* Harmondsworth: Pelican (paperback edition of Nakane (1970).

New, C. and Myers, A. (1986) *Managing Manufacturing Operations in the UK: 1975 to 1985.* Bedford: Cranfield Institute of Management.

Nishiyama, T. (1981) *Japan Is Not Capitalist.* Tokyo: M. Kasa Shobo.

Nobes, C. (1985) International classification of financial reporting. In C. W. Nobes and R. H. Parker (eds), *Comparative International Accounting.* Oxford: Philip Allan.

Noda, Y. (1976) *Introduction to Japanese Law.* University of Tokyo Press.

OECD (1982) *Positive Adjustment Policies: Summary and Conclusions.* CPE/PAP.

OECD (1988/89) *Economic Survey: Japan.* Paris: OECD.

Ohkawa, K. and Rosovsky, H. (1973) *Japanese Economic Growth: Trend Accelerator in the Twentieth Century.* Oxford University Press.

Ohtsuka, M. (1981) The effectiveness of accounting information in capital markets: information effect of accounting announcements. *Business Accounting,* January.

Ohno, K., Ichikawa, H. and Kodama, A. (1975) Recent change in accounting standards in Japan. *The International Journal of Accounting,* Fall.

Peat Marwick (1986) *Taxation in Japan.* Tokyo: Peat Marwick.

Perera, M. H. B. (1989) Towards a framework to analyse the impact of culture. *The International Journal of Accounting,* 24 (1).

Price Waterhouse (1983) *Doing Business in Japan.* Tokyo: Price Waterhouse.

Puxty, A. G., Willmott, H. C., Cooper, D. J. and Lowe, T. (1987) Modes of regulation in advanced capitalism: locating accountancy in four countries. *Accounting Organizations and Society,* 12 (3).

Radebaugh, L. H. (1975) Environmental factors influencing the development of accounting objectives, standards and practices in Peru. *The International Journal of Accounting Education and Research,* Fall.

Ramseyer, J. M. (1986) Lawyers, foreign lawyers, and lawyer-substitutes: the market for regulation in Japan. *Harvard International Law Journal,* 27, Special Issue.

Reischauer, E. O. (1988) *The Japanese Today: Change and Continuity.* Tokyo: Charles E. Tuttle.

Roberts, J. G. (1973) *Mitsui.* New York: Weatherhill.

Robins, B. (1987) *Tokyo: A World Financial Centre.* London: Euromoney Publications.

Rohlen, T. P. (1974) *For Harmony and Strength: Japanese White Collar Organization in Anthropological Perspective.* Berkeley: University of California Press.

Rohlen, T. P. (1983) *Japan's High Schools.* Berkeley: University of California Press.

Sakakibara, S., Yamaji, H., Sakurai H., Shiroshita K. and Fukuda, S. (1988) *The Japanese Stock Market.* Westport, Conn: Praeger.

Sakurai, H. (1986) The information content of annual accounting information and market reaction to its announcement: empirical research on the Tokyo Stock Exchange. *Accounting*, 129 (3).

Sanders, T. H., Hatfield, H. R. and Moore, U. (1938) *A Statement of Accounting Principles*. New York: American Institute of Accountants.

Schonberger, R. (1982) *Japanese Manufacturing Techniques*. New York: Free Press.

Smith, R. J. (1984) *Japanese Society: Tradition, Self and the Social Order*. Cambridge University Press.

Smithers, A. (1987) *A Look at Fundamental Values in the Japanese Market and the Impact of Foreign Shareholders*. London: Warburg Securities, August.

Smithers, A. (1989a) *Fundamental Value in the Japanese Market*. London: Warburg Securities, 15 May.

Smithers, A. (1989b) *Return to Normality*. London: Warburg Securities, 26 September.

Steiner, K. and Steiner, F. (1981) *Political Opposition and Local Politics in Japan*. Princeton University Press.

Stigler, G. J. (1971) The theory of economic regulation. *Bell Journal of Economics and Management Science*, Fall, 3–21.

Stilling, P., Norton, R. and Hopkins, L. (1984) *World Accounting Survey*. London: Financial Times.

Stockwin, J. A. A. (1982) *Japan: Divided Politics in a Growth Economy*. London: Weidenfeld and Nicolson.

Sumiya, M. (1981) Reconstruction of the theory of Japanese labour relations. *Nihon Rodo Kyokai Zasshi*, 262, January.

Suzuki, Y. (1981) Why is the performance of the Japanese economy so much better? *Journal of Japanese Studies*.

Takatera, S. and Daigo, S. (1989) The impact of international pressures on Japanese accounting: a critical perspective on the emergent issues. In A. Hopwood (ed.), *International Pressures for Accounting Change*. Englewood Cliffs, NJ: Prentice Hall.

Takatera, S. and Yamamoto, M. (1987) The cultural significance of accounting in Japan. Paper presented at European Institute for Advanced Studies in Management, Brussels, December.

Takayanagi, K. (1963) A century of innovation: the development of Japanese law, 1868–1961. In A. T. von Mehren (ed.), *Law In Japan – the Legal Order in a Changing Society*. Cambridge, Mass: Harvard University Press.

Tarullo, D. K. (1986) The structure of US–Japan trade relations. *Harvard International Law Journal*, 27, Special Issue.

Tokutani, M. and Kawano, M. (1978) A note on the Japanese social accounting literature. *Accounting, Organizations and Society*.

Tokyo Stock Exchange (1984) *Listing Regulations of the Tokyo Stock Exchange*. Tokyo Stock Exchange.

Tokyo Stock Exchange (1986a) *Business Regulations of the Tokyo Stock Exchange*. Tokyo Stock Exchange.

Tokyo Stock Exchange (1986b) *Constitution of the Tokyo Stock Exchange*. Tokyo Stock Exchange.

Tokyo Stock Exchange (1986 to 1989) *Fact Book*. Tokyo Stock Exchange.

Tonkin, D. J. (1989) *World Survey of Published Accounts: An analysis of 200 Annual*

Reports from the World's Leading Companies. London: Lafferty Publications.

Uesugi, A. (1986) Japan's cartel system and its impact on international trade. *Harvard International Law Journal*, 27, Special Issue.

Upham, F. K. (1986) The legal framework of Japan's declining industries policy: the problem of transparency in administrative processes. *Harvard International Law Journal*, 27, Special Issue.

van Wolferen, K. (1989) *The Enigma of Japanese Power*. London: Macmillan.

Vogel, E. F. (1975) *Modern Japanese Organization and Decision-making*. Berkeley: University of California Press.

Wakiyama, T. (1986) The nature and tools of Japan's industrial policy. *Harvard International Law Journal*, 27, Special Issue.

Waldmeir, P. (1989) Japanese financial markets: walls improve view from abroad. *Financial Times*, 13 March.

Appendix A
Extracts from the English Version Accounts of Hitachi Ltd and its Consolidated Subsidiaries: Year Ended 31 March 1991*

Independent Auditors' Report

KPMG Peat Marwick

The Board of Directors
Hitachi, Ltd.:

We have audited the accompanying consolidated balance sheets (expressed in yen) of Hitachi, Ltd. and subsidiaries as of March 31, 1991 and 1990, and the related consolidated statements of income, surplus and cash flows for each of the years in the three-year period ended March 31, 1991. These consolidated financial statements are the responsibility of the Company's management. Our responsibility is to express an opinion on these consolidated financial statements based on our audits.

We conducted our audits in accordance with generally accepted auditing standards. Those standards require that we plan and perform the audit to obtain reasonable assurance about whether the financial statements are free of material misstatement. An audit includes examining, on a test basis, evidence supporting the amounts and disclosures in the financial statements. An audit also includes assessing the accounting principles used and significant estimates made by management, as well as evaluating the overall financial statement presentation. We believe that our audits provide a reasonable basis for our opinion.

The segment information required to be disclosed in financial statements under United States generally accepted accounting principles is not presented in the accompanying consolidated financial statements. Foreign issuers are presently exempted from such disclosure requirement in Securities and Exchange Act filings with the United States Securities and Exchange Commission.

In our opinion, except for the omission of the segment information discussed in the preceding paragraph, the consolidated financial statements referred to above present fairly, in all material respects, the financial position of Hitachi, Ltd. and subsidiaries at March 31, 1991 and 1990, and the results of their operations and their cash flows for each of the years in the three-year period ended March 31, 1991 in conformity with United States generally accepted accounting principles.

The accompanying consolidated financial statements as of and for the year ended March 31, 1991 have been translated into United States dollars solely for the convenience of the reader. We have reviewed the translation and, in our opinion, the consolidated financial statements expressed in yen have been translated into United States dollars on the basis set forth in note 2 of the notes to consolidated financial statements.

KPMG Peat Marwick

KPMG Peat Marwick
Tokyo, Japan
May 20, 1991

*Copyright © Hitachi Ltd, 1991

Consolidated Balance Sheets
Hitachi, Ltd. and Subsidiaries
March 31, 1991 and 1990

Assets	Millions of yen		Thousands of U.S. dollars (note 2)
	1991	1990	1991
Current assets:			
Cash and cash equivalents...	¥1,648,460	¥1,853,734	$11,691,206
Short-term investments (note 3)..	384,909	324,784	2,729,851
Trade receivables, net of allowance for doubtful receivables and unearned income—1991 ¥25,666 million ($182,028 thousand); 1990 ¥23,660 million:			
Notes...	481,258	433,037	3,413,177
Accounts..	1,352,641	1,161,228	9,593,199
Inventories (note 4)..	1,597,129	1,355,007	11,327,156
Prepaid expenses and other current assets (note 10)............................	286,559	263,112	2,032,333
Total current assets..	5,750,956	5,390,902	40,786,922
Noncurrent receivables and restricted funds (note 5)......................	155,680	134,868	1,104,113
Investments and advances, including affiliated companies (note 3).............	420,178	358,736	2,979,986
Property, plant and equipment (note 8):			
Land..	251,755	225,918	1,785,497
Buildings..	1,017,059	872,128	7,213,184
Machinery and equipment...	3,356,157	3,042,851	23,802,532
Construction in progress...	89,474	64,942	634,567
	4,714,445	4,205,839	33,435,780
Less accumulated depreciation	2,728,719	2,496,948	19,352,617
Net property, plant and equipment	1,985,726	1,708,891	14,083,163
Other assets (notes 7 and 10)..	213,581	211,689	1,514,759
	¥8,526,121	¥7,805,086	$60,468,943

See accompanying notes to consolidated financial statements.

	Millions of yen		Thousands of U.S. dollars (note 2)
Liabilities and Stockholders' Equity	1991	1990	1991
Current liabilities:			
Short-term bank loans (note 8)	¥ 861,859	¥ 781,590	$ 6,112,475
Current installments of long-term debt (note 8)	53,056	46,790	376,284
Trade payables:			
Notes	335,938	317,389	2,382,539
Accounts	723,182	611,276	5,128,950
Accrued expenses	587,664	553,679	4,167,830
Income taxes (note 10)	155,717	157,179	1,104,376
Advances received	495,183	434,234	3,511,936
Employees' deposits	125,310	127,864	888,723
Other current liabilities	356,423	284,906	2,527,823
Total current liabilities	3,694,332	3,314,907	26,200,936
Long-term debt (note 8)	891,022	886,798	6,319,305
Retirement and severance benefits (note 9)	520,108	493,955	3,688,709
Total liabilities	5,105,462	4,695,660	36,208,950
Minority interests	609,518	548,591	4,322,823
Stockholders' equity:			
Common stock, ¥50 ($0.35) par value. Authorized 10,000,000,000 shares; issued 3,273,675,718 shares in 1991, and 3,072,846,556 shares in 1990 (notes 8 and 11)	269,747	246,913	1,913,099
Capital surplus	410,381	357,775	2,910,503
Legal reserve (note 12)	66,519	60,021	471,766
Retained earnings (notes 8 and 12)	2,093,902	1,911,144	14,850,369
Foreign currency translation adjustments	(29,408)	(15,018)	(208,567)
Total stockholders' equity	2,811,141	2,560,835	19,937,170
Commitments and contingencies (note 13)			
	¥8,526,121	¥7,805,086	$60,468,943

Consolidated Statements of Income
Hitachi, Ltd. and Subsidiaries
Years ended March 31, 1991, 1990 and 1989

	1991	1990	1989	Thousands of U.S. dollars (note 2) 1991
		Millions of yen		
Net sales (note 5)	¥7,736,961	¥7,077,855	¥6,401,417	$54,872,064
Cost of sales	5,417,159	5,023,533	4,552,089	38,419,568
Gross profit	2,319,802	2,054,322	1,849,328	16,452,496
Selling, general and administrative expenses	1,813,383	1,553,218	1,416,142	12,860,872
Operating income	506,419	501,104	433,186	3,591,624
Other income (note 15):				
Interest	173,692	151,488	118,597	1,231,858
Dividends	9,072	10,829	8,878	64,340
Other	22,153	14,760	15,751	157,114
	204,917	177,077	143,226	1,453,312
Other deductions (note 15):				
Interest and discount charges	129,886	97,047	71,438	921,177
Other	19,377	51,144	13,869	137,426
	149,263	148,191	85,307	1,058,603
Income before income taxes	562,073	529,990	491,105	3,986,333
Income taxes (note 10):				
Current	308,211	313,097	308,799	2,185,894
Deferred	(17,761)	(31,788)	(36,023)	(125,965)
	290,450	281,309	272,776	2,059,929
Income before minority interests	271,623	248,681	218,329	1,926,404
Minority interests	41,438	37,718	32,742	293,886
Net income	¥ 230,185	¥ 210,963	¥ 185,587	$ 1,632,518

	Yen			U.S. dollars (note 2)
Net income per share of common stock (note 1 (j))	¥65.96	¥61.71	¥56.14	$0.47

See accompanying notes to consolidated financial statements.

Consolidated Statements of Surplus

Hitachi, Ltd. and Subsidiaries
Years ended March 31, 1991, 1990 and 1989

		Millions of yen		Thousands of U.S. dollars (note 2)
	1991	1990	1989	1991
Capital surplus (note 11):				
Balance at beginning of year	¥ 357,775	¥ 302,651	¥ 232,865	$ 2,537,411
Conversion of convertible debentures	24,253	38,577	47,900	172,007
Increase arising from sale of subsidiaries' common stock, exercise of warrants and others	28,353	16,547	21,886	201,085
Balance at end of year	¥ 410,381	¥ 357,775	¥ 302,651	$ 2,910,503
Legal reserve (note 12):				
Balance at beginning of year	¥ 60,021	¥ 56,190	¥ 52,705	$ 425,681
Transfers from retained earnings	6,390	4,158	3,615	45,319
Transfers from (to) minority interests arising from conversion of subsidiaries' convertible debentures	3	(105)	(36)	21
Transfers from (to) minority interests arising from sale of subsidiaries' common stock, exercise of warrants and others	105	(222)	(94)	745
Balance at end of year	¥ 66,519	¥ 60,021	¥ 56,190	$ 471,766
Retained earnings (notes 8 and 12):				
Balance at beginning of year	¥1,911,144	¥1,740,285	¥1,590,976	$13,554,213
Net income	230,185	210,963	185,587	1,632,518
Cash dividends	(37,922)	(27,298)	(26,609)	(268,950)
Transfers to legal reserve	(6,390)	(4,158)	(3,615)	(45,319)
Transfers to minority interests arising from conversion of subsidiaries' convertible debentures	(377)	(3,806)	(1,029)	(2,674)
Transfers to minority interests arising from sale of subsidiaries' common stock, exercise of warrants and others	(2,738)	(4,842)	(5,025)	(19,419)
Balance at end of year	¥2,093,902	¥1,911,144	¥1,740,285	$14,850,369
Foreign currency translation adjustments:				
Balance at beginning of year	¥ (15,018)	¥ (36,920)	¥ (38,303)	$ (106,510)
Adjustments during the year	(14,390)	21,902	1,383	(102,057)
Balance at end of year	¥ (29,408)	¥ (15,018)	¥ (36,920)	$ (208,567)

See accompanying notes to consolidated financial statements.

Consolidated Statements of Cash Flows

Hitachi, Ltd. and Subsidiaries
Years ended March 31, 1991, 1990 and 1989

	1991	1990	1989	Thousands of U.S. dollars (note 2) 1991
		Millions of yen		
Cash flows from operating activities (note 17):				
Net income	¥ 230,185	¥ 210,963	¥ 185,587	$ 1,632,518
Adjustments to reconcile net income to net cash provided by operating activities:				
Depreciation	448,124	407,152	366,268	3,178,184
Deferred income taxes	(17,761)	(31,788)	(36,023)	(125,965)
Gain on sale of investments and subsidiaries' common stock	(21,255)	(2,394)	(9,436)	(150,745)
Income applicable to minority interests	41,438	37,718	32,742	293,886
(Increase) in receivables	(213,413)	(314,289)	(107,059)	(1,513,567)
(Increase) in inventories	(258,290)	(83,352)	(114,608)	(1,831,844)
(Increase) in prepaid expenses and other assets	(7,078)	(20,081)	(8,272)	(50,199)
Increase in payables	144,218	138,562	108,790	1,022,823
Increase in accrued expenses and retirement and severance benefits	60,560	102,519	112,733	429,504
Increase (decrease) in accrued income taxes	(1,052)	(33,280)	43,237	(7,461)
Increase in other liabilities	30,735	37,874	31,419	217,979
Other	(7,193)	11,505	10,126	(51,014)
Net cash provided by operating activities	429,218	461,109	615,504	3,044,099
Cash flows from investing activities (note 17):				
(Increase) decrease in short-term investments	(60,125)	60,301	(34,152)	(426,419)
Capital expenditures	(743,399)	(649,812)	(514,930)	(5,272,333)
Proceeds from disposition of rental assets and other property	47,719	58,565	40,245	338,433
Payment for acquisition, net of cash acquired	—	(47,130)	—	—
Proceeds from sale of investments and subsidiaries' common stock	26,271	3,039	20,324	186,319
Purchase of investments and subsidiaries' common stock	(45,745)	(22,559)	(35,420)	(324,433)
Other	(27,619)	(17,093)	(15,860)	(195,879)
Net cash used in investing activities	(802,898)	(614,689)	(539,793)	(5,694,312)
Cash flows from financing activities (note 17):				
Increase (decrease) in short-term borrowings	96,357	(69,601)	12,406	683,383
Proceeds from long-term debt	128,017	450,580	200,295	907,922
Payments on long-term debt	(44,971)	(33,281)	(54,606)	(318,943)
Proceeds from sale of common stock by subsidiaries	46,459	39,173	34,516	329,496
Dividends paid to shareholders	(37,783)	(27,221)	(26,565)	(267,965)
Dividends paid to minority shareholders of subsidiaries	(9,428)	(7,911)	(7,241)	(66,865)
Net cash provided by financing activities	178,651	351,739	158,805	1,267,028
Effect of exchange rate changes on cash and cash equivalents	(10,245)	17,247	(828)	(72,659)
Net increase (decrease) in cash and cash equivalents	(205,274)	215,406	233,688	(1,455,844)
Cash and cash equivalents at beginning of year	1,853,734	1,638,328	1,404,640	13,147,050
Cash and cash equivalents at end of year	¥1,648,460	¥1,853,734	¥1,638,328	$11,691,206

See accompanying notes to consolidated financial statements.

Notes to Consolidated Financial Statements

1. Basis of Presentation and Summary of Significant Accounting Policies

(a) Basis of Presentation
The Company and its domestic subsidiaries maintain their books of account in conformity with the financial accounting standards of Japan, and its foreign subsidiaries in conformity with those of the countries of their domicile.
The consolidated financial statements presented herein have been prepared in conformity with United States generally accepted accounting principles.

(b) Consolidation Policy
The consolidated financial statements include the accounts of the Company and those of its majority-owned subsidiaries, whether directly or indirectly controlled. Intercompany accounts and significant intercompany transactions have been eliminated in consolidation. The investments in affiliated companies are stated at their underlying equity value, and the appropriate portion of the earnings of such companies is included in consolidated income.

(c) Cash and Cash Equivalents
For the purpose of the Statement of Cash Flows, liquid short-term financial instruments with insignificant risk of changes in value which have maturities of generally three months or less when acquired are considered cash equivalents.

(d) Foreign Currency Translation
Foreign currency financial statements have been translated in accordance with Statement of Financial Accounting Standards (SFAS) No. 52 "Foreign Currency Translation." Under this standard, the assets and liabilities of the Company's subsidiaries located outside Japan are translated into Japanese yen at the rates of exchange in effect at the balance sheet date. Income and expense items are translated at the average exchange rates prevailing during the year. Gains and losses resulting from foreign currency transactions are included in other income (deductions), and those resulting from translation of financial statements are excluded from the consolidated statements of income and are accumulated in "Foreign currency translation adjustments."

(e) Short-term Investments and Investments and Advances
The portfolios of marketable equity securities included in short-term investments and in investments and advances are carried at the lower of cost or market. Realized gains or losses are determined by the average method. Other marketable securities classified as current assets, principally securities due within one year, and those included in investments and advances are carried at cost or less.

(f) Inventories
Inventories are stated at the lower of cost or market. Cost is determined by the specific identification method for job order inventories and generally by the average method for raw materials and other inventories.
Inventories include items associated with major contracts which, because of long-term processing requirements, have been or are expected to be performed over a period of more than twelve months. Those items as of March 31, 1991 and 1990 aggregated ¥458,460 million ($3,251,489 thousand) and ¥402,842 million, respectively. In general, income from such items is recognized at the time final shipments are made.

(g) Property, Plant and Equipment

Property, plant and equipment of the companies are stated at cost. Depreciation of property, plant and equipment is computed by the declining-balance method.

(h) Income Taxes

The companies recognize deferred income taxes resulting from timing differences between taxable income and income for financial statement purposes.

Income taxes have not been accrued for undistributed earnings of subsidiaries and affiliated companies as distributions of such earnings are either not taxable under present tax laws or are not material.

(i) Retirement and Severance Benefits

Effective April 1, 1989, the Company changed its method of accounting for unfunded retirement and severance benefit plans to conform with SFAS No. 87 "Employers' Accounting for Pensions." The net impact of this change on net income was not significant.

(j) Net Income Per Share

In computing net income per share, the average number of shares outstanding during each year and the number of shares issuable upon conversions of common share equivalents at the beginning of the year or at time of debt issuance, if later, have been used after giving retroactive effect to the free distribution of shares described in note 11.

(k) Future Application of New Accounting Standards

SFAS No. 96 "Accounting for Income Taxes" was issued in December 1987. This statement, as amended by SFAS No. 103, is effective for the year ending March 31, 1993, with earlier application permitted.

SFAS No. 96 requires a change in the accounting for income taxes by requiring a balance sheet rather than an income statement approach to account for the effect of income taxes that result from an enterprise's activities during the current and preceding years. At this time, the Company has not decided on an implementation date because the Financial Accounting Standards Board is considering to amend certain provisions of SFAS No. 96. However, if SFAS No. 96 had been implemented, certain portion of deferred tax assets would not be sustainable with the corresponding effect on retained earnings.

2. Basis of Financial Statement Translation

The accompanying consolidated financial statements are expressed in yen and, solely for the convenience of the reader, have been translated into United States dollars at the rate of ¥141−U.S.$1, the approximate exchange rate prevailing on the Tokyo Foreign Exchange Market as of March 29, 1991. This translation should not be construed as a representation that all amounts shown could be converted into U.S. dollars.

3. Marketable Equity Securities

The current and noncurrent portfolios of marketable equity securities included in short-term investments and in investments and advances, respectively, are summarized as follows:

| | Millions of yen | | Thousands of U.S. dollars |
	1991	1990	1991
Current portfolio:			
Cost	¥ 47,141	¥ 41,238	$ 334,333
Market	274,332	294,548	1,945,617
Gross unrealized gains	227,191	253,310	1,611,284
Noncurrent portfolio:			
Cost	87,857	85,754	623,099
Market	882,822	966,036	6,261,149
Gross unrealized gains	794,965	880,282	5,638,050

During the years ended March 31, 1991, 1990 and 1989, realized gains from sales of marketable equity securities were not significant.

4. Inventories

Inventories at March 31, 1991 and 1990 are summarized as follows:

| | Millions of yen | | Thousands of U.S. dollars |
	1991	1990	1991
Finished goods	¥ 420,579	¥ 370,164	$ 2,982,830
Work in process	1,006,371	840,534	7,137,383
Raw materials	170,179	144,309	1,206,943
	¥1,597,129	¥1,355,007	$11,327,156

5. Noncurrent Receivables and Restricted Funds

Noncurrent receivables and restricted funds at March 31, 1991 and 1990 are summarized as follows:

| | Millions of yen | | Thousands of U.S. dollars |
	1991	1990	1991
Housing loans to employees	¥ 41,028	¥ 44,298	$ 290,979
Trade receivables not due within one year, interest-bearing	29,886	22,175	211,957
Other receivables and restricted funds	84,766	68,395	601,177
	¥155,680	¥134,868	$1,104,113

The housing loans to employees are made with repayment terms ranging from 10 to 25 years.

The aggregated annual maturities of the noncurrent trade receivables after March 31, 1992 are as follows:

Year ending March 31	Millions of yen	Thousands of U.S. dollars
1993	¥17,990	$127,589
1994	5,001	35,468
1995	1,731	12,276
1996	1,087	7,709
Subsequent to 1996	4,077	28,915
	¥29,886	$211,957

Sales on an installment contract basis for the years ended March 31, 1991, 1990 and 1989 totaled ¥31,203 million ($221,298 thousand), ¥27,190 million and ¥26,294 million, respectively.

6. Majority-owned Subsidiaries

The following financial information is required to be disclosed by SFAS No. 94, in respect of the majority-owned subsidiaries that are now being consolidated to comply with the requirements of SFAS No. 94 from the year ended March 31, 1989.

	Millions of yen		Thousands of U.S. dollars
	1991	1990	1991
Current assets	¥1,311,876	¥1,170,832	$ 9,304,085
Other assets, principally property, plant and equipment	493,436	413,001	3,499,546
Total assets	1,805,312	1,583,833	12,803,631
Current liabilities	1,165,719	1,038,161	8,267,510
Long-term debt and retirement and severance benefits	233,928	186,569	1,659,064
Net assets	¥ 405,665	¥ 359,103	$ 2,877,057

	Millions of yen			Thousands of U.S. dollars
	1991	1990	1989	1991
Net sales	¥4,292,710	¥3,698,116	¥3,287,296	$30,444,752
Net income	44,260	37,264	34,671	313,901

7. Acquisition

On April 28, 1989, a subsidiary (80% owned by the Company) acquired all shares of National Advanced Systems Corporation (NAS) for ¥50,986 million. NAS distributes and maintains computer mainframes and related peripherals. The results of operations of the acquired NAS business from the acquisition date have been included in the consolidated financial statements. The acquisition has been accounted for as a purchase and, accordingly, the purchase price has been allocated to assets acquired and liabilities assumed based on their fair value at the date of acquisition. The total acquisition cost exceeded the fair value of the net assets acquired, and the excess has been recorded as goodwill and is being amortized on a straight-line basis over 20 years. The effect of the acquisition on the Company's consolidated statement of income was not significant.

8. Long-term Debt

Long-term debt at March 31, 1991 and 1990 is summarized as follows:

	Millions of yen		Thousands of U.S. dollars
	1991	1990	1991
Mortgage debentures:			
Due 1991—1998, interest 2.5—7.1%, issued by subsidiaries............	¥ 8,837	¥ 4,573	$ 62,674
Unsecured notes, debentures and debentures with warrants:			
Due 1991—1998, interest 2.2—7.7%, issued by subsidiaries............	122,840	105,321	871,206
Unsecured convertible debentures:			
3rd series, due 1994, interest 3.4%............	5,311	10,500	37,666
4th series, due 1997, interest 2.7%............	8,892	15,710	63,064
5th series, due 2002, interest 1.7%............	34,785	67,255	246,702
6th series, due 2003, interest 1.3%............	118,602	119,179	841,149
7th series, due 2004, interest 1.4%............	247,572	248,116	1,755,830
Due 1990—2004, interest 1.4—5.0%, issued by subsidiaries............	121,251	132,497	859,936
Loans, principally from banks and insurance companies:			
Secured by various assets and mortgages on property, plant and equipment, maturing 1991—2006, interest 4.6—7.1%............	87,115	41,674	617,837
Unsecured, maturing 1990—2003, interest 4.5—7.924%............	188,873	188,763	1,339,525
	944,078	933,588	6,695,589
Less current installments............	53,056	46,790	376,284
	¥891,022	¥886,798	$6,319,305

The aggregate annual maturities of long-term debt after March 31, 1992 are as follows:

Year ending March 31	Millions of yen	Thousands of U.S. dollars
1993............	¥131,195	$ 930,461
1994............	96,984	687,830
1995............	29,195	207,057
1996............	35,808	253,957
Subsequent to 1996............	597,840	4,240,000
	¥891,022	$6,319,305

As is customary in Japan, both short-term and long-term bank loans are made under general agreements which provide that security and guarantees for present and future indebtedness will be given upon request of the bank, and that the bank shall have the right, as the obligations become due, or in the event of their default, to offset cash deposits against such obligations due the bank. The mortgage debenture trust agreements and certain secured and unsecured loan agreements provide, among other things, that the lenders or trustees shall have the right to have any distribution of earnings, including the payment of dividends and the issuance of additional capital stock, submitted to them for prior approval and also grant them the right to request additional security or mortgages on property, plant and equipment.

The unsecured convertible debentures due in the year 1994 are redeemable in whole or in part, at the option of the Company, from April 1, 1989 to March 31, 1993 at premiums ranging from 4% to 1%, and at par thereafter. The debentures are currently convertible into approximately 6,201,000 shares of common stock. Commencing March 31, 1990, the Company is required to make annual payments to the Trustee of ¥12 billion ($85 million) less the aggregate amounts of the debentures converted, repurchased or redeemed which have not been deducted before.

The unsecured convertible debentures due in the year 1997 are redeemable in whole or in part, at the option of the Company, from April 1, 1990 to March 31, 1996 at premiums ranging from 6% to 1%, and at par thereafter. The debentures are currently convertible into approximately 10,991,000 shares of common stock. Commencing March 31, 1991, the Company is required to make annual payments to the Trustee of ¥10 billion ($71 million) less the aggregate amounts of the debentures converted, repurchased or redeemed which have not been deducted before.

The unsecured convertible debentures due in the year 2002 are redeemable in whole or in part, at the option of the Company, from April 1, 1995 to March 31, 2001 at premiums ranging from 6% to 1%, and at par thereafter. The debentures are currently convertible into approximately 34,359,000 shares of common stock. Commencing March 31, 1996, the Company is required to make annual payments to the Trustee of ¥12 billion ($85 million) less the aggregate amounts of the debentures converted, repurchased or redeemed which have not been deducted before.

The unsecured convertible debentures due in the year 2003 are redeemable in whole or in part, at the option of the Company, from October 1, 1996 to September 30, 2002 at premiums ranging from 6% to 1%, and at par thereafter. The debentures are currently convertible into approximately 63,248,000 shares of common stock. Commencing September 30, 1997, the Company is required to make annual payments to the Trustee of ¥10 billion ($71 million) less the aggregate amounts of the debentures converted, repurchased or redeemed which have not been deducted before.

The unsecured convertible debentures due in the year 2004 are redeemable in whole or in part, at the option of the Company, from October 1, 1997 to September 30, 2003 at premiums ranging from 6% to 1%, and at par thereafter. The debentures are currently convertible into approximately 146,121,000 shares of common stock. Commencing September 30, 1998, the Company is required to make annual payments to the Trustee of ¥20 billion ($142 million) less the aggregate amounts of the debentures converted, repurchased or redeemed which have not been deducted before.

Pursuant to the terms of the indentures under which the debentures were issued, retained earnings amounting to approximately ¥1,639 billion ($11,624 million) are restricted as to payment of dividends.

9. Retirement and Severance Benefits

The Company and its domestic subsidiaries have a number of contributory and noncontributory pension plans to provide retirement and severance benefits to substantially all employees.

Principal pension plans are unfunded defined benefit pension plans. Under the plans, employees are entitled lump-sum payments based on current rate of pay and length of service upon retirement or termination of employment for reasons other than dismissal for cause. Through March 31, 1989, provision was made in the accompanying balance sheets for the estimated accrued liability under the plan. Effective April 1, 1989, the Company changed its method of accounting for the unfunded defined benefit pension plans to conform with SFAS No. 87. For the purpose of applying SFAS No. 87, the projected benefit obligation which is made equal to the larger vested benefit obligation is recognized as retirement and severance benefits on the accompanying balance sheets. Pension cost for the year is computed as the retirement and severance benefits paid plus or minus the change in the vested benefit obligation. For the year ended March 31, 1991 and 1990, net periodic pension cost consists of service cost of ¥67,365 million ($477,766 thousand) and ¥64,507 million, respectively.

Directors and certain employees are not covered by the programs described above. Benefits paid to such persons and meritorious service awards paid to employees in excess of the prescribed formula are charged to income as paid as it is not practicable to compute the liability for future payments since amounts vary with circumstances.

In addition to unfunded defined benefit pension plans, the Company and certain of its subsidiaries contribute to each Employees Pension Fund (EPF) which is stipulated by the Japanese Welfare Pension Insurance Law. The pension plans under the EPF are composed of the substitutional portion of Japanese Welfare Pension Insurance and the corporate portion which is the contributory defined benefit pension plan covering substantially all of their employees and provides the benefits in addition to the substitutional portion. The Company, certain of its subsidiaries and their employees contribute to each EPF together with the pension premium of the substitutional portion and corporate portion. The plan assets of each EPF can not be specifically allocated to the individual participants nor to the substitutional and corporate portions.
The benefits for the substitutional portion are based on standard remuneration scheduled by the Welfare Pension Insurance Law and the length of participation. The benefits of the corporate portion are based on the current rate of pay and the length of service. Under EPF pension plans, the participants are eligible for these benefits after a period of participation in the plan exceeding one month.
EPF contributions and cost for the substitutional portion are determined in accordance with the open aggregate cost method (actuarial funding method) as stipulated by the Welfare Pension Insurance Law. Contributions and cost for the corporate portion are determined in accordance with the entry age normal cost method (actuarial funding method). The pension cost of the corporate portion for the year ended March 31, 1991, 1990 and 1989 totaled ¥32,681 million ($231,780 thousand), ¥25,526 million and ¥19,542 million, respectively.
The Company decided not to apply accounting for single-employer defined benefit pension plans under SFAS No. 87 for those plans as the effects on the consolidated financial statements of the implementation of SFAS No. 87 are not significant, however, the following table summarizes the funded status for the EPF of the companies at March 31, 1990 and 1989 according to the actuarial funding method, which is the latest information available.

Funding status of the Company is as follows:

	Millions of yen		Thousands of U.S. dollars
	1990	1989	1990
The liability reserve calculated using:			
Aggregate cost method—discount rate at 5.5% and assumed rates of compensation increase at 2.4–3.4%	¥(163,488)	¥(146,034)	$(1,159,489)
Entry age normal cost method—discount rate at 5.5% and assumed rate of compensation increase at 3.2%	(191,349)	(156,796)	(1,357,085)
Fair value of plan assets, primarily fixed income securities and contract receivables from insurance companies	356,340	315,975	2,527,234
Fair value of plan assets in excess of the liability reserve	¥ 1,503	¥ 13,145	$ 10,660

The fair value of plan assets and liability reserve of certain domestic subsidiaries are as follows:

	Millions of yen		Thousands of U.S. dollars
	1990	1989	1990
Liability reserve	¥(173,295)	¥(142,827)	$(1,229,042)
Fair value of plan assets	176,958	152,042	1,255,021
Fair value of plan assets in excess of the liability reserve	¥ 3,663	¥ 9,215	$ 25,979

Prior service liabilities at March 31, 1990 and 1989 amounted to ¥166,491 million ($1,180,787 thousand), and ¥80,599 million, respectively. It is the policy of the companies to amortize prior service costs over periods not exceeding 20 years. Contributions to amortize the prior service costs for the years ended March 31, 1991, 1990 and 1989 totaled ¥16,087 million ($114,092 thousand), ¥11,919 million and ¥8,636 million, respectively.

The companies are not required to report by regulation the actuarial present value of either vested or nonvested accumulated plan benefits, and such information, therefore, is not available.

10. Income Taxes

The companies are subject to a number of taxes based on income, which in the aggregate resulted in a normal tax rate of approximately 51.2% in 1991, 53.9% in 1990, and 56.1% in 1989. The effective tax rate for the years ended March 31, 1991, 1990 and 1989 differs from the normal income tax rate for the following reasons:

	1991	1990	1989
Normal income tax rate	51.2%	53.9%	56.1%
Tax credits for dividends	—	(0.4)	(0.6)
Equity in earnings of associated companies	(0.8)	(1.3)	(0.6)
Expenses not deductible for tax purposes	2.5	2.1	2.2
Other	(1.2)	(1.2)	(1.6)
Effective income tax rate	51.7%	53.1%	55.5%

Deferred income taxes result from timing differences in the recognition of income and expenses for tax and financial statement purposes. The sources of these differences and their tax effect for the years ended March 31, 1991, 1990 and 1989 are as follows:

	Millions of yen			Thousands of U.S. dollars
	1991	1990	1989	1991
Provision for retirement and severance benefits	¥ (1,240)	¥ (5,431)	¥(14,021)	$ (8,795)
Other	(16,521)	(26,357)	(22,002)	(117,170)
	¥(17,761)	¥(31,788)	¥(36,023)	$(125,965)

Net deferred income taxes at March 31, 1991 and 1990 resulting from timing differences between taxable income and income for financial statement purposes are reflected in the accompanying balance sheets under the following captions:

	Millions of yen		Thousands of U.S. dollars
	1991	1990	1991
Prepaid expenses and other current assets	¥180,324	¥164,671	$1,278,894
Other assets	140,950	139,027	999,645
	¥321,274	¥303,698	$2,278,539

11. Common Stock

During the years ended March 31, 1991, 1990 and 1989, the Company issued 47,186,835, 55,160,608 and 96,032,273 shares, respectively, of common stock in connection with the conversion of debentures.

Conversions of convertible debt issued subsequent to October 1, 1982 into common stock were accounted for in accordance with the provisions of the Japanese Commercial Code by crediting one-half of the conversion price to each of the common stock account and the capital surplus account.

The Company made a free distribution of shares of its common stock on May 21, 1990 to stockholders of record at March 31, 1990 on the basis of one new share for each twenty shares held. This free distribution, totaling 153,642,327 shares, which was made for an amount in excess of the aggregate par value of the stated capital as of March 31, 1990, was accounted for in accordance with the applicable provisions of Japanese Commercial Code. A United States company issuing shares in comparable amounts would be required to account for the distribution as a stock dividend, and charge retained earnings with an amount equal to the fair value of the shares being issued and credit the amount to the appropriate capital accounts. The fair value of the shares issued, representing the market value of the shares on February 21, 1990, the day immediately prior to the announcement of the free share distribution, was ¥227,391 million.

12. Legal Reserve and Cash Dividends

The Commercial Code provides that an amount not less than 10% of cash dividends paid by the Company and its domestic subsidiaries be appropriated as a legal reserve until such reserve equals 25% of their respective stated capital amounts. The legal reserve may be used to reduce a deficit or it may be transferred to the stated capital.

Cash dividends and appropriations to the legal reserve charged to retained earnings during the years ended March 31, 1991, 1990 and 1989 represent dividends paid out during those years and the related appropriations to the legal reserve. The accompanying financial statements do not include any provision for the semi-annual dividend of ¥5.5 ($0.04) per share totaling ¥18,005 million ($127,695 thousand) subsequently proposed by the Board of Directors in respect of the year ended March 31, 1991.

13. Commitments and Contingencies

At March 31, 1991 outstanding commitments for the purchase of property, plant and equipment were approximately ¥108,728 million ($771,121 thousand).

The Company and its operating subsidiaries were contingently liable for loan guarantees, principally of customers, in the amount of approximately ¥32,697 million ($231,894 thousand) at March 31, 1991. In addition, Hitachi Credit Corporation, a financing subsidiary, was the guarantor of consumer loans totaling ¥340,921 million ($2,417,879 thousand) at March 31, 1991.

It is common practice in Japan for companies, in the ordinary course of business, to receive promissory notes in settlement of trade accounts receivable and to subsequently discount such notes to banks or to transfer them by endorsement to suppliers in settlement of accounts payable. At March 31, 1991 and 1990, the companies were contingently liable for trade notes discounted and endorsed in the following amounts:

	Millions of yen		Thousands of U.S. dollars
	1991	1990	1991
Notes discounted	¥ 71,803	¥ 75,511	$ 509,241
Notes endorsed	137,152	131,773	972,709
	¥208,955	¥207,284	$1,481,950

Notes discounted are accounted for as sales. The aggregate proceeds from notes discounted for the years ended March 31, 1991, 1990 and 1989 are not available; however, based on its financing policy, the Company believes that the balance of such contingent liabilities should not have significantly fluctuated during the year ended March 31, 1991.

There are several legal actions against the Company and certain subsidiaries. Management is of the opinion that damages, if any, resulting from these actions will not have a material effect on the Company's consolidated financial statements.

14. Foreign Exchange Contracts

The Company and its subsidiaries enter into various contracts in order to hedge foreign trade receivables. At March 31, 1991 major contracts designated as a hedge against foreign trade receivables are forward exchange contracts and forward range contracts totaling $1,075,722 thousand.

15. Significant Items in Other Income and Other Deductions

In October 1990, the Company sold a portion of its investment in Hitachi Software Engineering Co., Ltd., a consolidated subsidiary, in connection with that company's listing on the Tokyo Stock Exchange. The resulting gain of ¥19,899 million ($141,128 thousand) has been included in other income–other on the consolidated statement of income for the year ended March 31, 1991.

During 1991 and 1990, the Company planned to improve the product structure mainly by conversion of several products, relocation and consolidation of plants in consideration of economical situation and market needs. Based on this plan, in 1991 and 1990, the Company carried out an enhancement of the computer and related peripherals manufacturing operation. The ¥13,555 million ($96,135 thousand) and ¥13,495 million, related to the relocation of certain production facilities and asset write-offs have been charged to other deductions—other as restructuring costs in 1991 and 1990, respectively.

16. Supplementary Income Information

	Millions of yen			Thousands of U.S. dollars
	1991	1990	1989	1991
Research and development expense	¥490,708	¥429,470	¥373,511	$3,480,199
Provision for retirement and severance benefits and pension expense	122,579	109,707	119,218	869,355
Rent	144,685	121,444	103,853	1,026,135
Exchange gain (loss)	(1,007)	(22,348)	2,914	(7,142)

17. Supplementary Cash Flows Information

	Millions of yen			Thousands of U.S. dollars
	1991	1990	1989	1991
Cash paid during the year for:				
Interest	¥129,215	¥ 94,991	¥ 70,120	$ 916,418
Income taxes	309,263	342,724	265,562	2,193,355

	Millions of yen
	1990
A subsidiary (80% owned by the Company) acquired all shares of NAS for ¥50,986 million. In connection with the acquisition, liabilities were assumed as follows:	
Fair value of assets acquired	¥ 96,248
Cash paid for the capital stock	(50,986)
Liabilities assumed	¥ 45,262

Convertible debentures of ¥45,598 million ($323,390 thousand) in 1991, ¥55,095 million in 1990 and ¥82,119 million in 1989 were converted into common stock.

Five-Year Summary
Hitachi, Ltd. and Subsidiaries

	1991	1990	1989	1988	Millions of yen 1987
Net sales	¥7,736,961	¥7,077,855	¥6,401,417	¥5,716,962	¥5,543,247
Net income	230,185	210,963	185,587	136,806	98,676
Net income per share (yen)	65.96	61.71	56.14	42.03	31.86
Net income per ADS (representing 10 shares, yen)	660	617	561	420	319
Cash dividends	37,922	27,298	26,609	25,390	25,275
Depreciation charged to operations	448,124	407,152	366,268	345,843	376,928
Total assets	8,526,121	7,805,086	6,937,651	6,187,921	5,842,121
Net property, plant and equipment	1,985,726	1,708,891	1,473,549	1,353,607	1,384,886
Stockholders' equity per share (yen)	858.71	833.37	756.06	690.89	648.36

See note 2 of the accompanying notes to consolidated financial statements. For the convenience of the reader, the figures for 1987 and 1988 have been restated to comply with the requirements of Statement of Financial Accounting Standards (SFAS) No. 94 adopted in the year ended March 31, 1989.

Net sales
(Millions of yen)

87	5,543,247
88	5,716,962
89	6,401,417
90	7,077,855
91	7,736,961

Net income
(Millions of yen)

87	98,676
88	136,806
89	185,587
90	
91	

Net income per share
(Yen)

87	31.86
88	42.03
89	
90	
91	

Stockholders' equity per share
(Yen)

87	648.36
88	
89	
90	
91	

Appendix B
Summary of the Main Differences in Financial Reporting between Japan, and the UK and US

The following abbreviations are used:

AICPA American Institute of Certified Public Accountants
APB   Accounting Principles Board
ARB   Accounting Research Bulletin
CA   Companies Act 1985
CC   Commercial Code
FAS   Financial Accounting Standards
SE   Stock Exchange requirement
SEC   Securities and Exchange Commission
SEL   Securities and Exchange Law
SSAP   Statement of Standard Accounting Practice
S-X   Regulation S-X, Form and Content of Financial Statement

Japan	United Kingdom	United States
	Accounting concepts	
	Tax	
Income for tax purposes is based on the published financial statements. An extensive range of reserves have been used in the past	Tax rules are separate from the financial accounting regulations.	As for the UK.

Japan	United Kingdom	United States

although less common now.

Historical cost

Japan	United Kingdom	United States
Upward revaluations should not be incorporated into the accounts.	Revaluations permitted with the surplus being credited to a revaluation reserve (CA, Sch. 4, para. 34(2)).	Upward revaluations may not be incorporated into the accounts other than as supplementary information.

Financial accounts

Japan	United Kingdom	United States
The CC requires a balance sheet, income statement, proposal of appropriation of profit or disposition of loss and supplementary schedules. A business report should also be prepared. The SEL accounts are similar but more detailed although a business report is not required. In addition, a funds (cash) statement is required as part of the securities report and the registration report for subscription or sale of securities.	Similar to Japan except that a separate appropriation statement is not required and a directors' report should be prepared rather than a business report. In addition, a funds statement is required by SSAP 10.	No general requirement, in state or federal law. Publicly owned corporations and listed companies must prepare financial statements (S-X).

Fundamental concepts

Japan	United Kingdom	United States
1 Going concern 2 Accruals 3 Consistency 4 Form over substance in certain cases.	As for Japan although substance over form is recognized (CA, Sch. 4, para. 15; SSAP 2, para. 14).	As for the UK and Japan except that substance over form is important.

Japan

United Kingdom

United States

Balance sheet

General

Layout

Follow the US style with assets on the left and liabilities and capital on the right of the balance sheet in the CC accounts. Assets are divided into current assets followed by fixed assets and deferred charges. In the SEL accounts it is normal for a vertical format to be used.

Usually vertical (under CA, Sch. 4, para. 1(1), a company may adopt the alternative format – formats cannot be changed without justification).

Vertical.

Valuation rules

Usually stocks and securities are valued at cost or the lower of cost and market value. Market value when valuing stocks is interpreted as replacement cost or net realizable value. Fixed assets must be valued at historical cost.

State rules for valuation where fixed assets are revalued and when valuing work-in-progress (CA, s. 275). CA provides for historical cost (CA, Sch. 4, s. B) and alternative accounting rules (CA, Sch. 4, s. C) SSAPs 1, 9, 19, 22 and 23 have an input on these matters.

Value assets at historical cost except for inventories, which are stated at the lower of cost and market value (not defined as net realizable value).

Capital

Share capital represents the par value of outstanding shares. On new issues since 1 October 1982 the amount included under share capital should be the higher of the par value of new shares issued or an amount equal to not less than 50 per cent of the

Shares may be categorized and allocated different votes (CA, Sch. 4, para. 38(1)(b)).

As for the UK.

Japan	**United Kingdom**	**United States**
proceeds received on issue. Consequently, the share capital balance will not necessarily be simply the number of shares outstanding multiplied by the par value of shares. Shares do not need to have a par value.		
The excess of proceeds received from an issue of shares over their par value should be credited to capital reserve.	Premium on shares should be transferred to the share premium account (CA, Part I, s. 130).	Disclosed as paid-in capital in excess of par or stated value.

Purchase of own shares

Japan	**United Kingdom**	**United States**
Companies are not allowed to purchase their own shares except in certain cases, such as: 1 purchase for cancellation; 2 acquisition resulting from merger or business transfer. Purchases and sales of treasury stock are treated the same as other securities. Shown at acquisition cost as a separate item in current assets.	May purchase and cancel own shares (CA, ss. 160(4), 162(2)).	May purchase and either cancel or hold as treasury stock. ARB 43, chapter 18, and APB Opinion 6, para. 13. State laws vary and, where they differ from GAAP, state laws are followed.

Reserves

Japan	**United Kingdom**	**United States**
The CC stipulates that a company must allocate an amount equal to at least 10 per cent of cash disbursements paid for each accounting period until the reserve equals 25 per cent of share capital.	No equivalent concept.	As for the UK.

Japan

United Kingdom

United States

Legal reserves are categorized as capital reserve, and legal earned reserve.

No equivalent concept.

As for the UK.

Retained earnings are segregated into appropriated and unappropriated. Appropriated retained earnings consist of amounts appropriated for dividends, directors' bonuses, auditors' bonuses and other purposes. Under the CC, other reserves constitute unappropriated retained earnings and are available for distribution.

Dividends may be paid out of distributable reserves (CA, s. 261(1)).

Dividends may be paid out of retained earnings but subject to any other restrictions; for example, restrictions placed on distributions by lenders. State laws determine the amount of dividends permitted.

Free distributions or stock dividends are accounted for by a transfer of an amount equal to the par value of the shares issued from additional paid-in capital or legal reserves.

Normally accounted for by a transfer from distributable reserves equal to the nominal value of the shares.

An amount equal to the fair value of the shares should be transferred from retained earnings to share capital and share premium (ARB 43).

Deferred tax

The CC does not permit inter-period income tax allocations. However, such allocations are permitted in the consolidated accounts filed with the Ministry of Finance.

Partial provision based on the liability method for timing differences. Provision is required where a liability is expected to crystallize (SSAP 15).

Comprehensive method based on the liability method for all short-term and long-term timing differences. FASB 96 effective from 16 December 1988 with earlier application encouraged.

Japan	United Kingdom	United States

Long-term liabilities

Disclosures

Discounts and issuing expenses on bonds payable are capitalized as deferred charges and amortized or expensed as incurred under the CC. Bonds payable secured by mortgages should be identified. Long-term loans should be disclosed along with related mortgages as applicable. The liability for retirement and severance benefits in the balance sheet is usually understated.

Show the aggregate amount for each category split between amounts owing in excess of five years and amounts owing less than five years (CA, Sch. 4, Part 1).

For each issue or obligation:

1 the rate of interest;
2 date of maturity;
3 any contingencies;
4 priority;
5 convertibility;
6 aggregate amount of maturities and sinking fund requirements (FASB 5, paras. 18–19, and 47, para. 106; S-X, 5.02 (22)).

Separate disclosure of liabilities secured on assets of the company

Details of pledged assets should be provided in the supporting schedules under the CC. The book balance of each balance sheet heading of assets pledged and related liabilities should be disclosed.

Disclose all charges on the assets of the company to secure the liabilities of any other person, including, where practicable, the amount secured (4 Sch. 50 (1) CA).

State all assets pledged or otherwise subject to lien (FASB 5, paras. 18–19).

Current liabilities

Disclose separately:

1 notes payable, trade;
2 accounts payable, trade;
3 short-term loans payable;
4 current portions of long-term debt;
5 accounts payable other than trade;

Disclose separately:

1 debenture loans;
2 bank loans and overdrafts;
3 payments received on account;
4 trade creditors;
5 bills of exchange payable;
6 amounts owed to group

Disclose separately amounts payable to/on:

1 short-term borrowings;
2 factors;
3 holders of commercial paper;
4 trade creditors;
5 parents and subsidiaries;
6 other affiliates;

Japan

6 accrued expenses;
7 corporation and other taxes payable;
8 deferred income;
9 allowance for product guarantee;
10 allowance for loss on sales returns;
11 other current liabilities.

United Kingdom

companies;
7 amounts owed to related companies;
8 other creditors including taxation and social security;
9 accruals and deferred income.

(CA, Sch. 4, Part 1).

United States

7 underwriters, directors, employees, officers, promoters and all amounts for payroll, taxes, interest, other material items;
8 dividends declared, current portion of bonds, mortgages and similar debt;
9 any other item in excess of 5 per cent of total current liabilities.

(Regulation S-X, 5-02, 19-29 – amounts payable to related parties FASB 57).

Contingencies

Contingent liabilities that will lead to losses (not gains) must either be accrued and reported in the financial statements or disclosed in the notes. Examples include:

1 guarantees of indebtedness to others;
2 obligations related to product warranties and product defects;
3 pending or threatened litigation;
4 actual or possible claims and assessments;
5 possible loss on contracts obtained or accepted;
6 notes receivable discounted or endorsed.

Disclose the amount or estimated amount of that liability, its legal nature and whether any valuable security has been provided by the company in connection with that liability and if so, what (CA, Sch. 4, para. 50(2)).

The treatment of contingent losses depends upon the probability of the loss and ability to estimate it reasonably. Where a loss is considered remote no provision and no disclosure are provided. In other situations the contingency is disclosed in the notes to the accounts. Contingent gains are recognized on realization (FASB 5).

Japan	**United Kingdom**	**United States**

Fixed assets

Classification

Specified subdivision into tangible assets, intangible fixed assets and a third heading, 'investments and other assets', under the SEL or 'investments etc.' under the CC.

Split between intangibles, tangibles and investment with specified subdivision (CA, Sch, 4).

Split by major class, e.g. land, machinery and equipment, leasehold, or functional grouping such as revenue-producing equipment or industry categories. Subdivide intangibles (APBO 12 and APBO 22).

Disclosure of movements

Disclose the closing balance. Accumulated depreciation is shown in a footnote rather than as a deduction from the total under the SEL. The supporting schedules should show full details of movements.

Disclose opening and closing balances and revisions, acquisitions, disposals and transfers during the year (CA, Sch. 4, para. 42).

Disclose carrying value and depreciation and cost for each major class of tangible assets (APBO 12 and APBO 22).

Disclosure of valuation method

Disclose NBV and accumulated depreciation charged. Special depreciation allowable under tax law may be accounted for by a transfer from unappropriated retained earnings to a reserve in shareholders' equity although normally special depreciation will be treated as an expense.

Disclose purchase price or production cost (CA, Sch. 4, para. 17). Alternative accounting rules (CA, Sch. 4).

Disclose carrying basis method and period of amortization and accumulated amortization of intangibles (S-X, 5.02-15).

Revaluations

These are not permitted.

Yes (CA, Sch. 4, para. 34).

Not permitted (APB 6; ARB 43, chapter 9B).

Japan

United Kingdom

United States

Intangibles

Categorization

1 Legal rights such as patents, property rights and trade marks.
2 Goodwill.

1 Development costs.
2 Concessions, patents, licences, trade marks.
3 Goodwill.
4 Payments on account.

(CA, Sch. 4).

Classify by type (S-X, 5.02–15; APBO 17).

Disclosure

Disclose cost and amortized amount. Amortization is normally on a straight-line basis over the useful economic life with the exception of property rights which are not amortized. Under the CC goodwill should be written off within 5 years.

Write off goodwill to reserves on acquisition or amortize over its useful life (SSAP 22).

Amortize goodwill over its useful life not exceeding 40 years (APBO 7).

Subsidiary companies

Only the number and names of consolidated and unconsolidated subsidiaries are required to be given by SEL. No requirement to disclose:

1 a subsidiary's activities;
2 a subsidiary's location;
3 percentage shareholdings in subsidiaries.

Disclose for each subsidiary:

1 name;
2 where incorporated;
3 identity of each class and proportion of the allotted shares of that class.

(CA, Sch. 5).

Disclose the name of each subsidiary (ARB 51).

Investments

An associated company is generally defined as a company of which 20 per cent or more of the voting

(Related company) any body corporate in which there is a long-term capital interest and the company

Significant influence (APBO 18).

Japan

United Kingdom

United States

power is directly or indirectly owned by a parent company.

exercises control or influence. Generally at least 20 per cent of the equity voting rights and significant influence (SSAP 1).

Securities are those specified by SEL as:

1 government bonds;
2 local   government bonds;
3 debentures (corporate bonds);
4 equity stock, etc.

Marketable securities which are classified as current assets are those securities which are marketable and/or held for short-term investment purposes. Investment securities are those owned for investment purposes and include trade investments and investments in affiliates.

Amount attributable to listed shares. The aggregate market value of listed investments where it differs from the amount stated (CA, Sch. 4, para. 45).

Carry at the lower of cost or market value segregated between current and non-current portfolios (FAS 12).

Stocks and work-in-progress

Normally classified as follows:

1 merchandise;
2 finished goods;
3 semi-finished goods;
4 raw materials;
5 work-in-progress;
6 office and manufacturing supplies, etc.

Subheadings required as follows (CA, Sch. 4):

1 raw materials and consumables;
2 work-in-progress;
3 finished goods and goods for resale;
4 payments on account.

Classification appropriate to the business (SSAP 9).

Disclose different classes and basis on which determined (S-X, 5.02-6(a) and ARB 43, chapters 3A and 4).

Japan

United Kingdom

United States

All direct and overhead costs of manufacturing must be included in determining cost. Direct cost only is not acceptable in financial reporting. Standard cost may be used where cost is reasonably determined. Tax regulations specify that standard cost variances should not exceed 5 per cent of total production cost for the period.

Required (SSAP 9).

Include related production overheads (ARB 43, chapters 3A and 4). Normally apply percentage-of-completion method (ARB 45).

Valuation under historical cost accounting

Valued at either cost or lower of cost and market. Market value is normally replacement cost or net realizable value. Where the market price is significantly less than cost, stocks must be written down to market value unless recovery of the shortfall is certain. Stock pricing methods include:

1 individual cost;
2 FIFO;
3 latest purchase price to approximate FIFO;
4 LIFO;
5 weighted average;
6 moving average;
7 other.

Lower of cost and net realizable value (SSAP 9).

Lower of cost and market value. Market value is usually current replacement cost but market value cannot exceed net realizable value. Midpoint of NRV, RC, NRV less normal profit margin (ARB 43, chapters 3A and 4).

Debtors categorization

Disclosed as current assets under three headings:

Debtors is a main heading on the balance sheet. Sub-

Classify by source, segregating notes from

Japan	United Kingdom	United States
1 accounts receivables – trade; 2 notes receivable – trade. 3 miscellaneous debtors.	division required (CA, Sch. 4).	accounts receivable and unusual receivables such as tax refunds (S-X, 5.02-3).

Profit and loss account

Turnover

Disclose both sales and cost of sales. In the SEL accounts sales to affiliated companies exceeding 20 per cent of total sales should be disclosed separately in a footnote.	Disclose amount divided by different business classes (CA, Sch. 4, para. 55).	Disclose for each significant type (defined as 10 per cent of sales). Disclose method of recognizing sales (APB 22 and 13).

Other income

Disclose non-operating income, separately categorized as follows: 1 interest income; 2 dividend income; 3 miscellaneous income.	Disclose the amount of income from listed investments (CA, Sch. 4, para. 53).	Disclose amounts earned from dividends, interest income and sale of securities (FAS 12; S-X, 5-03.7).

Salaries, wages and related contributions

The CC requires a supplementary schedule disclosing the remuneration paid to directors and statutory auditors. The SEL accounts require disclosure of personnel expenses divided into directors' remuneration, basic salaries, bonuses, provision for retirement and severance benefits, legal welfare and other welfare.	Wages and salaries, social security costs, other pensions costs (CA, Sch. 4, para. 56).	No requirement to disclose.

Japan	United Kingdom	United States

Auditors' remuneration

Aggregate amount to the statutory auditors shown under appropriations of profit.	Required (CA, Sch. 4, para. 53).	Not required.

Hire charges

Disclose rental expenses.	Required (CA, Sch. 4, para. 53).	Disclose operating lease rental expenses (FAS 13).

Appropriations

A separate statement on the proposed appropriation of profit should be disclosed. This starts with unappropriated retained earnings being brought forward, reversal of reserves, or appropriations to legal earned reserve, cash dividends, other reserves and finally unappropriated profit.	Dividends may be made only out of distributable profits (CA, s. 263). Directors' report should recommend the dividend (CA, s. 235).	Dividends paid and declared on a per-share basis (APB 15.70).

Segmental information

Segmental information prepared and disclosed by a parent company on the group. Information should be divided into business and geographical segments. Disclosure includes information by business/industry by line of product; information by the location of parent and subsidiaries; and information on foreign turnover.	State turnover and profit or less for each different class of business (CA, Sch. 4, para. 55). Geographical analysis of profit (SE).	Split sales, revenues, cost of sales and expenses by type (10 per cent of sales) (APB 22). Income before tax should be split between domestic and foreign (FAS 14 and 21).

Japan

United Kingdom

United States

General

Disclose parent company name

Disclose the name of the parent company in the individual company financial statements.

Disclose the name of the ultimate holding company (CA, Sch. 5, para. 20).

Disclose the name of the ultimate holding company (ARB 51).

Disclose names of subsidiaries and associates

Only the names of the consolidated subsidiaries are provided in accordance with SEL. There is no requirement to disclose the following information on subsidiaries:

1 activities;
2 location;
3 percentage ownership.

Disclose names where incorporated, shares of each class held and the proportion of the nominal value of the allotted shares of that class represented by the shares held (CA, Sch. 5, para. 1).

Disclose names, shares held and proportion owned (ARB 51.01).

Directors' report

According to the CC, a 'business report' should include:

1 a description of principal business activities;
2 description of stocks;
3 divisional results;
4 relations with a parent company;
5 results of operations and changes in financial position for at least the last three years as well as an explanation of major trends and fluctuations;

Required (CA, s. 239) to contain a fair review of the development of the business and amount of dividend to be paid (CA, s. 235). State directors, principal activities of the company and any significant changes. Disclose changes in values, directors' shareholdings and other interests, contributions for political and charitable purposes, etc. (CA, s. 235).

Publicly owned companies must provide information on operations in different industries, foreign operations, export sales and its major customers (SEC).

Japan	United Kingdom	United States
6 significant company profits; 7 names of directors and statutory auditors; 8 top seven or more major shareholders; 9 major lenders; 10 subsequent events.		

Standard audit report

Japan	United Kingdom	United States
The contents of audit reports are specified by the CC, by the Law Concerning Special Cases to the CC for the Audit of Kabushiki Kaisha and the SEL.	Standard report issued by the Auditing Practices Committee of the CCAB.	Standard report for SEC registrants only.

Statement of sources and application of funds

Japan	United Kingdom	United States
A funds statement is only required as part of the securities report and registration statement for subscription or sale of securities.	Required for companies with a turnover in excess of £25,000 (SSAP 10).	Required for all profit-orientated businesses.

Earnings per share

Japan	United Kingdom	United States
There is a requirement to disclose EPS and net worth per share in the footnote to the balance sheet in accordance with the SEL. There is no requirement to disclose fully diluted EPS figures.	To be shown in the profit and loss account of listed companies (SSAP 3). Not required for banking, insurance and certain other companies.	Disclose if a publicly traded corporation provided it is not a wholly owned subsidiary (APBO 15; FAS 21).

Appendix C
Comparison of Japanese Accounting Practices with International Accounting Standards

International accounting standards

IAS 1 – Disclosure of accounting policies
Requires presentation of a two-year statement.

Requires disclosure of the facts and reasons if the going concern assumption is not followed.

IAS 2 – Valuation and presentation of inventories in the context of the historical cost system
Requires valuation at the lower of cost and net realizable value.

IAS 3 – Consolidated financial statements
Consolidated financial statements should be issued by a parent company.

A company in which a group does not have control, but in which a group owns more than half the equity capital but less than half the votes, may be treated as a subsidiary.

Japanese standards

No equivalent requirement.

There is no equivalent requirement.

Either the cost method or the lower of cost and market value method may be used. Market value is interpreted as replacement cost or net realizable value.

Consolidated financial statements are prepared only by large companies required by the Securities and Exchange Law and filed as supplementary information.

A subsidiary is a company, more than 50 per cent of the votes of which is substantially owned by a parent company.

International accounting standards

Japanese standards

IAS 4 – Depreciation accounting
The useful lives of major depreciable assets or classes of depreciable assets should be reviewed periodically, and depreciable rates should be adjusted for the current and future periods if expectations are significantly different from the previous estimates.

The useful lives are not required to be reviewed periodically. The useful lives stipulated by the Corporation Tax Law are mostly used by Japanese companies.

IAS 5 – Information to be disclosed in financial statements
Requires disclosure of various items, including pensions and retirement plans, etc. in financial settlements.

Under the Commercial Code, the notes in the financial statements are limited to valuation methods assets, the method for depreciation, and accrual basis for significant allowances, pledged assets, significant assets denominated in foreign currency, liabilities to directors or statutory auditors, contingent liabilities and other significant items. Small companies whose share capital does not exceed ¥100 million may omit these notes (excluding the excess of deferred pre-operating costs and deferred research and development costs over legal reserves).

IAS 7 – Statement of changes in financial position
Required as part of the financial statements.

There is no requirement. However, a company whose registration report for subscription or sale of securities is filed with the Minister of Finance, should prepare such a statement. It is commonly prepared as supplementary information.

IAS 8 – Unusual and prior period items and changes in accounting policies
Prior period items should be either (1) reported by adjusting the opening retained earnings and restating prior years' financial statements, or (2) disclosed in the profit and loss account as part of net income.

Only (2) is applied in Japan.

International accounting standards

Japanese standards

Unusual items shoud be included in net income.

Material losses on assets arising as a result of a natural calamity which cannot be covered by net income in the current year or current retained earnings less appropriated earnings may be deferred as an asset in the balance sheet provided that it is permitted by specific laws or regulations.

IAS 9 – Accounting for research and development activities

Requires research costs to be charged in the year in which incurred but development costs may be deferred in exceptional circumstances.

Research and development costs may be deferred.

Deferred development costs should be amortized on a systematic basis.

The Commercial Code requires that deferred costs should be amortized over a period not exceeding five years.

Deferred costs should be reviewd at the end of each year.

There is no equivalent requirement.

The total of research and development costs should be disclosed.

Not required. The amortization method should be disclosed.

IAS 10 – Contingencies and events occurring after the balance sheet date

Requires disclosure in cases where it is probable that a contingent gain will be realized.

There is no equivalent requirement.

Dividends which are proposed or declared after the balance sheet date should be either adjusted or disclosed.

Not required.

IAS 11 – Accounting for construction contracts

Where both the percentage of completion and the completed contract methods are simultaneously used, the amount of work-in-progress should be separately disclosed.

There is no equivalent requirement.

International accounting standards

Japanese standards

IAS 12 – Accounting for taxes on income
Requires tax effect accounting, using either the deferral or the liability method.

As the Commercial Code does not permit deferred tax debits, tax effect accounting cannot be used at the individual company level. Tax effect accounting is optional only when the timing differences arise on consolidation. The deferral method is commonly followed rather than the liability method. Disclosure is not required, however.

IAS 14 – Reporting financial information by segment
Requires segment information in financial statements of publicly traded companies and other economically significant entities including subsidiaries.

Additional segmental reporting is required by the SEL. The regulation was published in 1988 with effect from 1990.

IAS 15 – Information reflecting the effects of changing prices
Requires disclosure of the adjusted amount for changing prices on depreciation, cost of sales, monetary items and the overall effects of such adjustments as supplementary information.

No equivalent standard although the Opinion on Disclosure of Financial Information for Changing Price Level Accounting was issued in 1980 by the Business Accounting Deliberation Council.

IAS 16 – Accounting for property, plant and equipment
The gross carrying amount of an asset should be either the historical cost or the revalued amount.

In principle historical cost should be used.

Requires disclosure of the revaluation method including the policy on the frequency of revaluations.

There is no equivalent requirement.

IAS 17 – Accounting for leases

In 1988 new regulations stipulated that all companies must either capitalize finance leases or disclose the information in the notes in accordance with the Commercial Code.

International accounting standards

IAS 20 – Accounting for government grants and disclosure of government assistance
Government grants related to assets should be accounted for either as deferred income or as a deduction from related assets.

IAS 21 – Accounting for the effects of changes in foreign exchange rates
Long-term monetary items at the balance sheet date should be translated at the closing rate. Exchange differences should be recognized in income in the current period, but may be deferred and amortized on a systematic basis.
When translating foreign currency financial statements whose activities are relatively self-contained and integrated, the closing rate method should normally be used. The temporal method should be used for a foreign operation whose activities are integral to the operations of the parent.

The restate–translate method should be used for the financial statements of a foreign entity which is affected by high rates of inflation. Alternatively, the temporal method may be used.

IAS 22 – Accounting for business combinations
Permits immediate write-off of goodwill against shareholders' equity.

IAS 23 – Capitalization of borrowing costs
Borrowing costs include amortization of discount or premium on the issues of

Japanese standards

Government grants related to assets may be accounted for as a deduction from those assets.

Long-term monetary items should be translated at the historical rates. Accordingly, there is no exchange difference.

The temporal method should be used for a foreign branch provided that long-term monetary items are translated at the historical rate. A modified temporal method should be used for a foreign subsidiary or associate provided that long-term monetary items are translated at the historical rates. Under the modified temporal method, net income and retained earnings should be translated at the closing rate and exchange differences resulting from the translation of balance sheet items should be charged or credited to assets or liabilities as appropriate.
There is no equivalent requirement.

Write-off within five years is commonly applied.

Borrowing costs are limited only to interest costs incurred from borrowing.

International accounting standards

Japanese standards

debt securities, amortization of ancillary costs for the arrangement of borrowing, etc.

Borrowing costs of property, plant and equipment, investments in enterprises, inventory that requires a significant period of time to bring to a saleable condition, and real estate and other long-term development projects are capitalized.

Capitalization of borrowing costs is limited to tangible depreciable assets.

The capitalization rate should be determined.

Borrowing costs for the acquisition of particular assets are capitalized with the assets. Accordingly, the capitalization rate is not required to be calculated.

IAS 25 – Accounting for investments
Long-term investments should be stated at cost or revalued amounts.

Long-term investments other than shares in subsidiary companies must be stated at either cost or the lower of cost and market value. Shares in subsidiary companies should be stated at cost. However, where market value is significantly less than cost, marketable securities (including shares in subsidiary companies and long-term investments) should be carried at cost less any reduction in value unless the shortfall will be recovered.

Appendix D
Summary of the Main Principles Issued by BADC

The important announcements regarding accounting and auditing issued by BADC are as follows:

1 Business Accounting Principles (established in 1949, amended in 1982).
2 Auditing Standards (General, Field Work and Reporting Standards). The General and Field Work Principles were published in 1950 and amended in 1956. The Reporting Principles were published in 1956. Amendments to the General Principles were made in 1982, to the Field Work Principles in 1989, and Reporting Principles in 1982.
3 Cost Accounting Principles (Standards) (established in 1962).
4 Accounting Principles for Consolidated Financial Statements (established in 1975, amended in 1982).
5 Accounting Principles (Standards) for Interim Financial Statements (established in 1977, amended in 1982).
6 Accounting Principles (Standards) for Foreign Currency Transactions, etc. (established in 1979, amended in 1983).

Appendix E
Summary of the Main Recommendations Issued by the JICPA

There are a number of opinions, statements and comments on various accounting and auditing matters which have been issued by the President, Vice-President and Executive Directors of the Institute, and by directors of the inquiry office and a number of Institute Committees.

As of 1989, among others, the following statements have been issued by the Audit Committee:

Expressing of Auditor's Opinion on Accrued Severance Indemnities (March 1962).

Auditor's Report on Initial Registration Statements (May 1963).

Accounting for and Reporting on Depreciation (July 1963, amended in March 1984).

Accounting for and Reporting on Allowance for Doubtful Accounts (December 1964, amended in April 1976).

Confirmation of Receivables (October 1965).

Observation of Inventories (October 1965).

Representation in the Scope Paragraph of the Auditor's Report on Registration Statements (January 1972, partly amended in March 1984).

Standardization of Audit Working Papers (December 1973).

Criteria for Determining Materiality (October 1974).

Auditing Procedures for Commercial Code Purposes (April 1975).

Changes in Accounting Principles or Procedures due to Reasonable Cause (May 1975, amended in September 1982).

Valuation of Investments in Common Stock of and Advances to Subsidiaries or Affiliated Companies (March 1976).

Use of the Work and Reports of Other Independent Auditors (April 1977, partly amended in March 1984).

Example of Auditor's Report on Consolidated Financial Statements (April 1977).

Auditing Gains Resulting from Sales of Land or Equipment between Affiliated Companies (August 1977).

Auditor's Report on Interim Financial Statements (November 1977).

Provisional Guidelines for Auditing Consolidated Financial Statements (January 1978, partly amended in September 1982).

Example of an Auditor's Report on Initial Consolidated Financial Statements (March 1978).

Provisional Guidelines for Auditing Interim Financial Statements (September 1978, partly amended in September 1982).

Changes in Estimated Useful Lives of Depreciable Assets and Disclosure thereof (April 1979).

Accounting for, Reporting on and Auditing a Change to an Approved Pension Plan (April 1979).

Auditing Bonuses to Employees (January 1980).

Accounting for, Reporting on and Auditing Accrued Severance Indemnities due to Revisions of Corporation Income Taxes (April 1980).

Consistency of Accounting Treatments Used in Semi-Annual Financial Statements and Annual Financial Statements (August 1980, partly amended in March 1984).

List of Interim Auditing Procedures (December 1980).

Audits based on amendments to the Commercial Code (September 1982, partly amended in January 1989).

Illustration of an Auditor's Report based on the Commercial Code (September 1982, partly amended in January 1989).

Audit of Special Reserves Stipulated in the Special Taxation Measures Law (September 1982).

Audit of Advanced Depreciation (March 1983).

Audit of Subsequent Events (March 1983).

Accounting for and Reporting on Various Taxes (December 1983).

Provisional Guideline for Auditing Short-term Receivables and Payables in Foreign Currencies (January 1984).

Disclosure of Additional Information about Financial and Managemental Condition of Enterprise (March 1985).

Revision of Outline and Illustration of Letter from Auditor to Underwriter (July 1987).

Audit of Account for Specified Trust Deposits (March 1988).

Fullness and Reinforcement of Auditing Procedures on Financial Statement Items with High Risk Relatively (October 1988).

Appendix F
Business Accounting Principles

TABLE OF CONTENTS

FINANCIAL   ACCOUNTING   STANDARDS   FOR

BUSINESS   ENTERPRISES

I. GENERAL   STANDARDS

1. (Principle of true and fair reporting)
Financial   accounting   for   business   enterprises
should provide a true and fair report of the financial
position   and   of   the   results   of   operations   of   a
business enterprise.

2. (Principle of orderly bookkeeping)
Financial   accounting   for   business   enterprises
should   encompass   the   maintenance   of   accurate
accounting records of all transactions   in   accordance
with   the   principle   of   orderly   bookkeeping.
(Supplement 1)

3. (Principle of distinction between   capital   surplus
   and earned surplus)
Capital surplus and earned surplus should   be   kept
separate.   (Supplement 2)

4. (Principle of clear disclosure)
Financial   accounting   for   business   enterprises
should, through financial statements,   present clearly
essential accounting facts to interested   parties   and
present   them   in a manner that will not be misleading
in their interpretation of the financial status of the
business enterprise.   (Supplements 1,1-2,1-3 and 1-4)

5. (Principle of consistency)
Accounting   principles   and   practices   should   be
consistently applied between fiscal periods and should
not be changed without justifiable reason.(Supplements
1-2 and 3)

6. (Principle of concept of prudence)
Financial   accounting   for   business   enterprises
should   include   prudent   accounting practices   in
providing for possible unfavorable   effects   upon   the
financial   condition   of   a   business   enterprise.
(Supplement 4)

7. (Principle of single source)
When several different forms of financial statements are required for such purposes as a shareholders' meeting, credit rating, tax reporting, etc., the contents of the financial statements should be prepared from reliable accounting records and the presentation of facts should be the same for each presentation and should not be distorted by considering the enterprise's policies.

II. INCOME STATEMENT STANDARDS

NATURE OF INCOME STATEMENT

1. The income statement should describe all revenue and related expenses that belong to an accounting period so as to present fairly the results of operations of a business enterprise, and should present ordinary income and, by adding to or deducting from it extraordinary income or loss, net income of a business enterprise.

> A. All revenue and expenses should be recorded on the accrual basis and should be properly allocated to the appropriate periods. However, unrealized profit should not be recognized as current income.
> Prepaid expenses and deferred income should be excluded from the computation of current income but accrued expenses and accrued income should be included in the computation of current income. (Supplement 5)
>
> B. Revenue and expenses should be stated in gross amounts, so that, as a general rule, neither any part nor all of them should be eliminated from the income statement by being offset against each other.
>
> C. Revenue and expenses should be classified clearly according to their nature and source. Revenue items and related expense items should be presented in the income statement so as to match expenses with revenue.

- 2 -

CATEGORY OF INCOME STATEMENT

2. The income statement should be divided into categories of operating income, ordinary income and net income.

A. The category of operating income includes revenue and expenses arising from the operations of a business enterprise in order to arrive at the operating income.

If a business enterprise operates more than one line of business, the revenue and expenses from each main line of business should be stated separately.

B. The category of ordinary income, which follows the operating income, includes revenue and expenses arising from sources other than from business operations such as interest and discounts, gains or losses on the sale of marketable securities. Other income or loss items that are not extraordinary items should be included to arrive at ordinary income.

C. Following ordinary income, the category of net income is presented and includes certain prior period adjustments, gains or losses on the sale of fixed assets and other extraordinary items to arrive at net income.

D. Following net income, retained earnings brought forward are stated to arrive at unappropriated retained earnings.

OPERATING INCOME

3. The category of operating income includes sales for the accounting period and the related cost of sales to compute gross profit. Selling, general and administrative expenses are deducted therefrom to arrive at operating income.

A. If a business enterprise sells merchandise and other inventories and also renders services, sales from merchandise and other inventories and income from services are to be shown separately.

- 3 -

B. Sales should be limited to those recognized through the sale of merchandise and other inventories or the rendering of services in accordance with the realization principle. However, for long-term construction contracts in process, rationally estimated revenue may be included in the computation of current income. (Supplements 6 and 7)

C. The cost of sales represents the purchase costs or manufacturing costs of merchandise and other inventories that are matched against revenue. In the trading business, cost of sales is presented by adding to the beginning balance of merchandise the purchase costs for the period and deducting from the above total the ending balance of merchandise. In the manufacturing industry, cost of sales is presented by adding to the beginning balance of finished goods the manufacturing costs of finished goods for the period and deducting from the above total the ending balance of finished goods. (Supplements 8, 9 and 10)

D. Gross profit is to be presented by deducting cost of sales from sales.
    Gross profit from services rendered is to be presented by deducting service costs incurred from service income.

E. Intracompany profits arising from transfers of inventories and other assets between departmental segments of the same business enterprise should be eliminated from the computation of sales and cost of sales. (Supplement 11)

F. Operating income should be presented by deducting selling, general and administrative expenses from gross profit. Selling, general and administrative expenses should be included in the operating income category under a proper caption and should not be included in cost of sales or the ending balance of inventories. However, for long-term construction contracts, selling, general and administrative expenses may be allocated to the construction contract work on an appropriate ratio and included in cost of sales and the ending balance of contracts in process.

- 4 -

NON-OPERATING INCOME OR EXPENSES

4. Non-operating income or expenses should be presented separately. Non-operating income should include such items as interest and discount income, gains on sales of marketable securities, etc., while non-operating expenses should include such items as interest and discount expenses, losses on sales of marketable securities, valuation losses on marketable securities, etc.

ORDINARY INCOME

5. Ordinary income is to be presented by adding non-operating income to operating income and deducting non-operating expenses from the above total.

EXTRAORDINARY INCOME OR LOSS

6. Extraordinary income or loss should be presented separately. Extraordinary income should include such items as prior period adjustments, gains on sales of fixed assets, etc., and extraordinary loss should include such items as prior period adjustments, losses on sales of fixed assets, casualty losses, etc. (Supplement 12)

INCOME BEFORE TAXES

7. Income before taxes should be presented by adding extraordinary income to ordinary income and deducting any extraordinary loss from the above total.

NET INCOME

8. Net income should be presented by deducting the amount of corporate income tax, inhabitants tax and other taxes that are chargeable to the current period. (Supplement 13)

UNAPPROPRIATED RETAINED EARNINGS

9. Unappropriated retained earnings are to be presented by adding to or deducting from net income the retained earnings brought forward, any reversals of appropriated retained earnings upon attainment of the specific purpose for which the appropriation had been made, interim dividends declared, the legal reserve as required in relation to interim dividends and other similar items.

III. BALANCE SHEET STANDARDS

NATURE OF BALANCE SHEET

1. The balance sheet should include all assets, liabilities, and shareholders' equity of the enterprise as of the balance sheet date and should fairly present them to shareholders, creditors and other interested parties so as to show clearly the financial position of a business enterprise. Certain immaterial assets and liabilities may not be recorded, only when such practices are in accordance with the principle of orderly bookkeeping. (Supplement 1)

    A. Assets, liabilities and shareholders' equity shown on the balance sheet should be presented after considering their appropriate category, arrangement and classification, and should be valued appropriately.

    B. Assets, liabilities and shareholders' equity should be shown in gross amounts. Neither any part nor all of them should be eliminated from the balance sheet by offsetting assets against liabilities or shareholders' equity.

    C. The following items, if considered material in interpreting the financial condition of a business enterprise, should be disclosed in the notes to the balance sheet: balance of notes receivable discounted or endorsed, contingent liabilities for guarantees of indebtedness, assets pledged as collateral against obligations, net income and net assets per share, etc.

- 6 -

D. Certain expenses that pertain to future periods may be included in the assets category of the balance sheet for allocation to future periods. (Supplement 15)

E. The total amount of assets should be equal to the total amount of liabilities and shareholders' equity.

CATEGORY OF BALANCE SHEET

2. The balance sheet should be separated into three major categories: assets, liabilities, and shareholders' equity. Assets should be further classified into current assets, fixed assets and deferred charges. Liabilities should be classified into current liabilities and non-current liabilities.

ARRANGEMENT OF BALANCE SHEET

3. Captions of assets and liabilities are to be arranged so that the most liquid assets and liabilities are presented first, as a general rule.

CLASSIFICATION OF BALANCE SHEET

4. Assets, liabilities and shareholders' equity should be clearly classified in the balance sheet in conformity with predetermined principles as follows:

(1) Assets
Assets should be classified into current assets, fixed assets and deferred charges. Suspense payments and other suspense items should be presented under appropriate captions that clarify their nature. (Supplement 16)

A. The following items are to be included in current assets: cash on hand and in banks, marketable securities held for a short-term, notes receivable, accounts receivable and other receivables arising in the normal course of operations with trade customers; merchandise, finished goods, semi-finished goods, raw

- 7 -

materials,   work   in   process   and   other
inventories,   and other receivables due   within
one year.

Prepaid expenses   which   are to be   expensed
within one year belong in current assets.

Notes receivable,   accounts   receivable   and
other receivables classified as current   assets
should   be segregated between trade receivables
from customers arising in the normal course   of
operations and other receivables.

B. Fixed   assets   should   be   classified   into
tangible fixed assets,   intangible fixed assets
and investments and other assets.

The following items should be classified   as
tangible fixed assets: buildings,   structures,
machinery, ships,   vehicles,   tools,   furniture
and fixtures,   land,   construction in progress,
etc.

Goodwill,   patents, leaseholds, trade marks,
etc.   should be classified as intangible   fixed
assets.

The following items should be classified   as
investments and other assets: investments   in
subsidiaries   and   other   investments   in
securities that   do   not   belong in   current
assets,   investments   in   equities   other than
stock ownership,   long-term   loans   and   other
non-current   assets   that   do   not   belong   in
tangible fixed assets,   intangible fixed assets
or deferred charges.

Accumulated depreciation of   tangible   fixed
assets   should   be   shown   in   principle   as   a
deduction   from   the   acquisition   cost under a
separate   caption   for   each   of   the   assets.
(Supplement 17)

Intangible fixed assets should be stated   at
their unamortized balance.

C. The   following   items   belong   in   deferred
charges: organization   costs,   preoperating
costs,   new stock issuing costs,   bond issuing
costs,   bond   discounts,   development   costs,
research and   experiment   costs,   and interest
paid   to   shareholders   as   dividends   during
construction   as   permitted   by   the Commercial
Code.   These assets should be stated   at   their

unamortized balance. (Supplement 15)

D. Allowances for doubtful notes receivable, accounts receivable and other receivables should be shown in principle as a deduction from the amount of receivables or the acquisition cost on an individual basis for each of the above captions. (Supplements 17 and 18)

Receivables from directors, statutory auditors and employees within a business enterprise and receivables from a parent or subsidiaries should be presented under certain appropriate captions separately from other receivables. Otherwise, the details of such receivables should be clearly disclosed in the notes.

(2) Liabilities

Liabilities should be classified into current liabilities or non-current liabilities. Suspense receipts and other suspense items should be presented under appropriate captions that clarify their nature. (Supplement 16)

A. Notes payable, accounts payable and other payables arising in the normal course of operations with vendors and other payables that become due within one year belong in current liabilities.

Notes payable, accounts payable and other payables that belong in current liabilities should be segregated between payables to vendors arising in the normal course of operations and other payables.

Reserves, such as reserve for employees' bonuses, reserve for guarantee on construction, reserve for repairs and other reserves that are expected to be due within one year belong in current liabilities. (Supplement 18)

B. Bonds, long-term loans payable and other long-term payables belong in non-current liabilities.

Reserves, such as reserve for retirement allowance, reserve for periodical repairs and other reserves that fall due beyond one year

- 9 -

belong in non-current liabilities. (Supplement 18)

C. Payables to directors, statutory auditors and employees within a business enterprise and payables to a parent and subsidiaries should be presented under certain appropriate captions separately from other payables. Otherwise, the details of such payables should be clearly disclosed in the notes.

(3) Shareholders' equity
Shareholders' equity should be classified into capital stock and surplus items. (Supplement 19)

A. The category of capital stock includes only the legal capital of a business enterprise. The number of issued shares should be disclosed in the notes by class of stock such as common stock, preferred stock, etc.

B. Surplus items should be classified into capital reserves, legal reserve and retained earnings.
The following items are to be presented as capital reserves: paid-in surplus, gain from reductions in capital stock and gain from merger transactions.
Retained earnings are to be presented as appropriated retained earnings and unappropriated retained earnings.

C. Consideration or subscription deposits for new stock to be issued after the closing date for subscriptions should be shown separately under an appropriate caption next to capital stock.

D. Certain reserves that are prescribed by law and are similar to the capital reserve or legal reserve should be presented in a separate caption under capital reserve or legal reserve.

VALUATION OF ASSETS IN THE BALANCE SHEET

5. The valuation of assets shown in the balance sheet should primarily be on the basis of their acquisition cost.

The acquisition cost of assets should be allocated to each applicable fiscal period based on a suitable allocation of cost for the respective type of asset. The acquisition cost of tangible fixed assets should be allocated to each fiscal period over their useful lives using prescribed depreciation methods such as the straight-line method, declining-balance method or other acceptable methods. The acquisition cost of intangible fixed assets should be allocated to each fiscal period based on an appropriate amortization method over the estimated useful lives of the intangible fixed assets. Likewise, the acquisition cost of deferred charges should be amortized at an equal amount or more. (Supplement 20)

A. Merchandise, finished goods, semi-finished goods, raw materials, work in process and other inventories as shown in the balance sheet are to be stated at their acquisition cost. Acquisition costs may be determined on the basis of actual purchase price or manufacturing costs plus handling and other incidental charges, to which one of the following costing methods should be applied: specific identification, FIFO, LIFO, average cost or other acceptable methods. However, if the market value is substantially lower than the acquisition cost, inventories should be stated at the market value unless the decline is due to a temporary condition. (Supplements 9, 10 and 21)

Inventories may be stated at the market value only when the market value declines below acquisition cost. (Supplement 10)

B. Securities as shown in the balance sheet are to be stated at their acquisition cost, which is primarily determined on the basis of purchase price plus brokerage commission and other incidental charges, to which aggregate average cost or other acceptable methods should be applied. However, if the market value is substantially lower than cost, marketable securities should be stated at the market value except where the decline is due to a

- 11 -

temporary condition. Non-marketable stock should be written down to fair value where the value of the investment, reflecting the investor's equity in the net assets of the invested company, is substantially below the carrying value of the investment. (Supplement 22)

Marketable securities excluding investments in subsidiaries may be stated at their market value when the market value declines below the acquisition cost.

C. Notes receivable, accounts receivable and other receivables should be stated at the amount of the receivables or acquisition cost less any amounts normally considered uncollectible. (Supplement 23)

D. Tangible fixed assets as shown in the balance sheet should be stated at their acquisition cost less accumulated depreciation. The acquisition cost of tangible fixed assets includes handling and other incidental charges, in addition to the purchase price. Fixed assets which are acquired in exchange for capital stock should be valued at the issue price of the stock to investors. (Supplement 24)

Fully depreciated tangible fixed assets should be stated at residual value or nominal value until they are disposed of.

E. Intangible fixed assets should be stated at the amounts paid to acquire the assets concerned less accumulated amortization. (Supplement 25)

F. Assets donated or acquired free of charge should be valued at their fair value. (Supplement 24)

- 12 -

IV. SUPPLEMENTS   TO   FINANCIAL   ACCOUNTING   STANDARDS

FOR   BUSINESS   ENTERPRISES

SUPPLEMENT 1   APPLICATION OF MATERIALITY CONCEPT
(General Standards   2,   4   and   Balance
Sheet Standard 1)

Although   financial   accounting   for   business
enterprises   should present an accurate computation in
accordance with the prescribed   accounting   principles
and   procedures,   it   is   permissible   to apply other
convenient   methods   to   immaterial   items   without
recourse   to   fundamental   and   rigid   accounting
principles   and   procedures   since   the   objective   of
financial   accounting for business enterprises lies in
clarifying the   financial   condition   and   results   of
operations   of a business enterprise and in presenting
interested parties with the facts in such a   way   that
will   not be misleading in their interpretation of the
financial status of a business   enterprise.   In   this
case,   recourse to such convenient methods is regarded
as being in accordance with the principle   of   orderly
bookkeeping.

The concept of materiality is   also   applicable   to
the presentation of financial statements.

Examples to which the concept of materiality may be
applied are as follows:

(1) Certain supplies,   expendable tools, furnitures
and fixtures and other supplies may be   treated   as
having   been   expensed   when purchased or used,   if
they are considered immaterial.

(2) Certain prepaid expenses,   accrued   income,
accrued expenses and deferred income may be handled
as current period items,   if   they   are   considered
immaterial.

(3) Certain reserves may not be provided   for,   if
they are considered immaterial.

(4) Certain incidental charges which are includible
in the acquisition costs   of   inventories   such   as
handling charges,   customs,   buying credit charges,
transfer   costs,   warehousing   costs   and   other

incidental charges, may be excluded from the
acquisition cost of inventories, if they are
considered immaterial.

(5) The current portion of long-term receivables or
payables to be settled on an installment basis may
be included in fixed assets or non-current
liabilities, if they are considered immaterial.

SUPPLEMENT 1-2   DISCLOSURE OF SIGNIFICANT ACCOUNTING
                 POLICIES
                 (General Standards 4 and 5)

Significant accounting policies should be noted in
the financial statements.
Accounting policies are accounting principles and
practices and presentation methods adopted so as to
present fairly the financial position and the results
of operations of a business enterprise in preparing
the income statement and balance sheet.
Examples of accounting policies are as follows:

(1) Basis and method of valuation of securities
(2) Basis and method of valuation of inventories
(3) Depreciation method for fixed assets
(4) Accounting for deferred charges
(5) Method of translation into Japanese yen of
    assets or liabilities in foreign currencies
(6) Objectives and basis of recording reserves
(7) Basis of recording expenses and revenue

Accounting policies for which there is no
alternative need not be noted in the financial
statement.

SUPPLEMENT 1-3   DISCLOSURE OF SIGNIFICANT SUBSEQUENT
                 EVENTS
                 (General Standard 4)

Significant subsequent events which have occurred
up to the date of preparation of the income statement
and balance sheet should be noted in the financial
statements.
Subsequent events are events occurring after the
balance sheet date and affecting the financial

- 14 -

position and the results of operations for the following period and thereafter.

It is useful as supplementary information in understanding the financial position and the results of operations in the future of a given business enterprise to disclose significant subsequent events in the notes.

Examples of significant subsequent events are as follows:

(1) Occurrence of substantial damage by fire, flood, etc.
(2) Increase or reduction in capital stock and issuance or early redemption of bonds
(3) Merger of companies, sale or purchase of important operations
(4) Occurrence or solution of important litigation
(5) Bankruptcy of important customers

SUPPLEMENT 1-4   PRESENTATION OF NOTES
             (General Standard 4)

Notes regarding significant accounting policies should be stated immediately following the income statement and balance sheet.

Other notes should be stated following the significant accounting policies.

SUPPLEMENT 2   DISTINCTION BETWEEN CAPITAL TRANSACTIONS
            AND REVENUE-EXPENSE TRANSACTIONS
            (General Standard 3)

(1) Capital surplus arises from capital transactions, and earned surplus arises from revenue-expense transactions, i.e., the amounts retained from net income. If both surpluses are combined, the financial position and the results of operations of a business enterprise will not be presented fairly. Therefore, for example, it is not permissible to deduct issuing costs from paid-in surplus resulting from a new stock issue.

(2) The amount of capital surplus which is permitted to be allocated to capital reserves under the Commercial Code is limited. Therefore, the amount of

- 15 -

capital surplus except for capital reserves and similar reserves prescribed by law, if any, is to be included in the category of retained earnings.

SUPPLEMENT 3   CONSISTENCY IN FINANCIAL ACCOUNTING
(General Standard 5)

Consistency in financial accounting for a business enterprise comes into question only when there exist two or more acceptable alternative accounting principles and practices for one accounting fact.

If a business enterprise does not apply accounting principles and practices consistently between periods, a different profit figure would result from the same accounting fact. Also, there would be a lack of interperiod comparability of financial statements which would consequently mislead interested parties in evaluating the financial conditions of a business enterprise.

Therefore, except for a justifiable change, the accounting principles and practices adopted by management in the preparation of financial statements should be applied consistently between accounting periods.

Furthermore, a justifiable change in accounting principles and practices, which has a material effect on the financial statements, should be disclosed in the notes thereto.

SUPPLEMENT 4   CONCEPT OF PRUDENCE
(General Standard 6)

Financial accounting for business enterprises should be based upon prudent accounting practices in providing against unfavorable effects of future events. However, the fair presentation of the financial position and the results of operations of a business enterprise should not be distorted through the application of excessively conservative accounting practices.

- 16 -

SUPPLEMENT 5   PREPAID   EXPENSES,   DEFERRED   INCOME,
ACCRUED EXPENSES AND ACCRUED INCOME ·
(Income Statement Standard 1.A.,   2nd
paragraph)

(1) Prepaid Expenses
Prepaid expenses represent considerations paid for
services that have not yet been rendered where such
services will be rendered continuously based on a
certain contract. They should, therefore, be excluded
from the determination of current income and be stated
as an asset, since they will be expensed in future
periods. Furthermore, such prepaid expenses should be
distinguished from advance payments made under the
terms of a contract for other than the rendering of
services.

(2) Deferred Income
Deferred income represents considerations received
in advance for services yet to be rendered where such
services will be rendered continuously based on a
certain contract.   Such deferred   income should,
therefore, be excluded from the determination of
current income and should be classified as   a
liability, since the income will be realized in future
periods.   Furthermore,   deferred income should be
distinguished from advances received under the terms
of a contract for other than the rendering of
services.

(3) Accrued Expenses
Accrued expenses represent any consideration yet
to be paid for services that have already been
received where such services will   be   rendered
continuously based on a certain contract.   They
should, therefore, be included in current income and
should be recorded as a liability, since the expenses
have already been incurred in the current period.
Furthermore, accrued expenses should be distinguished
from payables under the terms of a contract for other
than the rendering of services.

(4) Accrued Income
Accrued income represents any consideration yet to
be received for services that have already been
rendered where such services will be rendered
continuously based on a certain contract.   Accrued

- 17 -

income should, therefore, be included in the determination of current income and should be recorded as an asset, since the income has already been earned in the current period. Furthermore, accrued income should be distinguished from receivables under the terms of a contract for other than the rendering of services.

SUPPLEMENT 6   APPLICATION OF REALIZATION PRINCIPLE
               (Income Statement Standard 3.B)

In applying the realization principle to revenue from sales, the following methods are to be adopted for consignment sales, sales on approval, subscription sales, installment sales and other sales prescribed by a specific sales contract.

(1) Consignment Sales
     Revenue from consignment sales should be recognized when a consignee sells the consigned goods. A business enterprise should record the revenue from consigned goods for which sales have been made on or before the balance sheet date. Such fact becomes evident before the books have been closed by receiving sales advices (sales report) or other evidence. However, sales revenue may be alternatively recognized at the date when a business enterprise receives sales advices from the consignee, if such sales advices are issued with each sale.

(2) Sales on Approval
     Revenue from sales on approval should be recorded in the current period only when a customer approves of the goods purchased, since such revenue will be recognized when the intention to purchase is indicated.

(3) Subscription Sales
     When deposits for subscriptions are received in advance, revenue from subscription sales should be recorded in the current period only to the extent that the delivery of goods or rendering of services has been completed. The remaining portion of deposits should be recorded as a liability.

- 18 -

(4) Installment Sales
    Revenue from installment sales should be
recognized at the date of delivery of the
merchandise.
    Since collection of receivables on installment
sales are made over an extended period of time and
under the terms of an installment plan,
collectability is uncertain in comparison with
ordinary sales. Therefore, special consideration
is required in providing an appropriate allowance
for doubtful accounts, collection expenses for
outstanding accounts, warranty costs, etc.
Uncertainty and complexity are often encountered
in determining the above allowance. In order to
recognize revenue prudently, it may, therefore, be
permissible to recognize revenue at the date, in
lieu of the date of delivery, when the installment
payment becomes due or when the payment is
received.

SUPPLEMENT 7   REVENUE ON CONSTRUCTION CONTRACTS
               (Income Statement Standard 3.B.,   2nd
               sentence)

    In recognizing revenue from long-term construction
contracts, either the percentage-of-completion method
or the completed contract method may be applied.

(1) Percentage-Of-Completion Method
    Under this method revenue for the current
period is recognized at an appropriate percentage
of total revenue, and expenses are calculated at
the same percentage of the total estimated cost to
completion. The percentage is determined in
proportion to the estimated percentage of
completion at the end of each fiscal period.

(2) Completed-Contract Method
    Under this method revenue is recognized at the
date when the contract is completed and delivery
has been made.

- 19 -

SUPPLEMENT 8   MANUFACTURING COSTS OF FINISHED GOODS
               AND OTHER INVENTORIES
               (Income Statement Standard 3.C)

The manufacturing cost of finished goods and other inventories should be determined in accordance with appropriate cost accounting standards.

SUPPLEMENT 9   ACCOUNTING FOR COST VARIANCE
               (Income Statement Standard 3.C. and
               Balance Sheet Standard 5.A., 1st
               paragraph)

Where the cost variance is charged to cost of sales, this variance is to be stated separately under the cost of sales heading, as per the following form at:

Cost of Sales
1. Beginning balance of finished goods   XXX
2. Manufacturing cost of finished goods   XXX
               Total   XXX
3. Ending balance of finished goods   XXX
   Standard (or predetermined) cost of
   sales   XXX
4. Cost variance   XXX XXX

Where the cost variance is allocated to applicable items of inventory, such variances should be included in each respective amount of inventory in the balance sheet.

SUPPLEMENT 10   VALUATION LOSSES OF INVENTORY
                (Income Statement Standard 3.C. and
                Balance Sheet Standard 5.A.)

(1) Valuation losses arising from applying "the lower of cost or market" method to merchandise, finished goods, raw materials and other inventories should be shown separately under the cost of sales category or the non-operating expenses category.

(2) Valuation losses arising from a substantial decline in market value below cost (as described in the Balance Sheet Standard 5.A., 2nd sentence) should

- 20 -

be shown under the category of non-operating expenses or extraordinary losses.

(3) Valuation losses arising from deterioration in quality, obsolescence or other reasons should be shown under the category of non-operating expenses or extraordinary losses if such losses are considered not to have the nature of "cost". If such losses are considered to have the nature of "cost", they should be shown separately under the heading of manufacturing cost, cost of sales or selling expense.

SUPPLEMENT 11   INTRACOMPANY   PROFITS   AND   THEIR
ELIMINATION FROM THE INCOME STATEMENT
(Income Statement Standard 3.E)

Unrealized intracompany profits arise from internal transactions between independent accounting units within a business enterprise such as the head office, branch offices, divisions, etc. Cost variances arising from the transfer of raw materials, semi-finished goods and other assets within the same accounting unit are not considered intracompany profits.

Intracompany profits are eliminated from the income statement of the company by subtracting intracompany sales from total sales and by subtracting intracompany purchases (or intracompany cost of sales) from total purchases (or total cost of sales). In addition, intracompany profits are eliminated from the related ending balance of inventories. A reasonably estimated amount may be used as the basis for these subtractions.

SUPPLEMENT 12   EXTRAORDINARY ITEMS
(Income Statement Standard 6)

Extraordinary items are as follows:

(1) Non-recurring items;
    a. Gain or loss on sale of fixed assets
    b. Gain or loss on sale of securities acquired for purposes other than resale
    c. Casualty loss

- 21 -

(2) Prior period adjustments;
   a. Adjustment of reserves provided in prior periods
   b. Adjustment of depreciation provided in prior periods
   c. Correction of inventory valuation made in prior periods
   d. Recovery of bad debts written off in prior periods.

Extraordinary items of an immaterial amount or of a recurring nature may be classified as ordinary income.

SUPPLEMENT 13   ADDITIONAL ASSESSMENTS (OR REFUNDS) OF CORPORATE INCOME TAXES
(Income Statement Standard 8)

Additional assessments (or refunds) of corporate income taxes caused by a tax authority's examination should be shown as being deducted from (or added to) the income before taxes. In this case, if the amount is considered immaterial it may be included in the corporate income taxes for the period, although as a general rule, it should be separated from taxes for the period.

(SUPPLEMENT 14   Eliminated)

SUPPLEMENT 15   CERTAIN EXPENSES AFFECTING FUTURE PERIODS
(Balance Sheet Standards 1.D. and 4.(1).C)

"Certain expenses affecting future periods" represent the amounts paid or made due for services already received but the benefit of which is expected to be realized in future periods.
In order to allocate such expenses reasonably over the periods in which the resulting benefit will be realized, they may be shown as deferred charges in the balance sheet.
Further, extraordinary losses such as those which are caused by a natural disaster, etc. on fixed

- 22 -

assets or assets essential to the business operations
may be deferred and shown as an asset on the balance
sheet only if they are so significant in amount that
they are in excess of net income, or unappropriated
retained earnings less estimated appropriations for
the period and if the deferral is permitted by law.

SUPPLEMENT 16 STANDARDS FOR DISTINGUISHING CURRENT
ASSETS OR LIABILITIES FROM FIXED ASSETS
OR NON-CURRENT LIABILITIES
(Balance Sheet Standards 4.(1) and (2))

Receivables and payables arising from the main
operations of a business enterprise such as notes
receivable, accounts receivable, advance payments,
notes payable, accounts payable, advances received,
etc. should be classified as current assets or
current liabilities. However, receivables from
companies in bankruptcy, reorganization and other
similar conditions, which are evidently not
collectible within one year, should be reclassified as
investments and other assets in the fixed assets
category.

Receivables and payables such as loans receivable,
loans payable, guaranty money paid, guaranty money
received, and other receivables and payables, arising
from other than the main operations of a business
enterprise, should be classified as current assets or
liabilities, if their receipt or payment falls due
within one year starting from the day following the
balance sheet date. If the receipts or payments fall
due over one year, they should be classified as
investments and other assets or non-current
liabilities.

Cash on hand and in banks should be classified as
current assets. Cash in banks that may be withdrawn
within one year starting from the day following the
balance sheet date, should be classified as current
assets and those which may be withdrawn after more
than one year should be classified as investments and
other assets.

Marketable securities held on a short-term basis
for temporary investment of funds should be classified
as current assets, and those that are not marketable
or that are held as long-term investments for the
purpose of exercising control over invested companies

should be classified as investments and other assets.

That portion of prepaid expenses that is to be amortized or written off within one year from the day following the balance sheet date should be classified as current assets, and that portion chargeable to an accounting period or periods after one year should be classified as investments and other assets. Accrued income should be classified as a current asset, and accrued expenses and deferred income should be classified as current liabilities.

Merchandise, finished goods, semi-finished goods, raw materials, work in process and other inventories should be classified as current assets. Those products that are in use for business purposes but not held for processing or selling should be classified as fixed assets.

If the residual useful lives of certain fixed assets are one year or less than one year, they should still be classified as fixed assets. Certain inventories that are held for base stock or owned on a long-term basis as excess stock should be classified as current assets.

SUPPLEMENT 17   PRESENTATION OF ALLOWANCE FOR DOUBTFUL
ACCOUNTS OR ACCUMULATED DEPRECIATION
(Balance Sheet Standards 4.(1).B., 5th
paragraph and 4.(1).D., 1st paragraph)

An allowance for doubtful accounts or accumulated depreciation should be shown as a deduction from the claims or tangible fixed assets to which it relates on an individual basis. However, the following methods are acceptable:

(1) An allowance for doubtful accounts or accumulated depreciation may be shown in a lump sum as a deduction from two or more accounts.

(2) An allowance for doubtful accounts or accumulated depreciation may be netted against related claims or fixed assets if the amounts deducted are disclosed.

SUPPLEMENT 18   RESERVES
                (Balance Sheet Standards 4.(1).D., 1st
                paragraph, 4.(2).A., 3rd paragraph and
                4.(2).B., 2nd paragraph)

Certain costs or losses expected to be incurred in future periods should be charged to income as expenses or losses by providing for a reserve in the liabilities or assets section. Such reserves should be provided when expenses are incurred for the current period or before, if it is probable that they will occur and if their amounts can be reasonably estimated.

Such reserves are as follows: Warranty reserve, reserve for sales rebates, reserve for sales returns, reserve for employees' bonuses, reserve for guaranty on construction, reserve for retirement allowance, reserve for repairs, reserve for periodical repairs, reserve for guaranty loss, reserve for reparations and allowance for doubtful accounts, etc.

Cost or losses regarding contingencies which are unlikely to occur should not be provided as a reserve.

SUPPLEMENT 19   SURPLUS
                (Balance Sheet Standard 4.(3))

The amount of net assets in excess of legal capital is called surplus.

Surplus includes capital surplus and earned surplus.

(1) Capital surplus:
    Paid-in surplus, gains from reductions in capital stock, gains from merger transactions, etc.

    Further, it is permissible not to treat as capital surplus the portion of gains from merger transactions corresponding to the earned surplus of the merged company.

(2) Earned surplus:
    Surplus retained from earnings.

SUPPLEMENT 20   METHODS OF DEPRECIATION
                (Balance Sheet   Standard   5.,   2nd
                paragraph)

The following are methods of depreciating fixed
assets:

(1) Straight-Line Method
An equal amount of depreciation is charged
against each period over the estimated useful
lives of the fixed asset.

(2) Declining-Balance Method
The amount of depreciation is computed by
multiplying the net book value of the asset at the
beginning of the period by a predetermined
percentage based on the estimated useful lives of
the fixed asset.

(3) Sum-Of-The-Years-Digits Method
The amount of depreciation is determined on a
decelerated basis as computed by arithmetical
progression in each period over the estimated
useful lives.

(4) Unit-Of-Production Method
The amount of depreciation is determined in
proportion to the unit output or rendering of
services over the estimated useful lives of the
fixed asset.
This method may be applied to fixed assets
such as equipment for mining, airplanes,
automobiles, etc., where the total available units
of production or service can be physically
predetermined and where depletion will occur in
proportion to the use of the fixed asset.

Further, for those fixed assets which consist of
an assembly of various parts and whose serviceability
is maintained by repetitious replacement of worn-out
parts, the replacement method may be employed. Under
this method the expense required for partial
replacement is treated as the expenditure.

SUPPLEMENT 21   VALUE OF INVENTORIES TO BE PRESENTED IN THE BALANCE SHEET
(Balance Sheet Standard 5.A., 1st paragraph)

(1) The following are acceptable methods for determining the value of inventories to be presented in the balance sheet.

a. Specific Identification Method
Inventory cost at the year-end is determined via the specific identification of actual costs with individual inventory units that have been recorded and stored separately from items with a different cost.

b. First-in, First-out Method (FIFO)
Inventory cost at the year-end is determined on the assumption that the first units received are the first ones sold or delivered and that inventories at the year end consist of those which are the most recently acquired.

c. Last-in, First-out Method (LIFO)
Inventory cost at the year-end is determined on the assumption that the most recently acquired units are the first ones sold or delivered and that the earliest items remain in year end inventories.

d. Average Cost Method
Inventories at the year-end are determined by calculating the average cost of acquired inventories.
The average cost may be calculated based on the periodic average method or the moving average method.

e. Retail Inventory Method
Inventory cost at the year-end is determined by applying each cost ratio to each retail price group of ending goods after categorizing different kinds of goods in accordance with the similarity of their mark-up ratio.
This method is applied in pricing certain

- 27 -

retailers' and wholesalers' inventories that involve large numbers of goods.

(2) The manufacturing cost of finished goods and the like may be determined by applying a predetermined cost or a standard cost in accordance with appropriate cost accounting standards.

SUPPLEMENT 22   VALUE OF BONDS TO BE PRESENTED IN THE BALANCE SHEET
(Balance Sheet Standard 5.B., 1st paragraph)

Company-owned bonds may be presented at an amount which includes a premium or discount from their face value if they were purchased at such cost. In this case, in order to present these in the balance sheet on a consistent basis, the premium or discount will periodically be added to or deducted from the value of bonds by way of corresponding credits or charges to income over the periods to the maturity date of the bonds.

SUPPLEMENT 23   VALUE OF RECEIVABLES TO BE PRESENTED IN THE BALANCE SHEET
(Balance Sheet Standard 5.C)

Receivables may be presented at acquisition cost, where they were acquired at an amount below face value, or in other similar cases. In such cases, the difference may be amortized on a consistent basis over the periods to the maturity date of the receivable.

SUPPLEMENT 24   ASSETS ACQUIRED WITH A GOVERNMENT SUBSIDY, ETC.
(Balance Sheet Standards 5.D., 1st paragraph and 5.F)

Where assets are acquired with a government subsidy and/or a contribution to assist construction, such subsidy, etc., may be deducted from the acquisition cost of the assets.
In this case, either of the following methods are

- 28 -

acceptable for presentation in the balance sheet:

(1) State the amount of the government subsidy as a deduction from the acquisition cost.

(2) State the net amount of the acquisition cost and disclose in the notes the amount deducted therefrom.

SUPPLEMENT 25 GOODWILL
          (Balance Sheet Standard 5.E)

Goodwill should be recognized in the balance sheet only when purchased with consideration or acquired via a merger, and should be amortized at an equal amount or more.

Appendix G
JICPA Recommended Forms for the Commercial Code Schedules

1. Schedule of changes in capital stock and statutory reserves

	Balance at beginning of period	Increase	Decrease	Balance at end of period
(Issued shares) Capital stock	(shares) ¥	(shares) ¥	(shares) ¥	(shares) ¥
Capital reserve				
Legal reserve				

2. Schedule of changes in bonds and other long and short-term borrowings

(1) Changes in bonds

Name of bonds	Total amount issued	Outstanding balance at beginning of period	Current issuance	Current retirement or conversion into capital stock	Outstanding balance at end of period (Current portion)
	¥	¥	¥	¥	¥ (¥)
					( )
Total	¥	¥	¥	¥	¥ (¥)

(2) Changes in borrowings

a. Changes in long-term borrowings

Lender	Balance at beginning of period	Increase	Decrease	Balance at end of period (Current portion)
	¥	¥	¥	¥ (¥)
				( )
Total	¥	¥	¥	¥ (¥)

b. Changes in short-term borrowings

Lender	Balance at beginning of period	Balance at end of period	Net changes
	¥	¥	¥
Current portion of long-term borrowings			
Total	¥	¥	¥

3. Schedule of changes in fixed assets and accumulated depreciation

	Kind of assets	Book value at beginning of period	Increase	Decrease	Depreciation	Book value at end of period	Accumulated depreciation at end of period	Ratio of accumulated depreciation over acquisition cost
Tangible fixed assets		¥	¥	¥	¥	¥	¥	
	Total							
Intangible fixed assets								
	Total							
Investments and other								
	Total							

4. Schedule of collateralized assets

Collateralized assets			Corresponding liabilities	
Kind of assets	Book value at end of period	Type of collateral	Description	Balance at end of period
	¥			¥
Total	¥		Total	¥

5. Schedule of debt guarantees

Guarantee	Amount guaranteed	Type of debt guaranteed
	¥	
Other, total		
Total	¥	

6. Schedule of reserves

Name of reserve	Balance at beginning of period	Provided	Used	Balance at end of period
	¥	¥	¥	¥

7. Schedule of amounts due from/due to controlling shareholder

(1) Schedule of amounts due from controlling shareholder

Name of controlling shareholder	Short-term receivables			Long-term receivables		
	Account title	Account title	Total	Account title	Account title	Total
	¥	¥	¥	¥	¥	¥

(2) Schedule of amounts due to controlling shareholder

Name of controlling shareholder	Short-term payables			Long-term payables		
	Account title	Account title	Total	Account title	Account title	Total
	¥	¥	¥	¥	¥	¥

Note: The controlling shareholder is an individual or a corporation having more than 50 percent of the issued shares of the Company.

8. Schedule of equity ownership in subsidiaries and the number of shares of the Company's stock held by those subsidiaries

Name of subsidiary	Balance at beginning of Period		Current changes		Balance at end of period			Number of shares of Company's stock held by subsidiary
	Number of shares	Book value	Number of shares	Amount	Number of shares	Acquisition cost	Book value	
		¥		¥		¥	¥	
Other, total								
Total		¥		¥		¥	¥	

9. Schedule of amounts due from subsidiaries

Name of subsidiaries	Short-term receivables			Long-term receivables		
	Account title	Account title	Total	Account title	Account title	Total
	¥	¥	¥	¥	¥	¥
Other, total						
Total	¥	¥	¥	¥	¥	¥

10. Schedule of transactions with directors, statutory auditor and controlling shareholders

Classifi-cation	Name	Details of transaction	Amount of transaction	Remarks
			¥	
Director				
Statutory auditor				
Controlling shareholder				

11. Schedule of remuneration paid to directors and statutory auditors

	Number of persons paid during the period	Amount paid during the period	Remarks
Directors		¥	
Statutory auditors			
Total		¥	

12. Schedule of the treasury stock and the parent company's stock held as collateral

Classification	Reason for holding collateral	Number of shares held as collateral
Treasury stock		shares
	Total	
Parent company's stock		shares
	Total	

Note: Companies are generally prohibited from holding treasury stock. (See P 13.)

13. Schedule of equity ownership in more than 25% owned investee companies and the number of shares of the Company's stock held by these investee companies

Name of investee company	Balance at beginning of period		Current changes		Balance at end of period			Number of shares of Company's stock held by investee company
	Number of shares	Book value	Number of shares	Amount	Number of shares	Acqui- sition cost	Book value	
		¥		¥		¥	¥	shares
Other, total								
Total		¥		¥		¥	¥	shares

14. Schedule of transactions with subsidiaries and changes in receivables and payables from/to subsidiaries.

(1) Schedule of transactions

Name of subsidiary	Sales	Purchases	
	¥	¥	¥
Other, total			
Total	¥	¥	¥

(2) Changes in receivables

Name of subsidiary	Short-term		Long-term	
	Balance at end of period	Net change from prior period	Balance at end of period	Net change from prior period
	¥	¥	¥	¥
Other, total				
Total	¥	¥	¥	¥

(3) Changes in payables

Name of subsidiary	Short-term		Long-term	
	Balance at end of period	Net change from prior period	Balance at end of period	Net change from prior period
	¥	¥	¥	¥
Other, total				
Total	¥	¥	¥	¥

15. Schedule of directors and statutory auditors who hold concurrent posts in other companies

	Name	Name of company where person holds concurrent post	Type of post	Remarks
Directors				
Statutory auditors				

16. Schedule of selling, general and administrative expenses

Account title	Amount	Remarks
	¥	
Total	¥	

Note: This schedule must be prepared so as to indicate to statutory auditors whether the directors of the Company have given an economic benefit of the Company to anyone without consideration.

17. Other important information

Note: If there is any additional information, other than that disclosed in these supporting schedules, which might be considered necessary to supplement the balance sheet, the income statement and the business report of the Company, such information should be disclosed herein.

Appendix H
Form and Contents of Supporting Schedules to the SEL Accounts as Laid Down by the Ministry of Finance Ordinance

4) Notes to financial statements

The SEL requires that the following matters be disclosed in the notes to the financial statements:

a. Items described in (a) through (n) for the Commercial Code requirements at pages 28 and 29, except (e) and (g), are also required for the SEL reports.

b. If "Cost or market valuation, whichever is the lower" is applied, this fact and amount of the write-down should be disclosed.

c. If assets are revalued during the current period, the fact, reasons therefor, date of the revaluation, book value of the assets immediately before revaluation, amount revalued, and method of accounting of the revaluation difference. During the subsequent four-year period, only the fact of revaluation and the date need be disclosed.

d. Total number of shares authorized and issued.

e. The amount subscribed for new shares, number of new shares to be issued, date of capital increase, and the amount to be transferred to capital reserve, if any.

f. Any deficit which was offset with capital or legal reserve within two years prior to the beginning of the period along with the name of such reserve, amount offset, and date of offset.

g. Net assets per share.

h. Types of major taxes, if provision for taxes is not presented in detail.

i. The amount of stock dividends, included in dividends.

j. Subsequent events.

5) Supporting schedules

In support of applicable financial statement items, the following schedules are required for commercial and industrial companies:

1..... Marketable securities
2..... Tangible fixed assets
3..... Intangible fixed assets
4..... Investments in affiliated companies
5..... Investments in equity of affiliated companies other than capital stock
6..... Loans to affiliated companies
7..... Bonds payable
8..... Long-term borrowings
9..... Borrowings to affiliated companies
10..... Capital stock
11..... Capital surplus
12..... Legal reserve and other appropriation
13..... Depreciation, depletion and amortization of fixed assets and deferred charges
14..... Reserves and allowances

The Ministry of Finance Ordinance prescribes the form and contents of the supporting schedules as shown below.

1. Schedule of marketable securities

	Company name	Par value	No. of shares	Acquisition cost	Book value	Remarks
Shares		¥		¥	¥	
	Total			¥	¥	

	Name of bonds	Total amount of face value	Acquisition cost	Book value	Remarks
Bonds		¥	¥	¥	
	Total	¥	¥	¥	

	Description	Acquisition cost	Book value	Remarks
Other securities		¥	¥	
	Total	¥	¥	

2. Schedule of tangible fixed assets

Kind of assets	Acquisition cost at beginning of period	Increase	Decrease	Acquisition cost at end of period	Accumulated depreciation	Book value at end of period	Remarks
	¥	¥	¥	¥	¥	¥	
Total	¥	¥	¥	¥	¥	¥	

3.   Schedule of intangible fixed assets

Kind of assets	Acquisition cost	Increase	Decreare	Accumulated amortization	Balance at end of period	Remarks
	¥	¥	¥	¥	¥	
Total	¥	¥	¥	¥	¥	

4.   Schedule of investments in affiliated companies

	Company name	Par value	Balance at beginning of period			Increase		Decrease		Balance at end of period			Remarks
			No. of shares	Acquisition cost	Book value	No. of shares	Amount	No. of shares	Amount	No. of shares	Amount	Book Value	
Shares		¥	¥	¥	¥	¥	¥	¥	¥	¥	¥	¥	
	Total			¥	¥		¥		¥		¥	¥	

	Name of bonds	Balance at beginning of period		Increase	Decrease	Balance at end of period		Remarks
		Acquisition cost	Book value			Acquisition cost	Book value	
Bonds		¥	¥	¥	¥	¥	¥	
	Total	¥	¥	¥	¥	¥	¥	

5. Schedule of investments in equity of affiliated companies other than capital stock

Name of affiliated companies	Balance at beginning of period	Increase	Decrease	Balance at end of period	Remarks
	¥	¥	¥	¥	
Total	¥	¥	¥	¥	

6. Schedule of loans to affiliated companies

Name of affiliated companies	Balance at beginning of period	Increase	Decrease	Balance at end of period	Remarks
	¥	¥	¥	¥	
Total	¥	¥	¥	¥	

7. Schedule of bonds payable

Name of bonds	Date of issue	Total amount issued	Redemption	Outstanding balance	Issuance price	Interest rate	Mortgage (kind, object and order)	Maturity date	Remarks
		¥	¥	¥	¥				
Total		¥	¥	¥					

8. Schedule of long-term borrowings

Lender	Balance at beginning of period	Increase	Decrease	Balance at end of period	Remarks
	¥	¥	¥	¥	
Total	¥	¥	¥	¥	

9. Schedule of borrowings to affiliated companies

Name of affiliated company	Balance at beginning of period	Increase	Decrease	Balance at end of period	Remarks
	¥	¥	¥	¥	
Total	¥	¥	¥	¥	

10. Schedule of capital stock

Shares issued		Kind	No. of shares issued	Amount transferred to capital stock	Name of Securities Exchange where shares are listed	Remarks
	Shares having par value			¥		
		Sub total		¥		
	Shares having no par value					
		Sub total		¥		
Amount of capital without issuance of shares						
Amount of capital stock				¥		
Transfer from reserves to capital stock	Amount transferred to capital stock		Remarks			
	¥					
	Total ¥					

11. Schedule of capital surplus

Classifi- cation	Balance at end of previous period	Amount offset against deficit	Increase	Decrease	Balance at end of period	Remarks
	¥	¥	¥	¥	¥	
Total	¥	¥	¥	¥	¥	

12. Schedule of legal reserve and other appropriation

Classification	Balance at end of previous period	Increase	Decrease	Balance at end of the period	Remarks
	¥	¥	¥	¥	
Total	¥	¥	¥	¥	

13. Schedule of depreciation, depletion and amortization of fixed assets and deferred charges

Kind of assets	Acquisition cost	Depreciation for the period	Accumulated depreciation	Balance at end of period	Ratio of accumulated depreciation over acquisition cost	Difference from the amount calculated under the company's depreciation policy	
						For the period	Accumulated amount
	¥	¥	¥	¥		¥	¥
Total	¥	¥	¥	¥		¥	¥

14. Schedule of reserves and allowances

Classification	Balance at beginning of period	Increase	Decrease		Balance at end of period	Remarks
			Used	Others		
	¥	¥	¥	¥	¥	

Appendix I
Chronology of Accounting in Japan

1865	Double-entry bookkeeping adopted by French naval accountant at the Yokosuka Steel Works (previously single-entry bookkeeping was generally used by merchant traders)
1868	[Meiji restoration]
1871	V. E. Braga employed, by the government, as a chief accountant at the mint established in Osaka
1873	The first book in Japanese on Western bookkeeping published by Y. Fukuzawa
	A. A. Shand's treatise *Ginko Boki Seiho* (*The Detailed Method of Bank Bookkeeping*) published by the Ministry of Finance
1875	W. G. Whitney engaged as teacher of accounting at the first commercial college (later became Hitotsubashi University)
1878	[Stock exchanges established in Tokyo and Osaka]
1887	The first Income Tax Law promulgated
1890	The first Commercial Code promulgated
1899	The Commercial Code amended
	The Income Tax Law (including corporation tax provisions) promulgated
1907	First group of professional accountants formed
1911	The Commercial Code revised
1923	The Commercial Code revised
1927	The Registered Public Accountants Law promulgated
1934	Working Rules for Financial Statements issued by the Ministry of Commerce and Industry
1937	[Outbreak of the Sino–Japanese war]
1938	The Commercial Code revised
1940	Working Rules for the Preparation of Financial Statements in Munitions Factories for the Navy, issued by the Ministry of Navy

Working Rules for the Preparation of Financial Statements in Munitions Factories for the Army, issued by the Ministry of Army

The Corporation Tax Law independently promulgated

1941   Tentative Standards for Manufacturing Companies' Balance Sheets, Profit and Loss Accounts and Inventories issued by the Planning Bureau

[Outbreak of Pacific war]

1945   [Acceptance of Potsdam Declaration]

1946   [GHQ of allied forces began to dissolve the *zaibatsu*]

1947   The Securities Exchange Commission established

Instructions on the Preparation of Financial Statements for Industrial and Commercial Companies issued by GHQ

Anti-Monopoly Law promulgated

Full revision to the Corporation Tax Law

The Securities and Exchange Law promulgated

1948   The Securities and Exchange Law established

The Investigation Committee on Business Accounting Systems of the Economic Stabilization Board (later to be known as the Business Accounting (Standards) Deliberation Council) established

The Registered Public Accountants Law superseded by the Certified Public Accountants Law

1949   The Business Accounting Principles and Working Rules for Financial Statements issued by the Investigation Committee on Business Accounting Systems

First Report of the Shoup Committee on the restructuring of the Japanese taxation system issued

CPA examinations introduced

The Japanese Institute of Certified Public Accountants established

1950   The Corporation Tax Law amended

The Asset Revaluation Law promulgated

The Commercial Code revised

The Securities and Exchange Law amended

Second Report of the Shoup Committee on taxation systems issued

Regulation Concering Terms, Formats and Preparation Methods of Financial Statements (Regulation Concerning Financial Statements) issued by the Securities Exchange Commission

Auditing Standards and Auditing Working Rules for the Preparation of Audit Reports issued by the Business Acounting Standards Deliberation Council

1951   Working Rules on Audit Certification issued by the Securities Exchange Commission

Audits by CPAs under Securities and Exchange Law commenced

The Certified Tax Accountants Law promulgated

Introduction of examinations to become a certified tax accountant

Opinion on the Reconciliation of the Commercial Code and the Business Accounting Principles issued by the Business Accounting Standards Deliberation Council

1952   The Japanese Federation of Certified Tax Accountants established

Opinion on the Reconciliation of the Tax Law and the Business Accounting Principles issued by the Business Accounting Standards Deliberation Council

The administration of the Business Accounting Standards Deliberation Council transferred to the Ministry of Finance and renamed the Business Accounting Deliberation Council (BADC)

The Securities Exchange Commission abolished and the administration of the Securities and Exchange Law transferred to the Finance Bureau of the Ministry of Finance

1954   Revision to the Business Accounting Principles and addition of Notes to the Principles

1956   Auditing Standards, Auditing Working Rules for the Preparation of Audit Reports amended and Auditing Working Rules for the Reporting of Audit Reports issued by BADC

1957   Ordinances on Audit Certification of Financial Statements issued by the Ministry of Finance

The Special Tax Measures Law promulgated

1960   Serial Opinions on the Reconciliation of the Business Accounting Principles and the related Laws issued by BADC

Tentative Statement on the Revision to the Commercial Code issued by the Ministry of Justice

1962   The Commercial Code revised

Cost Accounting Standards issued by BADC

Addition to Serial Opinions on the Reconciliation of the Business Accounting Principles and the related Laws

1963   Revision to the Business Accounting Principles

Full revision to Regulation Concerning Financial Statements (this became an Ordinance of the Ministry of Finance as a result of the abolition of the Securities Exchange Commission)

Regulation Concerning Accounts issued by the Ministry of Justice

1965   Comprehensive revision to the Auditing Standards and Working Rules for the Preparation of Audit Reports

Full revision to the Corporation Tax Law

[Bankruptcy of Sanyo Special Steel]

1966   Further revision to the Auditing Standards and Working Rules for Reporting of Audit Reports

Provisional Opinion on Consolidated Financial Statements issued by BADC

The Certified Public Accountants Law amended

Ordinance of Audit Corporations issued by the Ministry of Finance

Opinion on the Reconciliation of the Tax Law and the Business Accounting Principles issued by BADC

1967   Revision to the Corporation Tax Law

Title of registered public accountant abolished

First audit corporation (Ohta Audit Corporation) established

Opinion on Consolidated Financial Statements issued by BADC

1968   Specific Opinions on Accounting Problems issued by BADC

1969   Revised Draft of the Business Accounting Principles issued by BADC

1971   Addition to Specific Opinions by BADC

The Securities and Exchange Law revised

1972   Addition to Specific Opinions by BADC

1973   Ordinance on the Disclosure of Financial Position issued by the Ministry of Finance

Addition to Specific Opinion by BADC

[Formation of International Accounting Standards Committee]

[Oil crisis]

1974   The Commercial Code revised (Law Concerning the Special Case of Commercial Code for Audit of Kabushiki-Kaisha issued)

Audit by independent external auditor under the Commercial Code began

Revision to Regulation Concerning Accounts

Revision to the Business Accounting Principles

Revision to Regulation Concerning Financial Statements

1975   The Securities and Exchange Law revised

Accounting Principles for Consolidated Financial Statements issued by BADC

Revision to Regulation Concerning Accounts

Revision to Regulation Concerning Financial Statements

1976   Ordinances concerning Consolidated Financial Statements Regulations issued by the Ministry of Finance

Revision to Regulation Concerning Financial Statements

Auditing Working Rules for Preparation and Reporting of Audit Reports amended

1977   Opinion on Interim Financial Statements Included in Semi-Annual Reports

(Accounting Standards and Auditing Standards for Interim Financial Statements) issued by BADC

Ordinance Concerning Interim Financial Statements Regulations issued by the Ministry of Finance

Audits of interim financial statements by CPAs began

1978 First disclosure of consolidated financial statements

1979 Accounting Standards for Foreign Currency Transactions, etc. issued by BADC

1980 Opinion on Disclosure of Financial Information of Price-Level Changes issued by BADC

Opinion on Regulation Concerning Accounts issued by BADC

Revision to the Certified Tax Accountants Law

1981 Revision to the Commercial Code (including the Special Case Law in 1974)

The Securities and Exchange Law revised

1982 Revision to the Business Accounting Principles

Revision to Note to Accounting Principles for Consolidated Financial Statements

Revision to Regulation Concerning Accounts

Revision to Accounting Standards for Interim Financial Statements

Revision to Auditing Standards for Interim Financial Statements

Revision to Auditing Working Rules for Reporting of Audit Reports

Ordinance on Audit Reports of Large-sized Companies issued by the Ministry of Justice

Ordinance on Regulation Concerning Accounts for Special Industries issued by the Ministry of Justice

Revision to Regulation Concerning Financial Statements

Revision to Ordinances concerning Interim Financial Statements Regulations

1983 Revision to Auditing Working Rules for Preparation of Audit Reports

Mandatory application of the equity method under the Securities and Exchange Law

Interpretative Guidelines on Audit for Balance Sheet Events issued by BADC

Revision to the Certified Public Accountants Law

Revision to Accounting Standards for Foreign Currency Transactions, etc.

1985 Report on a Survey of External Audits for Small-sized Company issued by BADC

Ordinances Concerning the Standardization of Accounting Standards for the Credit Industries issued by the Ministry of International Trade and Industry

Revision to the Securities and Exchange Law

1986   Interim Report on the Improvement of Financial Information on the Disclosure System under the Securities and Exchange Law issued by BADC.

1987   Revision to Ordinance Concerning Consolidated Financial Statements Regulations

Survey Results on the Disclosure of Segmental Information issued by BADC

Revision to Regulation Concerning Financial Statements

1988   Revision to Ordinance on Regulation Concerning Accounts for Special Industries

Opinion on the Disclosure of Segmental Information issued by BADC

Revision to the Securities and Exchange Law

Revision to Regulation Concerning Accounts

The Consumption Tax Law promulgated

1989   Revision to Ordinance of the Securities and Exchange Law and the related ordinances (regulation on insider dealing)

Revision to Auditing Working Rules for Preparation of Audit Reports

Index